Common Core Bilingual and English Language Learners
A Resource for Educators

EDITORS

Guadalupe Valdés
Kate Menken
Mariana Castro

WITH 130 CONTRIBUTORS

CASLON PUBLISHING
PHILADELPHIA

Caslon, Inc.
825 N. 27th St.
Philadelphia, PA 19130

caslonpublishing.com

9 8 7 6 5 4 3 2 1

Library of Congress Cataloging-in-Publication Data

Common core, bilingual and English language learners : a resource for educators / Guadalupe Valdés, Kate Menken, Mariana Castro, editors ; with 130 Contributing Experts.
    pages cm
Includes bibliographical references and index.
Summary: "Provides 130 expert responses to 95 questions. Topics include sociopolitical context of reform; demographic changes; language for academic purposes; language teaching and learning in content areas; policy, leadership, and advocacy; programs and instruction; family and community involvement; changing roles of ESL educators; planning professional development; and assessment and accountability"— Provided by publisher.
ISBN 978-1-934000-17-5
1. English language—Study and teaching—Foreign speakers. 2. English language—Study and teaching—United States. 3. Education—Standards—United States. I. Valdés, Guadalupe, editor of compilation. II. Menken, Kate, editor of compilation. III. Castro, Mariana, editor of compilation.
PE1128.A2C6757 2015

428.0071'073—dc23

Printed in the United States of America.

Contributors

Jamal Abedi
Professor
School of Education
University of California–Davis
Davis, CA

Ujju Aggarwal
Sarah Lawrence College
Bronxville, NY

Erin Arango Escalante
Director
Early Years, WIDA
Wisconsin Center for Education Research
University of Wisconsin–Madison
Madison, WI

Alfredo J. Artiles
Ryan C. Harris Memorial Endowed Professor
    of Special Education
Mary Lou Fulton Teachers College
Arizona State University
Tempe, AZ

Laura Ascenzi-Moreno
Assistant Professor and Bilingual Program
    Head
School of Education
Brooklyn College–CUNY
Brooklyn, NY

Diane August
Managing Researcher
Education Program
American Institutes for Research
Washington, DC

Alison L. Bailey
Professor
Graduate School of Education
University of California–Los Angeles
Los Angeles, CA

Lilia Bartolomé
Professor
Department of Applied Linguistics
University of Massachusetts
Boston, MA

Karen Beeman
Education Specialist
Center for Teaching for Biliteracy

Penny Bird
Program Manager
American Indian Language Policy Research
    and Teacher Training Center
University of New Mexico
Albuquerque, NM

Rebecca Blum Martinez
Professor
Language, Literacy, & Sociocultural Studies
University of New Mexico
Albuquerque, NM

Tim Boals
Senior Research Scientist/WIDA Director
Wisconsin Center for Education Research
University of Wisconsin–Madison
Madison, WI

María Estela Brisk
Professor
Lynch School of Education
Boston College
Chestnut Hill, MA

George Bunch
Associate Professor
Education Department
University of California–Santa Cruz
Santa Cruz, CA

Sandra Butvilofsky
Research Associate
BUENO Center for Multicultural Education
University of Colorado–Boulder
Boulder, CO

Suresh Canagarajah
Edwin Erle Sparks Professor
Department of English
Penn State University
University Park, PA

David Cassels Johnson
Department of Teaching and Learning
University of Iowa
Ames, IA

Mariana Castro
Director of Academic Language and Literacy
    Initiatives
WIDA at the Wisconsin Center for Education
    Research
University of Wisconsin–Madison
Madison, WI

Sylvia Celedón-Pattichis
Professor
Language, Literacy, & Sociocultural Studies
University of New Mexico
Albuquerque, NM

Anne H. Charity Hudley
Professor
Community Studies
College of William and Mary
Williamsburg, VA

Nancy Commins
Clinical Professor
School of Education and Human Development
University of Colorado–Denver
Denver, CO

H. Gary Cook
Research Director
Wisconsin Center for Educational Research
University of Wisconsin–Madison
Madison, WI

Ayanna Cooper
Consultant
Atlanta, GA

Byron Darnall
Head Learner
Potter Gray Elementary School
Bowling Green, KY

Ester de Jong
Professor
School of Teaching and Learning
University of Florida
Gainesville, FL

L. Quentin Dixon
Associate Professor
Teaching, Learning and Culture
Texas A&M University
College Station, TX

Silvia Dorta-Duque de Reyes
Professor
LaGuardia Community College–CUNY
Education and Language Acquisition
    Department
Long Island City, NY

Margot Downs
Senior Professional Development
    Consultant
Wisconsin Center for Education Research
University of Wisconsin–Madison
Madison, WI

Andrea Dyrness
Associate Professor
Educational Studies
Trinity College
Hartford, CT

Carole Edelsky
Professor Emerita
Arizona State University
Tucson, AZ

Kathy Escamilla
Professor
School of Education
University of Colorado–Boulder
Boulder, CO

Marjorie Faulstich Orellana
Professor
Graduate School of Education
University of California–Los Angeles
Los Angeles, CA

Rebecca Field
Director
Language Education Division
Caslon Publishing
Philadelphia, PA

Nelson Flores
Assistant Professor
Graduate School of Education
University of Pennsylvania
Philadelphia, PA

Cathy Fox
ESL Writing Support Teacher/SIOP Coach
Central Falls School District
Central Falls, RI

Salvador Gabaldón
Director
Culturally Relevant Pedagogy
Tucson Unified School District
Tucson, AZ

Ofelia García
Professor
Graduate Center
City University of New York–CUNY
New York, NY

James Gee
Regents' Professor
Mary Lou Fulton Presidential Professor of
   Literacy Studies
Arizona State University
Tempe, AZ

Sarah Gil
School Leader at International High School
LaGuardia Community College
Long Island City, NY

Claude Goldenberg
Professor
Graduate School of Education
Stanford University
Stanford, CA

Mileidis Gort
Associate Professor
Ohio State University
Columbus, OH

Margo Gottlieb
Lead Developer
Wisconsin Center for Education Research
University of Wisconsin–Madison
Madison, WI

Michael F. Graves
Emeritus Professor
Curriculum and Instruction
University of Minnesota
Minneapolis, MN

Danielle A. Guzman-Orth
Educational Testing Service
Princeton, NJ

Kenji Hakuta
Professor
Graduate School of Education
Stanford University
Stanford, CA

Anna Halverson
Project Assistant
Wisconsin Center for Education Research
University of Wisconsin–Madison
Madison, WI

Young-chan Han
Family Involvement Specialist
Maryland State Department of Education
Baltimore, MD

Holly Hansen-Thomas
Associate Professor
Bilingual and ESL Education
Texas Woman's University
Denton, TX

Lisa Harmon-Martinez
English Language Arts Teacher and Dual
    Language Co-Coordinator
Albuquerque High School
Albuquerque, NM

Beth Harry
Professor
Department of Teaching and Learning
University of Miami
Coral Gables, FL

Margaret R. Hawkins
Professor
Department of Curriculum and
    Instruction
University of Wisconsin–Madison
Madison, WI

Margaret Heritage
Senior Scientist
WestEd
San Francisco, CA

Sera Jean Hernandez
Adjunct Instructor
California State University–San Bernardino
San Bernardino, CA

John Hilliard
Education Specialist
Illinois Resource Center
Arlington Heights, IL

Don Hones
Professor
College of Education and Human
    Services
University of Wisconsin–Oshkosh
Oshkosh, WI

Susan Hopewell
Assistant Professor
School of Education
University of Colorado–Boulder
Boulder, CO

Victoria K. Hunt
Dos Puentes Elementary School
New York, NY

Susana Ibarra Johnson
New Mexico Education Continua
Albuquerque, NM

Mishelle Jurado
Spanish Language Arts Teacher and Dual
    Language Co-Coordinator
Albuquerque High School
Albuquerque, NM

Jill Kerper Mora
Associate Professor Emerita
School of Teacher Education
San Diego State University
San Diego, CA

Amanda Kibler
Assistant Professor
Curry School of Education
University of Virginia
Charlottesville, VA

Michael W. Kirst
Professor Emeritus
Stanford University
Stanford, CA

Tatyana Kleyn
Associate Professor
The Graduate Center
City University of New York–CUNY
New York, NY

Stephen Krashen
Professor Emeritus
School of Education
University of Southern California
Los Angeles, CA

Heidi LaMare
Supervisor
Programs for English Learners
Bellevue School District
Bellevue, WA

Juliet Langman
Professor
Department of Bicultural–Bilingual
   Studies
University of Texas–San Antonio
San Antonio, TX

Diane Larsen-Freeman
Professor Emerita
School of Education
University of Michigan
Ann Arbor, MI

Magaly Lavadenz
Professor
Educational Leadership
Loyola Marymount University
Los Angeles, CA

Jobi Lawrence
Director, Title III
Education Program Consultant
Iowa Department of Education
Ames, IA

Ohkee Lee
Professor
Steinhardt School of Culture, Education, and
   Human Development
New York University
New York, NY

Stacey J. Lee
Professor
School of Education
University of Wisconsin–Madison
Madison, WI

Robert Linquanti
WestEd
San Francisco, CA

Robin Liten-Tejada
Secondary ESOL/HILT Specialist and
   Teacher
Arlington Public Schools
Arlington, VA

Lorena Llosa
Associate Professor
Steinhardt School of Culture, Education, and
   Human Development
New York University
New York, NY

Gilberto Lobo
Science Teacher
Dual Language Program
Truman Middle School
Albuquerque, NM

Alexis Lopez
Educational Testing Service
Princeton, NJ

Marylin Low
Acting Chief Program Officer and Principal
   Investigator
Pacific Islands Climate Change Education
   Partnership
Honolulu, HI

Lorena Mancilla
Senior Outreach Specialist
Wisconsin Center for Education Research
University of Wisconsin–Madison
Madison, WI

Joanne Marino
Title III Director, Retired
Wisconsin Center for Education Research
University of Wisconsin–Madison
Madison, WI

Barbara Marler
Director
Design and Development
Illinois Resource Center
Arlington Heights, IL

Julie Marsh
Associate Professor
Rossier School of Education
University of Southern California
Los Angeles, CA

Maya A. Martinez-Hart
Early Childhood Specialist
Wisconsin Center for Education Research
University of Wisconsin–Madison
Madison, WI

Douglas S. Massey
Henry G. Bryant Professor of Sociology and
    Public Affairs
Princeton University
Princeton, NJ

Suzanna McNamara
Co-Curriculum Developer
Graduate Center
City University of New York–CUNY
New York, NY

Kate Menken
Associate Professor
Department of Linguistics
Queens College–CUNY;
Research Fellow
Research Institute for the Study of Language in
    Urban Society
CUNY Graduate Center;
Co-Principal Investigator
CUNY–New York State Initiative for Emergent
    Bilinguals
New York, NY

Trish Morita-Mullaney
Assistant Professor
Department of Curriculum and Instruction
Purdue University
West Lafayette, IN

Judit Moschkovich
Professor
Education Department
University of California–Santa Cruz
Santa Cruz, CA

Olivia Mulcahy
Education Specialist
Illinois Resource Center
Arlington Heights, IL

Monty Neill
Executive Director
National Center for Fair and Open Testing
    (FairTest)
Jamaica Plain, MA

Shondel Nero
Associate Professor
Steinhardt School of Culture, Education, and
    Human Development
New York University
New York, NY

Diep Nguyen
Chair, Teacher Education Department
College of Education
Northeastern Illinois University
Chicago, IL

David Nieto
Division Administrator
Illinois State Board of Education
Chicago, IL

Edward M. Olivos
Associate Professor
Department of Education Studies
University of Oregon
Eugene, OR

C. Patrick Proctor
Associate Professor
Lynch School of Education
Boston College
Boston, MA

Mari Rasmussen
Assistant Professor
Department of Teacher Education
Dickinson State University
Dickinson, ND

Ruth Reinl
Consultant
Early Dual Language Learning Consulting, LLC
Middleton, WI

Christy Reveles
Director
Teaching and Learning
Wisconsin Center for Education Research
University of Wisconsin–Madison
Madison, WI

Kristina Robertson
Professional Development Specialist
Teaching and Learning
Wisconsin Center for Education Research
University of Wisconsin–Madison
Madison, WI

Katherine C. Rodela
Assistant Professor
Educational Leadership
Washington State University–Vancouver
Vancouver, WA

Rubén G. Rumbaut
Professor
Sociology Department
University of California–Irvine
Irvine, CA

Maria Santos
Co-Chair and Senior Advisor for Leadership
Graduate Center
City University of New York–CUNY
New York, NY

Jamie Schissel
Assistant Professor
Teacher Education
University of North Carolina–Greensboro
Greensboro, NC

Kate Seltzer
Adjunct Lecturer
Graduate Center
City University of New York–CUNY
New York, NY

Timothy Shanahan
Distinguished Professor Emeritus
Curriculum and Instruction
University of Illinois
Chicago, IL

Sheila M. Shannon
Associate Professor
Linguistically Diverse Education
University of Colorado–Denver
Denver, CO

Chris Sims
Associate Professor
College of Education
University of New Mexico
Albuquerque, NM

Annie Smith
Co-Curriculum Director
Graduate Center
City University of New York–CUNY
New York, NY

Catherine Snow
Patricia Albjerg Graham Professor
Graduate School of Education
Harvard University
Cambridge, MA

Guillermo Solano-Flores
Professor
School of Education
University of Colorado–Boulder
Boulder, CO

Ronald W. Solórzano
Professor
Department of Education
Occidental College
Los Angeles, CA

Shelly Spiegel-Coleman
Executive Director
Californians Together
Long Beach, CA

Lydia Stack
Content Specialist
Multilingual Pathways Department
San Francisco Unified School District
San Francisco, CA

Diane Staehr Fenner
President
DSF Consulting, LLC
Washington, DC

Lorrie Stoops Verplaetse
Professor and Coordinator
TESOL/Bilingual Education
Southern Connecticut State University
New Haven, CT

Claire E. Sylvan
Executive Director
International Network for Public Schools
New York, NY

Edward Tabet-Cubero
Deputy Director
Dual Language Education of New Mexico
Albuquerque, NM

Sultan Turkan
Associate Research Scientist
Educational Testing Service
Princeton, NJ

Cheryl Urow
Education Specialist
Center for Teaching for Biliteracy

Guadalupe Valdés
Professor
Stanford University;
Founding Partner
Understanding Language Initiative
Stanford, CA

Wilma Valero
Director
Programs for English Language Learners
Elgin Area School District
Elgin, IL

Patricia Velasco
Assistant Professor
Elementary and Early Childhood Education
Queens College–CUNY
Queens, NY

Aída Walqui
Director
Teacher Professional Development
WestEd
San Francisco, CA

Terrence G. Wiley
President
Center for Applied Linguistics
Washington, DC

Thad Williams
Doctoral Candidate
College of Education
University of Washington
Seattle, WA

Lilly Wong Fillmore
Professor Emeritus
School of Education
University of California–Berkeley
Berkeley, CA

Laura Wright
Senior Research Associate
Center for Applied Linguistics
Washington, DC

Wayne Wright
Assistant Professor
Department of Curriculum and
    Instruction
Purdue University
West Lafayette, IN

Josie Yanguas
Director
Illinois Resource Center
Arlington Heights, IL

Holly Yettick
Director
Education Week Research Center
Bethesda, MD

Debbie Zacarian
Founder
Debbie Zacarian, Ed.D. and Associates, LLC
Amherst, MA

Preface

Common Core, Bilingual and English Language Learners: A Resource for Educators is for pre-service and practicing administrators, teachers, coaches, staff developers, curriculum specialists, leadership teams, and policymakers who are trying to make sense of what the Common Core State Standards (CCSS) mean for diverse learners. To date, federal and state departments of education have provided little guidance for educators about how to include English language learners (ELLs) in CCSS implementation. We find confusion, controversy, and questioning among educators at the state, district, school, and classroom levels about how to proceed. In response, we (Valdés, Menken, and Castro) developed this book to begin to provide some concrete answers.

We began by compiling 95 questions that we have heard from practitioners in the field, and we organized these questions into seven chapters: (1) terrain and landscape; (2) fundamental language issues; (3) family and community participation; (4) policy, leadership, and advocacy, (5) teaching and learning; (6) professional learning; and (7) assessment and accountability. We know that there is no one right answer to the numerous questions educators have about CCSS and ELLs in diverse district, school, and community contexts. This book therefore includes 136 brief, user friendly responses from 130 experts that collectively represent a range of states, institutions, communities, researchers, policymakers, practitioners, and perspectives.

As the title indicates, this book focuses on students who are officially designated as *English language learners*, the term commonly used in U.S. schools and policy today. However, the editors prefer the term *emergent bilingual* (EB) to recognize students' bilingualism, and because the result of learning English at school is usually bilingualism (or even multilingualism) rather than English monolingualism. Students who speak language(s) other than English at home and who are learning English as a new or additional language at school draw on their home language(s) as they learn content, literacy, and language. As we see in many of the contributions to the book, a holistic perspective on language learning has important implications for mainstream and specialist educators who have ELLs/EBs in their classes, schools, and districts. The contributors also represent a broad range of perspectives, approaches, and contexts, and the terminology and approaches used reflect this diversity.

We also emphasize that *all* students are language learners who must learn new ways of using oral and written language for academic and disciplinary purposes. This includes ELLs/EBs who are new to English, simultaneous bilinguals who grow up using two (or more) languages at home, students who come to school speaking vernacular varieties of English, and students who speak standard varieties of English. All educators must therefore know how to prepare linguistically and culturally diverse learners to meet the same high language and literacy demands set out in the new standards. The language and literacy education fields have much to offer the general education field, and the experts contributing to this guide provide an accessible entry point to this work.

Shifting Terrain and Landscape

In an EducCore White Paper titled "The Common Core Changes Almost Everything" (included in this volume as 1.1), the distinguished educational policy expert, Michael Kirst, warns us that these new standards "will affect almost all key state and local education policies in fundamental ways." He points out that part of the challenge is that "the Common Core Standards are trying to implement a 21st-century vision of K–12 education using 20th-century local school structures, resources, and culture." Kirst further argues that the field of education currently lacks the integrated research and development to build the more effective teaching practices, tools, and resources that are needed to implement this completely new vision in teaching and learning.

For us, deciding what needs to be questioned and what can simply be assumed as correct or on target is an important challenge. There is much around us that is shifting, much that we fear, but also much that we may learn from. As practitioners, researchers, and policymakers who are concerned about the effects of the CCSS on ELLs/EBs, it is particularly important that we engage in critical conversations that will help clarify (1) points of confusion, (2) what may now be indefensible views, (3) implications of shifts of various types for instructional practices, (4) the effects of new assessments, and (5) the ways in which new CCSS-aligned standards policies might negatively and positively affect this particularly vulnerable group of students.

Not everyone agrees with this latest reform movement, particularly those on either end of the U.S. political landscape who question the CCSS, and several states have chosen to opt out of the Common Core altogether. The controversies surrounding the CCSS are likewise evident in the responses by the different contributors to this book, whose viewpoints run the gamut from full support to total opposition. One important purpose of this book is to actively engage all educators in these debates. At the same time, we recognize that educators serving ELLs/EBs in school systems and schools across the country are now charged with implementation of the CCSS. Accordingly, this book offers educators the support and guidance they need to evaluate the CCSS, while implementing the standards in ways that make sense for their ELL/EB students.

Critical Conversations

We see this practical guide as an invitation to conversations about the CCSS and ELLs/EBs. As editors, we are a central part of the conversation. Each of us has been working in different but complementary ways to support the education of ELLs/EBs throughout our careers.

Guadalupe Valdés lives in California, which currently has the largest number of ELLs/EBs, most of them Latino, and most of them from Mexico. She is a professor at Stanford University and a founding partner of Understanding Language, an initiative that focuses attention on the role of language in subject-area learning, with a focus on helping ELLs/EBs meet the new CCSS and Next Generation Science Standards (NGSS). Valdés' work over a period of 30 years has focused on the English–Spanish bilingualism of U.S. Latinos and on discovering and describing how two languages are developed, used, and maintained by individuals who become bilingual in immigrant communities. Valdés has strong views and passions and has engaged in many skirmishes and battles on behalf of what she views as the most vulnerable students in American schools. She worries about the ways that language is conceptualized by educators and about the damage that misunderstanding the goals of second language acquisition pedagogy can do to children.

Kate Menken lives and works in New York City, the most multilingual city in the United States, where she is an associate professor of linguistics at Queens College of the City University of New York (CUNY), and a research fellow at the Research Institute for the Study of Language in Urban Society at the CUNY Graduate Center. She is also co-principal investigator of the CUNY–New York State Initiative for Emergent Bilinguals, which develops the knowledge base of school principals and staff to transform language policies and practices in schools enrolling EBs. Menken opposes education reforms like the CCSS when they lead to English-only approaches in schools. She also opposes the test-based accountability that has overtaken previous standards-based reform efforts, especially the test-and-punish approach that can be harmful for EBs. Menken fears that the Common Core is continuing this approach. She encourages educators, policymakers, and administrators to become politically active and push for better policies for ELLs/EBs. Menken asks educators and administrators not simply to accept and implement the Common Core as is. Rather, she encourages administrators, and policymakers to prioritize the needs of ELL/EB students, which include protecting high-quality programs like bilingual education that draw on and strengthen students' home language practices.

Mariana Castro lives in Wisconsin and is currently Director of Academic Language and Literacy Initiatives for the World-class Instructional Design and Assessment (WIDA) Consortium, a consortium of 35 states and territories that have joined together to develop standards-based resources and assessments to support the language development and academic achievement of ELLs/EBs. Throughout her career, Mariana's work at the school, district, national, and international levels has focused on the roles of educators in supporting student learning. Her passion for education is energized by the amazing work of teachers who draw on the linguistic and cultural resources of students and communities in diverse contexts. Through the concrete examples from practitioners included in this text, Mariana hopes to further the development of strong collaborative partnerships, not only within teacher groups in schools but also among schools and communities in ways that integrate linguistic, cultural, and experiential funds of knowledge into instructional designs that expand all students' opportunities to learn.

As editors, we started the conversation by collecting questions that we heard from practitioners in the field. We furthered the conversation by inviting experts we know and whose work we admire to participate in this project. We view these experts' opinions as points of departure for addressing the confusion in the field and suggest concrete actions that educators can take to support student learning, curriculum, instruction, assessment, programming, professional learning, policy, and advocacy.

We ask you to imagine all of us in the room as you engage in discussions and explorations of the topics presented in this book. We invite you to disagree with us, to question us, and to convince us of your positions as you read the responses of researchers, administrators, and practitioners who are also deeply committed to the education of students new to English. We expect that the conversations you engage in will raise new questions about controversial issues, invite you to explore positions about which you feel strongly, and perhaps allow you to make new and different connections with what you know has worked in instruction for ELLs/EBs.

How to Use This Guide

This practical guide can be used by educators in many ways, including the following:

- As a reference that provides clear and concise answers to specific questions that individuals or groups of educators may have about a particular CCSS-related issue.
- As part of a professional development (PD) workshop, book study group, or university class. Groups may do a close reading of one or more questions and answers to identify, compare, and contrast different perspectives on an issue, and consider how to apply what they learn in specific school or community contexts.
- To identify concrete ways to use the CCSS to focus on the role of language in education for all students, particularly ELLs/EBs.
- To organize a CCSS-aligned curriculum development project that is responsive to the needs of the linguistically and culturally diverse learners.
- To broaden educators' understanding of what is involved in appropriating the CCSS in contexts of linguistic and cultural diversity by focusing attention on leadership, policy, programming, professional learning, parental and community participation, and advocacy—in addition to curriculum, instruction, assessment, and accountability.
- To support and guide local efforts to review, monitor, evaluate, and improve the extent to which they are providing opportunities to learn and the best possible services for the ELLs/EBs in their districts and schools. For example, leadership teams might focus on particular chapters to respond to a program audit or to prepare a professional learning plan.
- To galvanize school administrators and staff to consider anew how their school is implementing and/or resisting the CCSS and their assessments, and to make changes if implementation is anything less than ideal for ELLs/EBs.

These are just a few suggestions for how educators might use this resource to open spaces for creative and innovative ways to implement the CCSS at the local level. We hope that this book will support educators as agents of change as they address the implementation gap left by federal and state policymakers who have provided little guidance about CCSS implications for diverse learners.

Contents

Fundamental Language Issues   36

Introduction   36

Becoming Bilingual and Multilingual: Language Acquisition and Development   38

The Language Valued at School   47

Policy, Leadership, and Advocacy   106

Teaching and Learning 154

Introduction 154

7 Assessment and Accountability 240

Chapter 1

Terrain and Landscape

T he focus of this chapter is the shifting landscape and terrain that have accompanied the development and implementation of the Common Core State Standards (CCSS). The educational community is keenly aware of the many changes that have surrounded the implementation of the CCSS and of the many moving parts that may shift further. The standards themselves, by this time, are familiar to the general public and have been examined at length by educators at all levels. As is well known, this set of academic standards in English language arts (ELA) and mathematics outlines what students should know and be able to do at the end of each grade so that they can make progress on their journey to becoming college and career ready. While interpretations of what the standards mean vary across the country, it is agreed that major changes in instruction will be necessary if all children, including traditionally underserved students, are to "argue from evidence," and "reason abstractly and quantitatively" as the wording in the standards themselves appears to require.

At this writing, 44 states, the District of Columbia, and the Department of Defense Education Activity have accepted these standards and are moving forward with their implementation. At the state level, preparation for CCSS implementation has included the development of CCSS-aligned state standards (when such action was required by state laws) and the establishment of membership in one or both of the two consortia (Smarter Balanced Assessment Consortium [SBAC] and Partnership for the Assessment of Readiness for College and Careers [PARCC]) funded to develop assessment of the CCSS. Various states, moreover, have initiated extensive activities designed to support teachers in working with the CCSS by providing professional development focusing on the new disciplinary demands of the standards and by adopting or developing appropriate CCSS-aligned curriculum materials across the K–12 spectrum.

More recently, the national debate over the CCSS has intensified. Strong concerns have been expressed about the process of standards development and about possible negative effects of the standards on both teachers and students. For teachers and for students in classrooms whose performance will be measured by new assessments, however, there is a sense of urgency. In spite of increasing public discussions and debates, on Monday morning, schools and teachers must still be prepared to provide instruction for all children in the context of a shifting curricular and assessment terrain that may not settle completely for some time.

This shifting context is, of course, even more complex for students who are categorized as "limited English proficient (LEP)," as defined by the original Executive Order, "Improving Access to Services for Persons with Limited English Proficiency" and by the general guidance document issued by the Department of Justice on August 16, 2000. Subsequently, the No Child Left Behind (NCLB) Act of 2001 referred to this same group of students as "English language learners (ELLs)," and, as Menken (2010) points out, required them to make annual progress on two separate sets of standardized tests: (1) state tests of academic content designed for monolingual English-speaking students and (2) the state English language proficiency assessment developed for that purpose (e.g., CELDT in California, NYSESLAT in New York, ACCESS for ELLs in states that are part of the World-class Instructional Design and Assessment [WIDA] consortium). As the country moves to the broad implementation of the CCSS, it is important to emphasize that NCLB accountability requirements remain in place. States, moreover, must develop or adopt CCSS-aligned English language proficiency (ELP) standards that will inform the implementation of *new* ELP assessments for the classification and categorization of ELLs/emergent bilinguals (EBs). These state ELP standards will be an essential and defining element of the education of ELLs in the context of the CCSS for the foreseeable future and will dictate exactly how learning English is defined for this population.

As the following figure illustrates, state ELP standards must correspond to CCSS standards. As the figure also illustrates, the education of ELL students is governed by two different systems, (1) the system that is part of the CCSS and New Generation Science Standards (NGSS) implementation, and (2) the system specifically designed to manage ELLs' English language acquisition. As compared to monolingual students, ELLs carry the burden of additional testing because they are required to take two sets of state assessments.

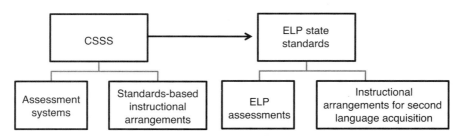

Relationship between Common Core State Standards (CCSS) and English language proficiency (ELP) standards.

State ELP standards and their assessments define and determine the expected progressions of English language acquisition; the elements and/or functions of language to be developed; and the levels of accuracy, complexity, or fluency to be attained. ELP assessments are aligned with these ELP standards and are designed to measure students' progress in moving through the stages of development as described in the ELP standards document. The ELP standards also inform the instructional arrangements that are put in place to ensure students' progress, the curricular frameworks that guide instruction, and the preparation offered to both language and content teachers so that they can effectively provide instruction for ELLs according to the perspectives on language and language development established by the ELP standards.

Much is changing; yet much remains the same: ELLs/EBs continue to be an afterthought. Students' resources in languages other than English have not been taken into account by the new standards, and education exclusively in English appears to be the underlying expectation of the discourses surrounding CCSS implementation.

In this chapter, experts explore a number of important issues and questions that directly affect the lives and futures of ELLs/EBs. The chapter is divided into two parts. First, we look broadly at the shifting landscape around the CCSS and ELLs/EBs, in terms of 21st-century educational goals and purposes, demographic changes in the United States, changing language policies for students officially designated as ELLs, and what we have learned about how these students have fared under NCLB accountability requirements. We begin with these broad issues because they can serve as a point of departure for explorations and discussions to stimulate thought and action as we move forward to better understand the challenges of educating children who are new to English.

The second section of the chapter explores some of the challenges and opportunities that the CCSS present to ELLs/EBs, their teachers, and the school systems responsible for providing their education. The CCSS are silent on the issue of educating ELLs/EBs, bilingualism, and bilingual education at the national level. This silence means that there is space for educators and policymakers at the state, district, and program level to create more equitable terrain in schools serving linguistically and culturally diverse students. Furthermore, the bilingual education laws are still in place in many U.S. states, and state, district, and school administrators and teachers need to understand how to implement the CCSS within their programs. The contributions in this section remind us that ELLs/EBs are the responsibility of all educators, and to consider a "reading" of the CCSS that views bilingualism as a point of departure for instruction. The contributions in this chapter, like the discussion questions and the topics for reflection and action at the end of the chapter, invite readers to explore the terrain and landscape in their states, districts, and schools through a bi/multilingual, sociocultural lens.

Shifting Landscape

1.1 How do reform efforts fit into our views about the goals and purposes of education?

- *Michael W. Kirst*

Common Core Changes Almost Everything

The full policy implications of the Common Core State Standards (CCSS) for mathematics and English language Arts (ELA) K–12 are just beginning to unfold across the 45 states (and Washington, DC) that are working to implement them. The CCSS will affect almost all key state and local education policies in fundamental ways. As we learned from the 1990–2005 era of systemic state standards-based reform, when academic standards change, so do policies related to student assessment and school accountability. Moreover, we must align and harmonize many other specific policies, including state curriculum frameworks, instructional materials, K–12 and college assessment, K–12 finance, professional development (PD), teacher evaluation/preparation, and preschool.

State and local policymakers must eliminate contradictions between policies and look for gaps where no policy currently exists. Examples are instructional transition from prekindergarten to kindergarten and newly aligned policies such as those concerning PD that have sufficient breadth and depth to cover all teachers.

In the past, the introduction of ambitious learning standards conflicted with assessment policy because existing multiple-choice assessments failed to measure the deeper learning needed by students and provided too little information to teachers about student performance. This conflict should be mitigated with the CCSS because an equal amount of effort is going into the development of next generation, computer-adaptive student assessment systems that will more robustly measure student learning against the standards.

Education policy is crafted within a complex educational governance structure that includes schools, school districts, and intermediate education agencies along with a wide variety of state and federal agencies. All of these agencies have overlapping responsibilities and must work together to create coherent education policies.

Standards, Frameworks, and Instructional Materials

The CCSS provide a consistent, clear understanding of what students are expected to learn from grades K–12 in the areas of mathematics and ELA (including literacy standards for history/social studies, science, and technical subjects). Although standards designate what students should learn at specific grade levels, local curriculum frameworks provide guidelines and research-based approaches to instruction to ensure optimal learning for all students. Frameworks also include guidance and criteria for publishers who are developing instructional materials aligned to the standards. Most local schools need to update, revise, and align English language development (ELD) standards for English language learners (ELLs) to meet the CCSS.

Local districts must determine curricular priorities and adopt supplemental and core materials for kindergarten through high school according to their specific needs for supporting student success. Common Core implementation will take more technology than is currently available in most schools because the deeper learning goals and assessments within the Common Core standards are enhanced using technology. Implementation of the CCSS will require new types of data on deeper learning and skill application that were not anticipated when most data systems were designed.

Assessment Programs

Local schools must address some key considerations, including the following:

- The extent to which local education agencies will develop assessments for grades and subjects not required by the Elementary and Secondary Education Act (ESEA).[1]
- The future of the high school exit examination requirements.
- The relationship between local secondary pupil assessments and college- and career-readiness standards in the CCSS.
- The roles of the state and local schools in developing diagnostic, interim, or formative assessments.
- The use, if any, of matrix sampling testing to minimize individual pupil testing time.
- The use of technology to enhance assessments and provide more rapid feedback to teachers, parents, and students.
- The assurance that assessments are fair, reliable, and valid for all pupils, including ELLs, students with disabilities, and pupils who may have limited access to technology.

Other Policies That Need to Be Aligned

Classroom implementation of the CCSS will require massive and deep PD aligned to the new learning expectations of these standards. Educators and administrators will need to overhaul teacher preparation programs and teacher professional standards to accommodate the new standards. Districts will need to revamp local teacher and principal evaluation systems during the transition to Common Core assessment starting in 2015. It will be some time before valid trend data on student assessments will be available for teacher/principal evaluation because prior state assessments featured traditional multiple-choice formats only.

Some educators are concerned that career and technical education (CTE) is not sufficiently represented in the CCSS. Consequently, districts need to redesign CTE occupation clusters to meet the CCSS. But how to measure student preparation for career readiness is largely unknown.

Districts must better integrate early childhood education with K–12 education. A better instructional progression from grades preK–2 could be an important boost for meeting the CCSS in primary grades. But in most localities, diverse public and private preschool providers and K–12 school systems do not have a close relationship.

---

[1]ESEA requires states to assess all pupils each year in grades 3–8 and at least once in high school in the subjects of ELA and mathematics. In addition, ESEA requires that the state assess the English language proficiency (ELP) of all ELL pupils in grades K–12. The results of these assessments are used for state and federal accountability purposes.

Aligned Policies between K–12 and Postsecondary Institutions

Inadequate K–12 preparation is one major cause of dismal college completion results, but inadequate college programs and policies also play a role. In addition, students' lack of money, long work hours, and social/family obligations are important contributors to low postsecondary completion results. Working alone, neither K–12 nor postsecondary education can solve the lack of student success. They must work together to accomplish their mutual goal of increasing rates of student college completion. Many of the problems with college preparation emanate from the growing disconnect between K–12 and higher education on issues of policy, finance, academic standards, and communication. The role of the senior year in high school as a platform for postsecondary general education is rarely discussed. Nor is there a widely shared conception of postsecondary general education that tightly links the academic content of high schools to the first two years of college.

The CCSS were designed in part to close the gap between K–12 and postsecondary education. For example, the new assessments now being developed will send students and parents reliable signals about college readiness in the primary and middle grades. Grade 11 assessments will provide clear guidance for an individual student's college readiness.

In sum, prior to the CCSS, the K–12 curriculum was largely unmoored from the freshman and sophomore college curriculum and from any continuous vision of general education. Policymakers for secondary and postsecondary schools worked in separate orbits that rarely intersected. The implementation of the CCSS provides a unique opportunity to strengthen alignment between K–12 and postsecondary education. The CCSS-aligned revision of the ACT and SAT that will be phased in by 2015 is a positive development for more coherent K–16 policy.

Accountability

All of the changes outlined here will require a major rethinking of state and local accountability systems and indicators. Educators will need to supplement test scores by new indices using multiple indicators. For example, California has several state priorities, including the following:

- Pupil achievement
- Pupil engagement
- School climate
- Parental involvement
- Access to a broad course of study

Moreover, Common Core assessments will measure a more robust array of academic attainment that includes metacognition elements that ask students to explain, prove, derive, construct, investigate, build, interpret, and estimate. Performance assessments have rarely been used in state or local accountability considerations but are an integral part of the CCSS.

Looking to the Future

Essentially, the CCSS are trying to implement a 21st-century vision of K–12 education using 20th-century local school structures, resources, and culture. The integrated research and development to build more effective teaching practice, tools, and resources is only now under way. In the previous era of standards-based reform, states and localities often spent less on local capacity building than was necessary to meet new accountability requirements.

The CCSS will require a major communications campaign to garner educator and public understanding and support. Local educators cannot view the new assessments as just another test or attempt to convert the CCSS to a scripted curriculum. Educators must understand how the CCSS will affect their careers and teaching practices. Surveys indicate very low public awareness of the CCSS, which will require a significant communications effort to overcome. A public backlash may occur if assessment scores drop during the initial phase of Common Core implementations or if technology problems hinder initial implementation.

The Common Core initiative is much more than just a new array of standards. It provides a new vision for teaching and learning that builds on reforms that states and districts began in the 1990s. Implementation will require sustained political support and the ability of educators to persist and change.

1.2 Who will the Common Core State Standards serve? How do they reflect 21st-century demographic realities?

■ *Rubén G. Rumbaut*

The Common Core State Standards (CCSS) are intended to guide the education of all children enrolled in U.S. schools for an unspecified period beginning in 2014. In evaluating the challenges to be faced by schools in implementing these standards and educating all children as required by No Child Left Behind (NCLB) mandates that remain in place, it is important to consider the evolving composition of the school population and projected changes in that population over time. This is particularly the case with regard to immigrant-origin children entering U.S. schools.

First, while the number of foreign-born students who arrive in the United States as young children is a relatively low proportion (under 5%) of all children under 18 in the country, children who are born in the United States to immigrant parents form a rapidly growing second generation. Together, this population of children being raised in immigrant families of diverse ethnic, class, and cultural backgrounds, largely speaking a language other than English at home, has transformed the composition of U.S. public schools, especially in areas of immigrant concentration. As the following figure shows, by 2012 more than a fourth (25.2%) of all U.S. children younger than 18 were either foreign born (3.8%) or members of the new second generation (21.4%). Since 1994 (when items on parental nativity added to the Current Population Survey permitted its measurement), the second generation's child share has grown from 13% to over 21%.

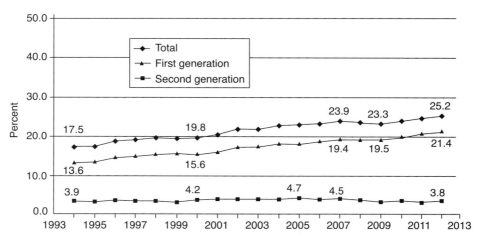

Percentage of U.S. children younger than 18 who are immigrants, by generation: 1994–2012. Immigrant children are those who have at least one foreign-born parent. First generation immigrants are those who were not born in the United States and second generation immigrants are those who were. (From *Child Trends'* original analyses of data from the Current Population Survey, March Supplement. Retrieved from http://www.childtrends.org/?indicators =immigrant-children)

The proportion of the total U.S. child population being raised in immigrant families is projected to continue to increase *regardless of future immigration.*

About half of the 40 million immigrants in the United States in 2010 came from Spanish-speaking Latin America (29% from Mexico alone), who in turn accounted for a plurality of the more than 50 million U.S. "Hispanics" in 2010. *Most* of the growth of the total U.S. population over the next half century, to 2060, will be accounted for solely by Hispanic population growth. (Between 1950 and 2000 most Hispanic population growth had been because of immigration; since 2000, however, it is mainly because of U.S. births.) This is a result of the demographic momentum generated by the youthful age structure and higher-than-replacement fertility of immigrant and Hispanic women in the United States, most notably (though not solely) Mexican-American women.

Meanwhile the rapidly aging baby-boom cohort (consisting mostly of non-Hispanic, white natives) is exiting out of the labor force at unprecedented numbers. Every day since 2011 about 18,000 have been reaching age 65, a pace that will continue alongside higher death rates until 2030. They are being replaced by young folks who disproportionately tend to be other than non-Hispanic whites. For this reason the United States within a generation, by around 2043, will become a "majority-minority" country, as California already did in 2000, and Texas more recently. Children three years and under now in the United States are already majority-minority, as will all children under 18 by 2020. They will increasingly form the American student body.

Beyond the sheer size of this growing population of immigrant-origin youth, there are important differences between groups of immigrants and their modes of incorporation. Legal status and education matter in critical ways. For example, 60% of all immigrants in the U.S. today are accounted for by only ten countries—five from Latin America, five from Asia. Over half of all immigrants from Mexico, El Salvador, Guatemala, and Honduras are undocumented, and over half of the adults from those countries have not completed high school. They share a common Spanish language, and are chiefly labor migrants with limited social mobility, including educational opportunities. They are the most isolated linguistically, economically, socially, legally and otherwise. They have been under systematic state persecution for years, living under a constant threat of detention and deportation and family disruption, although their children are constitutionally entitled to a U.S. public education through grade 12. Growing up under those circumstances and learning in the midst of instability is extraordinarily difficult. Multiple factors are arrayed against them.

In diametric contrast are immigrants entering from the largest Asian countries (India, China and Taiwan, the Philippines, South Korea). They tend to form a "brain drain" of professional immigrants: more than half of adult immigrants from those countries have college degrees (including 80% of those from India), and about a third have advanced degrees. While Asian groups also have a notable share of the undocumented (about 10%–15%, primarily visa "over-stayers"), they generally enter through regular legal channels. They are significantly more educated than the native majority in the United States, and also have lower fertility rates.

State-sponsored refugees form a third type: Vietnamese and Cubans are the largest, but also Cambodians, Laotians, Somalis, and from Bhutan, Iraq, and elsewhere. Refugees tend to have a mixed socioeconomic profile, with more educated immigrants arriving as part of a first wave and then becoming more representative of other social classes over time.

In terms of the challenges of educating the children of immigrants in the foreseeable future, the west and the south will be the areas of the country that will be proportionately most affected by the presence of immigrant-origin school children. New destinations show very rapid growth (e.g., Georgia, the Carolinas, Nevada, and Utah), but in absolute numbers their immigrant-origin populations remain much smaller than in the traditional receiving states (and metros) of California, New York-New Jersey, Texas, Florida, and Illinois. More importantly, the level of school segregation is higher than it was 50 years ago (notably in Southern California and New York). Under conditions of hypersegregation, there are fewer opportunities for immigrant-origin individuals to interact regularly with fluent monolingual speakers of English, a condition that is essential both for the acquisition of English and the development of fluent bilingualism.

■ *Douglas S. Massey*

The CCSS make no provision for the fact that a large share of U.S. students are first and second generation immigrants. Currently one fifth of all children under age 18 in the United States are immigrant children or the children of immigrants and the vast majority of these people are English language learners (ELLs) or emergent bilinguals

(EBs). By far the largest number is Spanish speakers and the largest number of Spanish speakers are from Mexico. Within Mexican households, parents generally have limited English proficiency and less than a secondary education, posing serious barriers to their children's learning in English. They will enter school with limited English ability and limited exposure to the kinds of knowledge and information that are typical in middle-class American families. In addition, 60 percent of all Mexican immigrant parents and more than two thirds of those from Central America are undocumented and thus fearful of contact with U.S. society and institutions and wary of taking advantage of services offered to their children, even if the children are U.S.-born citizens. In the past, the problems and difficulties associated with teaching common core standards to the children of immigrants were largely confined to a handful of immigrant-receiving states, such as California, New York, Texas, Illinois, New Jersey, and Florida. During the 1990s, however, immigration shifted from being a regional phenomenon to a national one, as immigrants from Mexico and Central America dispersed to all 50 states. The most rapidly growing immigrant populations are now in states such as North Carolina, South Carolina, Georgia, Nebraska, Iowa, and Kansas, not California. Thus the challenges of educating EBs and ELLs are not only greater in scale, given the large number of immigrant children, but more widely dispersed because of the new geography of immigration.

1.3 In what ways are the Common Core State Standards de facto language education policy?

- *Terrence G. Wiley*

Language policies are typically the result of planning designed to *prescribe* the language(s) or varieties of language and the purposes for which they will be used. In other words, language policies seek to shape, influence, or control language behavior. Often, they are depicted as solutions for solving purported communication problems. Language policies are frequently identified in a declared program with a defined set of criteria to establish norms for written and oral behavior. Traditionally, the planning of language polices involves two interrelated dimensions, *status planning* and *corpus planning*. Usually, the selection of a particular language or variety of language heightens its societal value or status. Corpus planning enhances status planning by focusing on language standardization, which involves the prescription and codification of language norms, particularly those related to grammar, spelling, styles, and registers of use (Wiley, 1996).

   In addition to status and corpus planning, a related area, *acquisition planning*, prescribes policies for spreading a language as well as norms for its use through education (Wiley, 1996). Obviously, schools play a significant role in attempting to prescribe, shape, influence, and control language behavior (Corson, 1999; Wiley, 2008). Thus, standards for the instruction in language arts (ELA) generally, or Common Core State Standards (CCSS) for English language arts specifically, are particularly relevant as examples of language policies.

Language planning is often depicted as being pragmatic, designed to produce positive benefits to language learners and society. Nevertheless, language planning encompasses a range of policy intentions and potential outcomes. These can *promote* or *accommodate* language learners, or *restrict* and *oppress* them. Despite the dominance of English, given the multilingual nature of U.S. society, policy prescriptions regarding the relationship between English and minority languages, as well as which language practices to emphasize, are particularly critical in education. When language standards are formulated, it is necessary to consider the linguistic and cultural backgrounds of all students who are the targeted recipients or clients of the educational services being provided. Because a large portion of students in the national population come from homes where languages other than English are spoken, their backgrounds and needs must be considered. Although ELA standards can be positive tools in planning instruction for language minority students, the history of curriculum planning provides reason for concern with respect to ensuring equitable instruction for all students (Wiley, 2005, 2008). Thus, we should scrutinize the extent to which the ELA CCSS reflect the needs and specific linguistic and cultural resources of all students.

Failure to take the ethnolinguistic needs and resources of all students into consideration can result in an implicit *monolingual-monocultural bias* against them (Wiley, 2005). Such a bias has been defined as "the practice of catering to the dominant or mainstream culture [while] providing no special consideration at all to persons from nonmainstream cultures" (Haas, 1992, p. 161). This bias can also create a false image of deficiency for language minority students. Consider how, even at the point of entry into the educational process, many students are labeled as being "at risk" prior to any instruction. Thus, because many students attend schools where there is a difference between the language or variety of language spoken in their homes and the English-mediated instruction they will receive at school, these children require status recognition of the linguistic resources of their homes and community, as well as accommodation in learning English, the dominant language. It is not apparent that these issues are adequately addressed in the ELA CCSS.

1.4 What has No Child Left Behind accomplished for students designated as English language learners? What do the Common Core State Standards and accountability requirements change?

■ *Wayne Wright*

Despite its lofty rhetoric, No Child Left Behind (NCLB) has accomplished very little for English language learners (ELLs), and evidence suggests it did more harm than good (Menken, 2008). At the very least, NCLB continued some of the mandates from prior versions of the Elementary and Secondary Education Act (ESEA) that required school districts to identify and serve ELL students. It may be argued that NCLB brought renewed attention to ELLs by holding states and schools directly accountable for their progress in learning and attaining English proficiency and meeting academic achievement standards. At worst, NCLB's elimination of the Title VII Bilingual Act, and its test-and-punishment approach to school reform, have led to narrowed instruction that focuses more on raising test scores and less on meeting the real language and academic needs of ELLs.

NCLB contains a fundamental contradiction by defining ELLs as students whose difficulties with English may be sufficient to deny their ability to pass state tests, but then mandating they pass the tests anyway. NCLB requires something we simply don't know how to do—test ELLs in a valid and reliable manner. In addition, NCLB contains a fatal flaw by holding schools accountable for an ELL subgroup, yet failing to account for movement into and out of the subgroup. This makes it increasingly impossible for the ELL subgroup to meet annual achievement objectives.

The Office of English Language Acquisition of the U.S. Department of Education submits a biannual report to Congress on the progress of ELLs in meeting annual language and academic achievement objectives set by each state. The most recent report with data up to 2010 shows the vast majority of states failed to meet their ELL objectives (U.S. Department of Education, 2013). In fact, only nine states met the objectives, and most have such small ELL populations, there were likely very few schools and districts that were actually held accountable for the ELL subgroup.

We are not able to draw any solid conclusions about ELL students' progress in learning English and academic content because the standards and assessments in each state vary widely, as do the results of these assessments. For example in 2010, state reports of the percentage of ELLs making progress in learning English ranged from a low of 20% to a high of 98%, while the percent attaining English proficiency ranged from a low of 5% to a high of 90%. Likewise, wide ranges are seen in the percentages of ELLs reaching the proficiency level or higher in reading/English language arts (9%–82%) and mathematics (12%–86%) (U.S. Department of Education, 2013). Such massive ranges tell us more about the states' inability to measure ELLs' English learning, proficiency, and academic achievement than they do about students' actual abilities.

With such abysmal results, there are few if any remaining defenders of NCLB. Yet Congress is long overdue in reauthorizing ESEA to make needed changes. As a workaround, the Obama Administration has extended ESEA flexibility waivers to well over half the states. These states agreed to new education reform priorities, including the development of college- and career-ready standards, English language proficiency (ELP) standards that correspond with them, and new tests to measure them. Rather than develop their own standards and assessments, nearly all states have elected to adopt the CCSS and join one of two consortia (Partnership for the Assessment of Readiness for College and Careers [PARCC] and Smarter Balanced Assessment Consortium [SBAC]) developing "next generation" assessments to measure the standards. Nearly all have also joined ELP standards and assessments consortia, with 35 joining World-class Instructional Design and Assessment (WIDA), and 11 joining ELPA21.

To be clear, the CCSS are not a federal initiative and do not replace NCLB, and ESEA flexibility does not waive all NCLB mandates. But CCSS states with waivers are required to lay out how they will use the new assessments to hold schools accountable, in addition to how teachers' performance evaluations will be directly tied to their students' test scores. A major concern is that the needs of ELLs were not considered in the design of the CCSS. Another concern is that in many states' waiver plans, ELLs are no longer tracked as a separate group, but lumped into a "super-subgroup" with other students with unique needs.

Thus, in short, reforms associated with the CCSS and ESEA flexibility waivers continue the failed test-and-punish approach of NCLB. They include even more rigorous standards and a new slate of unproven tests, based on a system that was not designed for ELLs, and in which ELLs' unique language and academic needs are further buried in super-subgroups. Educators must be ever vigilant to ensure that these new reform efforts do not leave ELLs even further behind than under NCLB.

Challenges and Opportunities

1.5 How are students designated as English language learners represented in the Common Core State Standards?

■ *David Nieto*

The Common Core State Standards (CCSS) initiative has created an ambivalent feeling in the field of education. Invested in the lofty goal of providing high standards for all students to meet the knowledge and skills required to be successful in a college or a career setting, the CCSS may represent a unique opportunity to ensure that students have access to a rigorous, all-encompassing, top-quality curriculum. However, there are voices, including teachers' unions such as New York's, which argue that the CCSS represent an attempt to exclusively prepare children for the market economy, teach them *what* to think rather than *how* to think, and absorb states in what has been described as "a race to the middle."

The National Governors Association Center for Best Practices and the Council of Chief State School Officers, authors of the CCSS, have made an effort to convey that the new standards represent a tool for states, districts, and schools to determine what students should master at each grade level and for "teachers [to] be better equipped to know exactly what they need to help students learn" (CCSS Initiative, 2012b).

It is undeniable that the authors have made efforts to provide research-based evidence in support of the new standards—"scholarly research; surveys on what skills are required of students entering college and workforce training programs; assessment data identifying college- and career-ready performance; and comparisons to standards from high-performing states and nations" (CCSS Initiative, 2012b)—and that the focus has shifted to ensure that students master knowledge and skills tightly aligned to college and career readiness.

The fact that the English language arts (ELA) standards are divided in five different strands—reading, writing, speaking and listening, and language—connected throughout the standards helps emphasize the importance of developing strong literacy skills across all the content areas. The call for a greater collaboration and a shared responsibility among teachers from all content areas is a breath of fresh air, especially with the mention of the "unique, time-honored place of ELA teachers in developing students' literacy skills" in an effort to promote reading proficiency in "complex informational text independently in a variety of content areas."[1]

However, given that all students' knowledge and skills will be measured against these rigorous and demanding high standards, the authors have missed a huge opportunity. They need to speak to the diverse challenges English learners (ELs) will face when exposed to these standards in the same way that they refer to the literacy needs of "all" students.

Although the CCSS authors state that "all students must have the opportunity to learn and meet the same high standards if they are to access the knowledge and skills necessary in their post–high school lives," they argue it is "beyond the scope of the Standards to define the full range of supports appropriate for English language learners and for students with special needs" (CCSS Initiative, 2012b). Furthermore, the standards are defined as a set of clear goals and expectations for knowledge and skills, but it is the responsibility of local teachers, principals, superintendents, and others to decide on how to best meet these standards.

It is common knowledge that the fastest growing and the lowest performing (as measured by standardized testing) group of students in our schools are ELs. And although it stands to reason that "no set of grade-specific standards can fully reflect the great variety in abilities, needs, learning rates, and achievement levels of students in any given classroom," releasing a set of more demanding standards, without contributing ways to better serve ELs in both English and content classrooms, equals setting up our students for failure. And then holding teachers responsible for devising "lesson plans and tailor[ing] instruction to the individual needs of the students in their classrooms," which, needless to say, include ELs, will lead to blaming those teachers for the failure.

The silence of the standards about the unique learning needs of ELs is representative of the importance assigned to them in the whole initiative. There is no mention of the "literacies" EL students bring into the classrooms and the "pivotal, unique and time-honored" role of the English as a second language (ESL)/bilingual teacher in serving these students. There is no encouragement for collaboration among content and EL specialist teachers and no reference to the importance of the role of the ELs' native language in the acquisition of the new standards' strands.

Unfortunately, in the case of ELs, the CCSS do not necessarily better equip teachers "to know exactly what they need to help students learn" (CCSS Initiative, 2012b). State and local policies need to take on this role to ensure that EL students' needs are met and teachers are better equipped to serve ELs during the implementation of the CCSS. Also, the new assessments being developed will not be a suitable measurement of EL students' knowledge and skills, but, sadly, in many cases, still a proxy for their English proficiency level.

---

[1] See http://www.corestandards.org/ELA-Literacy/introduction/key-design-consideration/

1.6 What do the Common Core State Standards mean for bilingual education?
■ *María Estela Brisk and C. Patrick Proctor*

The role of language in the Common Core State Standards (CCSS) is profound, and when instruction is delivered in English only, bilingual learners' access to these demanding standards can be curtailed considerably. With abundant research showing the success of well-implemented and high-quality bilingual education programs (August & Hakuta, 1997; Brisk, 2005, 2006; Cummins, 1999; Cummins & Corson, 1997; Gomez, Freeman, & Freeman, 2010; Lindholm-Leary, 2001), bilingual education that has the development of bilingualism and biliteracy as its goal should be considered a viable form of educational programming that will promote the attainment of standards set forth in the CCSS.

Benefits of Bilingual Programming
The use of students' native language by teachers and other students has been associated with better social skills and students' well-being in schools (Chang et al., 2007). Moreover, a bilingual setting defines "students' linguistic and cultural resources as assets" (Michael, Andrade, & Bartlett, 2007, p. 169), positioning students as successful from the start. In bilingual schools the norm is bilingualism, posing no threat to students' identity. In monolingual schools, students often struggle with cultural adaptation, unsure of whether they should or should not make apparent their other language and culture (Phelan, Davidson, & Yu, 1998). Further, the presence of bilingual personnel facilitates students' immediate connection with adults in the school without having to wait to master English. These professionals provide a strong inhouse model of academically successful bilingual adults (García & Bartlett, 2007; Michael, Andrade, & Bartlett, 2007). High-quality bilingual programs that promote learning *of* and *in* two languages are prime educational settings to support the new content and language demands of the CCSS. Specifically, these programs (1) facilitate language, literacy, and content-area learning by providing students with the opportunity to function in the language in which they can best carry out relevant tasks; and (2) promote high levels of bilingualism that may positively affect literacy and cognitive skills in a manner consistent with the demands of the CCSS.

Linguistic Facilitation
While bilingual programs have grown increasingly rare in recent years, they offer greater ease in implementing the CCSS for English-learning children because teaching and learning, particularly in the content areas, occur in the language in which students are most fully proficient. Thus, students are far more likely to be able to access the complex integration of language and content that characterizes the CCSS. The CCSS for oral language articulate that learners present their own thinking and understand others' perspectives (Bunch, 2013; Bunch, Kibler, & Pimentel, 2012). In environments that promote bilingualism, students are less likely to feel inhibited to participate because all

linguistic channels are open for use, which allows for free codeswitching and thus concentration on the topic, rather than struggling to find the words (García & Bartlett, 2007). Further, when bilingual learners are exposed to content instruction in the stronger language, they are more likely to grasp the concepts of instruction that will manifest in the second language as proficiency increases (Cummins, 1991).

Benefits of Bilingualism

In addition to the rather obvious notion that teaching children in their dominant language allows for greater curricular access, the cognitive benefits of balanced bilingualism and biliteracy may also have some bearing on meeting the CCSS. Specifically, the CCSS require students and teachers to pay strict attention to language, including its structure and use. Additionally, students must understand symbolic representation and solve cognitively challenging problems. In a recent meta-analysis of the cognitive correlates of bilingualism, Adesope, Lavin, Thompson, and Ungerleider (2010) found overall effects for bilingualism, irrespective of socioeconomic status, on two major areas: (1) metalinguistic and metacognitive awareness and (2) symbolic representation, attentional control, and problem solving. There are clear links to be made between the demands of the CCSS and the metalinguistic and cognitive correlates of well-developed bilingualism and biliteracy, which is often the goal of well-implemented bilingual programs.

Conclusion

High-quality bilingual education that promotes full development of two languages goes beyond just leveraging the native language of students in service of better English outcomes. It provides robust context to promote the demands of content and language learning of the CCSS by allowing students to use all their linguistic and cultural resources, while also preparing children to function in a global society.

■ *Nelson Flores and Ofelia García*

The CCSS have remained silent regarding bilingualism and bilingual education. The consequences of this silence are that the standards have been interpreted through an English-only lens. With the CCSS now in the initial stages of implementation, we have an opportunity to make bilingual education central to the conversation in ways that ensure that the CCSS build on—rather than ignore—the bilingualism of emergent bilingual (EB) students.

One way to do so is through the use of texts not only in English, but also in the students' home languages. For example, standard 1 for Reading Literature and Reading for Information in grade 6 asks students to grapple "with works of exceptional craft and thought whose range extends across genres, cultures, and centuries." Although it also mentions "seminal U.S. documents, the classics of American literature, and the timeless dramas of Shakespeare," which would seem to indicate the need for an English-only approach, a bilingual education program can teach these texts in the home language, gaining, as the standard continues, "a reservoir of literary and cultural knowledge, references, and images; the ability to evaluate intricate arguments; and the capacity to surmount the challenges posed by complex texts." In other words, students can build on the literacy abilities that they already have in their home language. They can also expand their understanding and learn to grapple with the craft and ideas in the texts, as they compare and contrast the bilingual texts.

Another way that the CCSS can be read in ways that build on the bilingualism of EB students is through an alignment of home language literacy development with the English language arts standards. Many EB students who are new to English are also emerging in their development of academic language, as used in U.S. schools. Therefore, many students will need scaffolding and differentiation to engage with grade-level texts even in their home language. The New York State Bilingual Common Core Initiative (NYSBCCI) is developing a resource that bilingual education teachers can use to meet the diverse needs of their students. The home language arts progressions are divided into five stages of literacy development: (1) entering, (2) emerging, (3) transitioning, (4) expanding, and (5) commanding. Each of these stages includes scaffolded performance indicators that outline the types of supports that students at this stage of academic literacy development in their home language need to engage with grade-level texts and to perform the language tasks that the CCSS in language arts demand.

Reflecting dynamic views of bilingualism that have emerged in recent years, the NYSBCCI is also developing new language arts progressions that bilingual teachers can use to identify appropriate scaffolds and supports to use with EBs at different levels of new language development, whether that be English for English language learners (ELLs)/EBs in transitional or dual language bilingual programs or another language for English-dominant EBs in dual language bilingual programs. Educators who view bilingualism as both a point of departure for language instruction and as a goal for all language learners can use both of these progressions creatively and in tandem in a wide range of bilingual instructional contexts.

Finally, the CCSS can be read in ways that build on the bilingualism of EB students by making their bilingual language practices central to the curriculum. For example, standard 6 for Speaking and Listening in grade 4 asks students to "differentiate between contexts that call for formal English and situations where informal discourse is appropriate." EBs can be supported in achieving this standard by reflecting on the dynamic ways that they use their two languages throughout their day. They may speak a formal variety of their home language with their parents, engage in bilingual interactions with their siblings, and use informal English with their monolingual peers. By analyzing their lived experience they can begin to build bridges to the metalanguage that the standard demands.

The CCSS claim the major goal to prepare students for the 21st century. The 21st century demands bilingual and multilingual competencies—competencies that EB students bring to the classroom. Rather than ignore these competencies, the CCSS must build on them to ensure that EBs are provided access to CCSS-aligned curricula to deepen understanding of texts and language use.

1.7 What are the challenges in identifying and categorizing English language learners/emergent bilinguals?

■ *Robert Linquanti and H. Gary Cook*

There are four key challenges in identifying and categorizing English language learners (ELLs). Before addressing them, let's clarify: We identify and categorize students as ELLs because they have unique educational needs related to fostering their academic uses of English while they learn in English. Their right to receive services addressing those needs is well-established under federal and state law (Linquanti & Cook, 2013). When states, districts, and schools use consistent, carefully determined criteria and procedures to identify and categorize ELLs, students are more likely to be accurately identified and equitably served no matter where they reside. The known benefits of consistent criteria imply moving toward a more common ELL definition *within* states, and over time, *across* states that share common English language proficiency (ELP) and/or academic assessments (Linquanti & Cook, 2013). The four challenges are:

1. *Accurately identifying students who are potentially ELLs.* Identification usually occurs by administering a home language survey (HLS) to the parent/guardian at the time of the student's enrollment. The purposes of the HLS are to: (a) identify students potentially requiring language and academic support services; (b) identify who to assess to determine ELL status; and (c) better understand students' language environments and use (Linquanti & Bailey, 2014). HLS survey questions should therefore focus on students' current language(s) use and frequency of English use and exposure.[1] Examples of questions that address these dimensions include
   - Which language(s) does your child currently understand?/speak?
   - Which language does your child usually use at home?/In school?/Outside of home/school?
   - Which language does your child usually hear at home?/In school?/Outside of home/school?

   Educators should employ clear procedures to consistently obtain and store this information, as well as consistent decision rules to interpret HLS answers. Those students found to be potential ELLs should be formally assessed to confirm (or not confirm) ELL status.

2. *Determining whether a potential ELL should be classified ELL or not.* This determination is usually made by administering some form of assessment. Most states use a placement test or screener, which is either a scaled down version of the summative ELP test or a commercially published ELP test. A few states administer their full ELP test (National Research Council, 2011). A major issue in classifying students as ELLs and placing them into language instruction programs is the variability in

---

[1] Just because a student speaks another language does *not* automatically make him or her either a *potential* or *actual* ELL; frequency of English exposure/use and the level of English proficiency, respectively, determine this.

screening instruments. For example, the World-class Instructional Design and Assessment (WIDA) Consortium provides member states a free ELP screener.[2] While most of the 34 WIDA states use this screener, many do not require it, and others allow districts to choose another screener. Different screeners may be based on different conceptions of ELP, and define what is "English proficient" differently. So even when states share common ELP standards and summative assessments, ELL classification procedures and tools can vary widely across states, and within a given state. As Linquanti and Cook (2013) suggest, there is a great need to establish common ELL classification policies, tools and procedures to standardize how ELLs are classified across districts within a state and across states within a consortium.

3. *Determining an English-proficient performance standard on the state's annual ELP test.* This performance standard—"how good is good enough"—is usually set by the state, but some states allow local educators to determine it (although usually they cannot go below the state standard.) What is an English-proficient performance standard? Linquanti and Cook (2013) argue that federal law provides valuable guidance on how to answer this question. The Elementary and Secondary Education Act within No Child Left Behind (NCLB, 2001) defines an ELL as a student "whose difficulty in speaking, reading, writing or understanding the English language *may* be sufficient to deny [them] the ability to meet the State's proficient level of achievement on State [content] assessments."[3] Note that the law does *not* say that an ELL must be proficient on content assessments to be considered English-proficient, but rather is no longer denied the *potential* to be academically proficient because of English. Multiple methods are available to compare ELLs' state content assessment and ELP assessment results, and identify this content proficiency potential, thus empirically identifying an English-proficient performance standard on the state ELP test (Cook, Linquanti, Chinen, & Jung, 2012).

Yet another challenge emerges in defining an English-proficient performance standard on ELP tests when looking across states and consortia: Weighting domains that comprise a composite score. Under federal law, all states must assess ELLs' listening, speaking, reading, and writing. States combine these four domain test results to create composite scores, but do so in different ways. For example, some states weight domains equally, while others weight literacy domains more than oral domains. This differential composite score weighting makes cross-state comparisons difficult. To improve comparability, states should provide a clear (empirically based) rationale for composite score weights. Also, Cook and MacDonald (2014) offer a reference set of ELP performance level descriptors to support linking and comparisons across state and consortia ELP tests. States and ELP assessment consortia will need to examine the relationship between ELP and content performance; and researchers need to conduct cross-state comparability studies of ELP test scores.

---

[2] The WIDA-ACCESS Placement Test (W-APT); see http://www.wida.us/assessment/w-apt/
[3] See NCLB, §9101 (25)(D)(i).

4. *Determining by what criteria an ELL should be reclassified (or exited) to former-ELL status.* In some states, this is identical to the third challenge because they use only the state ELP test result to determine eligibility to exit ELL status. In most states, however, multiple criteria are used for this decision, and in many of these states, local educators determine the criteria. This makes reclassification the most complicated challenge. Standardizing criteria, and allowing local educators to assess those criteria using methods that support statewide consistency, can help (Linquanti & Cook, 2013).

What criteria to use? One criterion should be the state ELP test result.[4] Other criteria should address ELLs' ability to successfully achieve in English-medium classrooms, and their opportunity to participate fully in society using English.[5] For these dimensions, educators can explore standardized assessment protocols (e.g., rubrics, rating scales) to observe and gather evidence of ELLs' use of receptive, productive and interactional language needed to carry out key academic disciplinary practices in the classroom, as well as to accomplish social/occupational goals within and beyond school. Doing this can help teachers more consistently collect evidence and evaluate ELL performance on these critical dimensions. This requires educators to collaborate and to examine the validity of inferences made from these methods. However, this can draw the attention of educators, students, and families to those language uses needed for life and work in the 21st century.

Finally, exit from ELL status is neither the whole story, nor the end of the story. Former ELL students are lifelong language learners, and will likely need periodic support to continue growing linguistically and academically. While the federal two-year monitoring requirement represents a minimum guideline, educators should monitor and support the progress of former ELLs for as long as they are in the school system.

1.8 What are the purposes of English language development standards?

■ *Kenji Hakuta*

Standards signal a desired set of end-goals for learning that serve multiple purposes:

- To communicate to students, teachers, and other constituents teaching and learning expectations
- To provide guidance and support for teacher preparation programs and in-service teacher professional development (PD)
- To inform publishers, creators of materials, and school administrators about learning expectations, and to guide school administrators and the appropriateness of materials and programs

---

[4] As explained previously, technical methods can help states choose an English-proficient performance standard that addresses the linguistic contribution to academic content test performance while not requiring a minimal level of performance on that academic content assessment.

[5] Two other dimensions in the federal definition for determining an ELL. See NCLB, §9101 (25)(D)(ii–iii).

- To guide specifications of the tests used to measure progress and report program outcomes
- To guide the initial identification and reclassification (exit) of students labeled "English learners (ELs)" (or "limited English proficient [LEP]"—as used in the federal definition)
- To set the framework for legal processes in the investigation and enforcement of federal civil rights protections for LEP students

Among these purposes, the present legal and policy environment privileges the purpose of assessment and accountability, and these set the motivations behind the articulation of English language proficiency (ELP) standards, to which these systems are aligned (Hakuta, 2011). The Elementary and Secondary Education Act (ESEA) (No Child Left Behind, 2001) requires disaggregated reporting on the state content tests for ELs under Title I, and also requires a separate set of assessments in ELP to be used for Title III accountability. Under current administration policy, ELP standards must "correspond" to the college- and career-ready standards of the state, which in most states are the Common Core State Standards (CCSS). Because the standards are written with the intent of meeting the needs of test specifications, they will likely reflect aspects of language that are more readily measurable in testing environments.

An additional challenge is the range of proficiencies that must be reflected, from beginning proficiency in English to full proficiency at each grade level. The problem space is quite different from standard writing for English language arts (ELA) or math, in which the range of at each grade level assumes instruction has taken place in prior grades. The presence of newcomers at each grade level (who, at the same time, vary considerably in their prior schooling) poses challenges not found in content standard writing.

A final major challenge is the disagreement among experts about the appropriate theory of language (forms, functions, and actions—see van Lier & Walqui, 2012a), as well as a theory about the necessary conditions for learning (behaviorist, cognitive, or interactional). The need to place a spotlight on the "correspondence" between ELP standards and the CCSS has resulted in the ascendency of functions and actions over form as the new ELP standards are being developed, but there is lack of agreement about how much explicit instruction of forms is necessary (Council of Chief State Schools Officers, 2012). Furthermore, forms are more measurable than functions and actions and, therefore, may be over-represented in standards that evolve with test development in mind.

■ *Tim Boals*

Think of language development standards as your blueprints for guiding curriculum, instruction, and assessment with respect to language development in classroom contexts, in particular for English language learners (ELLs). Language development standards are not limited to ELA, bilingual, or English as a second language classes, but are necessary to guide language and literacy development in *all* classrooms, with great frequency and intentionality. Within the context of their subject area, every teacher is a language and literacy teacher; we all must "attend to language," the medium through which content learning occurs. To do this, teachers need resources and ongoing PD to transform these blueprints into content and language rich lessons.

Well-written language development standards should provide models of language performance in a variety of instructional contexts, especially, but not exclusively, core subject areas like language arts, mathematics, science, and social studies. At their heart, these "performance models" illustrate language features or language functions, which are words or phrases that serve as examples of how we use language in practical ways to achieve a communicative purpose. "Describe" or "explain" are straightforward examples of language functions. Performance models should clearly link to classroom discourse, and, therefore, state and common content standards because these are the primary drivers of curriculum and lesson planning. Gottlieb and Ernst-Slavit (2014) remind us that content and language standards work together to "provide a full complement of grade-level content and language outcomes" (p. 16).

Language development standards, as delineated through language performance models, are illustrative of or tied to developmental milestones or benchmarks so that teachers can distinguish between what beginning, intermediate, and advanced language use looks like and where ELLs will likely move next in terms of increasingly complex language competencies. Lastly, but importantly, performance models should encourage teachers to scaffold language within socioculturally responsive contexts, in keeping with what Vygotzsky (1978) called the "zone of proximal development."

Language development standards function within standards and assessment systems, and therefore have the potential to inform ongoing classroom-based formative assessment. Because performance models provide examples of language at particular benchmarks or levels, they become tools for assessment, indicative of language progress within content-area contexts. Here, in particular, teachers will likely need interpretive tools and PD to assist them in becoming good judges or "raters" of ELL progress. National assessment consortia can play a crucial role in developing quality resources and PD tools consistent with language development and content standards that support teachers in improving instruction and monitoring growth.

While a significant departure from generic language instruction, using content-infused language development standards to guide instruction is just the beginning. In today's evolving world of work and increasingly diverse populous, we undoubtedly need students to become bilingual and biliterate. But we also hear the term "multiliterate" applied to students' abilities to handle a multiplicity of formats for making meaning beyond the traditional printed English word; this is the context of preparing students for 21st-century college and career opportunities. Language development standards serve to ensure that teachers "attend to language" in every content area and springboard expansive ways of making classrooms rich in language and literacy learning.

1.9 How should we refer to students who are acquiring English as an additional language?

- *Ofelia García*

U.S. students developing English as an additional language have always been described as lacking language and knowledge, and have seldom been recognized for the qualities they possess. Instead of having their potential acknowledged, they are marginalized, made inferior, and seen as limited. By naming them from a deficit perspective, such as limited English proficient (LEP) students or English language learners (ELLs), their capacities are ignored, and the possibility of schools building a multilingual U.S. citizenry is suppressed.

I argue that we should always refer to students who are acquiring English as *emergent bilinguals (EBs)*. Viewing them through a lens of promise, rather than deficiency, enables educators and policymakers to recognize their potential, while at the same time naming bilingualism as an important goal for U.S. society. Additionally, insisting on the emergence of bilingualism challenges old notions of language and bilingualism that are important in our globalized world. In what follows I discuss these three reasons for my preference of the term EB.

EB is a term full of future and promise, but it also recognizes the present. It acknowledges what students already have—their standards in other ways of using words and other knowledge frameworks. It leverages the students' existing standards so that other language features and other ways of understanding can emerge. Using EB, rather than ELL, acknowledges that isolating English from the students' conceptual and linguistic repertoire cannot possibly result in English language learning or in meeting content standards.

By naming bilingualism as an important goal and aspiration, the term EB moves us forward from the conversations we have had in the last half century. The remedial bilingual mentality of the past is no longer applicable in our globalized world. The transnationalism of migrants all over the world, as well as the simultaneity of interactions through sophisticated technology, have long ago debunked monolingualism as the end product of education and an educated elite. Immigrant students are in a privileged position to take on their roles as bilingual U.S. citizens. Naming their home language practices as a talent would mean that educators would no longer see these students as limited or deficient. It would also mean that the goal of a U.S. education would shift from a remedial one of simply teaching English to an expansive one of developing educated bilinguals.

Finally, the term EB signals an emergence of new understanding about language and bilingualism. Language has been increasingly seen as an emergent, complex, and adaptive system. Language is always emerging in creative ways as speakers interact with one another. For EBs, new ways of using language are always interacting with their own inner speech and the voices of others in their communities and families. Bilingualism cannot emerge unless it does so dynamically with other voices, extending the students' language repertoire instead of severing it from its roots. Thus, the term EB also proposes an understanding of these students' language practices that goes beyond two separate languages. It embraces an epistemology of *translanguaging* that poses that bilinguals develop only one language repertoire with features that are societally assigned to one language or another. This translanguaging epistemology can only then change the ways in which we educate these students.

Because of its potential for capturing the capacities of bilingual students, acknowledging the potential of bilingualism for U.S. society, and transforming the ways in which we educate students who are developing English, the term EB should be embraced by the U.S. educational system.

■ *Maria Santos*

LEP, ELLs, or EB, what is in a label and why do we need to be careful with the words we use to describe students? The labels placed on students who are acquiring English as an additional language can create mindsets, define opportunities, and determine investments. Labels not only affect how students are educated, they can also influence how students perceive themselves.

The LEP label tells us that a student is deficient in English as a determinant. It characterizes the student as lacking in English, a lack that needs to be fixed. The label negates any strengths students possess in other languages or any funds of knowledge they have related to academics. This labeling can constrain the educational program students receive, resulting in the programming of students into interventions that simplify language and isolate them from the academic and language demands of the Common Core. This branding can also create a negative stereotype for students acquiring English and lead to lower levels of engagement and effort with academic text. The label can also promote remedial education instead of grade level developmental opportunities in the core academics. As a result of this branding, investments are made in English language development (ELD) and remediation, which often lead to pulling students out of core academic learning opportunities.

The ELL label presents us with students who are developing in one language. It is growth focused and characterizes the students as learners of one language. This label has an ELD priority and is not invested in growing literacies in students' home languages. The parameters for growth are constrained to English and are minimally focused on core academic subjects. The label promotes attention to ELD in the educational programming as a priority for the students, resulting in labeling investments that prioritize ELD as stand-alone courses or as pull-out supports.

The EB label values the development of literacies in languages as well as in academics. The term embodies the characterization of students as learners of two languages and is growth focused, promoting the use of two languages in academic development. It recognizes the complexity of the learner's experience and affirms assets drawn from both languages. The aspiration is to develop literacies in both languages. The investment in both languages requires resources and expertise in a least two languages.

A more powerful label would be *emergent biliterate cross-cultural students,* which would not only value the development of literacies and academics in two languages but would have the goal of developing fully literate students, in addition to acknowledging the complexity of making sense of ideas and perspectives across cultures. The educational programs would be designed to build students' capacity to read, write, communicate, and understand thoughts and ideas in two languages and from diverse cultural perspectives.

The terms LEP and ELL identify a population of students in relation to the English language, narrowing and isolating language development from the complexity of understanding and meaning making. These two labels simplify and compartmentalize the learning exercise to the vocabulary, structures, and forms of languages. They are silent on cross-cultural understanding, which requires significant attention to critical thinking from the learner. The term EB more fully captures the language and academic demand of giving students the opportunity to participate in learning aligned to the Common Core. Yet EB falls short of promoting biliteracy, a highly valued skill in today's international and highly competitive economic society.

Labels are powerful and can be used as "frames" for negative mindsets/beliefs and to promote a deficit model of learners. Conversely, labels have the ability to flip this paradigm so that the frame is neutral or positive, benefiting the learner, creating a growth mindset, and bringing the language and culture of the learner as an asset to the forefront. The ways people, especially those in positions of power, use language lead to social consequences that either engage or marginalize those who do not conform to the established norms of a monolinguistic society. As I stated previously, these labels create mindsets, define opportunities and determine investments; these labels give those in power the position and permission to take action and create policies (investments) that benefit or are detrimental to this population of learners.

1.10 How have different groups of English language learners/emergent bilinguals been categorized and what issues are raised by these categorizations?

■ *Nelson Flores*

Official categories, such as English language learner (ELL), gloss over the tremendous diversity that exists within this large and heterogeneous group. They also erase the fact that these students are emergent bilinguals (EBs) who engage in translanguaging on a daily basis as they negotiate meaning in the many cultural contexts that they navigate. Unfortunately, these translanguaging practices are negated by a dichotomous view of language that positions some language practices as "academic" and others as "nonacademic." The result of this dichotomy is a failure to treat the dynamic bilingualism of ELLs as a vehicle for supporting their engagement with the Common Core State Standards (CCSS).

The stigmatization of the dynamic bilingualism of ELLs is perhaps best illustrated by the classification of a subgroup of these students as "non-nons"—nonspeakers of both

English and their home languages. The argument made in support of this linguistic impossibility is that these students come from linguistically impoverished households that failed to provide them with the foundations in academic language needed to be successful in school. This way of labeling ELLs can also be seen in the increasingly popular category of "long-term English language learners (LTELLs)"—students with official ELL status for seven or more years. As with non-nons, these students are said to have failed to master academic language in either English or their home languages. Students with interrupted formal education (SIFE) is another subgroup of ELLs that is framed in similar ways. These students have at least two years of interrupted schooling, with some arriving in the United States with little to no formal education.

All of these categories are well intentioned in that they seek to bring attention and support to ELLs who are struggling academically. Yet, a focus on what these students supposedly lack continues to perpetuate a deficit perspective—namely that these students lack necessary language and cannot effectively be educated until they have mastered it. This negates the complex linguistic repertoires these students use on a daily basis and leads to a missed opportunity to incorporate these complex repertoires into their academic socialization.

With the CCSS shift toward a view of language as a social practice it is essential that schools reconceptualize the ways that they frame the language practices of these students. Specifically, it is important to acknowledge that many of the social practices that the CCSS expect students to engage with and that are seen as "academic" overlap significantly with the social practices that students categorized as non-nons, LTELLs, and SIFE use on a daily basis to negotiate meaning in their complex linguistic worlds. For example, the sixth anchor standard of the Speaking and Listening standards is to "adapt speech to a variety of contexts and communicate tasks, demonstrating command of formal English when indicated or appropriate." The vagueness of what is meant by "formal English" notwithstanding, the fact of the matter is that all bilingual students (regardless of how they are categorized by schools) by necessity have learned to adapt their speech to a variety of contexts. These social practices can easily get overlooked when framing certain bilingual students as lacking academic language.

It is time to move away from a discussion of how certain subgroups of ELLs lack academic language toward a discussion of the complex translanguaging practices of these students and the communities where they reside. Only by doing this will it be possible to begin to develop linguistically responsive curricula that make the dynamic bilingualism of *all* bilingual students (regardless of how they are categorized) central to their academic socialization into the social practices required by the CCSS.

■ *Karen Beeman and Cheryl Urow*

For many years, one of the main premises of bilingual and dual language programs has been the idea that all students have a dominant language. This premise has led to decisions about student placement, the language(s) used for literacy instruction, and the allocation of content and language across the curriculum. While the idea of language dominance may make sense for sequential bilinguals who learn one language at home and then acquire a second language later in school, most students who are classified as ELLs no longer fit the description of a sequential bilingual. Rather, 75% of our current ELLs in elementary schools are better described as simultaneous bilinguals: individuals who have been exposed to two languages together, typically from birth to age 5 (Swanson, 2009). Their language development is described as bilingual first language acquisition (Potowski, 2013).

Although we find increasing understanding of simultaneous bilingualism, many bilingual and dual language programs continue to identify and place ELLs by first looking for "language dominance." For example, educators may use results of placement tests given separately in Spanish and then in English to describe some students as "low in both languages" or "semilingual," and the implications of this labeling can be damaging. Educators who view language practices from a monolingual perspective may counsel some students out of bilingual or dual language programs because they believe that students "know enough English" or are "confused." This reflects a lack of understanding about how students learn through two languages at school. In an attempt to determine a dominant language, the linguistic abilities of the students in English and Spanish are sometimes listed side by side to determine which language "wins." While it is critical to know what each student can do in each language, the notion that "he knows more colors in English than in Spanish, therefore he is English-dominant" ignores the rich linguistic background of these EBs.

Rather than categorizing students as English dominant, or Spanish dominant, we recommend that educators begin by looking at students from a holistic biliteracy perspective, and pay attention to the ways that students use oral and written language(s) at home, school, and in the community (e.g., English/Spanish/both). Educators will also need to keep track of whether students are designated as ELLs (as determined by the federally mandated test each state must administer) or non-ELLs for official school purposes. However, educators don't need to be constrained by these official designations. They can look for strategic ways to build on students' U.S. Spanish and English bilingual language practices and work toward the goal of bilingualism for all.

Bilingual and dual language programs are using more multilingual approaches, such as interviews with parents, documenting interactions with students in both languages, and using anecdotal evidence and formative assessments that capture what students can do in two languages to identify student language abilities. These districts are questioning the monolingual perspective that assesses student knowledge exclusively in one language and looks incorrectly at students as two monolinguals in one mind (Grosjean, 1989).

Many districts are shifting to a multilingual perspective that expects students to use their two languages together. We see increasing numbers of bilingual education programs structured in ways that build on students' strengths in their home and new languages, and guide students toward the goals of content learning and biliteracy development. Districts also purposefully carve out an instructional moment when the two languages are intentionally placed together. We call this instructional moment the Bridge (Beeman

& Urow, 2013), and it encourages students to compare and contrast their two languages (communication–*comunicación*) and develop metalinguistic awareness. Students are also assessed for content and language learning in two languages, side by side.

Challenging the idea of language dominance is important if we are to continue to build on what our students know and can do with language. Following a strength-based approach opens up a tremendous number of possibilities for all students, both sequential and simultaneous bilingual learners.

1.11 What kinds of variation do we find in the category "English language learner"?

■ *Rebecca Field*

The category "English language learner (ELL)" is incredibly diverse. Teachers and administrators can make better policy, programming, curriculum, instruction, and assessment decisions about how to implement the Common Core State Standards (CCSS) when they understand the diversity in their classes, schools, and communities. When educators focus on students as individuals who come to school with linguistic, cultural, and content-area expertise developed through personal experiences inside and outside of school, they can make informed choices that support student learning. To illustrate the kinds of diversity educators may find in their schools, this piece introduces profiles of three prototypical ELLs/emergent bilingual (EB) students who have reached the same composite level (3—intermediate) of English language development (ELD).[1] However, their specific linguistic, cultural, and educational experiences suggest the need for differentiated approaches so that each student can reach the same rigorous core content standards over time.

- **Julia is a Level 3 ELL who was born in the United States** to a Mexican family that speaks mostly Spanish at home and in the neighborhood. Julia has attended U.S. schools since kindergarten, and has been in pull-out ESL each year. There is no bilingual program at her school, and Julia has not learned to read and write in Spanish. According to the state English language proficiency (ELP) test, Julia is a Level 5 listening, Level 4 speaking, Level 3 reading, and Level 2 writing.
- **Ko Than Nu is a Level 3 ELL from Burma** who speaks Karen. Ko Than Nu is a refugee who has been in the United States for two years. He had no formal schooling before coming to the United States, nor had he learned to read or write. When Ko Than Nu arrived, he was placed in a newcomer/port of entry class that focused on literacy and numeracy development, with attention to the cultural norms of U.S. schools and society. According to the state ELP test, Ko Than Nu is Level 4 in listening and speaking and Level 2 in reading and writing in English.

---

[1] The state-mandated ELD/ELP (English language proficiency) systems vary, especially in terms of nomenclature. However, all systems yield data on ELLs' composite levels as well as their levels in reading, writing, listening, and speaking. Although no system is perfect, these data provide a useful starting point for educators.

- **Amitabh is a Level 3 ELL from India** who speaks Gujarati. Amitabh arrived in the United States in the middle of last year. He has a strong educational background that included English instruction every year in India. However, Amitabh's English instruction gave him little opportunity to speak English at school, and he has had little exposure to American English prior to his arrival. According to the state ELP test, Amitabh is a Level 2 listening, Level 1 speaking, Level 5 reading, and Level 4 writing.

Because ELD data are (or should be) readily available to all educators, let's start with this information. Reflecting its strength-based approach, the World-class Instructional Design and Assessment (WIDA) Consortium publishes a useful tool, the *Can-do Descriptors,* that allow educators to see at a glance what ELLs/EBs can do with reading, writing, listening, and speaking at different levels of ELD. On the following table, I have placed Julia, Ko Than Nu, and Amitabh on the can-do descriptors for grades preK–12.

For the given level of English language proficiency, **with support**, English language learners can:

Level 6 Reaching

	Level 1 Entering	Level 2 Beginning	Level 3 Developing	Level 4 Expanding	Level 5 Bridging
LISTENING	• Point to stated pictures, words, phrases • Follow one-step oral directions • Match oral statements to objects, figures or illustrations **Amitabh**	• Sort pictures, objects according to oral instructions • Follow two-step oral directions • Match information from oral descriptions to objects, illustrations **Amitabh**	• Locate, select, order information from oral descriptions • Follow multi-step oral directions • Categorize or sequence oral information using pictures, objects	• Compare/contrast functions, relationships from oral information • Analyze and apply oral information • Identify cause and effect from oral discourse **Ko Than Nu**	• Draw conclusions from oral information • Construct models based on oral discourse • Make connections from oral discourse **Julia**
SPEAKING	• Name objects, people, pictures • Answer WH- (who, what, when, where, which) questions **Amitabh**	• Ask WH- questions • Describe pictures, events, objects, people • Restate facts	• Formulate hypotheses, make predictions • Describe processes, procedures	• Discuss stories, issues, concepts • Give speeches, oral reports • Offer creative solutions to issues, problems **Julia; Ko Than Nu**	• Engage in debates • Explain phenomena, give examples, and justify responses • Express and defend points of view
READING	• Match icons and symbols to words, phrases or environmental print • Identify concepts about print and text features	• Locate and classify information • Identify facts and explicit messages • Select language patterns associated with facts **Ko Than Nu**	• Sequence pictures, events, processes • Identify main ideas • Use context clues to determine meaning of words **Julia**	• Interpret information or data • Find details that support main ideas • Identify word families, figures of speech	• Conduct research to glean information from multiple sources • Draw conclusions from explicit and implicit text **Amitabh**
WRITING	• Label objects, pictures, diagrams • Draw in response to a prompt • Produce icons, symbols, words, phrases to convey meaning	• Make lists • Produce drawings, phrases, short sentences, notes • Give information requested from oral or written directions **Julia; Ko Than Nu**	• Produce bare-bones expository or narrative texts • Compare/contrast information • Describe events, people, processes, procedures **Julia**	• Summarize information from graphics or notes • Edit and revise writing • Create original ideas or detailed responses **Amitabh**	• Apply information to new contexts • React to multiple genres and discourses • Author multiple forms/genres of writing

Courtesy of WIDA Consortium.

This simple example illustrates the need to look beyond the composite ELD level. Julia, Ko Than Nu, and Amitabh have all reached composite ELD Level 3, but their scores vary in listening, speaking, reading, and writing. This variation can be explained when we consider these students' language, literacy, cultural, and educational backgrounds.

Julia is an example of a large number of ELLs we find in U.S. schools who score higher in listening and speaking than in reading and writing in English. Julia can use English to converse with her friends, tell them what she did the night before, joke with them, and argue about who is the fastest runner. Julia can also use Spanish to talk with her parents and grandparents at home about what she did at school and to keep them apprised of her after-school plans, but she has not learned how to read and write in Spanish. As the most advanced speaker of English in her household, Julia takes on responsibilities as a language and cultural interpreter by answering phones, negotiating health and social service appointments for her parents and grandparents, and moving fluidly between Spanish and English as needed. Julia has a strong foundation in oral Spanish and English, and she is still developing the ways of using oral and written English in school settings to summarize a reading; demonstrate her understanding of a text with sufficient detail; and produce a strong, evidence-based argument in writing. Students like Julia are sometimes referred to as long-term ELLs (LTELLs) (Menken & Kleyn, 2010). However, with appropriate differentiated instruction and assessment (Fairbairn & Jones-Vo, 2010)—and time—teachers can expect students like Julia to succeed at school.

Like Julia, Ko Than Nu also scores higher in listening and speaking than he does in reading and writing on the state-mandated ELP test. He participates enthusiastically in everyday conversations in English with his peers and eagerly contributes orally in class discussions about topics that he knows something about.

Ko Than Nu had not had attended school before he came to the United States. He spent nearly ten years at a refugee camp in Thailand and he understands Thai in addition to Karen. He and his family now regularly attend a local Baptist church where English, Karen, and other languages from Burma are used. Ko Than Nu has not had the opportunity to learn to read and write in his home language, and he is far below grade level. Ko Than Nu is unsuccessful when the teacher asks him to read grade-level texts independently, and he struggles with colloquial English (e.g., "The boy was in a pickle" in a children's story). Because the cultural norms at school are new to Ko Than Nu, sometimes teachers think he has behavior problems. Ko Than Nu is an example of what is increasingly called SIFE (student with interrupted former education). These students need intensive and comprehensive support for literacy and numeracy development with attention to the cultural norms of U.S. schools and society.

We find students like Amitabh less frequently in U.S. schools, but his profile helps us avoid overgeneralizations and stereotypes about "intermediate ELLs." Amitabh's prior schooling provides him with a strong foundation for literacy and academic success in English and in Gujarati. Amitabh's family travels internationally every year to visit their relatives, and this year he will spend the summer break in India and England.

Because Amitabh's English instruction in India focused on grammar, reading, and writing, he is just beginning to develop oral "American" English. Because it is uncommon for ELLs to have stronger reading and writing skills than listening and speaking skills, teachers may not recognize Amitabh's content-area expertise or literacy strengths and they may treat him more like a beginning ELL in all domains.

Regardless of whether ELLs/EBs are in English-medium or bilingual instruction, home languages should be seen as a strength that educators can build on, and not as a problem to overcome. Fortunately, educators today can easily access powerful resources to help them understand more about the home languages of the bilingual learners in their classes, schools, and communities. For example, the New York State Initiative on Emergent Bilinguals (NYSIEB) in partnership with the City University of New York (CUNY) has identified the top ten languages in New York and developed a guide to help educators work with students from these language backgrounds (Funk, 2012). And in spring 2012, the New York State (NYS) Education Department launched the Bilingual Common Core Initiative that includes the development of the New Language Arts Progressions (NLAP) and Home Language Arts Progressions (HLAP) for every NYS Common Core Learning Standard in every grade. These resources provide concrete guidance for teachers about languages other than English, and about how to use students' home languages and new languages in the context of the CCSS English Language Arts Standards.

Experience leads to expertise. When educators learn about the experiences that their ELLs/EBs have had with language, literacy, and education inside and outside of school, they can make informed decisions about language policies, programming, curriculum, instruction, and assessment.

1.12 What spaces for bi/multilingualism can we find within the context of Common Core State Standards implementation?

■ *Tatyana Kleyn*

Misconceptions that the Common Core State Standards (CCSS) are to be taught in, through, and about English abound. At the same time, publishers are scrambling to develop Common Core–aligned and purportedly research-based curriculum with materials either only or mostly in English. However, there is nothing about the CCSS that demand an English-only approach. To the contrary, bringing in students' home languages not only helps them access the CCSS, but a bi/multilingual approach does so in a more enriching and holistic manner.

The CCSS require students to think critically, read analytically, and use language in sophisticated ways. For many students who are in the early stages of learning English, reaching these standards in English only will be an uphill and nearly impossible task. When we deny students the use of their full linguistic repertoire, that is, all the languages they use and know, it is like telling them to get from one place to another only using their left feet, and not their right. Clearly there are times when students need to focus on building one language, depending on the goal of the lesson or standard, but often we want students to focus on comprehension first and foremost—regardless of the language. For students who are emergent bilinguals (EBs), the best way to build understanding is through inclusion of the home language, because learning a concept is independent of any specific language.

There are also ways that languages other than English can enrich the learning of the CCSS for students who have bilingual and biliterate proficiencies. These students, who may never have been or are no longer labeled as "English language learners (ELLs)," should continue using their home languages as resources throughout their education, and learning the CCSS is no exception.

There is a range of ways to allow students to use their home languages to access the CCSS, and these differ by programs, resources, and students' language and literacy backgrounds. Within bilingual programs students learn in both languages, via instruction, discussion, resources, and tasks that could be completed in the home language, in English, or bi/multilingually. Within English as a second language and inclusive education programs, students can be provided resources in their home languages, allowed to use technology such as Google translate to access English texts (when authentic texts or translations are not available), and given opportunities to discuss concepts in home language peer groups.

Following are two examples of how specific CCSS were addressed bilingually within two levels and programs.

Grade 2 Bilingual (Spanish–English) Classroom

CCSS: RL.2.3 Describe how characters in a story respond to major events and challenges

Curriculum: Core knowledge listening and learning strand

Home language inclusion: Although this is an English read-aloud curriculum, the teacher scaffolds the lesson by periodically asking students to summarize what was just read in Spanish so that all students can comprehend the content while those who are bilingual can engage in the skill of summarizing in a different language. The teacher also explains key concepts and vocabulary in Spanish, checking for cognates, and asks students to turn and talk in Spanish and report to the class in English or Spanish.

Learning: Students have a better understanding of the text and can discuss how the character responds to major events and challenges. Some students can do this bilingually; others are able to do so in Spanish and still meet the lesson's CCSS.

Grade 11 Social Studies/English as a Second Language Classroom

CCSS: SL.11–12.2 Integrate multiple sources of information presented in diverse formats and media (e.g., visually, quantitatively, orally) to make informed decisions and solve problems, evaluating the credibility and accuracy of each source and noting any discrepancies among the data

Curriculum: Living undocumented: High school, college, and beyond film lesson

Home language inclusion: Students complete the anticipatory guide in English or Spanish and watch the short documentary with Spanish subtitles.

Learning: By previewing the key concepts in their home language and having access to the Spanish translations of the film, students become familiar with the content of the film and the perspectives within it. They can then evaluate (in English) the information presented in this film with a different film or text on the same topic.

DISCUSSION QUESTIONS

After reading this chapter, engage in dialogue with peer educators, including school principals, other administrators and supervisors, teachers of different subjects, specialists in different areas, paraprofessionals, and parents/community members to discuss the terrain and landscape surrounding CCSS implementation and ELLs/emergent bilinguals in your state/district/school/program. Here are some questions to reflect on individually, with a colleague, or ideally, as part of a professional learning community at your school. If you are in a school, the members of this group would comprise the school's ELL/EB leadership team, whose responsibility it is to collectively make the decisions that affect the education of ELLs/EBs.

1. Bring information about the demographics of your area and your school. Have there been changes? Is the population stable? Consider Rumbaut's and Massey's (see 1.2) positions about the increasing scale of the challenge of educating U.S. born children of immigrant origin. Talk about your experiences and share your insights about both challenges and possibilities.

2. What are the challenges of the CCSS for EBs/ELLs? Consider the opinions of Nieto (see 1.5), Brisk and Proctor, and Garcia and Flores (see 1.6). Does the group agree that EBs/ELLs are an afterthought? Make a list of the key considerations that your school and district need to consider in planning for the inclusion of EBs/ELLs in CCSS implementation.

3. Are the challenges of identifying and categorizing EBs/ELLs identified by Linquanti and Cook (see 1.7) an issue in your state or district? Which of the four challenges is the most serious? What solutions to the challenges would you propose?

4. García (see 1.9) argues that we should always refer to students who are acquiring English as "emergent bilinguals." Do you agree with García? Can you explain what "emergent" means?

TOPICS FOR REFLECTION AND ACTION

The following statements are organized around the big ideas of the chapter. Read through them and indicate the extent to which each applies to your community and your school. After you complete the survey, discuss your responses with your team. Then write down one to three reflection points that have emerged from your discussions. Finally, identify one to three concrete actions that you/your team can take.

DK don't know   1 strongly disagree   2 disagree   3 agree   4 strongly agree

PERSPECTIVES ON THE CCSS					
1. The challenges and changes that are part of the implementation of the CCSS are well known in the community and have been discussed extensively.	DK	1	2	3	4
2. The challenges and changes that are part of the implementation of the CCSS are well known in my school and discussed extensively.	DK	1	2	3	4
3. The challenges and changes for EBs/ELLs have been a central part of the discussion.	DK	1	2	3	4
4. Our school and district have done a good job of providing information about the standards and their related assessments.	DK	1	2	3	4

Perspectives on Change

5. The population of our community is changing and there are concerns and worries about how new families and new students will be integrated.	DK	1	2	3	4
6. Our school has done a lot with newcomers. We know a great deal about their linguistic resources and their needs.	DK	1	2	3	4
7. We have had programs in place to address the needs of EBs/ELLs and worry that CCSS implementation will change what we do well.	DK	1	2	3	4

EBs/ELLs

8. We are pleased with the ways in which EB/ELLs are categorized by our current state/district procedures.	DK	1	2	3	4
9. We have many debates about what to call students who are new to English.	DK	1	2	3	4

CCSS and EBs/ELLs

10. We are concerned that EB/ELLs are an afterthought for the CCSS	DK	1	2	3	4
11. We are determined to find ways to make EBs/ELLs successful in the current assessment and accountability landscape.	DK	1	2	3	4
12. We are eager to learn about instructional practices that can help us use students' full linguistic repertoires in the classroom.	DK	1	2	3	4

Reflections:

Action Steps:

2

Fundamental Language Issues

This chapter focuses on language itself. How language is conceptualized, how we think it is acquired, how we talk about it, and how we measure what we refer to as "language proficiency" matter a great deal. In this era of Common Core State Standards (CCSS) reform, language is of particular importance because achieving the new standards will make increased demands on all students' ability to use English to engage in standards-aligned disciplinary practices and to display subject matter competence and appropriate language practices on standardized performance assessments to be delivered via computers. Those of us who work with English language learners (ELLs)/ emergent bilinguals (EBs) are justifiably worried. We talk about the greater burdens that these students will face, and we are determined to be optimistic. We know, however, that ELLs/EBs were not directly considered when the standards were drafted, and we are concerned about the functional English language abilities and the specific knowledge about language that are assumed by English language proficiency (ELP) frameworks and assessments. At the same time, we know that ELLs/EBs bring with them important resources in their primary languages, resources that can be developed and built on to achieve high standards and prepare this country for an interconnected 21st-century world.

We have included this chapter because we want to invite our readers to once again think deeply about language and about the ways that we talk about language to each other, parents, and children. We are especially aware of the ways that ideologies of language—beliefs and "commonsense notions about the nature of language in the world" (Rumsey, 1990)—affect our policies and our pedagogies. We know, for example, that there are strong negative views in the United States about bilingualism and that the term "bilingual" is often still used as a euphemism for *poor* and *disadvantaged*. Many of us who work with ELLs/EBs have over years learned to challenge these views strongly.

The ways in which we came to accept commonly held views and beliefs about the superiority or inferiority of particular ways of speaking/writing in a single language or the validity of using resources from more than one language are often much less obvious. We have generally not seen such perspectives as ideological, and yet it is evident that implicit and explicit unquestioned notions of language directly influence our views about legitimate educational discourse. These notions matter because, as Kroskrity (2004) reminds us, "language ideologies represent the perception of language and discourse that is constructed in the interest of a specific social or cultural group." As Lippi-Green (2012) points out in *English with an Accent*, beliefs about language are similar to religious beliefs. They are both cherished and passed on and strongly defended.

Like Lippi-Green, the editors of this book suggest that if we, as educators and researchers, want to make certain that such beliefs do not harm the children that we work with, we must first begin with an examination of these beliefs, and with an awareness that ideologies of language are not neutral. Chapter 2, then, is an invitation to our readers to engage in a re-examination of existing popular views about language, including bilingualism/multilingualism, language mixing, pure and uncontaminated languages, native-like proficiencies, standardized varieties of language, and the non-empirical perspectives on language acquisition and development that are embodied in state ELP standards.

The chapter is divided into three sections. First, we review what we know about becoming bilingual and multilingual, and we consider competing perspectives on language acquisition and development. The second section focuses on the language that is valued in school. We discuss what educators need to know about language on the one hand and about expectations for language in the CCSS on the other hand. We look closely at what has been termed "academic language" because it is of central concern in the CCSS for all students. Applied linguists offer expertise that teachers and curriculum developers can build on, as well as cautions against oversimplifying this complex notion. Sociolinguists explain how language variation matters when working with linguistically diverse learners, including students who speak vernacular varieties of English (e.g., Ebonics, pidgins, creoles). The chapter concludes with a critical look at what we know—and what we don't yet know—about teaching and learning language at school. The contributions in this chapter, like the discussion questions and end-of-chapter activities, invite readers to make explicit and look critically at their perspectives on language, bilingualism, language acquisition, and language variation. Educators need a solid foundation in fundamental language issues in order to make sound decisions about teaching language for academic purposes to language learners at school.

Becoming Bilingual and Multilingual: Language Acquisition and Development

2.1 What is bilingualism/multilingualism?

- *Guadalupe Valdés*

Bilingualism/multilingualism is a common human condition that involves the use of more than one language for communication. It is characteristic of the majority of the world's population and results from the movement of peoples, including by conquest, colonization, migration, and trade. Bilingual/multilingual individuals share one key characteristic with each other: they have more than one language competence. They are able to function (i.e., speak, understand, read, or write) even to a very limited degree in more than one language. As this broad definition of bilingualism suggests, there are many different kinds and types of individuals who can be classified as bilingual/multilingual. At one end of the continuum, there are individuals who may be accepted as competent speakers of each of their languages by native speakers of those languages; and, at the other end of the continuum, there are bilinguals whose only ability in a second language may be limited to reading with the aid of a bilingual dictionary. For individuals who subscribe to a narrow definition of bilingualism, the term "bilingual" is used exclusively to describe a person who *is two monolinguals in one person,* who can do everything perfectly in two languages, and who can pass undetected among the speakers at each of the two languages. While absolutely equivalent abilities in two languages are theoretically possible, individuals seldom use two languages to carry the exact same functions. They do not develop identity strengths in both languages because they develop and use them in different ways. They may speak to a grandmother in Russian, share secrets with a sibling in English, tell jokes with cousins in both English and Russian, and read poetry and pray exclusively in Russian.

Individuals become bilingual/multilingual when the language that they speak does not suffice to meet all of their communicative needs. To engage in trade or to function in the workplace, for example, adults will often acquire key elements of a needed language by imitating their coworkers. As they use the language over time, they increase their proficiency to carry out the kinds of communicative tasks that are essential for them. Similarly, children who are raised in contexts where family or community members speak several languages acquire a complex linguistic repertoire that allows them to communicate effectively with these different individuals. Simply stated, bilingualism/multilingualism is a natural consequence of lived experience and of the necessity to communicate with others who do not share the same language.

Unfortunately, in many advanced societies, there are many myths and misunderstandings about bilingualism. In the United States, for example, American ideologies of bilingualism and monolingualism and theories about English language competencies and their acquisition and development permeate educational practice. The popular *and* the scholarly discourse on bilingualism reveal a multilayered set of themes that contribute directly to a version of reality where monolingualism is the normal and ideal human condition, and bilingualism is profoundly suspect. Embedded within the discourse of monolingualism are strong beliefs about (1) the dangers of early bilingualism, (2) the negative effects of "unbalanced" bilingualism on individuals, and (3) the expectation that "true" or "real" bilinguals will be identical to two native speakers in both their languages.

In the last several years, however, much has changed. The general U.S. public has been made aware of the cognitive benefits of bilingualism through articles in the *New York Times* and other widely read publications. Work by Bialystok (2011) has established that the executive function is fortified in bilingual individuals, leading to more efficient performance on executive control tasks, and that bilinguals continue to outperform monolinguals as they age, leading to a delay in the symptoms of dementia, particularly Alzheimer's disease. Work in psycholinguistics, moreover, has established that bilingual individuals are cognitively complex, unique speaker–hearers—never two monolinguals in one person (e.g., Grosjean, 1989).

In school settings, there is increasing recognition that immigrant students who must acquire English (the dominant societal language) to be educated through that language bring with them important linguistic resources that teachers can build on. Indeed, many scholars (e.g., Rodriguez, Carrasquillo, & Lee, 2014) speak of "the bilingual advantage" as providing both social and intellectual benefits that promote academic development.

The literature on bilingualism is rich and draws from psycholinguistic, linguistic, and sociolinguistic research with U.S. immigrant groups, as well as around the world. It is fundamental to educators' ability to understand, for example: (1) how languages are lived and developed, (2) why learning a second language in instructional settings is challenging, (3) how strengths developed in one language can transfer to the other, and (4) how classroom contexts can allow students to utilize their full communicative repertoires in the service of learning (García & Kleifgen, 2010).

2.2 How does a holistic perspective on (bi/multi)literacy help educators address the demands of the Common Core State Standards for English language learners/emergent bilinguals?

- *Susan Hopewell and Kathy Escamilla*

Holistic understandings of bilingualism are grounded in the idea that what is known and understood in one language contributes to what is known and understood in the other, and that all languages contribute to a single and universally accessible linguistic and cognitive system. From this perspective, languages and literacies are interdependent and mutually reinforcing. Put simply, the linguistic capacities of emergent bilingual learners are integrated, and we can never fully understand what a student comprehends and is able to do by examining only one language. Emergent bilingual (EB) learners use all of their linguistic resources when interacting with text and the world. What they know and understand may be distributed across languages.

While the Common Core State Standards (CCSS) are ostensibly concerned only with the development of *English* language arts, a holistic understanding of language and literacy acquisition compels us to examine ways in which nurturing, inviting, and celebrating bilingualism and biculturalism will ultimately expand EB students' opportunities to learn. A key step is for educators to learn and become knowledgeable about students' language and literacy backgrounds. How many and which languages do students know? Under what circumstances was the language acquired? (That is, to what extent are students able to read, write, speak, etc., in each language? Did students attend schools in which their languages were the medium of instruction?) What levels of proficiency are to be expected? Grouping students who share language and cultural backgrounds, and encouraging them to use their shared languages to negotiate text, will increase their abilities to apply their background knowledge and understanding to make sense of the learning objectives.

Research data indicate that EB students often have greater receptive (reading and listening) language abilities than productive (writing and speaking) language abilities. The result is that students often understand English language text better than they are able to express. Therefore, to the extent possible, allowing EB students to demonstrate English language text comprehension through whatever linguistic means are available to them may increase students' ability to communicate understanding which, in turn, increases our capacity to more quickly and confidently introduce them to increasingly complex and sophisticated texts. If we want students to accelerate in language and literacy acquisition, we must accept that holistic lenses provide greater opportunities for students to demonstrate their capacities, thereby increasing the likelihood that they can participate meaningfully in rigorous literacy instruction.

One unfortunate downside of the CCSS is the failure to recognize that biliteracy is ultimately a higher and more sophisticated form of literacy than monoliteracy. As such, it ought to be our goal that all students become biliterate, and that our standards develop *multilingual* language arts standards rather than being restricted to English only. As we self-reflect on our values as a nation, we would hope to see a commitment to holistic bilingualism that sets standards for all students to become biliterate. A starting premise would be to operate from the belief that *all* students are capable of learning in and through two languages.

As part of an innovative biliteracy model we call Literacy Squared, we have developed a holistic framework for biliteracy in which language and literacy instruction begins in two languages as early as kindergarten and is intentionally planned such that instruction is coordinated across languages (Escamilla et al., 2014). Language and literacy development are not conceived as specific to individual languages (which often results in duplicative instruction), but rather as integrated and synchronized disciplines. Both within and across languages, teachers strive to adopt a holistic pedagogy in which reading, writing, oracy, and metalanguage are attended to in balanced proportion. Assessment systems document students' trajectories toward biliteracy such that students are honored for the totality of what they can do, rather than being penalized for what they are not yet able to demonstrate in English.

2.3 How have different research perspectives viewed language development and language acquisition?

- *L. Quentin Dixon*

The terms "language proficiency," "language development," and "language acquisition" are commonly used when considering instructional issues related to English language learners (ELLs); for example, eligibility for bilingual or English as a second language (ESL) services generally relies on a determination of whether an English language learner has reached *proficiency* in English. But what do these terms mean? The Common Core State Standards (CCSS) do not define these terms; thus, we turn to conceptualizations from four different research traditions that have examined questions relating to "second language acquisition," the learning of a new language after a child or adult has already gained competence in their first or "native" language. Four broad research traditions have informed research and practice in second language acquisition greatly: foreign language education, child language research, sociocultural theory, and psycholinguistics. I briefly summarize the perspectives of these four general approaches on the terms "language proficiency," "language development," and "language acquisition."

Of the four groups, foreign language educators are probably the most concerned with defining and measuring language proficiency. However, foreign language educators tend to think of language proficiency as the mastery of what the foreign language teacher presented in the classroom, with the ideal being attainment of native speaker norms of grammatical competence and pronunciation. Progress in language development is marked by the elimination of grammatical errors. Language acquisition is seen as occurring when a student with high aptitude for language learning and high motivation pursues learning a language.

Child language researchers have long documented children's first language acquisition, and have recently turned to examining children's and adults' second language acquisition. Language proficiency is not a concept that is widely used by these researchers because it is the ongoing, lifelong process of language acquisition that is of interest to them. In contrast to foreign language educators who generally deplore errors, child language researchers see errors as important clues regarding the child's (or adult's) working hypotheses regarding the language being acquired. For example, young children or second language learners may say "I eated." To the child language researcher, such errors demonstrate the learner's acquisition of the general rule of marking past tense and may be a sign of progress in language development. Children and second language learners develop their language by updating these types of hypotheses as more language input is absorbed.

Similar to child language researchers, psycholinguists do not emphasize language proficiency. Rather, psycholinguists are interested in the mental processes necessary for language acquisition, which they see as fundamentally the same for first and second language acquisition, except that second language learners start with more information. Psycholinguists view language development as natural as long as there is input in the language and some effort to understand it.

Language proficiency for sociocultural theorists focuses on the appropriateness and effectiveness of communication rather than on the attainment of some elusive native-speaker standard in grammar and/or pronunciation. Unlike psycholinguists who see language exposure as key, sociocultural researchers emphasize the importance of social context to language development. They recognize that the status of a language or the social rewards for learning a language will influence how well a learner will acquire the language. For example, an English speaker who enjoys participating in discussions of the events of a recent *telenovela* with Spanish-speaking friends may acquire Spanish more quickly than an English speaker who is only using Spanish in a foreign language classroom. Language acquisition is depicted as a fundamentally social process that therefore also necessarily includes negotiating a new culture.

2.4 How has the acquisition/development of English been conceptualized for English language learners/emergent bilinguals? What are the implications of different ways of conceptualizing these processes?

■ **Diane Larsen-Freeman**

One conceptualization of English acquisition is that it is an individual cognitive process. It is seen to be the individual learner's task to figure out the rules of the linguistic system from the language to which he or she is exposed. For example, an English language learner (ELL) might have noticed that in English questions are formed by inverting the subject and the verb: You are from Mexico. Are you from Mexico? While the rising intonation of such questions is universal, the word order is not. According to a cognitive view of language acquisition, a learner has to figure out the word order rule and apply it to make his or her own questions and to comprehend the question of others. Such a view also holds that under propitious conditions, acquisition proceeds along a developmental continuum, known as an interlanguage. The use of the term "interlanguage" focuses attention on the systematic nature of ELLs' language production, rather than seeing it as random performance.

The language acquisition process has also been conceptualized socially. According to this view, language learning is not a strictly individual cognitive act, equivalent across all ELLs and situations. Rather, the acquisition process is presumed to be situated and social, with ELLs learning the local norms of social usage primarily through interaction with others (especially more knowledgeable others). Provided that the interactions are at an appropriate level, the ELLs' learning of English will be scaffolded, with the learners receiving support tailored to their communication goals. Social functions, such as extending an invitation or making a request, are also being learned through these interactions. Thus, the linguistic system is less in focus; instead, language is a means for doing something.

A third conceptualization, emergentism or a usage-based approach, combines cognitive and social views of learning. Language development is seen as an adaptive, dynamic process, involving changes in ELLs' emerging language resources as they adapt in response to new experiences and feedback. As ELLs use English to communicate with others, they discover constructions that are used to make meaning in context. The form–meaning constructions or patterns may or may not conform to traditional linguistic structures. For example, instead of the question formation we saw in the cognitive view, the patterns may be sentence stems such as "I believe/think/know that. . ." When ELLs are given abundant iterative opportunities to use the patterns in meaningful ways, they will come to assimilate the form–meaning constructions; by adapting these to new contexts of use, their language resources will develop.

Each of these views has advantages and disadvantages. A rule-based view of language acquisition runs the risk of ELLs knowing about English, particularly linguistic structures, but not necessarily being able to enact the knowledge, resulting in the inert knowledge problem. A social view of language broadens the view of language acquisition beyond the individual but remains narrow because it does not necessarily deal with the academic language and functions that ELLs need to learn to succeed. For instance, when it comes to the Common Core State Standards (CCSS), academic functions—such as constructing an argument from evidence, or developing a solution to a problem, not purely social ones—need to be mastered. As for a usage perspective on language acquisition, it is clear that engaging ELLs in using language meaningfully is important, but is not sufficient in and of itself. In terms of the CCSS, ELLs' attention must be drawn to the patterns that exist in academic language in both written and spoken texts.

■ *Catherine Snow*

Perhaps the most familiar representation of the course of language development for ELLs/emergent bilinguals (EBs) is that offered by Cummins (1981): Basic interpersonal communicative skills (BICS) emerge first, followed by cognitive academic language proficiency (CALP). This formulation was very helpful in alerting educators to the possibility that second language learners who sounded fluent might still struggle with many language tasks. Nonetheless, it was widely unrecognized that the BICS–CALP sequence is neither universal nor inevitable. It is a frequent sequence for young second language learners—those who acquire the second language orally in preschool or kindergarten settings with few literacy demands, and thus are exposed only to BICS-supportive language. Older learners, learners who are literate in a first language, and learners who have access to more explicit language instruction may well excel at the skills characterized as CALP before they have strong conversational skills.

Other oversimplifications are frequent in popular conceptions of second language learning. One is that the second language can be acquired without influence on the first language. We now know that, especially for younger learners, focusing on second language learning can compete with continued first language learning, unless the educational and home environment provide ongoing support for first language (and literacy) acquisition.

Another oversimplification is that the process of second language vocabulary acquisition is the same for all second language learners. There is a wide array in degree of challenge in learning second language vocabulary, depending on the relationship between the first and second languages, and the learner's degree of control over words in his or her first language. Young second language learners may just need to acquire new labels for familiar concepts (e.g., spoon as a new label for the familiar *cuchara)*, or labels in the second language for entirely new concepts (e.g., hypothesis, analysis, schism). Some of the new labels will require a new analysis of familiar concepts (e.g., the difference between roof and ceiling for *techo,* between fingers and toes for *dedos*) and others will require merging previously distinctive concepts (e.g., corner for both *esquina* and *rincon*). It is clear that the learning challenges here depend on the learner's first language knowledge and metalinguistic capacity. Some learners (e.g., Spanish speakers) can rely heavily on cognates between the first and second language, whereas for others (e.g., Vietnamese and Arabic speakers) cognates are rare.

And, of course, acquiring vocabulary goes far beyond learning word meanings. Knowing what "put" means is not enough; one needs to know that, in English, "put" requires mentioning both a direct object and a location, so "I put the food" and "I put in the refrigerator" are both ungrammatical sentences.

A major implication of these observations is that second language acquisition is a much more variable process than first language acquisition. First language acquisition can go faster or slower, but for normally developing children it is a relatively predictable process. Second language acquisition is influenced by a much wider array of factors: age, first language skills, relation of first to second language, literacy skills, and so on. Thus, educators require very high levels of skill and sensitivity to respond optimally to the widely varying needs of second language learners.

■ *Amanda Kibler*

Although the acquisition and development of English can be usefully discussed from multiple perspectives, this contribution focuses on how socially and socioculturally informed ways of viewing the process can be beneficial for teachers, administrators, learners, and others.

While there are several different theories, theorists, and researchers who utilize social and sociocultural perspectives, one key metaphor is that of acquisition/development being a process of *apprenticeship.* Just as an apprentice carpenter, for example, does not learn the trade simply by reading about carpentry, EB learners of English acquire the language by participating in real-life language and literacy activities that both support and stretch their proficiencies in English. In this way, language is acquired through use, not through distanced analytical language study. One must also consider the other people through whom our apprentice carpenter is learning her trade: she is likely learning from masters as well as fellow apprentices—perhaps teaching *them* something in the process too—and the strengths they bring are likely those she will also develop. With EB learners of English, we must likewise consider the ways in which teachers and peers are coconstructing knowledge, and the ways that peers' and teachers' interactions with a learner will shape his or her language acquisition. It is also important to recognize that the scaffolding teachers and peers would provide at the beginning of an apprenticeship process will change as learners develop expertise, making scaffolds both responsive and dynamic. And, finally, when considering our carpenter's apprenticeship, she is not simply learning the skills of a trade: through her interactions she is coming to understand (and possibly take on) the values, beliefs, and traditions of the community to which she is aspiring to be a member. EB learners of English are likewise socialized into language uses. As students come to understand the values and culture(s) behind the varieties of English they are acquiring, their sense of identity comes into play; they may accept or contest this socialization to various degrees based on who they want to be seen as by others or who they aspire to be. Thus, issues of power and agency in the classroom are also relevant.

Thinking about all that might be present in the carpentry workshop or job site at which our apprentice carpenter develops her expertise brings us to another useful metaphor from social perspectives: that of an ecological learning environment. Just like in any ecology, classrooms (among the many other contexts in which individuals use and acquire language) are interdependent and dynamic settings. What is important is not only the curriculum, or the teacher, or the students: it is how these resources operate in combination with each other that will determine to what extent students' language is actually able to "grow." This interdependence also underscores the important role that social interaction with other language users plays in learning, whether this occurs face-to-face or virtually; in oral or written form; or with teachers, peers, or others.

Yet "social" perspectives do not focus solely on what is popularly known (and sometimes misconstrued) as "social" language. Social perspectives can focus squarely on the language students needed to complete academic tasks. For example, in addressing a CCSS such as, "Determine an author's point of view or purpose in a text and explain how it is conveyed in the text" (English language arts [ELA], grade 6), social conceptualizations of language could lead teachers to ask questions that might include the following:

- How am I engaging students as apprentices?
  - How can I design activities that require students to engage in *giving* explanations, not just *learning about* how to say or write them?
  - How can I scaffold my support of students so that it is responsive to students' current levels of language development but also move students forward in their English language acquisition?
- What kind of ecological setting am I providing?
  - What sorts of interactions and experiences with texts, peers, and teachers would best help my learners of English understand what a point of view and purpose are, comprehend the text, and explain their ideas about a text's point of view or purpose?
  - What kinds of authentic examples and opportunities can I provide students so that they understand how explanations work and the kinds of language used to speak and write explanations in ways that are appropriate for ELA (or other) classrooms?

○ How am I drawing on who students are (or want to be) to create meaningful and motivating opportunities for them to acquire the English needed to complete academic tasks?

2.5 When we talk about language acquisition or language development, what is *it* that needs to be acquired?

■ *Suresh Canagarajah*

The notion that the target for an English language learner (ELL) is native-like ultimate attainment has been questioned recently. This is an inappropriate goal for many reasons. ELLs aspire to be competent multilingual speakers who can adapt English to the language repertoires they bring with them and use it for their purposes in contexts of linguacultural diversity. As ELLs adapt English to their multilingual identities, values, and interests, English will take a form (i.e., accent, idioms, structure, and discourse) that is different from that of native speakers. Furthermore, the proficiency they require is not that of English as an all-purpose language, but one that is complementary to the functions of the other languages they possess. In this sense, English may serve academic, professional, or social functions that are specific to their needs, with the grammars and discourses relevant to those functions. As ELLs shuttle between diverse functions, communities, and languages according to their communicative needs, in practices resembling codeswitching, they will also merge language items from English with other languages in their repertoire, resembling modes of language mixing.

Beyond these considerations of language identity and communicative purpose, there are complex considerations for what it means to know a language in the context of recent forms of globalization, migration, digital communication, and transnational relations. The variety and mix of languages in any particular context are becoming unpredictable. An ELL from a Spanish background in the United States might be speaking to a Singaporean 1.5-generation child who speaks Singaporean English, with a mix of Chinese and Malay words and grammatical structures. ELLs should know how to negotiate intelligibility and achieve communicative success with interlocutors with whom very few language features are shared.

Like people, languages are also mobile. Scholars have therefore redefined languages as mobile resources rather than as immobile systems (Blommaert, 2010). What this means is that language is not inflexibly structured into a monolithic system, owned by native speakers and associated with a territory that is the natural habitat for it. Instead, we have resources that people borrow from diverse mobile languages and merge with other diverse resources from different locations and communities. As people engage in communicative activity, these resources become sedimented into grammars (Pennycook, 2010). Language norms thus evolve situationally through social practice.

From this perspective, acquisition of form in a clearly defined grammatical system of English is insufficient for contemporary communication. What ELLs need is a competence that enables them to shuttle between communities and contexts, negotiating diverse English varieties, borrowing new language resources, and merging them with their existing repertoires according to their identities, values, and interests as they achieve intelligibility and communicative success. This type of competence is becoming known as *translingual* (Canagarajah, 2013), different from the traditional monolingual competence that separates languages and targets native norms for ultimate attainment. For translingual competence, we have to go beyond acquisition of form to the development of a complex language awareness that would help ELLs negotiate the unpredictable mix of language resources in any given context. Such an awareness would include intercultural competence, sociolinguistic sensitivity, pragmatic understanding, and critical thinking (Kramsch, 2014)—all of which would enable ELLs to negotiate language diversity and unpredictability in contexts of globalization and multilingualism.

The Language Valued at School

2.6 What do educators need to know about language as they make decisions about Common Core State Standards implementation?

- *Ofelia García*

The main point that educators preparing students who are developing English to meet the Common Core State Standards (CCSS) need to know is that there is no such thing as *A language*, or English or Spanish or Chinese. Of course, we speak and hear what we have learned to call English or Spanish, but *A language*, and especially what is known as "academic language," is a societal construction. As speakers, we have language with features that are, or are not, socially accepted at different times and spaces and that have been societally assigned to what is called *A language*.

Once educators understand the difference between *A language* and *language*, then their teaching has to focus on leveraging and using the language practices that students possess to expand them to encompass using language in the ways of school. This is especially so in the case of bilingual students whose language practices include features that are most often excluded from monolingual instruction or separated rigidly in bilingual education. I have developed these understandings in proposing a theory of *translanguaging* (García, 2009b; García & Wei, 2014).

Language is not a system of discrete skill sets, but a series of social practices and actions that are embedded in a web of social relations. Language in school emerges from the actions of state policymakers with certain perspectives and ideological positioning. Language, then, has to be reappropriated by actual language users in schools, and educators have to imbue their instruction with a critical perspective about how language is used.

The CCSS do not seem to have a coherent language theory. On the one hand, the English Language Arts (ELA) Standards seem to support a view of language as human action in the standards related to reading, writing, speaking, and listening. But on the other hand, the language standards seem to do totally the opposite, reinforcing the linear build-up of grammatical structures and vocabulary. While the reading, writing, speaking, and listening standards consider language as action and practice used in human relationships, the language standards emphasize language as a system of structures. The reading, writing, speaking, and listening standards do not (for the most part) decompose language into fragments that students are able to then "have," but as human action that they perform or "do" with others. The emphasis is on student participation in activity that simultaneously leads to increased understanding and more complex language use. But the language standards precisely propose that the knowledge of the conventions of standard English and vocabulary are isolated skills that can be acquired linearly.

The language theory inherent in the reading, writing, speaking, and listening standards is consonant with the ways in which language is used in the 21st century. Students are asked to use a greater variety of complex texts—oral, visual, quantitative, print, and nonprint—that technology has enabled. The purposes for which language is used have also changed—from recreation or factual declaration to analysis, interpretation, argument, and persuasion. Even language itself has gone from being acknowledged as simply the grammar and vocabulary of printed texts to include its many levels of meaning—figurative language, word relations, genres, and media. Finally, students are now being asked to perform language socially, through cooperative tasks. It is not enough to organize information on one's own and write as an individual. It is important to build on others' ideas, whether those of peers, teachers, or authors of texts, to find evidence to articulate one's own ideas, adjusting the presentation according to the different purposes or audiences. This in itself is a great leap forward from previous understandings of language.

And yet, the language theory inherent in the language standards takes a backward step. It proposes that there are a series of essential "rules" of English that must be taught explicitly. The language standards also suggest that language is simply a series of progressive skills.

The CCSS do not in any way connect the theory of language as human action that they formulate in their use of complex and content-rich texts and the grounding of language use in textual evidence, with that proposed in the language standards themselves. In seeing language as something to be "had" instead of something to be "done," the language standards particularly work against bilingual students whose language use is more complex and fluid than that of monolinguals.

If language is human action embodied in the social world of relationships, then educators must leverage the language practices that all bilingual students bring. Only then will bilingual students be able to extend their bilingual repertoire to also encompass the conventions of English that the CCSS require.

■ *Aída Walqui*

The current emphasis on deep learning and new standards present educators with immense challenges and opportunities. One of the most promising arenas of action is the one related to understanding of language and its effect on English language learners' (ELLs') education. To transform classrooms into stimulating arenas where ideas are exchanged, problematized, built on, and enhanced, second language teachers need to revisit how they conceptualize language, and recognize how these conceptualizations influence their classroom behavior. Only then will they be able to reorient their teaching and realize their students' immense potential. With this purpose in mind I will outline two very different views of language—which guide pedagogical practice today—and will counter them with the view of language as action.

Traditionally, formal theories studied language as a system of systems: a morphological system focused on words and their formation, a phonological system composed of sounds arranged in patterns, and a grammatical system ruling how words are organized into sentences. Because learning to use the second language (L2) meant learning to use its language systems, L2 classes emphasized learners' correct use of the structural aspects of language. This formal view of language has had a long and pervasive influence in L2 teaching. It led to the sequencing of lessons along a supposed organization going from simpler to more complex structures, and to the idea that if students have not "mastered" the structures to be studied in a course they need to retake the course.

Functional theories of language—which started in the 1970s—shifted the focus of language studies to meaning, what is done as language is used. In L2 teaching, a positive impact of communicative language teaching was a move away from the centrality of form and correctness to fluency and getting things done. A limitation, however, was the emphasis on the discrete accomplishment of functions (e.g., how to suggest, how to compliment) rather than on discourse.

A third view of language proposes that language is an integral part of all human action and as such it is inseparable from physical, social, and symbolic action. In the following example, to begin her writing course, an English as a second language teacher has prepared a project that invites students to study four different cases of brain injury. Teams of four students will work on one article each. After careful and well-supported reading and discussion, students will share their notes in a new group of four. There they will also learn about three other cases. Each student will keep notes in a chart, which will be used later on to develop a compare/contrast essay. This is part of the reporting conversation in one group:[1]

Carlos: His story was the beginning of the study of the biological basis of behavior.

Rosalía: OK, what happened to this person that caused brain impairment?

Carlos: A stumping rod may have penetrated Phineas Gage skull.

---

[1]Student names are pseudonyms. The transcript comes from Stacia Crescenzi's class at Lanier High School in Austin, Texas, September 2009.

Roberto: Did you put that he got that little thing through his head, right? (Makes a gesture signaling with his finger how the rod went through Phineas Gage's skull.)

Julián: Yeah.

Roberto: Awesome!

Carlos: The rod may have penetrated. . .

Roberto: Do you have to use a big word like that? I'm just gonna put "went through."

Rosalía: Why don't you put *p* and then a dot? (Crescenzi & Walqui, 2008, cited in Walqui & van Lier, 2010, p. 48)

In this excerpt we see language being used as action: students use their bodies to enhance communication; they build on what they know about each other to consolidate the relationships that bind them; they respond appropriately to what their peers say (although some comments would appear to deviate from the assignment, they are integral to the exchange); and they engage in symbolic action as they position themselves as resistors of a culture that requires them to use language that sounds phony to them. The teacher does not correct or redirect students; they are engaged; they are making sense of their readings; they are learning. As the semester goes on, students will gradually get accustomed to these new language uses, and in the process their agency—their sense of control and self-worth—and their academic skills will increase accordingly. In this class, language is viewed as subsuming form and function, integrating them in contextualized ways as students work through meaningful activities that engage their interest and encourage language growth "through perception, interaction, planning, research, discussion, and coconstruction of academic products of various kinds" (van Lier & Walqui, 2012b).

2.7 How have the language expectations for students and teachers at school changed with the adoption of the Common Core State Standards?

■ *Alison L. Bailey*

We want [students] to understand lectures and participate in academic conversations. We want them to comprehend challenging texts, make informed decisions based on information they have read, form rational opinions, and offer focused interpretations. We expect them to write with clarity, conviction, color, and sophisticated thought. In short we want them to express themselves intelligently, articulately and thoughtfully. (Cruz, 2004, p.14)

These high expectations expressed by Cruz, a secondary level teacher of English learners (ELs), predate the Common Core State Standards (CCSS) by several years and are indicative of how language expectations for students and teachers at school have not necessarily changed with widespread adoption of the CCSS and Next Generation Science Standards (NGSS). Rather, what may have changed is how *specific* those expectations have become in relation to the content-area knowledge, skills, and practices the new content standards articulate, and the ramifications this has for the educational experiences of ELs.

The notion that language and content knowledge and skills are simultaneously acquired by English learners is also not new. Content-based English as a second language (ESL) instruction was built on this premise as Snow, Met, and Genesee (1989) explained over two decades ago: "Content also provides a cognitive basis for language learning in that it provides real meaning that is an inherent feature of naturalistic language learning. Meaning provides conceptual or cognitive hangers on which language functions and structures can be hung. In the absence of real meaning, language structures and functions are likely to be learned as abstractions devoid of conceptual or communicative value" (p. 202).

Nevertheless, the knowledge, skills, and practices explicitly articulated for English language arts, mathematics and science have taken ELs and their teachers in new directions with regard to: (1) how language is seen to play a more visible role in the academic content learning now required of students, and (2) how ELs might best be educated in as inclusive an environment as possible.

As the Framework for English Language Proficiency Development states, "The CCSS as well as the NGSS spell out the sophisticated language competencies that students will need to perform across their respective academic subject areas." (Council of Chief State School Officers, 2012, p. ii). For some time, researchers and educators in the assessment and instructional arenas have attempted to define the word-, sentence- and discourse-level characteristics of English used in schools and *arguably* required for demonstrating academic success—the so-called "academic language register." Recently, research on discourse in teaching and learning mathematics has contributed to our understanding of the comprehension of mathematics explanations (e.g., Levenson, Tsamir, & Tirosh, 2010), and in science instruction the focus has been on the processes, discourses, and modes of reasoning shared by communities of scientists by which scientific knowledge is generated (e.g., Duschl, Schweingruber, & Shouse, 2007).

ELs may not only miss the requisite content material if they are schooled in ESL pull-out or sheltered English contexts, they may also miss the opportunity for exposure to the discourse practices of mathematics or science, and consequently may not have access to the challenging language of content-area instruction to the same degree as their English-speaking peers (e.g., Francis, Lesaux, & August, 2006).

With the advent of the CCSS and NGSS, the language demands inherent in content standards are taking a more central role in the education of ELs than the traditional English language development standards themselves. Unlike previous academic content standards, the CCSS and NGSS explicitly state what language and literacy are needed in support of achieving learning objectives. This situation holds true for *all* U.S. students, not just students acquiring English as an additional language. However, what makes these academic content standards particularly resonant for ELs and their teachers is the fact that rather than focus on learning language largely in *isolation* from content-area learning (and risk leaving students without access to the content and courses they need to graduate, e.g., Gándara, Rumberger, Maxwell-Jolly, & Callahan, 2003), students and teachers can use the content standards to more concretely and meaningfully connect language learning with specific content-learning goals that students are also required to meet. Moreover, *critical thinking, communication, collaboration,* and *creativity,* as articulated by the Partnership for 21st-Century Skills, are reflected in the new content standards (National Education Association, 2011), and each adds further demands for language learning in scholastic contexts.

Moving forward, students will need to acquire the linguistic acumen to take part in classroom interactions that support the deeper content learning presumably afforded by the CCSS and NGSS. For example, when partnered with others, students will need familiarity with language practices and routines to negotiate their involvement in activities, solve problems cooperatively, and discuss and support one another's ideas.

In turn, teachers will need to understand what language repertoires are necessary to support students' participation in such practices. Teaching English language in isolation from content classes, particularly if students are placed in form-focused programs, is unlikely to expose students to many opportunities for language and content integration at this level. In contrast, Bailey and Heritage (2014) report teachers can support effective student participation in negotiations during collaborative activities in content classes (e.g., building representations of their math learning), by modeling the use of modal verbs and causal embedding (e.g., We should do this part first because. . . ; If we do this part first then we could. . .).

In the future, however, we must scrutinize the almost exclusive value placed on the acquisition and assessment of new content knowledge using such language forms (e.g., Valdés, MacSwan, & Alvarez, 2009). Students may acquire new content knowledge without command of academic language (e.g., Bunch, 2006; Escamilla, 2012). Moreover, prior definitions of an academic language register may have constrained teachers' thinking about what ELs can and cannot do with language and perhaps have limited recognition of the language varieties used in school to specialized content vocabulary alone (Escamilla, 2012). In the future, teachers might be encouraged to also leverage the everyday communicative repertoires (e.g., translating, codeswitching) of their ELs for learning and assessing new content (e.g., Bailey & Orellana, 2015).

2.8 How has the concept of academic language been defined and interpreted? How can educators draw on this work as they implement the new standards?

■ *Terrence G. Wiley and Laura Wright*

Many researchers and policymakers who describe the shifts that the Common Core State Standards (CCSS) will mean for instruction emphasize the importance of "academic language," or more specifically of "academic English" (Alberti, 2012/2013; Zwiers, O'Hara, & Pritchard, 2013). What is meant by the term "academic language," however, remains hazy. Many definitions of academic language exist, but most are imprecise and default to folk notions of language and language development, emphasizing aspects such as "formality" or "complexity." Other definitions focus on aspects of language such as knowledge of specialized vocabulary that can be easily measured by standardized tests.

Many of these definitions stem from the work of Jim Cummins (e.g., Cummins 1986; Cummins & Man, 2007), who makes a distinction between the allegedly more cognitively demanding language of the school and the language used in so-called "basic" communication. This is popularly known as the basic interpersonal communication skills (BICS)–cognitive academic language proficiency (CALP) distinction. This distinction is based on the notion that school language is more cognitively challenging because it is decontextualized. It has also been assumed that that the acquisition of academic language leads to greater cognitive development, and that school language has special qualities that other forms of language do not.

Others, such as Gee (2000), contend that all language is contextual and embedded in social relationships noting that "all language is meaningful only in and through the [social] contexts in which it is used. All language is meaningful only on the basis of shared experiences and shared information. . . [that] they have gained in prior socioculturally significant interactions with others" (p. 63). Thus, alleged cognitive aspects of language cannot be isolated from the social contexts of their use. From this perspective, the notion of academic or school language becomes problematic. As Gee (2001) further notes: "There is, of course, no such thing as 'school language' or 'academic language' as single things. There are, rather, many different school languages, different styles of language used in different academic practices. There are, too, many different sorts of public-sphere language, different styles of language used for a variety of civic, economic, and political purposes. None of these many styles of language is 'decontextualized.' They are all—just like 'everyday' face-to-face language—'contextualized'" (p. 63).

This does not mean that the role of language in individual cognitive development is unimportant, but rather that school uses of language and literacy practices in academic contexts are best understood and analyzed as socially embedded, rather than as independent, cognitive proficiencies (Wiley & Rolstad, 2014). Because many children in schools come from a variety of cultures and socioeconomic backgrounds, it is important that instruction and school language practices be understood as socially embedded.

If we are to move beyond focusing on cognitive deficits and reports of a neverending achievement gap, we need to move beyond the notion that children cannot engage in intellectually stimulating work until after they have developed academic language. We need to support the efforts of educators to engage students in interesting, challenging work that leads and expands their linguistic repertoires and facilitates their development of literacy, rather than beginning with a focus on isolated tests of linguistic knowledge (Wiley & Rolstad, 2014; see also Valdés, 2004). Expanding students' linguistic repertoires to include the variety of ways language is valued in schools, such as language practices promoted by the CCSS, supports students becoming adept language users rather than viewing them as having linguistic deficiencies.

2.9 How is the term "academic language" helpful? How is it imprecise?

■ *Catherine Snow*

The term "academic language" is useful in signaling to teachers, parents, and students that the language used in school can be different from the language used in everyday communication. It is also useful in reminding us of the following:

- Language development is not completed at age 3, 5, or even 12.
- Continued oral language development becomes dependent on literacy after a certain point—in other words, we start to talk, for academic purposes, in ways influenced by what we read and how we write.
- Though children learn most of their language naturally in the context of rich and interesting conversations, they might need some explicit teaching of academic language forms.

It would be a mistake to think of academic language as a dialect or a register, another language variety that children need to learn. Instead, it is a set of features that may be used to a greater or lesser degree. Some academic language features are unlikely to occur except in written language. Consider a sentence like "Risk of failure has been proven to correlate with lack of practice." It includes many academic language features: passive voice, complex noun phrases, nonanimate sentence subject, and an embedded clause. Other academic language features, such as using sophisticated vocabulary (e.g, hypothesize, vary, nonetheless instead of the more casual guess, change, instead) may be used even in casual conversation.

Some approaches make a sharp distinction between disciplinary language and academic language. Disciplinary language is characterized by both vocabulary (e.g., photosynthesis, branches of government, and dodecahedron in biology, civics, and math, respectively) and certain other language features (particular discourse structures, argument forms, and specific uses for common words). Much disciplinary language is simultaneously academic. The distinction is important, though, because content-area teachers who may be conscious of the need to teach disciplinary vocabulary may be unaware that academic language used in discipline-specific ways can be puzzling to students. Asking students to explain in their own words what they have read or heard can reveal their misunderstandings or failures to appreciate the subtleties of the forms used for academic purposes.

■ *Okhee Lee and Lorena Llosa*

The term "academic language" has been helpful in drawing attention to the fact that proficiency in everyday language only is insufficient to ensure that English language learners (ELLs) will succeed in school. ELLs need to develop language that allows them to engage in the discourse of school in general and of academic disciplines in particular. The term "academic language" has also been helpful in that it engages and brings together several (traditionally separate) professional communities, including English as a second language (ESL) and bilingual educators, English and literacy educators, and content-area educators. This is particularly true because the Common Core State Standards (CCSS) for English language arts (ELA)/literacy and mathematics and the Next Generation Science Standards (NGSS) are language intensive for all students, not just for ELLs.

The challenge with this term is that it is imprecise in several ways. First, various communities of educators have different definitions of academic language (Valdés, 2004). Among communities of language educators, academic language is often defined as the lexical, grammatical, and discourse level features of the language needed to succeed in school. In practice, instruction on academic language has taken on different approaches, with most approaches focusing on either vocabulary knowledge (general academic and/or discipline-specific) or increasingly complex grammatical structures. In content-area communities, this term has been introduced more recently and thus its meaning is even less precise. When it is used, it is often interpreted as vocabulary, content, and/or processes in academic disciplines. For example, science educators may interpret academic language in terms of science vocabulary, science content, science inquiry or processes, or some combination of these.

Second, what is considered academic language varies from grade to grade. Students develop not only in their language ability but also in their cognitive and academic ability. As sophistication of language increases across grade levels, academic language also changes. In a similar manner, as sophistication of academic content increases across grade levels, the academic language of a discipline changes as well.

Finally, even though some features of academic language are considered to be relevant across content areas, some vary by content area. In school, the language used to teach and learn a particular content area, be it history, mathematics, biology, or English literature, draws from the disciplinary language and discourse conventions of the discipline. Disciplinary language is the language used by "real" historians, mathematicians, scientists, or professionals in their disciplines. Written materials used in science classrooms, for example, rarely represent the disciplinary language of professional scientists but rather use styles and levels of language intended for science learners. Thus, the language used in the science classroom represents the academic language of science, but this is not the same as the disciplinary language of science. However, as the grade level advances, academic language tends to mirror disciplinary language more closely.

To conclude, the term "academic language" is helpful in that it encourages all educators of all students to focus on language. This focus, however, should not be limited to specific vocabulary or grammatical structures. Rather, it should take on a view of language as action, one in which vocabulary, grammar, and discourse features are used in the context of communicative activities in school and in the service of learning academic disciplines specifically. Ultimately, helping students acquire academic language will involve providing them with opportunities to meaningfully engage with language as they make sense of academic content with appropriate supports for both language and content.

■ *James Gee*

The CCSS are fine. Indeed, they are more focused on reasoning, argumentation, and collaboration than were the old standards. The problem is not standards as such, but standards getting trapped in a system of testing that favors publishers and politicians more than children and families. Aside from this problem, though, there is another deep problem that bears on the very nature of language and the important notion of "equal opportunity to learn" (Moss, Pullin, Gee, & Haertel, 2007).

In a sense, all school learning is language learning (Gee, 2004; Halliday, 1993). All students—native English speakers and ELLs—have to learn the special varieties of language that represent and give access to "content." They have to learn the varieties of language connected to mathematics, science, literature, art, and technology. They need to be prepared to learn further sorts of specialist languages outside of school, whether this be the language of "modding" video games or the language of citizen science or an activist cause in which they may want to engage. All learning is about learning to "walk the walk and talk the talk" and the two cannot be separated. The special varieties of language that I have referred to here are often called "academic language" (academic varieties of language). However, because the language of *Yu-Gi-Oh* is as technical as any academic language form a child hears or reads early in school, I just call them all "specialist varieties of language." ("Specialist social languages" or "specialist registers" would be other terms we could use; see Gee, 2014.)

Current theories of the mind centered around "embodied cognition"—now well supported (Bergen, 2012; Gee, 2004)—argue that what gives meaning to language are goal-based, contextually sensitive mental simulations based on our experiences. Furthermore, the experiences necessary for thinking, reasoning, and comprehending well need to have been edited (foregrounded and backgrounded in certain ways) so that they are useful in preparing for future action and problem solving. Mentors with lots of previous experience need to help newcomers know what to focus on to help them see how words match up with experience and help order it. Words get situated meanings (the only really useful type of meaning) from experience, but language, in turn, regiments and orders experience (Gee, 1992/2014). Experience and language dance together or fall apart into meaninglessness. Without all this context, learners are not well prepared to understand new forms of talk and texts. They can only achieve relatively superficial verbal (definition-like) meanings.

Children who have had nowhere near the amount of experience with the world words are about—the experiences that give them situated meanings—and of the words as they are used to organize those experiences are at a great disadvantage in learning to talk, write, listen, and read new forms of language, whether this language is physics or *Yu-Gi-Oh*. They have had nowhere near the same opportunity to learn even if they have been handed the same texts. They cannot learn content well because they cannot marry language and experience in the cause of "language development." Demanding that a pole vaulter hit a higher standard without a pole is a meaningless—if not pernicious—standard, no matter how good it sounds.

Without a standard for equity based on experience, it does not really matter what other standards we have. We will just keep producing gaps and controversy without creating the vaunted equal opportunity the United States claims as a core value.

2.10 How can an understanding of language variation help educators address the demands of the Common Core State Standards for linguistically diverse learners?

■ *Lilia Bartolomé*

Teachers who have a sociolinguistic understanding of language variation can articulate the difficulties many linguistic minority students may face in meeting the Common Core State Standards (CCSS), particularly those that clearly reflect social and cultural discourse preferences. As I have learned in teaching my graduate sociolinguistics course, teachers struggle to move away from a prescriptive stance regarding what constitutes "correct" English to understand the legitimacy of language varieties (e.g., African-American vernacular English [AAVE], Chicano English, Spanglish) often considered "deficient" or "bastardized." In the course, we study language variation relative to socioeconomic class, ethnicity, gender, geographic region, and historical language contact situation. Teachers are fascinated when they analyze AAVE and Cape Verdean Creole and discover that each variety is a language in its own right, complete with a linguistic structure and a system of rules, principles, and parameters—just like any other standard language that reflects high social status.

A key learning moment occurs when a teacher comprehends the distinction between the purely linguistic aspects of a language and the social value attributed to it by society. In their classrooms, these teachers soon realize that they are unfairly burdened with the contradictory responsibility of having to both meet the CCSS *and* honor the discourse and preferred rhetorical styles of their culturally and linguistically diverse students. I say "unfairly" because the creators of standards and assessments develop one-size-fits-all measures that cannot capture the nuanced performance and English language development (ELD) of students from various linguistic minority groups. These teachers frequently express frustration and a sense of powerlessness when they realize that they cannot negotiate the CCSS or build in alternative modes of communication that acknowledge the language skills linguistic minority students bring to the classroom. Thus, they often defend their students by utilizing alternative (possibly teacher-authored), authentic assessments that more accurately demonstrate students' progress while concurrently working with them to additively appropriate standard and academic forms of oral and written English represented in the CCSS.

As these teachers come to understand the relationship between language and social status and power differentials more fully, it becomes clear to them that the CCSS document is written with the white, monolingual, middle-class, standard-English-speaking student in mind and thus serves to support the current English-only language policy in Massachusetts. In fact, the CCSS document itself simultaneously acknowledges and dismisses linguistic minorities by indicating that the standards can be met regardless of a student's ELD level or other circumstances, such as having little prior schooling and limited literacy in their native language.

Understanding the social, political, ideological, and pedagogical ramifications of language variation certainly produces more informed and critical teachers. Despite the rigidity of the CCSS and other state standards, these enlightened teachers struggle to embrace and build on their linguistic minority students' linguistic strengths and rhetorical preferences as a way to maximize their acquisition of standard academic language and preferred school discourse styles.

■ *Anne H. Charity Hudley*

The CCSS place a special focus on speaking and language, stating that "students must demonstrate command of the conventions of standard English grammar and usage when writing or speaking" (CCSS, 2015).

Yet, preliminary Common Core materials have a focus on correcting language features that are systematically part of well-documented English language varieties, including African American, Latin, and southern English. Without specific linguistic knowledge, educators may perpetuate linguistic structural inequalities whereby students who would be likely to get the items wrong can be easily predicted by the variety of English they speak as well as their ethnic and cultural backgrounds.

Furthermore, the Common Core linguistic item examples are presented as developmentally grounded, with no mention of inherent language variation. Educators who do not have a thorough understanding of the complex ways in which English is different both across and within specific varieties may identify students as having language deficits and delays rather than typical and predictable language differences. For example, while it is academically necessary for students to learn the morphemes suggested in Common Core Language Arts Appendix A, "Morphemes Represented in English Orthography, Examples of Derivational Suffixes in English" (CCSS, 2012a), no mention is made of the fact that most of the morphemic variations presented are well-documented characteristics of adult African-American English, including inherent variation in the presence and absence of: -s plural noun, -s third person singular, -ed past tense verbs, -en past participle, -'s possessive singular, and -er comparative adjectives. Confounding variety- and nonvariety-based differences will perplex educators as they develop teaching strategies and students, whose natural linguistic intuitions may be marked as deficits or delays.

Such issues are not confined just to grammar, phonology, and other intrinsic aspects of language. The Common Core emphasizes even more socially constructed notions of language, including agreed-upon rules for discussions (e.g., listening to others and taking turns when discussing topics and texts). Pragmatic rules vary by variety of English and are not explicitly taught. Yet, in the Common Core, such features are deemed— without comprehensive evidence— as "kindergarten level" skills, and no mention is made of linguistic and cultural variation.

Despite these challenges, educators may use aspects of the Common Core guidelines that recognize the flexibility of language to help students understand how language is used differently in various contexts. The Common Core recognizes that students must be able to use standardized English but that they must also be able to make informed, skillful choices among the many ways to express themselves through language in each situation that they encounter. Educators can use this recognition to shape a discussion on how to recognize varieties of English in the classroom in listening, writing and speaking, and how to use such skills to improve overall communication in both academic and nonacademic contexts.

The Common Core (2012c) states: "Students who are college and career ready in reading, writing, speaking, listening, and language 'actively seek to understand other perspectives and cultures through reading and listening, and they are able to communicate effectively with people of varied backgrounds'" (p. 7). Rather than glossing over linguistic and cultural variation within English, it will be critical to emphasize the importance of explicitly instructing students as to the norms and conventions of standardized English while at the same time building their understanding of varieties of English. If so, carefully developed Common Core materials may help educators prepare students for a wider variety of experiences in college and 21st-century careers.

2.11 Who are second dialect speakers in U.S. schools? What are their specific learning needs?

■ *Shondel Nero*

Defining who are speakers of nonstandard varieties of English is tricky. Elbow (2012) rightly argues that standard English is no-one's mother tongue. By that definition, most, if not all, English speakers—to a greater or lesser degree—speak a nonstandard variety of the language, and learn the standard variety in school. For the purposes of this book, however, speakers of nonstandard varieties of English in U.S. schools are defined as those students who primarily speak and/or write varieties of English that are not sanctioned by schools. Typically such varieties include syntactic, phonological, morphological, lexical features, meanings, and discourse norms that deviate from standard American English (e.g., African American vernacular English [AAVE], Caribbean Creole English [CCE], Hispanized English, southern vernacular English, Hawai'i Creole English, West African Pidgin English, or South Asian English).

In U.S. schools, speakers of nonstandard varieties of English are often thought to be doing poorly in school *because* of their use of nonprestige varieties of English. They are then given direct language instruction and are considered to be learning standard English as a second dialect rather than a second language. As can be seen from the preceding examples of nonstandard varieties of English, second dialect speakers are not a monolithic group. The degree of difference between their varieties of English and standard English varies based on factors such as the development of the variety itself; socioeconomic class, level, and type of formal schooling; language and literacy practices beyond school; social networks; and amount and nature of exposure to standard English. Students may also be speakers of more than one nonstandard variety of English (e.g., AAVE and CCE) because of cross-cultural interactions, use of social media, and dialect borrowing.

There are five salient characteristics that are common among most second dialect speakers:

1. They typically self-identify as native speakers of English, regardless of their actual proficiency in standardized forms of spoken or written English.
2. Many are struggling readers and writers of standard American English.
3. Those with low levels of literacy often face the same challenges in reading and writing as beginning level English as a second language (ESL) students.
4. Their vernacular is stigmatized and discouraged both in school and in their own communities.
5. They often exhibit ambivalent attitudes toward their own vernacular—simultaneously celebrating and denigrating it, depending on the context.

These characteristics create specific learning needs for second dialect speakers in schools. As students who perceive themselves as already *knowing* and *speaking* English they may not be as invested in English learning in the way a traditional second language student would, nor might they be aware of the difference between their *perceived* level of English literacy and their *actual* level. Such students, therefore, need first and foremost to heighten their language awareness so they can notice the differences among the grammar, words, and meanings of their dialect(s) and those of standard English. Sociolinguistic scholars and teachers have recommended contrastive approaches to highlight these differences and help students learn to codeswitch effectively (Wheeler, Swords, & Carpenter, 2004). This is important because many second dialect speakers may not even be aware that their dialect has a grammar. Second, the specific language needs of second dialect speakers must be distinguished from second language speakers, even though their needs partially overlap. Second dialect speakers usually have excellent *receptive* skills in English and, unlike second language speakers, they can grasp subtle nuances in the language. This is the case because they have been raised in the United States or in countries where English is an official and/or dominant language and the medium of instruction in school. Thus, second dialect speakers need more targeted instruction in *productive* standard English skills, especially in writing. To do so successfully, their reading skills must also be enhanced. Third, second dialect speakers need a classroom environment that affirms rather than stigmatizes dialect difference. Use of dialect literature, and explicit focus on language variation as normal, have been found to be effective means of validating dialects in the classroom (Nero & Ahmad, 2014).

Challenges of the Common Core State Standards Reform Efforts for Educating Second Dialect Speakers

The first challenge in the Common Core State Standards (CCSS) reform effort with respect to second dialect speakers is identifying them. U.S. education reform efforts have legal mandates with clearly stipulated requirements for identifying and supporting English language learners (ELLs), such as providing ESL or bilingual classes. However, there is no equivalent structured support system for identifying and supporting second dialect speakers on a national level. Such students are considered native English speakers, and it is up to individual school districts and classroom teachers, often with little or no training, to identify their unique linguistic needs and help them meet the CCSS. The risk in this situation is that teachers, lacking deep knowledge of the structures and usage of dialects, may rely on folk linguistic understandings of dialect and focus on surface level "errors," thereby misdiagnosing the students' needs. Furthermore, negative attitudes toward dialects can compound the problem because school districts may ignore or dismiss second dialect speakers simply as speakers of "bad" or "broken" English, and therefore either not address their needs at all or place them in special education or speech pathology classes for remediation. Occasionally, second dialect speakers, such as CCE speakers, are classified as ELLs and placed in ESL classes, much to their surprise. Because most second dialect speakers self-identify as speakers of English, they tend to feel stigmatized in ESL classes and resentful of such placements, which often do not address their needs.

It must be noted, however, that developing a valid diagnostic tool for second dialect speakers would be challenging given the wide range of dialects involved and the paucity of applied linguists with expertise in second dialect assessment.

One of the key requirements of the CCSS is that students be able to read increasingly complex texts independently as they progress through school. For second dialect speakers, this is particularly challenging because their taken-for-granted understanding of English may mask deeper misreadings of sophisticated text structure, grammar, and usage. Furthermore, language standard 3 of the CCSS requires that students have a strong command of usage choices in writing and speaking, as well as an awareness of varieties of English. English language arts teachers are often not equipped with the requisite sociolinguistic knowledge to effectively address differences in grammatical structures and usage between dialects and standard English, especially in the teaching of writing. This is a lacuna in teacher training that should be addressed. In the meantime, teachers must provide multiple opportunities for second dialect speakers to engage in sustained writing in a variety of genres and probe them for clarification where dialect features may impede intended meaning. Finally, although the CCSS require understanding of language varieties, usage, and choice, outcomes are measured by assessments that favor demonstrated proficiency in a narrowly defined standard variety of American English. As such, teachers feel pressured to tailor their teaching to engage this standard variety only, thereby excluding opportunities for second dialect speakers to display their knowledge through other complex language practices in which they regularly engage, such as code-meshing, dialect borrowing, or even drawing on other non-American varieties of standard English. Thus, there is a growing disparity between students' language practices and language assessment that merits further investigation.

Language Teaching and Learning

2.12 What do we know about the direct teaching of a second language to young children?

■ *Carole Edelsky*

It's a sad fact: much second language education is based on a couple of major errors. One is the view that language consists of discrete pieces (e.g., nouns, verbs, adjectives, sentences, grammatical rules for making verbs agree with subjects). The other is that learning is the flip side of teaching. Together, these two mistaken ideas are a one-two punch for young English language learners (ELLs). On the one hand, they lead to a superficial analysis of language into oversimplified forms and then explicit teaching and testing of those forms. On the other, they lead to the adult-centric fantasy that what we teach of a second language is a mirror for what kids learn. Those beliefs aren't merely foolish. They actually deprive children of what *would* help them learn the second language.

The main task for young ELLs is not learning the surface forms of English, such as which verb endings go with which subjects; it's learning how to *do* things with English for genuine social and intellectual reasons—that is, how to "do life" using the new language.

And how do children learn that? They learn by interacting with people who are using the new language with them for real purposes, not for giving and getting language lessons. They also learn by using the language they already know (their home language[s] and whatever they know of the new language) and, in the process, extending what they know. That is, it's by starting from the most basic and most concrete—the on-the-ground meanings of the real-life situation happening at the moment.

But to the detriment of learners, too much second language teaching focuses on what's least basic and most abstract—exercises with pieces of language in a situation that's hardest to learn a language in—one where there are too few opportunities to interact about too little that's of any interest.

This is the case in Arizona, where state law mandates structured English immersion—four hours per day of English language development (ELD) in a classroom where the only fluent English speaker is the teacher. The four hours are to be spent on pronunciation, the structure of words (morphology), vocabulary, and sentence construction. This policy expects that children will learn English because they are directly taught language abstractions (e.g., phonetic variation within phonemes, turning nouns into adjectives, etc.). But what has to be learned (a complex system for how to *use* English in life in and out of school) bears little relationship to a curriculum of discrete abstract forms laid out in some supposedly easy-to-hard sequence. Even more importantly, direct teaching is not how young children learn a second language in the first place (Faltis, 2013).

Instead of making sure young children have lots of time to work on engaging projects, so that they have something they *want* to talk about with people they want to talk *to*,

Arizona expects them to do worksheet-like activities on subject/verb agreement. Instead of a curriculum that asks learners to use English for a variety of social and intellectual purposes (e.g., getting into the game, planning a recycling drive, investigating connections between health and the location of neighborhood food stores), Arizona's law asks learners to concentrate on pronouncing *sit* with a short *i*. Instead of making sure young English learners work in groups with more and less advanced speakers of English, Arizona practices language segregation. The practical consequence is that young English learners in Arizona are deprived of the contexts they need for learning English and are also subjected to impoverished content. And everyone—English learners and monolingual English speakers—is denied opportunities to learn from each other. What a waste!

2.13 To what extent do the Common Core State Standards support the linguistic, emotional, and physical development of dual language learners in early childhood programs?

■ *Maya A. Martinez-Hart*

Developmentally, kindergarten age children are learning enthusiasts with maturing large and fine motor control, attention span, and impulse control; diverse interests and social skills; and maturing complexity of oral language and processing abilities. Dual language learners (DLLs) are no different. In addition to all these developing skills and abilities, they are learning and processing two or more languages and their associated cultures. However, the vast range of development among kindergarten age children poses challenges for teachers. "For young children to develop and learn optimally, [teachers] must be prepared to meet their diverse developmental, cultural, linguistic, and educational needs. . . . [E]ducators face the challenge of how to best respond to these needs" (NAEYC, 1995a).

The adoption and implementation of the Common Core State Standards (CCSS) in K–12 school systems has captured the attention of the early childhood practitioners. Nationally, the early childhood community considers early childhood years as birth to 8. Also the CCSS' narrow focus on English language arts, literacy, and mathematics leaves other areas of development implicit, at best, in the scope of learning. Different interpretations as to what is important for school readiness and success present dissonance between the early childhood community and the K–12 school systems.

With the highlighted emphasis on reading, and precursor skills such as phonemic awareness and letter sounds, preschool teachers are concerned about the potential for "push-down" of a narrow emphasis curriculum in an effort to align early learning standards and the CCSS. They worry that the curriculum may ignore ". . .the true complexity of growth. . .and children whose development is well within the normal range may be erroneously characterized as inadequate" (NAEYC, 1995a and b).

According to the CCSS, teachers can help determine how the goals of the standards will be reached and what other topics will need to be addressed. This flexibility provides powerful opportunities to shape instructional practices, the learning environment, and the ability to enrich curriculum, presenting a unique opportunity for teachers to support children's linguistic, social–emotional, and physical development, especially DLLs' language development needs.

Following developmentally appropriate practices guidelines, these suggestions could transform the academic curriculum focus on cognitive skills into a curriculum that pays attention to all the areas of development.

Creating a Caring Community of Learners

- Provide an environment where children can "see themselves" reflected in the environment and content.
- Promote positive social and emotional development.
- Hold attainable, scaffolded, developmentally appropriate expectations.

Teaching to Enhance Development and Learning

- Plan for intentional teaching of academic and social language, frequent opportunities for oral language development, and an environment filled with appropriate and accessible language supports.
- Implement the concept of translanguaging by making provisions to support the children's home languages as scaffolds for processing concept development in academic English.

Planning Curriculum to Achieve Important Goals

- Plan intentional self-directed play experiences as a vehicle for language skill development and practice.
- Plan for high-quality movement instruction with plenty of time to practice.

Assessing Children's Development and Learning

- Use strategic and purposeful formative assessment to continuously assess progress of academic language acquisition and development.
- Implement goals for all developmental domains.

Establish reciprocal relationships with families

- Build learning experiences based on what you learn about language use, beliefs, and uses of home literacy, family's strengths, and knowledge.

The CCSS (2012b) state that teachers must use "whatever tools, knowledge, experience, and professional judgment [are necessary] to meet the goals of the standards." This is the responsibility of teachers, as well as school and district leadership. The system must understand the importance of a curriculum that promotes development of all domains to engage children in meaningful participation and learning.

■ *Catherine Snow*

The CCSS focus on oral language and thinking skills to a much larger extent than many previous standards. While this is a desirable feature in general, it can of course constitute a dilemma for teachers of dual language and second language learners. At what point can second language learners be expected to display skills at the same level as their monolingual classmates?

Ideally, because the CCSS require more sophisticated language and thinking tasks for all students, they will stimulate greater use of mother tongues in the classroom. Students should be able to display their language and analytic skills in their strongest language, which may be a home rather than a school language, at least for young and recently arrived students. Students who use their mother tongue for preparation of second language performances will show greater sophistication and higher levels of performance in the second language, thus ending up more likely to meet the challenges of the CCSS.

2.14 What do we know about second language acquisition in instructional settings?

■ *Diane Larsen-Freeman*

It is important that English language learners (ELLs) be immersed in language they can understand, from which they can learn language implicitly. However, just being able to understand the language is insufficient, especially when it comes to more formal academic language. ELLs benefit from explicit instruction to develop new resources for making meaning, resources they will need in this era of the Common Core State Standards (CCSS). Explicit instructional practices, informed by second language acquisition (SLA) research, for enabling them to do so fall into three categories: consciousness-raising, practice, and corrective feedback.

Consciousness-raising refers to helping students notice or become aware of the language patterns and discourse practices of English. Students will naturally transfer their knowledge and skills from their home language. It is ideal to contrast ELLs' home language with English when this is possible. When it is not, recognizing ELLs' home language as a valuable resource and integrating ELLs' cultures into the classroom is important for supporting their sense of identity.

Other consciousness-raising activities include input enhancement, whereby the language that is in focus in a given text is highlighted or stressed. Importantly, while vocabulary and grammar structures are necessary to learn, knowledge of them is insufficient. When it comes to the CCSS, activities such as text analysis are beneficial. Teachers can use an appropriate amount of metalanguage (language to talk about language) to draw students' attention to patterns in a text that function to make meaning in a coherent and cohesive manner. Rather than unduly simplifying such texts, research has shown that elaborative simplification is superior to reductive simplification. Further, it is important that ELLs understand the thinking that goes behind the construction of text and discursive practices. This can be accomplished through the teacher's employing think-aloud protocols, reporting in real time how he or she is making sense of the text.

Consciousness-raising must be complemented by practice activities to ameliorate "the inert knowledge problem," whereby students have learned about the language but cannot use it. Encouraging active use of academic English is particularly important because ELLs are often reticent to participate in class activities. Peer interaction is beneficial in encouraging participation, and research has shown that doing so does not mean that ELLs will pick up "bad habits" from each other. Another important characteristic of effective practice activities is the opportunity to reactivate the same language again and again. For instance, students can conduct an experiment in small groups in a science class. Next, they can discuss what they did and what the outcome was; then, they can write it up in the form of a lab report. Multimodal iteration, such as this sequence, is extremely valuable.

Corrective feedback also has a role to play; however, feedback needs to be given to students in a judicious and affectively supportive manner. One way to offer effective feedback is to recast or reformulate what a student has said in a more appropriate way. However, teachers should not be overly concerned with accuracy of form because SLA research suggests that, at least in the early stages, more emphasis should be given to student success in making meaning. For instance, if a student in a math lesson says "X is big." "Y is small," a teacher can recast it by saying, "Yes. X is greater than Y."

It should be noted that the process of language acquisition is gradual and takes place over an extended period of time. Furthermore, the acquisition process is, like other development, nonlinear: sometimes there is progress, sometimes regress. As with all learners, ELLs learn at different rates and exhibit individual differences. For instance, ELLs' working memory, age, prior educational experience and literacy level, motivation, aptitude, and attitudes all play a role in their success; therefore, the argument for differentiated instruction is compelling.

Above all, it is important to recognize that ELLs are not English-deficient learners. They are emergent bilinguals (EBs), who will become multicompetent in more than one language, and this multicompetence represents an enormous cognitive, social, and personal resource.

■ *Claude Goldenberg*[1]

One of the fundamental issues in how we learn second languages is whether they can be *taught* or must be *aquired*. This might seem like a purely academic distinction, but it has real consequences for how we think about and help promote English learners (ELs)/EBs' English language development (ELD). If we assume that second languages

[1]Portions excerpted and condensed from Saunders, W., Goldenberg, C., & Marcelletti, D. (2013). Guidelines for English language development instruction. *American Educator, 37*(2), 13–25, 38–39. Available at http://files.eric.ed.gov/fulltext/EJ1014023.pdf

can (or should) be *taught*, then we focus on curriculum and instruction designed to teach specific aspects of the language (e.g., vocabulary, syntax, morphology, phonology, pragmatics) and how learners should combine these aspects to promote competent use of the target language. If, however, we assume that second languages must be *acquired*, then we focus much less (if at all) on curriculum and instruction and much more on providing students with opportunities that will give them ample and meaningful exposure to and use of the second language.

A third possibility is that this is not an either/or question and that, instead, second languages are learned through some combination of being taught *and* having opportunities to acquire. Existing research does not provide sufficient basis for determining the most effective methods of ELD instruction with total confidence, but there is considerable evidence that providing ELD instruction, in some form, is more beneficial than not providing it.

In the current educational climate, where ELD instruction is such a prominent topic for ELs/EBs, readers might find it difficult to conceive that three decades ago "Does second-language instruction make a difference?" (Long, 1983) was a viable question. A dominant view (then, for some time after, and still among some in the field) was Krashen's (1982) "monitor" hypothesis, which proposed that formal instruction is of limited utility for SLA. Instead, according to this view, large amounts of exposure to comprehensible input in authentic communicative contexts is critical. This hypothesis states that although second language instruction might help learners learn some rules, language forms, and the like, this type of learning is not very useful for language *acquisition*—that is, being able to speak and understand a language in natural conversations and authentic contexts—in contrast to *learning* and being able to apply rules of the language in contrived situations. A review published 30 years ago of studies comparing second language instruction with second language exposure concluded that instruction indeed aided second language learning for learners of various ages and levels (Long 1983). There are undoubtedly benefits to exposure—that is, living, working, and going to school with speakers of a target language; in fact, it is probably impossible to attain a high level of proficiency without such learning opportunities. But second language instruction has added benefits.

Norris and Ortega's (2000) meta-analysis revisited this question and asked: How effective is second language instruction overall and in comparison with exposure and communication with speakers of a second language? The review found that focused second language instruction designed to teach specific aspects of the second language is more effective than conditions that do not provide focused second language instruction (including exposure only, minimally focused instruction, or minimal exposure). Students who received focused second language instruction made more than five times the gains of students who did not (Norris & Ortega 2000).

For a more thorough treatment of the research base, see Saunders, W. M., & Goldenberg, C. (2010). Research to guide English language development instruction. In D. Dolson & L. Burnham-Massey (Eds.), *Improving education for English Learners: Research-based approaches* (pp. 21–81). Sacramento, CA: CDE Press.

However, there are several limitations of this meta-analysis with respect to its applicability to K–12 ELD contexts. First, of the 79 studies Norris and Ortega reviewed, nearly four fifths involved college-age or adult learners; only 6% involved high school, 13% middle or junior high school, and 1%—just one study—involved elementary school. Second, most (59%) were conducted in foreign language instructional contexts and fewer than a third (29%) in second language instructional contexts, that is, where students are learning the dominant societal language and, presumably, have more opportunities for exposure outside of instructional settings. Third, the great majority of the studies were of short duration. The average "treatment" lasted just over four hours and was more laboratory-like than long-term, classroom-like. Finally, most studies were narrow in scope—teaching a specific feature of language (e.g., verb tense, adverb placement, relative pronouns, or wh- questions).

Thus, the most robust conclusion from this meta-analysis—that the most effective way to help older second language learners learn a language form or rule in the short term is to teach it explicitly—is of somewhat limited utility in EL/EB school contexts. We do not know empirically whether a semester or a year or multiple years of such instruction on a scope and sequence of language forms and rules would produce higher levels of second language proficiency in young learners than some other approach—for example, one emphasizing language *acquisition* in more authentic and communicative contexts—also sustained over time. So the fundamental challenge posed by Krashen to instructed second language learning has not been fully resolved in favor of either the learning or the acquisition perspective.

Despite these caveats, however, the available data point to the value of teaching language explicitly. Although the "learning perspective" has a limited empirical base, the "acquisition perspective" has nothing even comparable. Moreover, and despite necessary caution in drawing analogies between language and literacy instruction, comparable findings have emerged about the value to ELs of explicit instruction in English reading skills (August & Shanahan, 2006; Genesee, Lindholm-Leary, Saunders, & Christian, 2006) in contrast to providing learners with opportunities and exposure intended to promote literacy *acquisition* without adequate explicit instruction.

An important study by Tong, Lara-Alecio, Irby, Mathes, and Kwok (2008) confirmed the general conclusion about the value of instructed second language for accelerating ELD. Tong et al. found that providing kindergarten and grade 1 students with an "English-oracy intervention" resulted in more accelerated ELD growth compared with students in control schools who received typical "English as a second language (ESL) instruction." The ELD intervention, which was equally effective with students in either English immersion or bilingual education, comprised (a) daily tutorials with a published ELD program; (b) storytelling and retelling with authentic, culturally relevant literature and leveled questions from easy to difficult; and (c) an academic oral language activity using a "question of the day."

The study is important in demonstrating the value added by direct and focused ELD instruction even in an English immersion context where students receive instruction in English throughout the day. Again, the study has its limitations, such as it only included children in kindergarten and first grade. But, again, the evidence is consistent that instructed settings can play a productive role in aiding second language acquisition.

2.15 What are language learning progressions and why are they important to educators?

■ *Alison L. Bailey and Margaret Heritage*

Learning progressions are descriptions of how learning in a domain develops from its most rudimentary form through increasingly sophisticated forms as a result of instruction and experience (Heritage, 2008). The idea behind progressions is that they provide the detail of the significant steps along the path or paths that lead to the desired goals of schooling. Unlike end-of-grade level standards, progressions are not prescriptive. Rather, they lay out a sequence of "expected tendencies" in student learning along a continuum of developing expertise (Confrey & Maloney, 2010).

One primary way that researchers develop progressions is to first create a hypothetical description based on extensive reviews of the empirical literature on learning in a specific domain, and then to conduct empirical validation studies of their hypothesis. For example, tasks are given to students to determine that the hypothesized progression is a representation of how learning develops in reality (Mosher, 2011).

In contrast, standards development is typically informed by the disciplinary knowledge and professional experience of educators and other constituents. Generally, standards are not subjected to empirical validation (e.g., subjected to rigorous study of their efficacy for student learning). More typically, they undergo a process of establishing "face validity," whereby experts and other professionals come to consensus that the standards are reasonable and defensible end-of-grade level expectations for students (Corcoran, Mosher, & Rogat, 2009).

Language learning progressions can present a more detailed description than English language development (ELD) standards of how language tends to evolve from its earliest forms and practices (e.g., from sentence fragments and participation in predictable routines) through increasingly mature forms and practices (e.g., to multiclausal utterances and extended expressive discourse over a period of schooling).

The new content standards in mathematics, English language arts (ELA), and science place increased demands on what students must do with language in content-area learning (Council of Chief State School Officers, 2012). These demands have particular implications for students who are English language learners (ELLs) because ELLs are learning language at the same time as they are acquiring content knowledge. For this reason, language learning progressions do not exist in isolation. Rather, they answer the question, "What language competencies underpin the acquisition of [academic] concepts and skills?" (Bailey & Heritage, 2010, p. 3). By answering this question, language learning progressions provide teachers and students with a pathway that supports both content and language learning.

To date, there are too few comprehensive longitudinal studies of school-age children's language to derive the hypotheses that have traditionally formed the bases of learning progressions. Consequently, the development of language learning progressions involves an inductive step to generate empirical data across age/grade and a spectrum of language backgrounds. An example of such an approach is the Dynamic Language Learning Progressions (DLLP) project.

Researchers in this project initially began by developing language progressions for explanation, a productive language practice that cuts across the academic domains in the new content standards. First, researchers generated data from a sample of students with a wide range of English language experiences, including monolingual English-speaking students and students first encountering English in a formal schooling context. Then they conducted linguistic analyses of students' explanations, which informed progression development (Bailey, Reynolds Kelly, Heritage, Jones, & Blackstock-Bernstein, 2013). As a result, the progression was empirically derived and then subjected to further validation through a pilot study of teachers' use of the progression. Taking this approach will require creating unique learning progressions for the different language practices encountered in school, for example, arguing from evidence and recounting events.

Students' language development along a progression will be largely dependent on quality learning opportunities, combined with attentiveness on the part of teachers and students to where individual students' current language development lies on the progression as learning is occurring. This kind of attention and pedagogy holds promise for increased language learning in the content areas for all students, and especially for ELLs.

■ *Patricia Velasco*

In New York State, the Common Core Standards (CCSS) are known as the Common Core Learning Standards (CCLS). The New York State Bilingual Common Core Initiative (BCCI) (http://www.engageny.org/resource/new-york-state-bilingual-common-core-initiative) is a resource that provides scaffolding descriptors and supports to address the CCLS in the bilingual population.

Bilingual Common Core Initiative Language Arts Progressions

Within the BCCI there are five levels of language proficiency—entering, emerging, transitioning, expanding, and commanding—referred to as "the progressions." The term "progressions" was deliberately chosen to convey a sense that language development is an ongoing process, characterized by fluidity and flexibility. The five levels of language proficiency are not to be construed as fixed categories.

The progressions present two visions for bilingual classrooms: New Language Arts Progressions (NLAP) and Home Language Arts Progressions (HLAP). The NLAP address language growth in the language being acquired. In the first three stages of language development, students can approach a task in the home and/or new language. The HLAP differ from the NLAP by focusing more strongly on literacy development. Many students come into home language arts classrooms with strong oral language skills but with varying degrees of literacy knowledge in their home language. A student in this situation would expect to receive different types and degrees of scaffolding, depending on the language of instruction. When used together, the NLAP and HLAP convey a dynamic sense of bilingualism and a roadmap to develop bilingual Common Core skills in emergent and proficient bilinguals.

The NLAP and the HLAP build on the work of the New York State Native Language Arts Learning Standards (2004) and World-class Instructional Design and Assessment (WIDA) (2012). Their purpose is the development of language in academic settings.

Academic Language Features: World-class Instructional Design and Assessment and the Common Core State Standards

WIDA presents six levels of language proficiency: entering, emerging, developing, expanding, bridging, and reaching. This last level, though, represents the end of the continuum rather than another level of language proficiency. Essentially, students who are considered to have reached the sixth level meet all the level 5 criteria.

WIDA organizes social, instructional, and academic language into three levels: discourse (linguistic complexity), sentence (language forms and conventions), and word/phrase (or vocabulary) (WIDA, 2012). WIDA does not allocate fixed words and sentence patterns to particular grade levels. Teachers are expected to address these aspects depending on the content area being developed. This is not the case with the language standards that are part of the ELA in the CCSS.

The language standards in the CCSS are addressed by grade level, reflecting a sense that their mastery is anticipated and expected. Language Standard 1: Conventions of Standard English for grade 3 states: "(a) Explain the function of nouns, pronouns, verbs, adjectives, and adverbs in general and their functions in particular sentences." For grade 4 the same standard states: "Use relative pronouns (who, whose, whom, which, that. . .) and relative adverbs (where, when, why. . .)." One cannot avoid thinking that there is a sense of arbitrariness, and a subjective sense of language development.

Development of Language for Academic Purposes: Gradual, not Necessarily Linear

Undoubtedly, language and literacy development require attention, quality reading materials, and authentic opportunities to develop receptive (listening and reading) and productive (speaking and writing) skills. As all teachers know, this development is a gradual, but not necessarily linear, process. Language is learned naturally and in context, not arranged in an easy-to-difficult sequence.

Conclusion

Language plays a central role in communication with other people and with ourselves. Social and educational variables, experiential factors, attitude, personality, age, and motivation all affect language learning. Bilingual teaching requires being cognizant of all these factors while developing content knowledge and gaining a firmer grasp on the language that is an intrinsic component of the content. Orchestrating these complex demands requires fluidity and flexibility. It requires that teachers have the confidence to react and adjust their pedagogical practices to the changing circumstances that characterize all students, particularly bilingual ones.

2.16 How might existing language progressions help or hinder English language learners/emergent bilinguals in meeting the demands of the Common Core State Standards?

- *Claude Goldenberg[1]*

Learning progressions have generated considerable interest over the past few years (e.g., Alonzo & Gotwals, 2012; Sztajn, Confrey, Wilson, & Edgington, 2012; Wilson, 2009). Curriculum must be sequenced in some way; it therefore makes sense to try and determine whether some learning sequences are more productive than others. Moreover, because formative assessments that track students' learning progress help improve achievement by providing feedback to students and relevant information to teachers (Black & Wiliam, 1998), formative assessments based on well-specified learning progressions might be especially productive.

English learners (ELs) and their teachers face what we are coming to understand is a formidable challenge, particularly in the Common Core era. EL students must learn the high-level academic content all students must learn, while learning the language itself at a very high level (Wong Fillmore & Fillmore, 2012). Under these circumstances, students and teachers need a great deal of support in implementing appropriate curriculum, instruction, and assessment. Developing *language* learning progressions that help guide teachers and students along a challenging and complex linguistic terrain might be an important step forward.

What do we know about the utility of learning progressions when applied to *language development*? We have a few hints. In the field of second language acquisition (SLA) there are "developmental sequences" (Lightbown & Spada, 2011)—sequences of development that seem to have a natural "acquisition order" (Gass, 2013) that all learners seem to go through. Developmental sequences have been described for acquisition of forms such as grammatical morphemes, negations, questions, and relative clauses. For example, second language learners first use relative clauses referring to nouns in the subject ("The boy who was tall played basketball") and the direct object positions ("The play that we saw was boring"); later they use relative clauses to modify indirect objects ("The girl who[m] you gave the gift to was surprised") and objects of prepositions ("I saw the movie that Maria was telling us about").

On the one hand there might be limits on the extent to which instruction can meaningfully influence the course or pace of developmental sequences (Gass, 2013; Lightbown & Spada, 2011). But on the other, we have examples of second language learners being taught a more difficult or advanced form (e.g., object-of-preposition relative clause) then being able to generalize to an easier, less advanced form (e.g., subject and direct object relative clauses), suggesting the sequence is not necessarily invariant (Gass, 2013). Although it might be useful for second language teachers to understand typical developmental sequences of specific language forms, it would be wrong to assume that language learning progressions cannot be influenced by classroom instruction (Gass, 2013).

---

[1] My thanks to Bill Saunders for his invaluable help on this article.

What about other aspects of language, such as pragmatic functions? Pragmatic functions, especially those important in classroom settings, are becoming increasingly important for all students—including those acquiring English as a second language. The Commom Core expects students to accomplish increasingly complex goals with language—not just *know* and be able to speak and understand the language or correctly use specific grammatical forms. Students are expected to do such things as justify, persuade, explain to different audiences, convey complex ideas, and gather information from different sources and evaluate their credibility. No language learning progressions such as those for grammatical morphemes and relative clauses have been developed and empirically tested for these language functions. Until they are, it is difficult to know what their utility is.

The authors of the Common Core State Standards (CCSS) have identified "progressive language skills,"[2] which might be a starting point for developing sets of language learning progressions to help guide language curriculum and instruction in the Common Core environment. These identified skills comprise a mixture of grammatical forms (e.g., subject-verb agreement) and pragmatic functions (e.g., choosing words and phrases for effect). It is unclear, however, what research actually supports these "progressive language skills" and the targeted grade levels for introduction and initial mastery.

Despite the potential utility of these identified skills, we are clearly far from being able to advocate using language learning progressions to guide instruction for ELs/emergent bilinguals (EBs). Here are some of the issues to consider:

1. How do we know whether a language learning progression actually describes a modal progression through some dimension of language? Determining learning progressions will invariably involve judgments based on probability, that is, although we might be able to describe a "typical" progression, there will be plenty of exceptions. What is the margin of error we are willing to accept? What criterion do we use to determine whether we can claim something as a bona fide language learning progression—if it describes a majority of cases? 75%? 80%? What if the language learning progression describes some learners but not others? Here's a cautionary tale from science teaching. Steedle and Shavelson (2012) found that a learning progression describing students' understanding of force and velocity worked fairly well to describe the response patterns of two types of students: those with nearly accurate scientific understanding and those with naïve prescientific understanding. For all other students in between, the language progression items did not successfully diagnose what position they occupied along the learning dimension; responses were not sufficiently consistent with the stated (presumed) learning progression levels. How much inconsistency can we tolerate as we construct language learning progressions and levels within them?

---

[2] Common Core State Standards for English Language Arts & Literacy in History/Social Studies, Science, and Technical Subjects—Appendix A: Research Supporting Key Elements of the Standards, pp. 29–31. Available at corestandards.org/ELA-Literacy/

2. Even if we successfully define a modal or typical progression through some content domain or dimension of language, on what basis do we make the leap to inferring that this *descriptive progression* should be a *prescriptive teaching sequence*? It's clearly a leap. We know that children babble before they begin to speak, and many scribble before engaging in conventional writing. Does that mean we should teach young children to babble and scribble? Is there a danger of creating a lock-step progression that teachers then follow too rigidly, assuming that children have to go through each and every level before reaching some target level of performance?

3. Most important: what evidence do we have that if teachers use language learning progressions their students will enjoy better learning outcomes? The preceding theoretical concerns pale in comparison to this question, because if we can show that using language learning progressions can actually promote student language acquisition, at least along some dimensions if not all, then none of these other concerns matter. What will matter at that point is how we get this technology into the hands and heads of teachers and support its consistent and productive use.

If language learning progression are to play a role in the education of ELs, several things must happen:

- Plausible progressions related to important classroom language functions must be identified.
- The progressions must be observed in use in classrooms as they help guide and inform instruction, if indeed they do.
- Use of the progressions must be evaluated with respect to (1) the extent to which they help both teachers and students understand learning goals and tasks, and (2) whether they help enhance language and achievement outcomes for students.

In other words, what we need is a proof of concept, a plausible demonstration that if we determine viable language learning progressions for some domain of language, then train teachers how to use them, they might be advantageous to student learning. Only then can we begin to think in realistic terms about whether language learning progressions help—or hinder—ELs/EBs in meeting the demands of the CCSS.

DISCUSSION QUESTIONS

After reading this chapter, engage in dialogue with peer educators, including school principals, other administrators and supervisors, teachers of different subjects, specialists in different areas, paraprofessionals, and parents/community members to discuss fundamental language issues in relation to CCSS implementation and ELLs/EBs in your state/district/school/program. Here are some questions to reflect on individually, with a colleague, or ideally, as part of a professional learning community at your school. If you are in a school, the members of this group would comprise the school's ELL/EB leadership team, whose responsibility it is to collectively make the decisions that affect the education of ELLs/EBs.

1. Invite everyone to talk about the languages that they speak. Do they consider themselves bilingual? Why or why not? How did they acquire the languages that they use? Where did they learn them and with whom? What memories do they have about the acquisition process? What are their feelings about the languages that they use?

2. How is a second language acquired? Ask members of the group to imagine that they want to learn another language. What would they have to do in order to learn it well enough to do specific things in that language (e.g., to travel successfully in another country, to buy and sell things in a face-to-face context, to teach their subject matter in a school in that country, to argue about politics, to write a short story or an academic article in that language)? What would the role of instruction be in each case? What kinds of and how much exposure to speakers/users of the language would be required? How long do different individuals think that the process would take?

3. Now turn your discussion to the U.S. school context and to the CCSS. Do you and your colleagues use the term "academic language"? Does everyone define it similarly? Make a list of definitions that are proposed. How are these definitions different? How are they useful? What problems do they raise for teachers and for students?

4. Consider the discussion in the "Language Valued at School" section. Talk about the readings on language variation. Ask people to talk about the ways that language is used in their part of the country (south, north, east, west). What did they first notice was different in the way that people in different parts of the United States (or the English-speaking world) talk? Then ask people to think about the ways that they speak to different people in different situations (e.g., speaking to a toddler, speaking to male buddies about a sports event, speaking to a group of fellow teachers about practice). What is the same and what is different in these ways of speaking? Finally, ask people to talk about ways of speaking that are not highly valued. Who speaks that way? Where are they acceptable and not acceptable? Where and for what purposes might they be effective? What would be involved in learning to speak in these ways if one spoke a high-prestige variety of English?

TOPICS FOR REFLECTION AND ACTION

The following statements are organized around the big ideas of the chapter. Read through them and indicate the extent to which each applies to your community and your school. After you complete the survey, discuss your responses with your team. Then write down one to three reflection points that have emerged from your discussions. Finally, identify one to three concrete actions that you/your team can take.

DK don't know   1 strongly disagree   2 disagree   3 agree   4 strongly agree

PERSPECTIVES ON LANGUAGE					
1. Most of my colleagues and I have a good understanding of bilingualism. We view it as a resource rather than as a handicap.	DK	1	2	3	4
2. We know how many of our colleagues use more than one language in their everyday lives and do not confuse ethnic background with language proficiency.	DK	1	2	3	4
3. When my colleagues and I talk about language, we know that we are talking about the same thing.	DK	1	2	3	4
4. It is possible that teachers at my school have very different ideas about what we mean by the term "academic language."	DK	1	2	3	4
Perspectives on Language Acquisition					
5. We disagree about how second languages are acquired. Some of us believe in the apprenticeship models and others of us are convinced that language has to be "taught" directly.	DK	1	2	3	4
6. Our programs for "teaching" English as a second language are congruent with our beliefs about second language acquisition.	DK	1	2	3	4
7. Content teachers in our school expect that EBs/ELLs have completed their acquisition of English before they are enrolled in regular classes with fluent speakers of English.	DK	1	2	3	4
Language Variation					
8. Our school community has a deep awareness of how and why language varies and why particular ways of speaking are more valued than others.	DK	1	2	3	4
9. We have many debates about whether to allow students to use nonstandard varieties of English in the classroom.	DK	1	2	3	4
10. We have many debates about allowing students to use their full linguistic repertoires including non-English languages in the classroom.	DK	1	2	3	4

Reflection:

Action Steps:

Family and Community Participation

F amilies and community organizations are often identified as partners in education because they share the work of teaching and learning about our world. We
know that when parents are involved in education, students and schools improve. We
also know, however, that many complex issues and questions arise when we consider the
how, who, and the why of parent involvement.

For English language learners (ELLs)/emergent bilinguals (EBs), families and communities offer cultural and linguistic experiences that may differ from those of schools
or other formal learning spaces. Respectful collaboration between families, teachers,
and communities can lead to better understanding and partnerships that benefit these
children, their families, schools, and communities. On the one hand, educators need
to communicate with families and communities to inform them of what goes on in
schools and formal learning spaces. We can think of this as one-way communication.
Just as importantly, two-way communication between families and schools, as well as
between schools and communities, can increase educators' understanding about student's home language practices, learning experiences, and funds of knowledge in ways
that can inform decision making at school. These dynamic connections deepen educators' understanding about the ways in which ELLs/EBs know and apply concepts and
ideas and use language and learn across various contexts. Moreover, because families
and communities are constant factors in ELLs'/EBs' lives, they are among the most influential partners our schools could have in the education of children.

Unfortunately, however, even when families and communities are recognized as key
partners in education, the way educators have historically approached these school–
family or school–community partnerships has often been ineffective and even damaging. Some of these relationships are set in environments where there is unequal power and
privilege, which may be invisible to school staff who have power and privilege but very
real to families from diverse language and cultural backgrounds who may be in marginalized positions at school and in society. Other times, schools employ cultural assim-
ilation approaches or use culturally inappropriate practices in the name of parent "involvement" in their children's education through parent trainings or "parent-education"

programs. While these types of activities are well intentioned, the one-way information they provide reflects an assumption that parents come as blank slates or that they must leave their own cultural norms at the door and assume new cultural ways of parenting that, at times, conflict with their own. As educators, we have the opportunity to create meaningful partnerships that focus on the children and their education and that disturb the unequal power relationships between home, school, and community.

This chapter is about creating spaces for meaningful partnerships with families and communities. We explore relationships among schools and families and communities from various perspectives, and we include contributions from a wide range of contexts. The first section of the chapter highlights the importance of families and communities in the education of ELLs/EBs with concrete examples of meaningful engagement strategies that involve parents in the education of their children and work to elevate the status of families and communities at school. The second section considers shifting views of relationships between families and schools. Educators are invited to look critically at the nature of family–school and school–community relations in their context, question who owns the decision making at school, who actually engages with the school, and who has privilege and power. We see examples of the development of relationships between schools and families that go beyond the traditional one-way practices, which have been historically ineffective in creating strong ties between schools and families. Meaningful two-way communicative practices serve to inform families as much as to inform schools.

While our work with families and communities is far from perfect, there exist, throughout the country, spaces where deficit and exclusive ideologies about parent engagement are being contested and where educators are implementing innovative ways to work with families through meaningful engagement and equitable partnerships. While this may sound idyllic, meaningful collaboration with families and communities is not always easy and fulfilling. Most often these relationships are challenging and require a constant state of change and negotiation.

The value of the examples provided in this chapter will not be in taking the strategies and replicating them in other sites ignoring the particular contexts in which they are being used, but instead, in understanding how the particular contexts and situations guided families, communities, and schools to make specific decisions and adopt those strategies. Knowing the communities and the families of our students and identifying the needs and resources we have available, whether we are in rural or urban environments, or whether we are working with immigrants, first, or even second, generation families, is the first step into action that results in meaningful engagement of the various people invested in the education of our children.

Engaging Diverse Families and Communities in Education

3.1 Why is it important to discuss the role of families and communities in the education of English language learners/emergent bilinguals relative to the Common Core State Standards?

■ *Debbie Zacarian*

The advantages of family–school engagement and community involvement are well known (Espinosa, 2010; Henderson, Mapp, Johnson, & Davies, 2007; Zacarian, 2011, 2013; Zacarian & Silverstone, 2015). However, we might not think of their special relevance for families from linguistically and culturally diverse experiences—especially families whose life, cultural, and prior schooling experiences are quite distinct from our own. Let's look at an example of the differences in action by exploring a common school event—Open House held at a local urban high school.

> Mr. and Mrs. Santiago recently moved to the area from El Salvador to live with a distant relative and work in a local restaurant. Their son is a freshman in high school and is overwhelmed with his studies. To make matters more stressful for him, he recently learned that he is required to take two important "state" tests. When his parents ask him about school, he bursts out crying and tells them of his fear that he will be asked to leave school, as he knows that he will not do well on the tests. Through serendipity, his parents learn of the Open House event that will be held at their son's high school and have taken precious time from work to attend the event. Their intent is to speak with his teachers to find out what they can do to keep their son in school. When they arrive, they are given an abbreviated schedule of their son's classes and told to attend ten-minute session overviews of each one. After an hour of passively listening to his teachers speak in a language that they do not understand well, they return home. When their son asks them what to do, they too are afraid that he will be asked to leave. Before the state tests occur, he becomes one of the many English learners who are chronically absent.

Like the Santiagos, many families of English learners (ELs) are unfamiliar with the cultural norms and expectations of American public schools. While "Open House" is a familiar cultural event that has existed for generations (Lawrence-Lightfoot, 2005), it may be unfamiliar to many of the families with whom we work. The example shows the amount of misconceptions and misunderstandings that can occur (Zacarian, 2011; Zacarian & Silverstone, 2015). This, coupled with the realities of standards and accountability, should make family engagement and community involvement a top priority among this segment of our schools.

To do this, we have to consider ways that will supportively build and maintain these elements as core to what we do. The following four components from Zacarian (2011) and Zacarian & Silverstone (2015) are drawn from Henderson et al. (2007), Espinosa (2010), Delpit (2006), and Zacarian (2004, 2006, 2007a and b, 2008a and b).

1. **Bridging the cultural divide**. Educators should evaluate the various school routines and practices that occur and seek ways to make them transparent, meaningful, and

accessible. For example, state assessments and standards are routine and should be made known to families. Equally important is learning about families' cultures to support involvement that coincide with their ways of being and acting. For example, many ELs and their families are from collectivist cultures that believe strongly in relationships and community membership as important ways of being and acting. This cultural approach is distinct from the dominant U.S. cultural view, in which independence and competition are highly valued (DeCapua & Marshall, 2011; Zacarian & Haynes, 2012).

2. **Infusing advocacy as part of the core.** It is important to support families in their child's education. Helping families to become advocates for this purpose is essential. As in the earlier example, had the Santiagos known about Open House and the state tests, they may have been in a much better position to advocate for their son. Bilingual educators, support staff, translators, and community members from EL communities are essential for this work.

3. **Linking parent involvement to learning.** Students spend more time out of school than they do in school. It is essential to secure ways for families to engage in their child's education and in activities that are connected with learning. A means for doing this is to provide students with real-life examples and projects that relate to the academic standards and to secure activities (e.g., a family interview about a school topic) that can occur at home.

4. **Working together for the common good of students.** Creating a welcoming environment for students, their families, and the community (particularly communities that are new to a city or town or that are still disconnected from it) should also be core to what we do. To make this work well requires us to build close connections between our school, community services and agencies, and the families of our ELs to best ensure that we work together for the well-being and academic success of our students.

■ *Diep Nguyen*

The Common Core State Standards (CCSS) provide guideposts for districts and schools when setting learning goals for students. These standards are also used as the foundations for state assessments to measure student achievement in core-content subjects and keep schools accountable.

Providing Information: Common Core State Standards and English Language Development Standards-Based Curricula and Assessments

In my experience as a school administrator, parents of emergent bilinguals (EBs) on the whole are less likely than their counterparts to be informed about the program of instruction and major curricular changes in their local schools. This lack of information, in addition to parents' beliefs and attitudes about bilingual programs, often deepen the gap between home and school and negatively affect EBs' learning and achievement (King & Fogle, 2006). Parents and families of EBs need to be informed about the planning and implementation of the standard-based curriculum that are driven by the CCSS for several reasons:

- According to the No Child Left Behind (NCLB) Act of 2001, §3302, parents have the right to be informed about the program of instruction designed for their students. This information needs to be in a language that parents can understand. Because the CCSS are overloaded with specialized educational language, it is important to provide essential information about the CCSS for parents. While parents do not need to know the details of every content standard and how they are aligned with each other, they need to be informed about the grade-level goals and expectations in each core subject and how their child is instructed to meet those goals. The purpose is to help parents understand the learning expectations for their child based on the new standards.

- School districts take different approaches to align their local curricula to the CCSS. It is important to describe the approach the district is taking for curriculum recalibrating and the rationale behind it, especially when taking into consideration the English language learning trajectory of their EB students. EB parents need to know how the school curriculum integrates content subject learning with English or other second language development to help their EBs meet the CCSS. This knowledge will help parents of EBs feel more confident about supporting their child to meet both the academic and language challenges of CCSS-based curricula.

- Because EB parents are concerned that their children are successful academically while attaining English proficiency, the explanation of how the district is aligning the curriculum for English language development (ELD) standards for ELs in addition to CCSS is of particular importance. EBs' parents need to know that the program of instruction implemented with EB students takes into consideration their English language learning goals and intentionally builds English language proficiency, while addressing the academic content target. The purpose here is to let parents know that both language development and academic content learning are important for their children to meet the CCSS.

To this end, the myriad of CCSS and ELD standards can be summarized and converted to an easy to understand yearly curriculum map for each core content at each grade level. Parents will be able to use this map to monitor their child's progress throughout the year both in terms of the student's language development targets and their academic goals.

In an attempt to help teachers understand what EL students can do within each content subject, depending on their language proficiency, the World-class Instructional Design and Assessment (WIDA) consortium published the *Can Do* descriptors (2009) for specific grade levels for core subjects. Using a similar approach, a school district can organize workshops and prepare literature to inform and demonstrate to EB parents how to use their child's ELD level to estimate what the student can do in each academic subject in English to meet the CCSS. This knowledge can empower parents to encourage and support their children in ELD and academic learning.

Because the CCSS will be accompanied by a new high-stakes academic achievement test, parents need to be informed about this new assessment and the role it will play in their children's learning and evaluation. Parents also need to be informed about critical assessments that their child will be required to participate in and the rationale for each.

While not all assessments need to be explained, parents can be benefit from knowing how their child's learning is monitored and how assessment data are systemically used to evaluate their child's progress and achievement.

There are many ways of informing EBs' parents, including curricular information meetings, webinars, parent–teacher meetings, and other written and electronic means. However, information needs to be shared in a way that is accessible and comprehensible to EBs' parents, and parents should have the chance to raise questions and concerns. Utilizing both formal and informal means of communication will help reach the maximum number of parents and families who need the information.

Engaging Community and Parent Leaders in the Process of Implementing and Calibrating the Curriculum to Meet Emergent Bilinguals' Needs

Parents and families of EBs not only need to be informed of the changes made to their students' program of study, they also need to become engaged in the implementation of CCSS and ELD standards. Parents of EBs bring to the discussion cultural and linguistic insights that inform our decisions as educators when differentiating instruction and planning the curriculum for EBs.

In any group of parents, informal leaders emerge. These individuals can become liaisons and advocates for the schools among their peers and in the community. EB parent engagement often begins with the careful cultivation of informal relationships with specific individuals and inviting them to take on a leadership role to help the school implement a specific project that benefits their children. In the case of the CCSS, these parent leaders can be invited to be at the table to inform educators of sociocultural or linguistic needs of EBs that may be overlooked when implementing the new standards-based curricula.

Fenner (2014), in her review of research on ELs' parental involvement, concludes that one way of increasing EBs' family involvement is to increase their advocacy capacity. The most obvious group of EB parent leaders and advocates can be found in the mandatory bilingual parent advisory committee (BPAC) in each school district receiving Title III funding. The role of the BPAC is to provide advice and oversight of the program of instruction implemented for EBs in the program. This group of leaders, as they work collaboratively with teachers and administrators to monitor and improve educational programs, can provide support and serve as critical friends and advocates for the school districts in their implementation of CCSS and ELD standards-based programs for EBs.

Educators need to recognize that some EB parents and community leaders are quite concerned about the fairness of state mandated testing of EB students. Many take on active roles in questioning the validity of such assessments. These leaders would welcome the opportunity to be at the table with educational leaders of their local schools to discuss and find ways to implement fair and valid assessments for EBs. While it takes more preparation and information sharing to include parent leaders in the planning of district level curricula, they can serve as advisors and critical friends to help educators improve local programs. Every district I served in had a parent advisory group that provided input for the superintendent or the leadership team on districtwide concerns or new initiatives. EB parents serving on these advisory groups often raised concerns about students that others overlooked, particularly when it involved language needs or sociocultural conflicts. They often serve as the liaison between the school district and local ethnic community leaders and facilitate the process for sharing school information with other EB parents. School districts that have instituted such an advisory body from the community have found that EB parent and community leaders in this advisory group help to ensure that the needs of EBs are addressed in critical decisions with regard to implementing CCSS and ELD standards.

3.2 What are some culturally and linguistically appropriate practices when communicating with families of English language learners/emergent bilinguals?

■ *Sheila M. Shannon*

The first encounters parents have when they enroll their children in schools are often with school staff such as secretaries. For English-speaking, white, middle-class parents this initial encounter is typically seamless. The staff will do its best to understand their interests. Requirements and expectations are familiar to these parents and they expect to be served. On the other hand, the adults of immigrant families who enroll children in school find themselves in an unfamiliar context. Often they do have sufficient command of the English language to understand what is being communicated to them.

Language is not the only issue that makes communication in schools challenging to immigrant parents and staff alike. Classic studies (e.g., Brice Heath, 1983) have shown that in white, middle-class, English-speaking families, children are brought up in ways that mimic schools. They have been socialized from the earliest age to be read to, to read, and to participate in organized activities, from soccer to ballet, in school-like settings. Children of immigrants may have had experiences that are substantially different. Some of those differences are grounded in the cultural contexts of other places. For example, many children of Mexican immigrants (the largest number of bilingual children in the United States) come from large extended families that may have been divided and separated by immigration. Their lives from a very early age may have involved mobility, instability, and uncertainty. Entering the schoolhouse door for the first time could be a daunting challenge filled with more uncertainty.

Nearly 30 years after the last major immigration reform (Immigration Reform and Control Act, 1986) Congress is divided and there are now an estimated 11 million people in the United States who are unauthorized. Many are immigrant parents with children in school. The already complicated encounter with language and cultural differences is further exacerbated by anxieties around detection and deportation. It is imperative that school staff understands that the 1982 *Plyler v Doe* ruling of the U.S. Supreme Court guarantees that public schools may not restrict registration of children for immigration status (Olivas, 2012). The most practical application of that law is to ensure that school staff do not ask about immigration status of children or their parents. It is imperative that the school culture be one where all families are welcome and no one is turned away.

Some facts can help sketch the face of immigrants. The majority of immigrant families (not *all*) are from Mexico. Most children of immigrants are U.S.-born citizens. Increasingly, these children come to school already bilingual. Despite differences, all children and their families need a safe and secure place in school where they can learn and be treated with dignity and respect.

Dual language programs are particularly vulnerable when it comes to accommodating parents in schools. Typically in these programs, half the students are from white, English-speaking families while the other half are from Mexican, Spanish-speaking families. While many programs profess a goal of bilingualism and biculturalism for all, reaching that goal with this mix incites a dilemma of interest convergence (Shannon, 2011). School staff need to understand that the needs and interests of the "naturally ready for school" families do not eclipse those of the children of immigrants.

I recommend that the school leadership and teachers make parent recruitment and education a priority. Parents need to be informed and educated about their rights and responsibilities and the services available to their children. Particularly in dual language schools, parents and families need to be aware of the social experiment they are participating in. Those with power need to be shown how to share it and those who are vulnerable need to be shown how they can accept it.

■ *Marjorie Faulstich Orellana*

The families of English learner (EL) students or emerging bilinguals (EBs) are sometimes immigrants who are navigating new linguistic and cultural contexts every day. Most immigrant families pool their linguistic and cultural resources to do so. Family members work collectively to read and interpret written documents, fill out forms, make phone calls, and speak to and for many different people. This practice is referred to as language brokering (Morales & Hanson, 2005). Some rely on their children to broker language for them, and to explain cultural practices, values, and norms (Orellana, 2009).

When school staff communicate with families, family language brokering practices should be taken into account. Find out who serves as family language brokers or how families work together to navigate the everyday demands of life in an English-speaking world. Even when school materials are available in the home language, and even when a translator is available to speak with families, schools recognize the fact that families are used to working together to make sense of language and culture. They may like to have bilingual family members participate in meetings with school staff, even when a professional translator is available. Allowing for different configurations of family meetings is important.

Often teachers, like parents, rely on children to be language brokers. Even very young children—and children who are themselves classified as ELs—may be expected to be translators and interpretors. But as any bilingual adult knows, translation work is hard! Thus, teachers should support children in their brokering work. When you ask a child to translate, speak clearly and in short segments. Give the child time to process the information and to clarify its meaning. Invite questions. Notice the hesitations and pauses; step in and help by rephrasing things. Be sure to thank the child for his or her work.

Keep in mind that even when a translator is needed, parents may understand more than they let on. Parents will be following teachers' body language and facial expressions. They may comprehend more than they can speak, and they may be able to speak more than they do. Remember that parents are not passive participants. Allow time for them to formulate their ideas. Invite them to speak, not just listen. Typically in parent–teacher conferences, teachers present their ideas to parents and only at the end do they invite questions. Why not reverse things, and invite parents to ask questions up front? This can help orient you to what parents' concerns may be, and it helps to bring parents in as active participants in the conversation.

Keep in mind that the challenges of communication are not just about language. Parents are trying to understand how schools work, what they value, how they are organized and structured, and what they expect of parents. These may not be the same things that schools expected of parents in their countries of origin. School staff can help by making the school's cultural values more explicit for families.

3.3 How can educators create opportunities for families to engage in equitable school participation in linguistically and culturally appropriate ways?

■ *Young-chan Han*

In a dynamically changing cultural landscape, actively engaging diverse students and families in education requires intentional partnerships between home, school, and community. To create meaningful partnerships and ensure equal educational opportunities for immigrant families, it is critical that educators gain insight into the lives of immigrant families to better understand their needs and challenges/barriers. When the barriers are identified and removed, students and families can fully access and participate in educational programs, as seen in the following example:

> Leila is a 12-year-old Haitian student attending a local middle school. She had an opportunity to attend an overnight field trip. Were it not for her teacher learning why Leila did not turn in her permission slip along with the $75 fee on time, she would have missed this great learning opportunity. The teacher found out that Leila's father was still in Haiti and her mother worked two jobs. With the support of the English as a second langague teacher, Leila's teacher connected with a Haitian interpreter. The interpreter called the mom's work place, and the next day the interpreter visited the mom at work during her break to provide

information about the field trip. The mother understood the importance of the trip and signed the form. However, the fee was a barrier for the mom, so she asked if it could be paid in increments because she got paid every two weeks. Wanting to help, the parent-teacher association (PTA) offered to cover the fee. Without the intentional support and partnerships created among the interpreter, PTA, and teachers, Leila would have missed out on a valuable learning experience.

As immigrant families acclimate to U.S. culture, parents generally fall into four stages of involvement: *cultural survivors, cultural learners, cultural connectors*, and *cultural leaders* (Han, 2012). Cultural survivors face multiple challenges and their priority is to meet the family's basic needs. Leila's mom was a cultural survivor. Although she deeply valued education, because of language, long work hours, and lack of understanding about the U.S. school system she did not know about the value of field trips or how to fill out the permission slip. As families become more familiar with the new school culture and the U.S. educational system, they become cultural learners. Cultural learners are engaged in learning about U.S. schools —instruction, curriculum, assessment, school cultures, and so forth. With the help of interpreters schools can effectively communicate with parents on topics, including Common Core State Standards (CCSS). Cultural connectors have a greater familiarity and comfort level navigating the school system and are able to connect others (survivors and learners) with needed resources and programs and assist immigrant families with transition into the new culture. Parents at this stage continue to learn about U.S. education. For Leila's parent, the Haitian interpreter served as a cultural connector. Cultural leaders are the face/leaders of their ethnic/language community. They actively seek leadership opportunities and are engaged in advocating for cultural survivors and learners.

Programs, services, and support for parents of immigrant families should be determined by the stage of parental involvement. The needs of cultural survivors are very different from the needs of cultural connectors and leaders. When families face multiple challenges because of language, culture, and socioeconomic status (cultural survivors and learners), students and parents often miss out on educational opportunities. Using interpreters, meeting parents in their communities, providing for essential educational needs, and helping families understand the U.S. educational system, will help remove barriers and more fully engage immigrant families in education. There is power in putting practices in place appropriate to students' and families' needs.

■ *Penny Bird and Chris Sims*

In New Mexico we are fortunate that the language families within the Athabascan, Keres, Tewa, Tiwa, Towa, and Zuni tribes are still being spoken and used among the state's 22 tribes. We educators also have the New Mexico Indian Education Act (NMIEA) that was legislated in 2003 to first, "ensure equitable and culturally relevant learning environments, educational opportunities, and culturally relevant instructional materials for American Indian students enrolled in public schools; and second, "to ensure maintenance of native languages." The NMIEA also states that it "ensures that the Department of

Education partners with tribes to increase tribal involvement and control over schools and the education of students located in tribal communities; and ensure that parents; . . . tribal departments of education; . . . community-based organizations; . . . the department of education; . . . universities; and tribal, state, and local policymakers work together to find ways to improve educational opportunities for American Indian students, which includes [notifying] tribes of all curricula development for their approval and support."

These purposes of the NMIEA are the very expectations that tribes in New Mexico want implemented by the public schools that serve their children. From the tribal perspective, the NMIEA was recognition of their tribal sovereignty and authority for determining the conduct and provision of educational programs. They saw this as a means for schools, in partnership with tribal communities, to create enhanced educational activities, resources, and curricula. However, the implementation of the NMIEA has been inconsistent, and in certain instances unsupported. While the act holds great merit for encouraging systemic culturally based reform, it has not been fully funded nor is there knowledgeable oversight and accountablity for implementing it in the schools. Although this is an example of a "safe practice" in the school-based safety zone because it appears to create a culturally responsive infrastructure, the power structures in the state marginalize and deny full implementation.

The challenge this poses to local school boards, administrators, teachers, tribes, and parents is in agreeing how the act can be implemented in light of the limitations placed on the schools through the grading and labeling begun under past No Child Left Behind (NCLB) designations, and now continuing with the implementation of the CCSS. Too often the schools indigenous, bilingual, and English language learner (ELL) students attend are those designated as "needing improvement" and/or slated for "restructuring" because of the adoption of measures of student progress that have been based primarily on a single test instrument that the state requires. Therefore, the prescribed solution is for the schools to select from a menu of services that the New Mexico Public Education Department deems as appropriately research-based to "turn the school around." These services do not include the expansion of language- or culture-based knowledge, but rather, the reduction of time and resources for these elements of the instructional program.

In one school district, the parents, with support from local tribal officials, coordinated full-scale voter turnout to elect a school board that would support their efforts to implement an immersion Navajo language program in the schools. The board hired a superintendent who supported their efforts. However, the non-Indian member on the board fomented fear among the non-Indian population of the district and even proposed a separate school district to separate themselves from the Indian population who hampered their progress on making "adequate yearly progress."

While this is a very simplistic answer to a whole array of contributing factors that exist in our educational environments, the success of the CCSS in the education of our children can be met if the circumstances in which schools and tribes interact and decide what is best for the children are changed. Unless educational leaders, including departments of education at the state level, work in partnership with tribes, education for our children cannot be successful. The CCSS are seen as the new panacea for schools and students to achieve so that we have more critical thinkers to delve deeper into the substance and content of curricula that everyone is supposed to know. If the "critical thinkers"—read policymakers and administrators—cannot get past racial or cultural barriers, then the solutions will continue to be seen as superficial and ineffective.

3.4 How can rural communities ensure that immigrant and refugee families participate in how their schools choose to implement the Common Core State Standards?

■ *Margaret R. Hawkins and Stacey J. Lee*

The growth of immigrant and newcomer populations in the United States is extending beyond traditional gateway locations as immigrants increasingly settle in small towns and rural areas. While schools nationwide are preparing to use the Common Core State Standards (CCSS), and struggling with what implementation means for students with limited English proficiency, issues and challenges are significantly different for rural schools and districts. Many such communities function in isolation, with no existing pathway or knowledge base for designing programs and structuring language and academic support for English learners (ELs), limited resources (conceptual, material, and human) on which to draw, and limited historical encounters between the "majority" population and those from diverse language and cultural backgrounds. Here we present issues and suggestions drawn from a study we conducted exploring how rural school and districts respond to the needs of new immigrant and refugee populations.

The CCSS, nested as they are in a climate of accountability and assessment, call attention to ELs: with mandates for tracking *all* student progress, ELs cannot be overlooked or denied services. Further, the focus on academic language mandates that educators attend to language in instruction. However, a focus on standards and assessment does not help educators with little or no prior training in supporting language and academic development for newcomers to do so effectively. In fact, one clear finding from our study is that the focus on assessment and accountability provides a disincentive to work with ELs. As mainstream teachers were held accountable for student performances on standardized content tests and assessments, they feared that the poor scores ELs might achieve (because of insufficient command of English) would reflect negatively on them, and thus that newcomer students with limited English proficiency ought to be the responsibility of someone else. This encouraged a de facto segregation, where only the very limited number of staff designated as English as a second language (ESL) or bilingual teachers had responsibility for planning and implementing EL instruction.

Perhaps the most persistent finding among rural school personnel, including those with preparation to support ELs, was a deficit view of these learners and their families. As ELs failed to adequately master grade-level material, blame often fell on students and families. Deficit perspectives prevented educators from connecting with students, families, and cultures. Yet we know, from a multitude of research, scholarship, and practice, that *all* students learn by integrating new concepts (and language) into their existing knowledge and experiences, thus expanding their repertoires. The CCSS, with their intensive focus on classroom achievement (including content learning and academic language), may unintentionally increase challenges to building on students' funds of knowledge (González, Moll, & Amanti, 2005).

How can mainstream educators with little experience with diversity connect with, include, and learn from newcomer students and families? First, schools and districts must make spaces for collaboration with all constituents—administrators, staff, community members, parents, and students—willing to learn and negotiate together. One rural district we studied hired a former student from an immigrant family to serve as a bilingual resource specialist, and her knowledge of both the immigrant community and the schools was beneficial in building bridges between home and school. Taking this one step further, schools and districts would be well advised to invest in "grow your own" programs by partnering with universities to educate minority community members in preparation for careers as educators. Further, schools could collaborate with local community-based organizations in multiple ways, such as joint educational endeavors (e.g., providing English language support, GED preparation, and/or vocational training to families) as did a few of the districts we saw. One, in particular, partnered with a local mosque to provide services. In this way, school personnel learn about cultural beliefs and practices of the community, and community members know that their beliefs and institutions are visible and respected.

Relatedly, diversity itself must be seen as asset; mainstream students and staff have much to learn and gain from diverse others in school and community contexts. The CCSS provide learning goals, but do not provide a how-to map. For rural communities with limited prior experience in educating ELs, the CCSS offer an unprecedented opportunity to rethink relations and practices and open spaces to create sustainable and equitable partnerships from the ground up.

3.5 How can community organizations support and negotiate the work of schools around the Common Core State Standards for young dual language learners?

■ *Ruth Reinl*

Community organizations take on a very different role in supporting our youngest dual language learners (DLLs), birth–5 years, regarding the K–12 Common Core State Standards (CCSS) than they do for K–12 students. At the K–12 level, community organizations provide *supplemental* educational programing for students who spend the majority of their day learning within the public school setting. In contrast, early development and learning experiences for preschoolers take place primarily within the context of their families and Early Care and Education (ECE) programs, the majority of which are located within community-based settings that may or may not be located in, or associated with, public schools. In this sense, community-based ECE programs, such as Early Head Start, Head Start, 3- and 4-year-old kindergarten, preschools, childcare centers, and family child care, take on a *central* role in programming and guiding pre-schoolers' early educational experiences. This distinction is important because it reframes the question to: "How can community-based ECE programs *and* K–12 public schools *navigate and support each other* in preparing our youngest learners to meet the requirements of the CCSS?" In other words, how can we create a two-way bridge between these very different, yet integral, systems for the educational success of our youngest DLLs?

It is important to note that CCSS do not yet exist for the preschool population. States have, however, adopted early learning standards (ELS) that map out expectations for children's development and early learning in preparation for children's entry into 5-year-old kindergarten. In some instances, states have also aligned their ELS with the CCSS to further ensure children's school "readiness." The Office of Head Start has also created the Child Development and Early Learning Framework that provides guidelines for the development and learning of children in Head Start programs where many DLLs are enrolled. Because ECE programs are located in a multitude of community settings, have different federal and state requirements regarding DLLs, and have very different funding sources, uniformity of practice is challenging from state to state, from community to community within the same state, and from program to program within the same community. Nevertheless, there is general agreement in the ECE field that effective preschool programming uses ELS to guide curriculum decisions as well as instructional and assessment practices for *all* children—including DLLs.

For our youngest DLLs to have the greatest chance of success with the CCSS, it is critical that ECE programs and K–12 schools establish concrete mechanisms for on-going communication and exchanges of information at both the systemic and community levels. Administrators, practitioners, and teachers in each system hold different yet equally important expertise regarding DLLs' development and learning as well as knowledge about their present performance and future expectations—especially as they relate to the CCSS. ECE practitioners have forged vital relationships with the families of DLLs and have critical knowledge of the children's language development and learning. As such, ECE practitioners are important resources for connecting families of DLLs with schools and for providing K–5 teachers with essential information on DLLs' language development and learning. In turn, K–12 schools often have greater access to resources and knowledge regarding dual language learning and can provide invaluable information and training to ECE programs regarding relevant language and literacy supports for DLLs.

Establishing formal communities of practice (COP) in which ECE practitioners and teachers of DLLs, birth–8 years, meet regularly as equal partners to share their expertise and inform their practice for meeting the cultural and linguistic needs of DLLs, is an important step in preparing our youngest DLLs for success in meeting the CCSS on school entry. Of course, professional liaisons at the systemic level between ECE administrators, K–12 administrators, and community leaders are essential to making this a concrete, on-going reality. A two-way bridge, where knowledge and expertise flow equitably across systems and where an "up-down" educational approach (rather than the current "push down" approach) to child development and learning is valued and implemented, is definitely worth building and maintaining for the future success of DLLs in the CCSS.

Shifting Views of the Relationship between Families and Schools

3.6 How are parents of English language learners/emergent bilinguals seen by schools and "parent-education" programs?

- *Katherine C. Rodela*

Often parents of English language learners (ELLs)/emergent bilinguals (EBs) are seen from the *deficit perspective* by schools and parent-education programs. This means that parents of ELLs/EBs are seen as unable or unwilling to support their children in school because, according to the deficit perspective, their home environments lack the needed educational and linguistic resources to ensure their children's success in U.S. schools. School officials may perceive deficits of ELLs/EBs and their families based on language, racial, class, or cultural differences. For example, an educator might say something like: "Well, her child is at-risk because the mother does not speak English at home." Another might say, "In their culture, they do not participate in children's education." Underneath these comments are beliefs about families, their cultures, and their knowledge of U.S. schools.

There are three main reasons why the deficit perspective is harmful in schools and parent education programs:

1. **It dismisses diverse parent and family strengths.** The deficit perspective emphasizes what the families and children *do not have*, rather than what they do have. Frequently the rich cultural, linguistic, and educational resources immigrant families bring with them are ignored or dismissed as irrelevant to U.S. school success. Extensive sociocultural research of families and strengths-based approaches to working with culturally and linguistically diverse families contradicts the deficit perspective (for a recent review see Baquedano-López, Alexander, & Hernandez, 2013).

2. **It stems from a mainstream, middle-class European-American worldview of the poor and makes unfair value judgments about cultural differences.** The deficit perspective reflects the cultural worlds and values of schools and middle-class educators, leaders, researchers, and policymakers. Comments about what parents "should" do at home or how parents "should" be involved in their children's education presuppose knowledge of school expectations and particular values. Beneath ideas about how parents should be engaged in schools are fundamental cultural ideas about what constitute "good" and "bad" parenting. Cultural differences abound between school officials and families of ELLs/EBs; but cultural differences themselves are not a problem. What is a problem is assigning value judgments to such differences. This is exactly what the deficit perspective does, resulting in views of parents of ELLs/EBs

as disinterested or uninvolved, though they may work very hard to promote their children's well-being, education, and success.

3. **It undermines true collaboration and partnership**. The deficit perspective undermines the collaborative work many educators wish to engage in with parents of ELLs/EBs. Typically, educators and leaders are unaware that they hold deficit views of low-income families of color. Because the deficit perspective is so ingrained in how Americans think about low-income people, a major step in combating it and seeking true partnership with parents is to acknowledge how it works in schools and outreach programs. The deficit perspective thrives in an environment where issues of inequality and differences of race, class, ability, gender, immigration, and language among others cannot be talked about freely and critically. Parent and family knowledge, strengths, and leadership abilities must be acknowledged on their own terms and for their own goals.

Helpful questions teachers and educational leaders should consider when analyzing their parent involvement efforts include the following:

- How is parent involvement defined in our school/district?
- How are we making space for diverse parents to define their own involvement or educational experiences?
- What are our goals in engaging parents? (Why is it important?)
- How are families of ELLs/EBs participating? (Are we providing adequate translation services and childcare supports, or making our school welcoming to all family members regardless of their immigration status?)
- How are we acknowledging alternative forms of parent involvement or leadership in and around schools? (Adapted from Rodela, 2013)

3.7 How and why are immigrant families seen as both the source of and the solution to the challenges that their children experience in school?

■ *Katherine C. Rodela*

Immigrant families are seen as both the source of and solution to the school challenges their children experience. This is an aspect of the deficit perspective and directly blames families for children's problems, such as high school dropout, low grades or test scores, poor attendance, behavioral issues, or lack of kindergarten readiness skills, within schools. Most studies of immigrant parent involvement start with student underachievement as a rationale for why parents should be involved in schools. Many of us have heard colleagues say things like: "If only we could get the family involved, he would do his homework." or "Her mom never comes to conferences or responds to my emails!" Embedded in these statements are two assumptions: (1) a parent is key to a child's school success; and (2) a parent can also be the source of a child's failure. Parents are expected to be involved in visible ways (e.g. volunteering, meetings, at-home educational activities). Parents who did not go to school in the United States will not intuitively understand school expectations of them. The deficit perspective comes into play. Blame is placed on parents who are unfamiliar with mainstream middle-class American school norms and values.

Example from Early School Years

Perceptions of parent involvement in the early school years provide clear examples of how immigrant families are seen as both the source of and solution to children's school challenges. School readiness is seen as a direct result of parent engagement in preschool years. Did parents read aloud and build vocabulary? Did they teach numbers or colors? Did they build children's self-esteem and brain connections? These questions are laden with mainstream, middle-class U.S. beliefs about good parenting and how to talk to children and support school goals. The practices listed among these questions are not universal, nor do they necessarily predict teacher evaluations of kindergarten readiness (Ready & Wright, 2011). Also, with increased emphasis on complex, linguistically demanding tasks in the Common Core (e.g., argumentation), cultural differences in adult–child talk may exacerbate the blame placed on parents who supposedly do not speak enough to their children.

Immigrant Parents Are *Not* the Source of or Solution to Children's School Challenges

The deficit perspective's major flaw is its focus on individual solutions to educational problems. The message that immigrant families are the source of and solution to children's school challenges masks educational inequalities and unequal material conditions between middle-class and low-income families. Focusing on immigrant parents as the solution deflects from what educational leaders, policymakers, and communities can do to address inequalities like "overcrowding, deteriorating facilities, inadequate funding, high staff turnover, lack of up-to-date textbooks, and children performing below grade level" (Gold, Simon, & Brown, 2002, p. 5). In essence, it blames the victims.

Changing How Immigrant Families Are Seen in Our Schools

A major step educators can take to confront this issue is to push against parental involvement as a panacea for success. This does not mean dismissing the role immigrant families may play in advances for educational equity, but reconsidering why parental involvement is seen as lacking. We can ask ourselves: Why are we involving parents? How will we acknowledge the agency and work they already do at home? Educators can challenge assumptions that parents and teachers can be partners without first acknowledging unequal power dynamics between them. This is especially true between middle-class, college-educated teachers and low-income, immigrant parents who do not hold professional credentials. Just because we say we are partners does not make it true. Finally, educators and school leaders can push for collaboration with grassroots community organizations to help bridge distances between schools and immigrant families.

3.8 How can well-intentioned school practices limit parental participation/ leadership? How can educators address this challenge when working with parents of English language learners/emergent bilinguals?

■ *Andrea Dyrness*

As educators, we often think that including parents means *providing information*, making sure parents are up to speed on the policies, practices, and procedures in our school and classrooms. This concept of parental inclusion is not only limiting, it is often fatal to meaningful parental involvement and leadership. It positions the educator–parent relationship on a one-way street where the parent is the recipient of technical information that is controlled by the educator. With the introduction of the Common Core and myriad federal and state testing policies affecting K–12 teaching, the amount of technical information to be conveyed has exploded, making the information-dispensing model of parental involvement more burdensome than ever. Of course parents need to be aware of what is happening in their children's schools, but parent meetings structured primarily around giving information are fatal to the collaborative spirit and relationship-building that make school communities thrive. This is especially true in schools serving high concentrations of immigrant families from diverse cultural and linguistic backgrounds. If inclusion is conceived as transmitting technical information to parents of diverse educational backgrounds who speak English as their second language, the prospect of including them is daunting indeed. But research on immigrant parents has shown that *relationship-building* is a more important prerequisite for effective parent involvement than transmitting information. This insight suggests two fundamental principles for educators: (1) We should get to know parents as members of cultural communities with rich life histories, values, and goals for their children; and (2) we should recognize the ways our professional training often prevents us from doing this.

How many times have we facilitated or attended parent meetings where we never hear parents' voices? When our preoccupation with communicating information has left no time for parents to discuss, share, or reveal themselves? Professionals stand in the way of community when we attempt to set the terms of parent participation in limiting ways—requiring parents to divert their concerns to a "complaint box," limiting them to questions about our topics, or teaching them how to help their children without first finding out what they already know or want to know. When we offer advice or solicit input only in predefined areas of institutional interest (e.g. discipline, or homework) we reduce the opportunities for genuine engagement. But if we invite parents into a dialogue about their own questions and goals for their children, we open up the possibilities for meaningful exchange and collaboration within the school. Educators who care about the development and participation of immigrant parents support spaces where parents can meet their own goals of self-realization and community-building. How can we create these spaces? Identify the parent leaders in the community who already have strong relationships with other parents and may also have community organizing experience. Ask for their advice and partnership in running meetings. Think about how you like to be included when you attend meetings, and model those practices. And, finally, seek partnerships with community organizations who have experience creating safe spaces for adults and families.

The good news is that these principles do not involve more work or more meetings for educators. Rather, they call for *a different kind of meeting*, in which educators are learners of parents' worlds, and our relationships guide our work together. When we truly come to know the parents we are working with, where they have been and where they hope to go, we can more effectively mediate between professional expectations and the needs of families, and engage them as partners in our mutual quest for a fuller humanity.

3.9 In what ways can school policies limit authentic involvement of English language learners'/emergent bilinguals' parents, and how can this be addressed?

■ *Sera Jean Hernandez*

Schools have historically underestimated and underutilized English language learner (ELL) parents' ability and willingness to assist in their children's academic success. This largely stems from the deficit perspective of linguistically and culturally diverse parents inherent in federal policies (e.g., early childhood programs) that target them before their children enter school and while their children are in school (e.g., family literacy, parenting, and English as a second language [ESL] classes). These initiatives prescribe ways for families to interact, usually centering on changing the language and literacy practices within the home. At the heart of these programs is the belief that by remedying parent deficiencies (e.g., lack of English proficiency) educational outcomes will improve. Even when programs are intended to be inclusive and supportive of parents, this deficit perspective ignores the knowledge base of families and overlooks historical and present social conditions that play a role in how or why ELL parents are involved in their children's education.

In my research in Title I schools in California, I note how language and education policies simultaneously facilitate and impede partnerships between ELL homes and schools. The tensions surrounding the policies exist because parents are often asked to participate in schools to engage in accountability and auditing practices. Some administrators shared their concern with the checklist of parent involvement practices dictated by No Child Left Behind (NCLB) provisions (e.g., annual Title I meeting for parents, school–family compacts) that stifled authentic interactions and created barriers for meaningful parent participation. The school–family compacts, for example, relegate parent responsibility to marginal spaces that include monitoring attendance, homework completion, and TV watching, limiting a parent's role to one of surveillance, or as a compliance officer of the school system (Mapp, 2012). One principal, however, used the state-mandated English Learner Advisory Committee (ELAC) as a vehicle to encourage ELL parents to take on leadership roles within and outside of the committee.

The training they received in ELL policies through ELAC, coupled with strong relationships with the principal and ELAC teachers, spurred engagement in school activities that were supportive of the school and also parent-led and initiated.

To better serve bilingual families, policymakers must shift from viewing ELL parents as problems or simply participants, to seeing them as informed and empowered decision makers in their children's education. Educators need to distinguish between the practice of being in compliance with parent involvement legislation and creating local plans to build authentic, parent-led partnerships with the school community. Additionally, parent involvement should not be limited to how parents can further the school's agenda. Teachers and administrators must ask: How are parents perceived or represented in current policy and practice? Are parents simply being asked to comply with the school's agenda? Is there a space for ELL parents to voice their hopes and concerns?

The implementation of the Common Core State Standards (CCSS) can either serve as a springboard for authentic partnerships between ELL parents and educators or lead us down a road of more of the same prescriptive parent involvement policy that at many levels runs the risk of excluding ELL parents from their children's education. It is critical that ELL parents are at the center of the transition to the CCSS, and that their participation extends beyond accountability roles that ensure CCSS programs and curricula are in compliance. ELL parents contribute to their children's development throughout their lives. At the very least, their role in helping their children become bilingual—one of the most important 21st-century skills—should be recognized and supported by schools. Ultimately, they are their children's primary socialization agents and are guided, like us, by what they believe to be the best for their children.

3.10 Why might parental leadership be particularly important relative to the Common Core State Standards and high-stakes testing?

- *Ujju Aggarwal*

There is an emerging movement against high-stakes testing. This is, by all accounts, a good thing and speaks to the accumulation of collective harm that parents, teachers, and students have been subjected to as a result of the expansion of high-stakes testing and the one-size-fits-all drive to standards. Indeed, over the past years there have been an increasing number of parents—including middle and lower income, native-born and immigrant, and politically conservative and progressive—who have spoken out and taken a stand against high-stakes tests. The cries from the various forces are divergent. Politically conservative forces claim that the Common Core is representative of "big government" while middle-income parents often cite the harm that an increased emphasis on testing has caused children who, as they importantly note, should not have their youth marked by stress and anxiety.

Yet what becomes important during a time of such convergence is the critical perspective offered by low-income immigrant parents and parents of color about the historical and long-term inequities associated with high-stakes testing. To be sure, how "harm" is defined affects how we seek to transform a given injustice. As Katz (2011) has observed, neoliberal education reforms that focus on educational "outcomes" measured through the mechanisms like high-stakes tests are increasingly coupled with an emphasis on parental care. Kohn (1998) explains such an emphasis can easily become misconstrued, as the structures of support and security that produce the particular concerns about education held by middle-class parents become conflated with the academic success of their children and reified as *appropriate* care. When it comes to the Common Core, this dynamic has resulted in obfuscation of a specific continuity of impact that is about social reproduction and inequality mediated by race, class, and migration. The point is not to maintain the status quo and get rid of testing, but to understand how a challenge to testing provides an opportunity to also challenge the status quo.

To center the voices and perspectives of low-income immigrant parents, resources are needed to support and facilitate their leadership and organization (rather than "parent training" initiatives). Low-income immigrant parents and parents of color have long been seen as a "problem to be fixed" and the inequalities that plague our public education system are often attributed to values, aspirations, and capacities of students' families. Indeed, failing schools and broken homes could be a chorus for the ways that social policies in the wake of *Brown v. Board of Education* have attempted to reform poor immigrant parents and parents of color. These reforms have been based on changing the behaviors—and thus the cultures—of families rather than the structures or the conditions that create poverty or educational inequality. The Common Core builds on this logic and tells English language learners (ELLs) that their families and their home cultures and languages are of little value to their academic success. Given this reality, it is necessary to address the immediate effects of the Common Core on ELLs and their families through a combination of services, advocacy, and organizing. One way to do this is by supporting local leaderships' efforts to develop programs that create an intentional and structured space that (1) provides an opportunity for low-income immigrant parents to reflect, learn, and build analysis together; and (2) provides an opportunity for ELLs to recognize that their home, families, language, and cultures are sources of learning and knowledge.

3.11 How can schools ensure that families and communities are part of decision making in educational issues involving English language learners/emergent bilinguals?

■ *Edward M. Olivos*

Back in the mid-1990s I was working in California as an elementary bilingual education teacher. During this decade, state voters overwhelmingly passed a series of anti-immigrant and anti-Latino state initiatives—including Proposition 227 in 1998—the measure that significantly limited bilingual education in the state. It was during this period that I became convinced that local families and communities must play a more active role in educational decision making, rather than constantly being the recipients of others' policies and politics.

The Common Core State Standards (CCSS) are no exception to the rule of over-looking, or completely ignoring, English language learner (ELL) communities in top-down decision-making processes. With the dramatic increase of ELLs and immigrant families in our public schools during the last 20 years, policymakers and corporations are using this opportunity to promote agendas that have not been vetted by the communities they are purported to serve.

Using my 20 plus years of working with ELL and immigrant families there are a few principles and ideas that educators should keep in mind if they are sincerely interested in including these families in decision-making processes.

First, there is no way to ensure that these families will be heard or that their advice will actually be heeded. As I've argued in the past, not all parent groups are treated equally by school officials nor do these authorities hold the same expectations for all parents (Olivos, Jiménez-Castellanos, & Ochoa, 2011). In fact, some parent groups (e.g., immigrant, working-class, non-English-speaking) are at a significant disadvantage when dealing with the schools. Given these realities, this is the most logical place from which to begin the process of being part of the decision-making processes.

Bicultural ("minority") parents need allies, and those allies must come from the school system. Public education in our country is confusing for those of us born and raised here, so one can only imagine how it must be for an immigrant family or a family that has not had much experience with formal education. These "insider" allies must therefore be folks who are willing to share honest, and to the extent possible, unfiltered information with the parents. These allies must also be people that the parents trust. Above all, the parents must feel assured that the work being done is for the benefit of the children and not some external or personal agenda.

In addition to allies, bicultural parents need to understand, for example, how the U.S. school system functions and how it is constantly changing. Why are these "reforms" happening? Who is promoting them? Who are the players? What are the implications? How do they go from policy to practice? We used to call this process "demystifying" the school system for parents. We would work with parents to demonstrate that there are indeed opportunities (some very structured, controlled, and rigid, but opportunities nonetheless) to provide feedback and suggestions. And while those suggestions may not be integrated into the final policy, at the very least their concerns have been recorded and in some cases have become public record.

Finally, bicultural parents need to be realistic, given time and power constraints. Not every effort will reap dividends or the desired changes. But, in the long run, the voice of the community is being recorded. If this voice is consistent, policymakers will come to realize that there are indeed individuals in the community who have questions and wish to be heard. One of the worst things a community can do is to remain silent, for in the eyes of policymakers this silence is often interpreted as consent and, in worse case scenarios, as apathy.

3.12 What are key issues that require attention in informing parents about special education policies and practices?

■ *Alfredo J. Artiles and Beth Harry*

Special education policies and practices are complex and often presented to families and the general public in nonaccessible ways. For this reason, parents must remember that (1) *knowledge is power* and (2) *participation matters*. Thus, parents must be well informed and involved in school practices relating to special education, particularly if their children speak English as a second language. This is crucial advice because students of color, including emergent bilinguals (EBs), are at a higher risk of disability identification. The evidence suggests that such heightened probability is not explained solely by student factors, such as child poverty and its attendant sequeala (Harry & Klingner, 2014). The following table outlines key rights and responsibilities of parents and schools.

When EBs struggle to learn, teachers and school administrators develop explanations for their performance. Teachers sometimes assume a that a disability is the cause of EBs' learning difficulties; a common consequence is an assessment referral to special education. In other cases, teachers wonder if lack of English proficiency might be causing students' academic struggles; thus, teachers decide to "give time" to students, hoping they will catch up as they improve their English skills. Rushing to a special education referral or just waiting and doing nothing are problematic because either decision could result in a disability misidentification or lost opportunities to intervene early before a formal referral is pursued. In subsequent sections, we offer guidelines and suggestions to navigate these dilemmas.

School Districts Are Required To	Parents Are Entitled To
• Invite parents to participate in meetings related to identification, evaluation and placement • Inform parents in writing of any intent to initiate or change the identification, assessment, or placement of their child • Inform parents about available resources that may assist them in understanding the content of written school notices, and provide the notices in the parents' native language and in a format that can be understood by them • Provide parents with a copy of all procedural safeguards, which fully explains their legal rights and responsibilities	• Give written permission for the referral, evaluation, re-evaluation, and placement of their child in special education • Review all education records related to identification, evaluation and placement, • Be provided with an interpreter if the native language is not English • Contribute information to all initial or subsequent assessments, discussions, and decisions • Request an independent evaluation at no cost to them, if they disagree with the diagnosis or evaluation conducted by the district • Be included in the determination of eligibility and placement, and to receive a copy of the evaluation of the report and documentation of the determination of the disability • Receive regular progress reports once the child is placed in a special education program

From Artiles and Harry, 2004.

Where Can Families, Schools, and Communities Find Specific Special Education Resources to Advocate for English Language Learners/Emergent Bilinguals?

The Individuals with Disabilities Education Act (IDEA) is the law that requires school districts to identify children who have disabilities and provide them with appropriate services at no cost to the parent. These services can be an excellent resource for children who need them, but there are also several concerns that parents of children who are learning English (also known as English learners [ELs] or EBs) should be made aware of. Educators and community advocates should create opportunities for parents to learn about the entire process of special education referral, evaluation, and placement and the role they can play in it. Download free resources on the intersections of disability with linguistic and cultural differences at http://ea.niusileadscape.org/lc/Category/disproportionality

How Can Educators Help Families Navigate the Processes of Identification, Individualized Education Plan Development, and Implementation?

In the following subsections, we outline several considerations that parents should be informed about. (Download free resources at http://ea.niusileadscape.org/lc/Search ?search_query=english+learners&search=Search)

Are the Child's Difficulties with School Learning Related to a Disability or to the English Learning Process?

The first questions to ask are whether the child is receiving quality classroom instruction and whether that instruction recognizes and builds on his or her strengths in his or her home language, as well as his or her first-language literacy resources and practices. Parents need to be sure that the child is being taught in a manner that includes attention to his or her learning of English and that builds on his or her native language strengths. Parents can ask to observe in the child's classroom and can invite an advocate who understands classroom instruction to observe with them. They can ask if opportunities to "develop the conversational and academic language proficiency needed to understand classroom language use (e.g., teacher talk and the language of texts and related materials) across the content areas" are provided (Ortiz & Artiles, 2010, p. 254). Educators should monitor whether students' educational achievement is better in one language than the other. Teachers should also vary "the nature and complexity of tasks and products, using multiple levels and kinds of texts and materials, modifying the pace and level of instruction, utilizing flexible grouping strategies, and allowing for alternative modes of responses or ways for students to show what they learn" (Ortiz & Artiles, 2010, p. 255).

Although some states are now debating whether to use the Common Core State Standards (CCSS), virtually all states have adopted them—the exceptions are Indiana, Oklahoma, and South Carolina (Gewertz, 2014; Ujifusa, 2014). Therefore, the use of the CCSS will likely mediate how curriculum is structured and assessed for EBs; hence, these standards will shape the learning opportunities these students have under this new accountability regime. We return to this issue in the next subsection.

Referral for Special Education Evaluation

If the child has been receiving effective instruction and is still not achieving at his or her age level, the school may want to refer the child for an evaluation to see if a disability exists. An evaluation for special education requires the parents' written permission. Parents can give, or decline to give, permission. If they disagree with the result of the school district evaluation, they are entitled to seek an independent evaluation at cost to the school district. The evaluation must be performed in the child's dominant language and his or her educational achievement must be assessed in both languages. Other considerations include the following (Artiles & Harry, 2004, p. 6):

- Are the parents and people with expertise on cultural diversity included in the team?
- Does the assessment plan include multiple perspectives? For example, are multiple instruments used and do different professionals participate? Are the difficulties assessed in multiple settings? How are the difficulties handled and what are the consequences across such settings?
- For ELs, assess dominant language to determine if the disability is manifested in the dominant language. Dominance is reflected in the language that is better developed or the language in which a child shows the greatest level of skill.
- Information on language proficiency in the first language and in English should be collected.
- Educational achievement information must be collected in both first and second language.
- The assessment team must obtain information from parents about their perceptions of the child's problem, and about the values, beliefs, and expectations they may have about the child's learning or behavioral difficulties.
- Test translations or the use of interpreters when assessing ELs have serious limitations. If the school can't avoid using either of these approaches, do the following:
  ○ Have the school document the skills of interpreters.
  ○ Request that the team rely on multiple sources of information (formal and informal assessment procedures) so that decisions are not based on single instruments or scores to make eligibility decisions.
  ○ The team should use peers from the same group as norms.
  ○ If tests are invalid, ask the assessment team to look for patterns of performance within subtests instead of relying on absolute scores.

Academic performance is a crucial source of information in diagnostic decisions. Enduring questions with EBs include the extent to which academic assessments conflate lack of English proficiency with learning difficulties, or whether these measures underestimate or misread the ability levels of this population. Although particular measures of academic performance will be used for diagnostic purposes (whether from response to intervention [RtI] databases or an individual assessment conducted with a specialist), data from Common Core assessments will also be included in an EB's evaluation dossier. Several issues related to Common Core assessments are worth noting.

For instance, some states will follow the Smarter Balanced Assessment Consortium (SBAC), whereas others will rely on the Partnership for Assessment of Readiness for College and Careers (PARCC). The tests developed by these two consortia depend heavily on technology and are purportedly more inclusive for students with special needs and EBs, because tests will include universal design tools, such as English glossaries, highlighting and zooming capabilities, notepads, spell check, videos with American Sign language, calculators, and Braille options, among others (Gewertz, 2014; Heitin, 2014). These are welcome advances in test accommodations for the purpose of educational equity with EBs and special needs learners.

On the other hand, these tools create different equity concerns. For instance, does the reliance on technological tools give unfair advantage to affluent kids who have greater exposure and practice with technology? Will practice with these tools make a difference in the performance of EBs? In addition, the SBAC will allow read-aloud accommodations after grade 6, whereas the PARCC will permit it at any grade level (Sawchuk, 2014). The SBAC will allow students to use read-aloud accommodations when accessing the glossary, while PARCC will let students use paper-based glossaries (Heitin, 2014). How do these test features and constraints mediate the academic performance of struggling EBs? Will unfair language demands be unintentionally imposed on these groups as a result of the features of these assessments? To what extent will these equity issues affect the chances of special education misidentification or underidentification for EBs? Some states follow English-only rules while others require giving tests in Spanish (Heitin, 2014). How do these policy environments interact with the use of these assessment systems and what will be the consequences for the evaluation of EBs for special education placement? Parents and advocates must raise some of these considerations.

Placement in a Special Education Program

If the evaluation results in a special education program or special education services recommendation, parents must participate in the decision (Ortiz & Artiles, 2010). Parents must be invited to a meeting in which an individualized education plan (IEP) is developed based on the evaluation's results. All information about the placement process, the parents' and child's legal rights, and the evaluation results must be provided in writing as well as in person wherever possible. Notices must be provided in the parent's primary language wherever feasible, and a professional interpreter must be provided for the meeting if the parent needs one. Parents should not agree to let the child's siblings be the interpreters because this can be very unreliable and is too heavy a responsibility for a child to carry. The date set for the meeting must take into account the parent's schedule and availability and the parent is entitled to bring an advocate to the meeting. This can be a person provided by a parent advocacy agency or it can be a friend who has first-hand knowledge of the special education system, such as a teacher, a therapist, or another parent of a child with a disability.

The IEP will include decisions about exactly what services the child is to receive, such as individualized or small group instruction; specialized therapies such as speech, occupational, or physical therapy; or transportation to school. The parent is expected to participate in making the decisions about services and school placement and, once the IEP is signed, it is a legal document that the school must follow and must review with the parents every year. Every three years, the child is entitled to a full re-evaluation.

Part B of IDEA requires that the child be placed in the "least restrictive environment" possible for that child's needs. This rule means that the first option should be placement in a program with other children who do not have disabilities. A general guideline for this option is that special education services should not remove the child from the general education classroom for more than 60% of the day; however, this decision is made based on the unique circumstances and learning needs of each student. The underlying understanding is that the child must receive every opportunity to learn and advance in the general school curriculum to allow for his or her exit from the special education program as soon as he or she is able. If the school district is using the CCSS, then the child must be instructed within this curriculum, and as stated previously, assessment accommodations can be used to allow EBs to perform under equitable conditions.

In summary, it is the responsibility of school personnel to see that parents are fully informed of all these processes. However, advocacy organizations and community groups, such as churches or action groups, do need to take the initiative to reach out to members with informational fliers, ads in public media, meetings, and group counseling to ensure that families of children who are EBs are aware of and are accessing their rights under the law.

DISCUSSION QUESTIONS

After reading this chapter, engage in dialogue with peer educators, including school principals, other administrators and supervisors, teachers of different subjects, specialists in different areas, paraprofessionals, and parents/community members to discuss family and community participation in decisionmaking about CCSS implementation at the local level. Here are some questions to reflect on individually, with a colleague, or, ideally, as part of a professional learning community at your school. If you are in a school, the members of this group would comprise the school's ELL/EB leadership team, whose responsibility it is to collectively make the decisions that impact the education of ELLs/emergent bilinguals.

1. What has been your school's (or organization's) experience in establishing partnerships with families? Talk with your colleagues about the key issues you have encountered. Which of the authors in this section address those issues? What strategies or approaches do they offer that could be implemented in your school? What resources would your school need to implement such strategies or approaches?

2. Collect artifacts (e.g., assessment score reports, newsletters, handbooks) used by your school (or organization) for communicating with parents and community members. What are some ways that information about your school's routines, practices, and

data are made accessible and meaningful to families and community members? What evidence do you have that families and community members can access this information and find it meaningful? How can these methods of communication be improved?

3. How and what do you learn from your students' families, culture, environment, and ways of knowing and learning? How do you use this information to make your school (or organization) a welcoming space for your students' families? How do you use it in the creation of curriculum and beyond?

4. Aggarwal (see 3.10) suggests that recent social reforms, including educational initiatives like the CCSS, have been based on "changing the behaviors—and thus the cultures—of families, rather than the structures or the conditions that create poverty and social inequality." Do you agree with this statement? Can you provide examples of how you see this being carried out or contested in your school (or district)? What are some specific ways that you ensure (or could ensure) that your students' families and their cultures are respected and supported? How does your work relate to poverty and social inequality?

TOPICS FOR REFLECTION AND ACTION

The following statements are organized around the big ideas of the chapter. Read through them and indicate the extent to which each applies to your community and your school. After you complete the survey, discuss your responses with your team. Then write down one to three reflection points that have emerged from your discussions. Finally, identify one to three concrete actions that you/your team can take.

DK don't know   1 strongly disagree   2 disagree   3 agree   4 strongly agree

Engaging Diverse Families and Communities in Education					
1. We know and understand how to create environments that are culturally and linguistically accessible to the families of ELL/EB students in our school and classrooms.	DK	1	2	3	4
2. We create systems and practices and communicate to the families of ELL/EB students in accessible and meaningful ways, using our knowledge and understanding of our students, their families, and their communities.	DK	1	2	3	4
3. We know (and have evidence) that the families of our ELL/EB students feel welcomed at our school.	DK	1	2	3	4
4. Our school offers meaningful opportunities for administrators, staff, families, and community members to discuss (potential) positive and negative effects of the CCSS on ELL/EB students.	DK	1	2	3	4
4.1 (Subsequent statement, if you choose 3 *or* 4 for question 4.) These discussion opportunities are facilitated in mutual, bidirectional ways (not a one-way presentation by the school).	DK	1	2	3	4
5. Our school offers meaningful opportunities for administrators, staff, families, and community members to discuss our goals and visions for CCSS implementation for ELL/EB students	DK	1	2	3	4

ENGAGING DIVERSE FAMILIES AND COMMUNITIES IN EDUCATION *cont.*					
5.1 (Subsequent statement, if you choose 3 *or* 4 for question 5.) These discussion opportunities are facilitated in mutual, bidirectional ways (not a one-way presentation by the school).	DK	1	2	3	4

Shifting Views of the Relationship between Family and Schools

6. Families of ELL/EB students are partners in decision making and goal setting towards educational improvement of our schools.	DK	1	2	3	4
7. Families of ELL/EB students play an active role in the educational improvement of our schools.	DK	1	2	3	4
8. I can identify local groups and organizations working toward the educational improvement of ELL/EB students, including those students who are immigrants.	DK	1	2	3	4
9. Our school (district) works with local groups and organizations to ensure educational parity and continuous improvement in the education of ELL/EB students, including immigrant students.	DK	1	2	3	4
9.1 (Subsequent statement, if you choose 3 *or* 4 for question 9.) Our school (district) works with local groups and organizations in regards to CCSS policy and its implementation in the educational programs offered to ELL/EB students, including immigrants.	DK	1	2	3	4

Reflection:

Action Steps:

Policy, Leadership, and Advocacy

he fluidity of the Common Core State Standards (CCSS) is readily apparent. Educators and administrators at every level of our educational system, from state education agencies to school districts to schools and into individual classrooms, are working tirelessly to interpret the CCSS' demands for emergent bilinguals (EBs) and negotiate their implementation in ways that are consistent with research, policies, and practices proven effective in the education of this student population. While seen as an opportunity by some to ensure that EBs are also able to attain these new and rigorous standards that have been set, many concerns have been raised about the lack of information or guidance by the CCSS pertaining to the education of EBs, especially that the standards might undermine the provision for bilingual education. Educators, leaders, and advocates are thus unraveling the implications of the CCSS for the education of EBs as they are put into practice. Educational leaders are considering ways to ensure that the CCSS do not hinder the progress of these students in attaining the bilingual language practices necessary to succeed in school and the same academic content knowledge that is required of their English monolingual peers. In other words, as policy is turned into practice within schools, efforts to date have focused on moving the education of EBs from the periphery to the core of the Common Core.

No Child Left Behind (NCLB) is federal education policy that was passed into law by Congress in 2001 and remains in effect. The CCSS are a state-led policy initiative that does not supplant the requirements of current federal education policy. Even so, these two policies have much in common. Like NCLB, the CCSS were developed for all students but have many repercussions for EBs. Because the test-based accountability requirements of NCLB remain in place, the CCSS promise to greatly affect EBs and their education as states implement new, extremely high-stakes assessments to evaluate student attainment of the CCSS. Accordingly, these assessments will be used to evaluate students, teachers, schools, school districts, and states. The CCSS are already shaping what is taught to EBs, how it is taught, and in which language(s) it is taught; therefore, the CCSS are actually de facto language policy, as clarified by Wiley in Chapter 1 (see 1.3). As past experience with NCLB would dictate, this education reform, which was mainly intended for English monolinguals, is likely to result in numerous language policy by-products.

At present, the CCSS are being both embraced and contested by educators and administrators responsible for serving EB students, who are called on to interpret the meaning of the standards and then translate them into new educational programming, pedagogies, and curricula for EBs. In so doing, these key players are generating a new set of language education policies for schools, as educators make meaning of the standards and determine how they ought to play out in curriculum and instruction. The reality is that most educational policies are rarely implemented exactly as policymakers intend (Cuban, 1998; Menken & García, 2010) because they are changed as educators attempt to make sense of them. Accordingly, it is important to understand that the CCSS are not a singular static policy to be interpreted at face value; rather, the standards as policy are living and fluid, and there is space for educators to ensure that the standards and their assessments are implemented in ways that provide the best possible education for EBs. Specifically, a strong theme that emerges from the authors' responses in this chapter is that the CCSS and bilingual education are not mutually excusive, even though new policy focuses solely on English.

Building on the presentation of language policy issues pertaining to the CCSS that were first laid out in Chapter 1, this chapter considers the many complexities involved in implementing the CCSS, and how the CCSS as language education policy are being negotiated in the education of EBs at all different levels of the educational system. The first set of questions in this chapter probe the ways that the CCSS are being negotiated from the "top-down" to the "bottom-up," by examining how the Common Core has turned into state, school district, and school policies, and identify considerations for educators to ensure that the CCSS are implemented in beneficial ways for EBs and their languages. What emerges in this section is an exploration of how educational leaders are responding to the CCSS, highlighting the critical role of state and school leadership in translating the CCSS into effective practices for EBs. The next section of this chapter examines programming for EBs under the CCSS, with attention to the new demands placed on English as a second language and bilingual teachers, offering school leaders and teachers direction in terms of what to hold onto and what to let go as we face new policy mandates. The final section focuses on advocacy, a central element of these conversations, as advocates are mobilizing to make sure that EBs' needs are considered and addressed. The sections in this chapter combine to offer critical considerations for educators and policymakers at every level of the U.S. educational system, as they decide how to implement the CCSS in schools serving EBs.

Policy Negotiations from "Top-down" to "Bottom-up"

4.1 What does the process of language education policy development look like at the state level, and why is it important relative to the Common Core State Standards?

- *David Cassels Johnson, Heidi LaMare, and Thad Williams*

Washington State is notable for its language policy, which explicitly promotes bilingual education. Under the Transitional Bilingual Instructional Program (TBIP), school districts receive funding for English language learner (ELL) education and are given five program options: (1) dual language or two-way immersion, (2) developmental bilingual education (late-exit), (3) transitional bilingual education (early-exit), (4) sheltered instruction (or content-based English as a second language), and (5) newcomer programs. From the 2004–2005 school year to the 2010–2011 school year, the number of ELLs enrolled in bilingual education programs—including dual language, late-exit bilingual education, and early-exit bilingual education—increased by 96%. Growth in these programs has drastically outpaced enrollments in the English-only sheltered instruction program promoted in Washington, which has grown by 9%. The greatest growth has occurred in the dual language programs—more than tripling in student enrollment. As might be noted, the name of the policy is something of a misnomer because it funds more than just *bilingual* education, transitional or otherwise (and there are historical reasons for that, see Johnson & Johnson, 2014).

While the state provides funding for a variety of programs, it is up to school districts to decide which programs are in the best interest of their students. In the Bellevue School District, we offer dual language programs because we believe in language policy that promotes multiple languages as a resource for all teaching and learning. Choosing an additive model of instruction for our students has been an overt act to raise awareness about the value of language in our language rich and very diverse region of the United States. As the student enrollment increases in dual language programs, a need for high-quality content-area language instruction is amplified. For example, teachers in Spanish–English programs are required to pay explicit attention to both the Spanish and English language demands necessary to understand ideas being presented as part of the language arts standards. Similarly, a teacher of a grade 10 ELL student in a social studies class must have a deep understanding of language demands to create accessible content. While a dual language teacher may think about language development each and every lesson, the content teacher may be evolving into this new awareness.

The Office of Superintendent of Public Instruction (OSPI) in Washington State has embraced the Common Core State Standards (CCSS) and a variety of resources have been put in place to scaffold educators while the standards are adopted in ways that benefit ELLs. At the state level, OSPI has developed clear standards—which are helpfully aligned with the English language proficiency (ELP) standards—and offers training on these standards. Additionally, OSPI policies and initiatives support other state

---

Capacity Building

Professional development that includes
- Differentiated content-area specific workshops that are presented and attended by content and language specialists
- Shared responsibility for ELL students (by ELL and content specialists)
- Alignment with CCSS and ELP standards

Collaboration that includes
- Curriculum mapping
- Joint course development
- Joint lesson planning/teaching/assessment development
- Specific expertise of content teachers, instructional coaches, administrators, and ELL specialists
- Development of ELP/CCSS–aligned units (see ELL Stanford sample units)
- Use of the CCSS anchor standards as a central point

---

organizations such as the Washington Association of Bilingual Education (WABE). For example, they provide regional and statewide workshops and conferences that focus on adopting CCSS and ELP standards in practical ways that benefit ELLs. In the Bellevue School District, this has meant that our professional development (PD) is more closely aligned with that of the state.

As educators incorporate the CCSS in ways that support multilingual education they must consider what the implementation looks like at all levels and structures. Through the use of ELP standards, districts, schools, and instructional leaders can make meaningful decisions around PD, while classroom teachers can make better-informed decisions and identify the language demands and skills needed to progress toward and meet the CCSS. Two broad areas stand out and provide the focus for our districts' work to build capacity for student success: PD and collaboration (see box).

While the CCSS will certainly present many challenges to many school districts, we believe that, with ongoing PD and collaboration, the interaction between Washington State language policy and CCSS will help us accommodate ELLs in multilingual programs.

■ *Jobi Lawrence and Byron Darnall*

There are a variety of policy decisions at the state level that affect local education efforts, and historically those decisions have been made from a "top-down" perspective without any connection to educators, students, or parents. In general, state law and code have been developed void of any collaboration with the constituents who will be most affected by those policies. One of the greatest challenges in language policy development at the state level is to bring the right people to the table, at the right time, with the right data, to make the best possible decisions to affect teaching and learning for English learners (ELs). In theory this appears to be relatively simple; however, it becomes highly complex in practice because the needs of various constituents create competing priorities.

According to Fullan (2011),

> In the United States, the strategy is to drive reform by better standards, assessment, monitoring, intervention, and teacher development. I believe these ambitious and admirable nationwide goals will not be met with the strategies being used. No successful system in the world has ever led with these drivers—they are ineffective because they do not change the day-to-day culture of school.

To develop policies that have the potential for changing the day-to-day culture of the school, it is necessary to select a driver that ensures broad-based constituent ownership of the change process. A "top-down" approach to policy development will be insufficient to meet this goal. Collaborative inquiry, a process of high-level contituent engagement in the presence of high-quality data, has the potential for being the most effective driver for policy development and education reform.

To illustrate Iowa's concerted effort to engage collaborative inquiry as a driver of future language policy development, a brief discussion of the recent ELL Taskforce work will be presented and utilized to highlight key aspects of the process.

The Iowa Department of Education (DOE) recently commissioned an ELL Taskforce, at the request of legislators, in response to a grassroots effort by local education agencies lobbying for increased funding for ELs. District lobbyists worked closely with a variety of community-based organizations to propose an increase in percentage of weighted funding, as well as additional years that EL students could receive such funding, under Iowa code. In response to the request, legislators asked for evidence that additional funding would ensure positive EL student outcomes, as well as data related to the tracking and monitoring of EL categorical funding. In short, legislators requested assurance that more money would produce better EL student results and that adequate monitoring and tracking mechanisms were in place to know what the additional funding would be spent on. The DOE recognized the competing needs, and responded with the formation of the ELL Taskforce. This Taskforce was composed of school administrators and representatives from area education agencies (AEAs), organizations representing K–12 educators, higher education, and the business community. The overarching goal of the ELL Taskforce was to bring all constituents together to understand Iowa's current EL context and to create shared ownership of both the current reality and a shared vision for the future. The deliverable of the ELL Taskforce was a report to the DOE that would be used to inform legislators and future legislation.

The ELL Taskforce focused on five broad areas: deep data study of Iowa ELs, multistate comparison of Iowa and other similar states, research-based practices for language instruction education programs, weighted funding, and monitoring of categorical funding. Over the course of six months the ELL Taskforce engaged in collaborative inquiry to develop a set of recommendations that were sorted into priority levels based on a five-year strategic planning timeline. The collaborative inquiry process utilized by the ELL Task Force yielded several positive outcomes in addition to the formal report and associated recommendations. These secondary outcomes include, but are not limited to, the following:

- Individual constituents gained a deeper understanding of multiple perspectives and recognized that some level of compromise would be required of each constituent to move Iowa forward.
- Every constituent group recognized the need to "own" a piece of where we are now in relationship to EL policy and practice statewide.
- Taskforce members developed an awareness of the need for both "top-down" decisions and "bottom-up" (grassroots) advocacy and the intricacies of balancing both.
- Recognition that "connecting the dots" is crucial for moving statewide policy work forward, and that a "top-down" approach would not suffice.
- A collective understanding that it is difficult to get each group to see the "needs/ perspectives" of the other groups, but that until that conversation is mediated, the status quo is the likely outcome.
- Recognition that while we have gained traction on some priorities, others will have to wait until we produce the results necessary to inform data-driven conversations.
- Consensus that it takes finding the middle ground and staying the course to affect long-term sustainable change. All ELL Taskforce members now understand that language policy reform will be a long haul and that it will take years for the "fruit" of the Taskforce labor to ripen.

Based on this illustrative example, it is highly recommended that state-level officials utilize drivers, such as collaborative inquiry, to engage constituents in the development of policies and legislation in an effort to minimize the current disconnect between policy and practice.

4.2 How might the Seal of Biliteracy be used strategically to promote biliteracy within the context of the Common Core State Standards?

- *Shelly Spiegel-Coleman and Magaly Lavadenz*

> Biliteracy awards advance the district's commitment that every student graduates prepared and equipped with the knowledge and skills to participate successfully in college, career, and a diverse 21st-century society. Additionally, the awards build upon the rich linguistic and cultural assets of the district and communicate that mastery of two or more languages is an important skill that is advantageous in an ever-shrinking global society.
> —Los Angeles Unified School District's Policy Resolution for the Seal of Biliteracy (2010)

This statement provides an example of a locally proposed language policy leading to the approval of the Seal of Biliteracy in Los Angeles Unified School District. School board resolutions such as these had emerged prior to the passage of Assembly Bill (AB) 815 (Brownley). California's legislation is a formal acknowledgement via a special insignia by the California Department of Education (DOE) of high school graduates' proficiency in one language in addition to English. In this entry, we provide a description of the trajectory of local language planning and policies that resulted from a network of regional and statewide advocacy efforts leading to the implementation of the State Seal of Biliteracy (SSB) in California. We discuss the implications of the expansion of California's

Seal of Biliteracy from locally determined multilingual language planning efforts to an official statewide language policy that suggests a shift from monolingual, English-only ideologies towards the recognition of the benefits of bilingualism and biliteracy across several states in the nation.

Reversing English-Only Education Policies in California

Since the passage of California's voter-led initiative Proposition 227 in 1998, multiple researchers and data reports reveal that achievement gaps between English learners (ELs) and their native-English-speaking peers have increased (Gold, 2006; Parrish, Linquanti, Merickel, Quick, Laird, & Esra, 2002). The "miseducation" of ELs in California, stemming from the aftermath of Proposition 227 and similar initiatives, created highly restrictive language and education policies that resulted in limited parental access to bilingual education programs. Many bilingual program options were replaced by the rampant expansion of widely diverse types of structured English immersion programs and decreased opportunities for emergent bilingual (EB) learners to develop biliteracy from the beginning of their schooling experiences (McField, 2013).

Modeled after the local practice of awarding a Seal of Bilingual Competency in Glendale (California) Unified School District, a district renowned for its multilingual programs and EL achievement (Olsen & Spiegel-Coleman, 2010), AB 815 (Brownley) established the SSB in 2010. As part of the legislation, state funds were appropriated to establish the official SSB, marked as a gold, embossed insignia affixed to the student's transcript or diploma of a qualified high school graduate.

The first year that graduates in California's public schools have been able to earn the SSB was 2012; 168 early-adopting districts opted to participate in the program and recognized over 10,000 students in the first year. By 2013, over 195 districts participated and 21,655 students qualified for the SSB.

Coinciding with local and statewide advocacy efforts for the bill was the attention given to the Common Core State Standards (CCSS) defining college and career readiness and the preparation of students for a global economy, as seen in part in the Partnership for 21st-Century Learning (Manger, Soule, & Wesolowski, 2011). While not specifically identifying ELs as a focal group or addressing the linguistic and cultural resources that they contribute to the central concepts within globalization or 21st-century learning, the implicit alignments were not lost on the advocacy groups. Indeed, the intersection between the recommendations of Partnership for 21st Century Learning and the college and career readiness called for in the CCSS facilitated the momentum toward proposing and aligning legislative efforts leading to AB 815.

The inclusion of language study in the realm of high school curriculum was not totally new in California's see-saw language and schooling policies; bilingual schooling was mandated in elementary schools since the 1920s and had existed informally in the times of westward expansion and in colonial times:

> In every city, which according to the federal census of 1920 has at least 500,000 inhabitants, the school board shall establish and maintain at least one public school in which along with

the courses in English Language prescribed and permitted for the elementary schools there shall also be taught French, Spanish, Italian and German, or one of them. (California Education Code 1967, § 660–663, quoted in Kloss, 1998, p.236)

This section of the California Education Code (EC) was repealed in 1965 and replaced with EC 51220 (c), making foreign language teaching mandatory in all public schools no later than grade 7. Currently, prerequisite requirements for California public universities' systems include a three-year language component, providing an opportunity for high school students to be eligible for the Seal.

Requirements for the California State Seal of Biliteracy

Established as evidence of high school graduates' attainment of a high level of proficiency in speaking, reading, and writing in one or more languages in addition to English, the SSB appears as a distinct addition to the transcript or diploma of the graduating senior and is a statement of accomplishment for future employers and for college admissions. It is awarded by the State Superintendent of Public Instruction in accordance with specified criteria set forth in the legislation. Participation by school districts is voluntary. The relatively low-cost implementation at the district level includes applying the state's criteria and procedures to identify and ensure the graduates' qualifications in meeting the criteria.

The following box describes the types of assessments and/or evidence that schools and districts may use to recommend students for the SSB. Once identified at the local level, the names of eligible students are then forwarded to the California DOE.

Strategies for Establishing Multilingual State Pathways for Biliteracy

As an advocacy coalition composed of 25 educational, community, and civil rights organizations across the state, Californians Together was founded in 1998 with a

---

Student Requirements for Eligibility for the California State Seal of Biliteracy

1. Completion of all English language arts requirements for graduation with an overall grade point average of 2.0 or above in those classes.
2. Passing the California Standards Test in English language arts administered in grade 11 at the "proficient" level.
3. Proficiency in one or more languages in addition to English, demonstrated through **one** of the following methods:
   - Passing a foreign language Advanced Placement examination with a score of 3 or higher or an International Baccalaureate examination with a score of 4 or higher.
   - Successful completion of a four-year high school course of study in a foreign (world) language and attainment of an overall grade point average of 3.0 or above in that course of study.
   - Passing a district-created examination of a foreign (world) language that the district certifies meets the rigor of a four-year course of study in a world language.
   - Passing the Scholastic Assessment Test (SAT) II foreign language exam with a score of 600 or higher.

Retrieved from http://www.cde.ca.gov/sp/el/er/sealofbiliteracy.asp

commitment to ensure quality education for the state's 1.5 million ELs. Created shortly after the passage of Proposition 227, Californians Together has sponsored and/or collaborated in many legislative bills, as well as provided key testimonies to public education policy bodies, the state legislature, and other governmental agencies to ensure equity in law and practice in addition to the SSB. Additionally, Californians Together provides supports for implementing Seals of Biliteracy through webinars, online resources for best practice, and partnerships with districts and county offices of education. Between 2008 and 2010, Californians Together provided training across the state for school district teams to guide implementation of locally designed Seals of Biliteracy. Those initial 55 school districts based their criteria on suggestions in the Seal of Biliteracy booklet that accompanied the training. These districts, plus widespread community support, provided momentum to carry the SSB forward through the legislative process.

District Implementation Steps for Seal of Biliteracy[1]

The process of creating a local Seal of Biliteracy policy might begin with assembling a working group or taskforce of district staff and EL and world language teachers, to think through how the award might work in their community and who potential supporters might be. A common approach that has been implemented across several districts is to deliver a small working group–drafted policy statement tying the Seal of Biliteracy to a board resolution for 21st-century learning and to the district's strategic plan for implementing 21st-century education (such as the one by Los Angeles Unified School District at the beginning of this article). The passage of a locally defined policy establishing the award thus becomes part of a broader district commitment to education for the new century.

Establishing Board Approval for a Seal of Biliteracy

- Clarify purpose(s) and rationale for giving the Seal. The rationale needs to resonate with your school, community, district, and state.
- Determine the level of pathway awards to be granted: preschool, elementary, middle school, high school.
- Define criteria for granting award.
- Develop outreach and application process.
- Identify the award process and presentation.
- Seek endorsements; spread the word.

As the official adoption of SSB is being implemented throughout the state, a general practice seems to be that the process for identifying eligible high school students for the Seal includes assigning the task of implementation explicitly to personnel who become responsible in identifying, monitoring, and communicating the names of the recipients

---

[1] Retrieved from http://sealofbiliteracy.org

to the California DOE. Additionally, districts that intend to award the SSB follow two steps:[2]

1. Complete the California SSB requirements checklist (Appendix A).
2. Complete the insignia request form. School district and charter school staff are to complete this form and submit it to the California DOE EL Support Division to request the diploma insignias for eligible students.

Reversing the Tide: A Return to Multilingualism

California, along with other states throughout the nation and in the original thirteen colonies, has a long and largely unknown tradition of public bilingual schooling (Kloss, 1998). At the time of this writing, California has been joined by New York, Texas, Illinois, Washington, New Mexico, and Louisiana in adopting SSBs. Legislation is pending in Florida, Massachusetts, and Maryland and is being discussed in several other states. The move to establish the Seal of Biliteracy for all students in these states represents a shift in priorities for public schooling and an exciting trajectory for school reform that is a result of purposeful and collective political action. The passage of AB 815 is both a clear interruption of previous English-only policies and a pedagogical innovation for California public schools. Nonetheless, because the Seal is predominantly focusing on high school graduates, pathways to biliteracy through the entire preK–12 pipeline have yet to be officially established. To encourage both breadth and depth in the recognition of local efforts, and to build on the momentum of the SSB, a new legislative agenda is being developed to recognize districts that have established multiple preK–12 pathways to biliteracy. Launched at the annual conference of the California Association for Bilingual Education in April 2014, the California Campaign for Biliteracy seeks to support the development of preK–12 programs that will prepare students with proficiency in two or more languages so they may speak to, from, and across multiple communities, populations, and nations and be fully qualified for the SSB on high school graduation. The overwhelming success of the Seal of Biliteracy in California and other states points to renewed energies in returning to the U.S.' bilingual traditions and a resurgence in revitalizing multilingualism in a nation where rich linguistic histories have been long repressed.

■ *John Hilliard, Olivia Mulcahy, and Josie Yanguas*

The authors of the CCSS do not speak to two-language learning directly, nor do they include more than cursory attention to learners of English as a second language (ESL). However, the CCSS do not preclude districts from expanding their vision to integrate the goal of biliteracy. In fact, the CCSS set expectations to which bilingual approaches to instruction can contribute significantly.

---

[2] These documents are available electronically at http://www.cde.ca.gov/sp/el/er/sealofbiliteracy.asp

The CCSS do raise the issue of attending to multiple literacies (e.g., literacies across content areas, technological/multimedia literacies). Elements of the CCSS (e.g., academic language) allude to the importance of understanding the intertwined nature of content and language learning. The CCSS emphasize college and career readiness, critical thinking, problem solving, and flexibility in accessing concepts from a number of perspectives. This emphasis provides some fertile ground and a compelling rationale for the cultivation of two-language learning, not only as a critical goal in and of itself, but as a means of meeting the goals of the CCSS as they stand.

Lack of awareness, misunderstanding, ideology, and traditional practices have often led us to underestimate the importance of learning two languages. However, academic research, mainstream media, and increasing numbers of employers encourage us to use bilingual instruction as a powerful strategy for academic success and bilingualism/ biliteracy. Pathways to biliteracy are a clear benefit in the context of the CCSS for all students, including English-speaking students who are learning a world language; heritage speakers of a language other than English (LOTE) who are reclaiming, embracing, and developing their heritage language; and students who are identified as ELs and continue to develop their home language(s). Two-language learners learn to transfer the knowledge, understanding, and skills that they learn in one language to the other, and they develop cognitive flexibilities linked to bilingualism. Two-language learning also brings strong social, emotional, cultural, economic, political, and diplomatic benefits to individuals and society.

The adoption of a Seal of Biliteracy by a state acknowledges the value of reaching a certain level of proficiency in more than one language, and it recognizes educational objectives that go above and beyond the scope of the CCSS. But besides its practical function of honoring the achievement of individuals who demonstrate biliteracy and flagging biliterate high school graduates for potential employers or colleges, such a seal can become a powerful tool to advocate for biliteracy for all students if it inspires us to

- Become more cognizant and appreciative of the rich linguistic resources of our students who already speak a LOTE, and more cognizant and appreciative of the benefits of learning a LOTE to students who otherwise would only speak English.
- Design programs and adopt potent practices to help ELs and other two-language learners better leverage their LOTE as an asset and continue their LOTE development and open up more pathways for any student to become a learner of two languages.
- Reflect on and intentionally nourish connections between developing more than one language and developing healthier intercultural understanding.
- Revisit and amplify our definition of college and career readiness to include multilingualism and multiculturalism and, therefore, create more synergy with colleges and employers seeking candidates with these experiences, understandings, and skills.
- Create greater market demand for curricular materials, instructional resources, and assessment tools specifically for programs that promote biliteracy and focus developers'/ vendors' attention in this area—creating a richer variety of linguistically and culturally appropriate options for teachers, schools, and districts to choose from.

- Design and align federal, state, and local policies to better reflect what 40 years of research confirms about bilingualism and to best serve the needs of students in today's schools.

For the Seal of Biliteracy to be relevant to the widest number of high school students, our definition of (bi)literacy must be expanded beyond the traditional focus on reading and writing in English language arts instruction to include an integrative view of reading, writing, listening, and speaking within and across two languages. Paired literacy, or relating reading and writing in two languages side-by-side over time, is a key component of biliteracy instruction and assessment. Effective biliteracy instruction is holistic and comprehensive, and includes an explicit focus on oracy, reading, writing, and metalinguistic awareness (Escamilla et al., 2014). A broader perspective of (bi)literacy can help set up clearly defined paths for learners who begin their journey to bilingualism from different starting points in different contexts.

All of our students are language learners; however, students enter our schools with widely varying experiences, knowledge, and skills in one, and sometimes in a second (and third. . .), language. Educators who implement the Seal of Biliteracy in their states, districts, and schools need to clearly articulate which students can earn the Seal on their diplomas. For example, is the Seal of Biliteracy an option for all students, or only those enrolled in high school bilingual programs? Can students who are enrolled in world language or heritage language programs pursue the Seal of Biliteracy? Is the Seal an option for students who do not have access to instructional support for LOTE at school but who may have developed biliteracy in another context? Can any language pairs (e.g., English, Mandarin) be included, or can students only earn the Seal of Biliteracy using Spanish and English?

The requirements/criteria to be used for the Seal of Biliteracy are tied to how a state or district defines and assesses both literacy and biliteracy for which students in what programs. There are different pathways to biliteracy. Students start at different places and their two-language learning travels along different trajectories. This rich variation could be identified, supported, developed, and documented as part of research and action surrounding the Seal of Biliteracy. Teachers could gather evidence of students' oral and written language development in two languages for college and career purposes, and in so doing help us understand what it means to develop biliteracy for academic purposes. Districts and schools could collect longitudinal evidence of students' biliteracy development, and educators could use that evidence for a wide range of purposes beyond formatively and summatively assessing student learning— including professional development, program evaluation, policy formulation, and advocacy.

We are in the early stages of developing and implementing the Seal of Biliteracy in states, districts, and schools, and we see considerable variation in the requirements for the Seal. For example, at a statewide level such as in California, student requirements for the Seal explicitly include passing high school courses in a foreign language for four years, as well as taking a standardized language assessment test such as Advanced Placement (AP), or a language SAT. School districts that have already implemented a Seal of

Biliteracy at the local level (e.g., Albuquerque, NM and Woodstock, IL) also include taking content-area courses at the high school in a second language for four years. In the case of these two district examples, there is also recognition that not all students in these language tracks may complete all requirements. In these instances, districts make distinctions of different levels of the Seal of Biliteracy.

In the case of ELs at the high school level, some states are considering the use of English language development (ELD) assessments that capture a student's academic language proficiency within the content areas. This is different from using a standardized English language arts assessment that captures a student's content-area knowledge and skills. An argument can be made that both of these types of assessments should be employed to capture a fuller range of literacy, that is, students have the academic language to capture content, as well as the content knowledge and skills themselves.

We know that there are other ways to determine if a student is bilingual and biliterate, such as through performance-based or common assessments. Such assessments may include answering questions in a live interview or an oral presentation on a particular topic. We also know that students can be on pathways to bilingualism and biliteracy at the elementary (preK–8) level. In those instances, more authentic artifacts, such as oral presentations, reading logs, essays, and participation in a dual language program, are possible indicators that school districts can use.

Guiding Questions for Developing Seal Requirements

- Are assessments authentic and appropriate (designed for the particular language learners to whom they will be administered)?
- Are all four domains (listening, reading, speaking, and writing) addressed evenly or are some domains weighted more than others?
- Will requirements include both traditional measures of language/literacy development and measures of language/literacies developed in the content areas or other contexts?
- What portion of the Seal of Biliteracy requirements will be outcomes-based (e.g., standardized measures, performance assessment, portfolio artifacts)? What, if any, portion will set minimums for time/credit/experience?
- What measurement tools are currently available (e.g., AP exam), and which will need to be developed (e.g., portfolio content requirements and rubrics)?
- Are the requirements rigorous but reasonably attainable in relation to the programs and supports that are in place for students?
- Is there equitable access to two-language learning and opportunity to achieve the Seal of Biliteracy?
- Are the expectations balanced or do they favor some types of language learners over others?

If we hope to provide opportunities for any and all of these students to start, or continue, on a path to robust and balanced biliteracy, we must create programs that are responsive to who these students are as language learners and lead them through a coherent progression of language learning. We need to take stock of the offerings in our schools, and we may discover that our work includes the following:

- Building and refining programs for ELs and dual language, heritage, and world language programs to serve any kind of learner in every neighborhood
- Examining how we might create stronger connections across these programs and innovative partnerships with resources in the community (e.g., ethnic-based "Saturday schools") to create coherent preK–12 pathways that maximize opportunities for deep and authentic language learning
- Revisiting the criteria we use for program quality and core curricula to begin integrating expectations for two-language learning
- Reflecting on our own entrenched notions about bilingualism and working to elevate the status of LOTE at school, in the community, and throughout society

Ultimately, adopting a Seal of Biliteracy, and embracing the vision that it could be achieved by any student, calls us to redefine our understanding of language education and reimagine our school systems as places where multilingualism is part of a landscape where we nurture our students' linguistic resources and cultivate new languages to add to their repertoires.

4.3 Why is it important for schools to develop school language policies relative to the Common Core State Standards?

■ *Ester de Jong and Mileidis Gort*

Language policy in schools can be narrowly interpreted as a set of formal decisions about which language can be used as a formal medium of instruction. Through this lens, districts have to address the question of what program model to implement to best meet the needs of emergent bilinguals (EBs). Dual language education programs are one effective way to meet the demands as outlined in the Common Core State Standards (CCSS), particularly given the differences between the expectations for how students use language and literacy in the CCSS and prior standards, and the integrated model of learning represented in the CCSS—where language, literacy, and content overlap significantly. For example, the CCSS require that students (1) read and comprehend texts, particularly informational texts, with increasing levels of complexity; (2) gather, comprehend, evaluate, synthesize, and report on information and ideas, using text-based evidence; (3) write to persuade and explain; and (4) use their oral language skills to work collaboratively, understand multiple perspectives, and present their own ideas (Bunch, Kibler, & Pimentel, 2012). As Brisk and Proctor (2012) argue, the cognitive advantages of bilingualism have been well documented and students in dual language education programs consistently outperform comparable peers on academic achievement tests in English as well as the partner language (Lindholm-Leary, 2001; Thomas, Collier, & Collier, 2011). Moreover, bilingual education teachers have extensive experience with negotiating the relationship between language and content in instruction through content-based and thematic language teaching approaches (e.g., Freeman, Freeman, & Mercuri, 2005; Howard & Sugarman, 2007). Step one for districts is to articulate their approach to programming for EBs so that the education offered to this group of students is consistent and coherent with sufficient support both in terms of material resources and teacher expertise (Horwitz et al., 2009).

Language policy in schools affects more than just the medium of instruction and program model, however. As the CCSS are being implemented, schools have to make decisions about curriculum content and materials, the status and role of different varieties (more and less standard) of English and other languages, the language(s) of assessment, and so forth (de Jong, 2012). As part of their policy framework, teachers and administrators need to collaborate on developing a framework where the school's values and mission are made explicit so that further instructional decision-making processes can be aligned effectively. Corson (1999), for example, identifies several components to include in a school-based language policy: professional development (PD), personnel, home–school communication, language testing and program evaluation, parent involvement and community participation, and curriculum content related to (attitudes toward) diverse students and bilingualism.

Because the CCSS do not highlight students' home language resources and the role they play in ensuring equal access to quality education, educators who work with EBs must articulate a language policy for their school(s) that explicitly takes a *language-as-resource* orientation (Ruiz, 1984). A broadly defined language policy can be used as a tool to address the linguistic and cultural strengths that EB students bring to school and identify effective ways of expanding these students' linguistic and cultural repertoires. For example, Barbieri elementary school in Framingham, Massachusetts implemented a differentiated two-way immersion (TWI) program that provided limited initial access to Spanish to native English speakers in grades 1 and 2 and undermined the sociocultural and academic integration of both English and Spanish speakers. Reflecting on program evaluations, the school decided that, to be aligned with the research on TWI and improve academic achievement for their Spanish speakers, an 80:20 model would be a better approach. This would increase exposure and use of Spanish for all students and integrate them from the beginning of the program. This program decision came during a time when revised No Child Left Behind policy resulted in increased testing in English (both language proficiency and academic achievement). The staff understood that improving test scores in English and meeting state mandates would not happen as a result of simply increasing the amount of English; rather, they critically examined the program and quality of English and Spanish instruction to better align it with effective practices for EBs. A *language*—or rather, *bilingual-as-resource* orientation—served as a shield that helped teachers and administrators at Barbieri negotiate "top-down" reforms and protect programming for EBs from external pressures.

4.4 What might the process of language education policy development look like at the district and school levels relative to the Common Core State Standards?

■ *Rebecca Field and Kate Menken*

Since the adoption of the Common Core State Standards (CCSS), administrators are challenged to ensure that all of their constituents (teachers, support staff, parents, students, community partners) understand and support the ways that they organize their programs and practices for English language learners (ELLs)/emergent bilinguals (EBs) at the local level. The effort to clearly articulate how these students are to reach the same high standards as their English monolingual peers in the school or district is complicated by the confusion, controversy, variation, and change in and about effective programs, practices, and assessments for ELLs/EBs. This is compounded by the reality that the CCSS do not address linguistic diversity at all, but are monolingual in their orientation, raising concerns for how they will affect bilingual education programs. Moreover, the CCSS leave it to states and districts to determine how the standards and their assessments will be implemented for ELLs/EBs.

A school district or school language policy and implementation plan can help educators navigate complexities such as these. A strong language policy will act as an umbrella to protect the educational priorities of a given district or school, rather than leaving them vulnerable to top-down mandates that oppose or undermine their vision. For instance, a school or district language policy that promotes multilingualism serves as the guiding force driving all decisions about how the CCSS are to be interpreted, negotiated, and implemented locally.

A district or school language policy addresses all decisions to be made about language, such as which language(s) will be used in instruction and how languages are to be taught. It brings all members of a given school or even district together through a coherent and cohesive school- or districtwide vision for ELLs/EBs that is mutually accepted and implemented in every classroom. It sets out what the school intends to do about areas of concern and includes provisions for follow-up, monitoring, and revision of the policy itself in light of changing circumstances. A language policy is a dynamic action statement that changes along with the dynamic context of a school (Corson, 1999).

An effective language policy and implementation plan should (1) comply with all federal, state, and local policies and accountability requirements; (2) respond to local community needs, interests, and concerns; (3) promote the development and implementation of educationally sound programs that deliver valid and reliable results for all language learners; (4) be understood and supported by all constituents (administrators, teachers, students, parents, community members); and (5) drive decision making on the local level. The language policy should begin with a mission statement that clearly articulates the district's or school's stance toward languages other than English (LOTEs). Districts and schools that are committed to maintaining and developing LOTEs, not only for ELLs/EBs but also for English monolinguals, must reflect this mission in all of their policies and procedures. This commitment is critical in the context of the CCSS.

Most schools and districts typically do not have one explicit, coherent language policy that is endorsed by the school board and supported by a written implementation plan that includes procedures guiding all aspects of education (in a readily accessible format). However, all schools do have language policies that guide practice at the local school level. These language policies are not necessarily explicitly written but they are implicit in the practices that we can observe within and across schools in the district. In many places we find gaps, confusion, or contradictions in the policies and procedures that are to guide the language education of ELLs/EBs and English monolinguals, and we see this happening with the implementation of the CCSS at every decision-making level.

To date, states have adopted the CCSS in English language arts, mathematics, and science. In response to concerns about what the CCSS mean for bilingual education, some states have taken to explicitly refering to the *English* language arts standards as *language* arts standards, thus promoting bilingual education by making it clear that the standards can be reached in one or more languages. So, for example, in a Spanish–English dual language bilingual program, the language policy would include a concrete language allocation plan that expects biliteracy and explicitly articulates how Spanish and English are to be used for instructional purposes during the language arts block (e.g., see Escamilla et al., 2014). Language policies also clarify what languages teachers are to use for what purposes across content areas within the model of bilingual education implemented in their context (Beeman & Urow, 2013). Reflecting a more holistic, dynamic notion of bilingualism (García, 2009a), language allocation plans encourage the intentional and strategic use of translanguaging (García, Ibarra Johnson, & Seltzer, in preparation). Likewise, plans for CCSS-aligned professional development (PD) need to include structured opportunities for all teachers to learn to draw on students' home and new languages to shelter and differentiate core-content instruction (see 5.12).

The City University of New York–New York State Initiative for Emergent Bilinguals (CUNY–NYSIEB) offers one example of local efforts to develop school language policies that promote multilingualism in schools. The primary purpose of CUNY–NYSIEB is for principals serving large populations of ELLs/EBs in underperforming schools to expand their knowledge base and receive support in the education of these students. The overall goal is to improve programs and practices for ELLs/EBs in these schools in ways that adhere to the two guiding principles of CUNY–NYSIEB: (1) bilingualism is to be seen as a resource in education; and (2) schools must promote a schoolwide ecology of multilingualism. Toward that end, each school participating in the project creates an emergent bilingual leadership team that includes the school principal and other key administrators, teachers across a range of subjects, and parents of ELLs/EBs. The team works together to develop a school improvement plan for ELLs/EBs, which serves as the school's new language education policy. In the final stage of the project, the new policy is adopted and implemented schoolwide. As documented in García and Menken (2015), the majority of the 43 schools that have participated in the project have shifted their school's language policies, educational practices, and ideologies toward language in ways that embrace bilingualism as a resource and value multilingualism in schools.

Moving Forward

If your district/school already has a strong language policy and implementation plan in place, we recommend you use it to guide your decisions about CCSS implementation. If there is no coherent language policy in place, then we recommend that you use the CCSS implementation as an opportunity to develop a bi/multilingual language policy around an issue that matters in your context.

Because writing a language policy and implementation plan is a large, time-consuming task, it is useful to divide into taskforces with specific, clearly defined charges such as

- Defining programs for language learners that are approved in the district (bilingual; English-medium, ideally with home language supports; home language; world language) with reference to the research base that supports these program models.
- Outlining how a given school is to implement the program(s) they have selected, with appropriate adaptations to ensure it meets the needs of the school, student population, and community.
- Listing instructional approaches that should be found in all classes that serve ELLs/EBs (e.g., sheltered instruction, differentiated instruction).
- Describing the components of the district's assessment and accountability system with attention to the needs of language learners, ensuring that it will not undermine a given school's language policy.
- Identifying the needs of particular groups of ELLs/EBs (e.g., struggling readers and writers, long-term ELLs, special education).
- Planning PD.
- Setting up outreach and advocacy.

The language policy that emerges should be a short, concise document that lays out general goals, definitions, and principles guiding decision making, and it should be submitted to the school board for approval. The language policy and implementation plan should be revisited on a regular basis and revised as necessary by the leadership team. A state/district/school/program would use its dynamic language policy to frame local efforts to customize and differentiate all new educational decisions, including CCSS implementation.

4.5 What might the process of language education policy development look like at the school and classroom levels relative to the Common Core State Standards?

■ *Mishelle Jurado and Lisa Harmon-Martinez*

As the oldest public high school in Albuquerque, New Mexico, Albuquerque High School (AHS) has experienced myriad changes in the 134 years since welcoming its first students. AHS is again changing and growing in new and exciting ways, as the dual language program expands to include both of us, Mishelle Jurado (a bilingual, Spanish language arts [SLA] teacher) and Lisa Harmon-Martinez (a monolingual, English language arts [ELA] teacher), as coordinators. Additionally, we have created a new language arts department, to include ELA and SLA educators working together to support emerging bilinguals (EBs) at all grade levels. This change is a direct result of a long journey toward a true high school dual language model, in which Spanish language development (SLD) is on par with English language development (ELD). Our efforts are also bolstered by new research that proves the importance of a strong dual language education, not only for English language learners (ELLs) but also for the native English speakers in our program. As we move toward the newly adopted Common Core State Standards (CCSS), in addition to the World-class Instructional Design and Assessment's (WIDA's) existing ELD and new SLD standards. we see an opportunity to align our school's curriculum for EB students through professional development (PD) and collaboration in our language arts department.

While we are pleased that the CCSS include language standards in the speaking and listening strands, EBs are seemingly only addenda to the CCSS. Unfortunately, we recognize that Spanish is sometimes devalued as a language in the United States; this then informs the biases of educators who teach in English and even in Spanish, which then creates issues when developing a healthy and positive student identity. However, we are continually moving farther from the view of SLA classes as an elective with a modern–classical focus, and are therefore working hard to elevate the status of Spanish by crafting a rigorous and engaging curriculum that rivals its ELA counterparts. In addition to valuing students' sociocultural and linguistic background, by implementing our vision students who take both ELA and SLA are now doubly fortified in the development of their language skills because they receive two class hours of language arts instruction aligned to the Common Core. This is an improvement on past classes that had modern and classical language standards that did not meet the same language expectations that the Common Core requires in language arts. Our assertion is that our students will achieve the designation of proficiency or higher in either language on standardized tests required by the state.

Recent research by Thomas and Collier, *Dual Language Education for a Transformed World* (2012), featuring AHS students' smiling faces on the cover, cites the importance of student access to language arts classes in both languages. While we agree with the separation of language instruction, meaning each language has its designated class, we are fully aware that our students use both languages simultaneously to acquire and negotiate meaning of language and content in the classroom. It is also clear that the standards, rigor, and academic expectations should be the same in both language arts classes, to support the instruction in either English or Spanish that students receive in their other core-content and elective classes. Additionally, teachers outside of the language arts department participate in PD targeting language demands in their content areas; the CCSS speaking and listening standards are essential to these efforts.

We are also beginning a collaborative effort in grade 12 to align the strategies used in the English and Spanish Advanced Placement (AP) literature classes. While our curriculum varies greatly, the skills required by the AP exam are still largely the same, in that students must analyze the author's craft. Using our work both as a model and a backward-planning approach to vertical alignment, with the CCSS as our focus, we are working toward increasing the rigor demanded by the CCSS and the support to be successful.

With our students in mind, and their future as U.S. bilinguals at stake, we are taking a brave step forward together to improve access to equitable language development and instruction.

4.6 What preparation do administrators need to implement the Common Core State Standards in schools serving English language learners/emergent bilinguals?

■ *Barbara Marler*

The challenges facing a school administrator charged with implementing the Common Core State Standards (CCSS) are numerous. When rolling out the CCSS in a school that serves English language learners (ELLs)/emergent bilinguals (EBs), those same challenges remain, and without knowledge about English as a second or other language (ESL or ESOL) and bilingual instruction, these challenges can be overwhelming. Without this foundational knowledge, school leaders may abdicate this aspect of their responsibilities, leaving instructional leadership around this student population to the ESL/ESOL or bilingual teachers. Such administrators may also forge blindly ahead, believing that what they know about their special education population or their low socioeconomic population can accurately be applied to this group. There is a better way. A CCSS rollout can actually benefit ELLs/EBs, enriching their learning and development, enhancing their academic and linguistic performance, promoting research-based pedagogy and instructional methodology, and building greater capacity among all teachers to meet the needs of these students.

Decisions about CCSS implementation reflect orientations toward language and culture in education. A sociocultural orientation is reflected in linguistically and culturally responsive curriculum, instruction, and assessment that builds on student and community strengths and resources in ways that benefit all learners.

As schools implement the CCSS, many tasks present themselves and advance to the top of the priority list: alignment of curriculum, development of curricular maps, design of graphic representations of curricular scope and sequence, compilation of curricular guides, design of suggested instructional activities, creation of common assessments and corresponding rubrics, and so forth. The exchange of ideas among educators around learning and instruction is essential to the completion of these tasks. At the very minimum, an instructional leader wants to be a part of those conversations and no doubt wants to assert influence as to the outcomes. Leaders in these professional conversations need to know about processes of second language acquisition and biliteracy development. Professional learning communities need to use and understand research-based pedagogy and methods associated with sustained content and language learning in an ESL/ESOL/bilingual instructional context. The school administrator, as an instructional leader, should work toward ensuring that all educators can work with linguistically and culturally diverse students as they work on the tasks associated with the CCSS rollout.

Knowledge of the commonalities between the CCSS and the English language development standards is also important. In a bilingual program (transitional, maintenance, heritage, or dual), a third set of standards comes into play: the non-native or non-English language arts standards. A school administrator who is able to show and illustrate the crossover between these sets of standards and to suggest methods for content and language differentiation can build capacity among all teachers in the school. General education teachers will grow in their skill and expertise to set reasonable expectations, create comprehensible and meaningful lessons, differentiate for language proficiency levels, and design valid and reliable assessments for the ELLs/EBs they teach. They will also learn how to increase the academic language proficiencies of the native-English-speaking students. ESL/ESOL/bilingual teachers will grow in their ability to connect content and language instruction at all levels.

■ *Victoria K. Hunt and Tatyana Kleyn*

School administrators play a central role in guiding how teachers approach the CCSS for their ELLs/EBs. Their views of these students and bilingual instruction can affect the degree to which students are either given access to the new standards through their full linguistic repertoire or provided with English-only instruction that creates unnecessary obstacles to learning and becoming bilingual and biliterate.

Understanding the Heterogeneity of English Language Learners/Emergent Bilinguals

Although the CCSS are for all students, educators cannot approach the standards in the same way for each child. This is especially true for students who are EBs, a heterogeneous group along different places of the bilingual and biliterate continuum (Menken, 2013). Administrators should distinguish between ELL/EB subgroups and, to be effective, should see these students through the strengths (e.g., their home languages and background experiences) they bring. This understanding must then be communicated and explored by the school's faculty, regardless of the program or students they teach.

It is also important that administrators understand the various language-learning needs of EBs. Students with strong academic knowledge and complex speaking patterns in their home languages will be able to explain their understanding in that language. With the right supports, these students will also be able to do this in their new language. Students who have had less exposure to academic discourse in their home language will need more linguistic supports to explain their understanding; however, these students should also be exposed to new and challenging concepts. EBs should have opportunities to think critically as they develop academic language and literacy in either language. One example of considering the Common Core in relation to language learning is New York's Bilingual Common Core Progressions that have been developed for the new and home languages (https://www.engageny.org/resource/new-york-state-bilingual-common-core-initiative). They provide a structured tool for scaffolding languages while supporting the CCSS.

It is not possible to wait until ELL/EBs know the target language to use critical thinking skills; instead, strategies to support their ideas, opinions, and ways of finding evidence to support their thinking through the text must be enacted. It is imperative that their education not be limited to a focus on basic skills or English only.

Understanding the Common Core State Standards as Rigorous Concepts Approached across Languages

Administrators need to be instructional leaders who understand both the larger objectives and details of the CCSS, apart from simply supporting the implementation of a Common Core–aligned curricula. It is important to find ways to ensure that students from diverse language backgrounds are learning the Common Core via scaffolds and participating and working at the required level. This is not easy; but it is necessary as they learn in a new language. Administrators and faculty should also view the CCSS as a set of concepts and skills that can be approached not only through English, but also through students' home languages. The following example highlights the difficulties that EBs can face in articulating their content learning through academic language.

> A kindergarten Spanish–English two-way dual language bilingual class was learning about 2D and 3D shapes and their relationships. An English-dominant student with a high degree of academic language proficiency and a Spanish-dominant student with less academic proficiency in Spanish were comparing a sphere and a cone in Spanish. Both students understood that both shapes could roll because they were round in parts, and that the sphere could roll in any direction because it was completely round while the cone could only roll in a circle. The English-dominant child did not know all the related Spanish vocabulary, but he was able to explain that "*Esfera pueda rodar en cualquier dirección pero el cono no puede porque no rondar en todos los lados.*" ("The sphere can roll in whichever direction, but the cone can't because it isn't round on all sides.") The Spanish-dominant child could only say, "*La cosa puede ser así pero esa cosa no puede porque no es así en todos lados.*" ("The thing can go like this, but this thing can't go like this because it's not like this on all sides.") Both understood the concept deeply, but the child with less developed academic language did not have the linguistic ability to explain the concept in a detailed manner.

Asking teachers to analyze this scenario or a similar one at their school, with the goal of meeting the CCSS while supporting content and language development, could lead to rich conversations and effective planning for ELLs/EBs.

Building a Culture of Collaborative Leadership

School leaders should not lead this work individually, but must create collaborations and avenues for experts in their schools to work together to ensure equitable and bilingual practices are put in place across disciplines (Hunt, 2011). Addressing the CCSS, and the education of ELLs/EBs, should be approached by building on the teachers' strengths, just as teachers should build on their students' linguistic, cultural, and academic backgrounds.

4.7 How can schools use instructional teams that build on teacher and student strengths to appropriately implement the Common Core State Standards?

■ *Sarah Gil and Claire E. Sylvan*

Recently arrived immigrants to U.S. secondary schools have a wealth of diverse strengths, experiences, and capacities to achieve educational success with the Common Core State Standards (CCSS). They also face tremendous challenges to obtaining a high school diploma—hurdles that are linguistic, academic, and cultural. To succeed in educating these students in the short time they have to attend public high school, schools and educational programs must be designed to leverage their strengths and accelerate their learning.

Internationals Network for Public Schools (Internationals) is an organization that supports, develops, and networks 19 secondary schools/academies that all face this challenge. Our schools share a common educational approach for educating recently arrived immigrant students from 119 countries and over 90 language backgrounds that is designed to leverage their diverse strengths. Virtually all Internationals' students at the time of admission to an Internationals school have been in the United States under four years and have low levels of English proficiency. Our schools' goal is to prepare these students for college, careers, and full participation in democratic society.

Key to leveraging the students' strengths and building the teachers' capacity is our interdisciplinary team structure. This structure is critical for providing the deep support needed for students to access academic content. There are several key elements that allow us to create cohorts of students who travel together for their academic experience: (1) students are grouped heterogeneously and work collaboratively on projects; (2) language and content learning is integrated in all classes; (3) experiential learning is emphasized; (4) teams of teachers have autonomy to design instruction; and (5) teachers' learning and organizational structure mirror that of the students. The foundation that holds all this together is the team structure. It allows both students and teachers to build on the *strengths* of their group members and supports tackling complex tasks, including Common Core–aligned learning, while limiting the linguistic difficulty for students.

All students are grouped heterogeneously, regardless of their English level, prior academic experience, home language, length of time in the United States, and so forth. These cohort clusters of 80–100 students are subdivided into equally heterogeneous strands of 25–30 students. A team of (at a minimum) four teachers: an English/English as a second language, math, science, and history teacher form an interdisciplinary instructional team that can discuss the best ways to form small groups, so that students can work on carefully developed collaborative projects that incorporate both academic and linguistic content. Our students *always* need linguistic and academic scaffolding, but working in groups also allows them to use their diverse strengths, including existing academic and linguistic (e.g., native languages) knowledge by working together. As we approach incorporating texts within the CCSS, we structure supports across a team (all teachers working on similar linguistic and/or content focus) to support students, lowering the second-language demands while retaining rigorous and complex cognitive goals.

Consider this example. In a combined grades 9 and 10 cluster. the life science and history teachers create a rich collaboration addressing evolution and eugenics. They plan their work together, studying texts by and about different perspectives. This work culminates in a debate where students take on the role of a person, like biologist Charles Darwin; multiple intelligences theorist Howard Gardner; forced sterilization victim Leilani Muir; and proponent of voluntary sterilization of poor women, former Louisiana State legislator John LaBruzzo, to name a few. The students present arguments on what government's role should be in encouraging the reproduction of certain types of people and discouraging the reproduction of other types of people.

The content is compelling and incorporates support for reading diverse texts, thesis generating, and argumentation, all competencies at the center of the CCSS. At the same time, the activity differentiates for students based on interest, skill, and language proficiency. Students choose from nine different roles, generate two to four arguments that they refine in expert groups supported by graphic organizers, and confer during project time with the teachers. The most English proficient students stretch their abilities by debating in character as they facilitate. The unit closes with students reflecting in writing on the experience and its impact on their perspectives of government's role in eugenic policies. Without interdisciplinary teacher team collaboration, emergent bilinguals miss opportunities for deeply considering the implication of content as they negotiate meaning and ambiguity and use newly acquired academic language. Thoughtful planning that supports language development and the divergent thinking the CCSS demands is successfully achieved by teachers on instructional teams who can create experiences that individual teachers cannot provide, and the embedded assessments allow students to deeply demonstrate their knowledge in ways CCSS–aligned tests can only hope to approximate.

4.8 How should educational leaders evaluate teachers who work with English language learners/emergent bilinguals?

■ *Edward Tabet-Cubero*

Teacher evaluation approaches have not necessarily been linked directly to the adoption of the Common Core State Standards (CCSS). However, under the Obama Administration's Elementary and Secondary Education Act (ESEA)/No Child Left Behind (NCLB) waivers, redesigned teacher evaluation systems and the adoption of the CCSS go hand in hand. Two primary considerations need to be taken into account when evaluating teachers of emerging bilingual (EB) students. First, if the accountability system is linked to students' standardized test results, then the system must take into account not only content-area achievement, but also growth in student language proficiency. Second, the teacher observation component of such evaluations systems must include specific elements of sheltered instruction to meet the distinct learning needs of EBs, elements that do not readily appear in most teacher evaluation systems.

When it comes to teacher evaluation systems, many local and state education agencies have adopted teacher performance standards that are similar to, or directly derived from, Danielson's (2007) *Enhancing Professional Practice: A Framework for Teaching,* 2nd Edition. Although not originally intended as a formal teacher evaluation tool, it has become one of the most commonly referred to resources for teacher evaluation system development. The Danielson Framework divides teacher practice into four domains: (1) planning and preparation, (2) classroom environment, (3) instruction, and (4) professional responsibilities. Although most teacher evaluation frameworks include elements on differentiation to meet the needs of diverse learners, the majority are void of direct references to language and culture. Therefore, significant revisions and/or augmentations must be made for any set of teacher evaluation competencies/standards to be relevant and effective for teachers of EB students.

The commonly adhered to adage "good teaching is good teaching" does not ring true for the teaching of EB students. If that were the case, linguistically and culturally diverse students would not be suffering from such a tremendous gap in achievement with their native-English-speaking peers. The same holds true for teacher evaluation practices. There are specific elements of effective general classroom instruction, but in the case of EB teachers there are very specific skills related to language and culture that must be the area of focus.

Take for example an instructional element that is included under the planning and preparation and instruction domains in most teacher evaluation systems—*differentiation.* Teacher planning for differentiated instruction to meet the needs of diverse learners is typically focused on students' varying levels of content and reading proficiencies, and sometimes their individual learning styles. However, key to effectively differentiating instruction for EBs is an understanding of students' varying language proficiency levels in English and in their home language(s). Teachers of EBs need to take great care to differentiate linguistic input and output based on students' language proficiency, all while ensuring students meet rigorous grade-level content standards.

Another commonly evaluated teacher competency is "demonstrating knowledge of students." For teachers of linguistically and culturally diverse students, this would include not only an understanding of content and language proficiency, but a focus on students' cultures as well. Culturally responsive instruction receives little to no attention in most teacher evaluation systems. These are just a couple of the myriad considerations that should be considered when evaluating teachers of EB students.

For teacher evaluation systems to be relevant and effective for teachers of EB students, significant revisions to current systems must be made. Districts and states should not construct entirely separate observation protocols for teachers of diverse students, rather they should infuse language and culture throughout the systems they are implementing. Dual Language Education of New Mexico has identified eight components of sheltered instruction that could serve as a starting point for state and local education agencies looking to revise their current teacher evaluation systems. The eight components of sheltered instruction are the following:

1. Focus on language
2. Plan for peer interaction
3. Support meaning with realia
4. Activate prior knowledge and/or create shared knowledge
5. Make text accessible
6. Develop student learning strategies
7. Bridge the two languages
8. Affirm identity (Kriteman and Tabet-Cubero, 2014)

Examples of Teacher Evaluation Systems

Two examples of teacher evaluation systems that have effectively infused language and culture throughout come from the Woodburn School District in Woodburn, OR, and the New Mexico State Bilingual Advisory Council's ELL Crosswalk of NMTEACH. In the Woodburn School District's case, the Executive Director of Human Resources, Steve Williams, gathered a diverse group of teachers and administrators, several with specific expertise in culturally and linguistically responsive instruction, and developed the *WSD Performance Supervision and Evaluation of Licensed Teaching Professionals* handbook (Woodburn School District #103, 2011). From initial research, to standards writing, to actual implementation, the process took three years to complete. The final document is loosely based on Danielson's framework, but with clearly articulated considerations of language and culture embedded throughout. The following two tables show examples of standards elements from the Woodburn document that demonstrate how EBs' needs were considered.

Domain 1: Planning and Preparation
Standard 2: Demonstrating Knowledge of Students

Element	Deficient	Basic	Proficient	Exemplary
2C. Knowledge of students' skills, knowledge, language acquisition, and language proficiency	Teacher displays little or no knowledge of students' skills, knowledge, language acquisition, and language proficiency—or does not indicate that such knowledge is valuable.	Teacher recognizes the values of understanding students' skills, knowledge, language acquisition, and language proficiency but displays this knowledge only for class as a whole.	Teacher displays understanding of individual students' skills, knowledge, language acquisition, and language proficiency and has a strategy for maintaining such information.	Teacher displays understanding of individual students' skills, knowledge, language acquisition, and language proficiency and has a strategy for utilizing that information to improve instruction.

Domain 2: Classroom Environment
Standard 8: Creating an Environment That Supports 1st and 2nd Language Development

Element	Deficient	Basic	Proficient	Exemplary
8B. Language development and multiculturalism	There are few language development resources and materials available, either posted on the walls or in the classroom. Environment promotes neither diversity nor language development.	There is a growing body of language development resources and materials available to students. However, there is little or no apparent connection between the environment and language development.	There is a considerable body of language development resources and materials available to students. Environment clearly supports and contributes to both language development and diversity.	There is considerable body of language development resources and materials available, which have been selected, organized, and maintained by students. The environment clearly serves as a motivational tool in the language development and valuing of diversity of all students.

Similarly, as a part of its ESEA waiver requirements, the New Mexico Public Education Department crafted a Danielson-based teacher evaluation system titled NMTEACH. Noting that 71% of New Mexico's student population is identified as linguistically or culturally diverse, the State Bilingual Advisory Council conducted an ELL crosswalk of the NMTEACH document and developed a supplemental document and set of recommendations for the New Mexico Public Education Deparment to meet their diverse students' needs. The following table shows some examples.

Examples from the New Mexico State Bilingual Advisory Council's Recommendations

Element	Descriptors	Sheltered Instruction for ELLs Crosswalk	Evidence: Look-Fors
2B. Organizing physical space	• To what level do all students have equal access to learning resources and materials? • To what level does the classroom environment support the day's lesson?	The classroom environment includes posting of content and language objectives, culturally and linguistically relevant materials, student work, visuals, and graphics that make learning comprehensible.	• Instructional materials are available in the child's home language and/or reflect the culture of ELLs. • Content and language objectives for lesson are explicit and posted.
3A. Communicating with students in a manner that is appropriate to their culture and level of development	• To what level are directions clearly delivered and understandable? • To what level is *content* communicated in a clear, concise manner?	Teacher uses features of comprehensible input throughout the lesson as follows: • Academic tasks are explained clearly in L1 or L2. • A variety of specific sheltered instruction techniques make *content* concepts clear. • Teacher's speech nurtures *language* development and advances ELLs' proficiency level. • Teacher's explanations of academic tasks are clear and clarified in L1/L2 when needed.	• The teacher has students who are bilingually proficient and use the native *language* to clarify directions and concepts being taught to other ELLs. • Teacher uses modeling, visuals, hands-on activities, demonstrations, gestures, and body language, with repeated exposure to key concepts. • The teacher's rate, enunciation, and complexity of speech are appropriate for students' English language development levels, based in ACCESS score. • Teacher avoids use of jargon, and focuses on/explains idioms.

Considering that EBs represent the fastest growing subgroup in U.S. public schools, educators and policymakers must consider these students' distinct learning needs. These considerations are particularly important in policies, such as teacher evaluation, that relate to classroom instruction. Once again the adage that "good teaching is good teaching" simply does not hold true for EB teachers. Such teachers need to demonstrate a very specialized set of skills to ensure the success of their diverse learners.

Programming and Instruction

4.9 What are some of the critical components of educational programs for English language learners/emergent bilinguals? What types of resources are available for administrators to support this work?

■ *Mari Rasmussen*

"Kim, how was biology today?"

"Neeb, it's cold today. Where is your coat?"

"Lee, how do you say, 'It's cold out!' in Hmong?"

I was a student teacher working with high school English learners (ELs). Enthusiastic about my profession, and interested in my students, I occasionally abandoned the skill and drill, or "skill, drill, and kill," English as a second language (ESL) text to engage my students in real conversations. Unfortunately, my unorthodox behavior was frowned on by the university supervisor, a retired teacher hired to evaluate student teachers. "Do not further embarrass these poor refugees by making fun of them and pointing out their lack of English. Teach them correct grammar so that they can succeed," was her advice to me.

I was daunted by the directive of this well-meaning, but misinformed, evaluator; fortunately, I did not take it to heart. After several decades of working with ELs, teachers, and program administrators, I would argue that the critical components of successful programs for ELs involve several of the things I was attempting to do as a very inexperienced, but enthusiastic, ESL teacher. These components include the following:

- Educators who engage students in meaningful conversations
- Schools that foster a sense of community
- Schools that value the culture and language that ELs bring to the classroom
- Learning environments that develop academic skills within the context of conversation, community, and students' backgrounds
- Learning environments that foster a joy of learning through challenging activities, positive experiences, and shared laughter (Dewey, 1916; Goldenberg, 2013; Wisconsin Center for Educational Research, 2013).

Administrators face many challenges in implementing these components because of the emphasis on rigorous college- and career-ready standards and assessments, increasing

EL numbers, and limited budgets. How can they support these key components and what resources are available to them? What tools are needed to nurture meaningful student conversations, home language support, and the other components of a successful EL program?

While many resources are needed to support these components, key to their implementation is the availability of highly qualified, capable teachers. Research has demonstrated the important roles support and professional development (PD) play for teachers in student achievement (Yoon, Duncan, Lee, Scarloss, & Shapley, 2007). This support is even more essential when implementing these key components for unique student populations, such as ELs, and for successful EL programs (Téllez & Waxman, 2006). It is the teacher who needs to have the skills to arrange group work to involve ELs, facilitate academic conversations, and develop challenging learning activities. Teachers cannot do this in isolation, though. My research with EL teachers in rural and urban communities found that teachers know a lot about supporting their students successfully, and their voices can be just as meaningful as quantitative test score data. Without administrative and systemic support, however, the teachers' voices are unheard (Rasmussen, 2008).

Administrators play key roles in supporting teachers, scaffolding their PD, and serving as advocates for students and teachers in the implementation of the various components necessary for successful EL programs (Staehr Fenner, 2014). Administrators can also be key in supporting a positive learning environment schoolwide, one that values home language and culture, community spirit, and a joy of learning.

The resources available to administrators include institutions of higher education, technical assistance centers, and other entities dedicated to the support of educators assisting ELs to achieve high standards. Successful administrators work hand in hand with those who can provide the PD and technical assistance necessary to develop strategic plans, including face-to-face workshops, coaching support, professional learning communities, resource libraries (both physical and online), and schedules that allow for collaboration.

In summary, successful educational programs for ELs that promote academic achievement and English language development in this era of accountability involve a collaborative effort among a variety of educators, from administrators and practitioners to researchers and policymakers. It means working together to ensure that administrators have the resources they need to create learning environments that support teachers and lead to student success.

4.10 How can educators who work in bilingual/dual language programs implement the Common Core State Standards in their states, districts, and schools?

- *Silvia Dorta-Duque de Reyes and Jill Kerper Mora[1]*

National Level

The Council of Chief State School Officers (CCSSO), the California Department of Education (CDE), and the San Diego County Office of Education (SDCOE) jointly sponsored and funded the Common Core Translation Project (CCTP) as a commitment to providing leadership, assistance, and resources so that every student has access to an education that meets world-class standards. The Spanish translation and linguistic augmentation of the Common Core State Standards (CCSS) supports standards-based instruction because it presents a framework for schools and teachers to ensure that all students are exposed to rigorous content and prepared to contribute positively to an increasingly complex world. The linguistic augmentation provides a structure and specific detail to address points of learning, skills, and concepts that are specific to Spanish language and literacy, as well as transferable language constructs between English and Spanish. The linguistic augmentation is based on the conventions for oral and written Spanish from the Real Academia de la Lengua Española (RAE) promulgated in 2010. The intent is to promote, through quality curriculum and instruction, the same expectations and level of rigor for Spanish usage as educators expect for English usage. Both the Common Core en Español standards and the Common Core Matemáticas en Español are blueprints to a parallel, aligned, and equitable architecture for biliteracy. They make a significant contribution to education reform because they can be used as a guide for equitable assessment and curriculum development.

The creation of these standards represents a consensus of pedagogical norms and objectives leading to proficient biliteracy. An extensive peer review process was conducted in 2012. There were over 40 participants representing teachers, district and county offices of education, and CDE administrators, as well as parents and community representatives from throughout California, Florida, and New York. The Mexican-American Legal and Education Fund (MALDEF) was also present to witness the process. This process focused on important outcomes, such as ensuring that the document was

- Comprehensible by the intended audience of educators, parents, general public and publishers
- Equivalent in content to the English standards
- Comprehensive in its specific linguistic adaptation for Spanish
- Cohesive in terms of Spanish throughout all grade levels.

---

[1] This response draws on our experiences working in California at the district, county, state, and university levels to develop Common Core en Español.

A webpage (http://commoncore-espanol.com/) was constructed to make the CCSS en Español available online to all.

State Level

The pedagogical implications of the Common Core en Español are affirmed in the English language/English Language Development Framework (2014). Instructional Quality Commissioners (framework committee members) voiced strong support:

> It should be noted that literacy and language proficiency in languages other than English are highly desirable and advantageous for California's students and the state. The State Superintendent of Public Instruction and the State Board of Education recognize biliteracy as a precious resource in our state, one that should be encouraged and nurtured. In effect since 2012, the State Seal of Biliteracy is awarded to high school graduates who have attained a high level of proficiency in speaking, reading, and writing in one or more languages in addition to English. As Superintendent Torlakson emphasized, "Fluency in a second language helps our students be well prepared to compete in a global marketplace. The gold seal on their high school diplomas recognizes and celebrates a second language as an asset, not just for themselves, but also for our state, nation, and world. In the pursuit of a biliterate and multiliterate citizenry, California has the opportunity to build on the linguistic assets that our ELs bring to public schools while also supporting the acquisition of biliteracy and multiliteracy in students whose home language is English." (CA ELA/ELD Framework, p. 2)

This pedagogical shift at the state level opens the door to many opportunities because it also implies a systemwide policy shift that affirms biliteracy as an asset. The challenge, as with all systems, is the willingness of decision makers to take the lead in making the changes necessary for realizing the vision called for in the framework. As we move into the era of local accountability control, it is urgent to have advocacy and representation for biliteracy.

Implementing the Common Core en Español systemwide will require equitable assessment, curriculum, and instructional resources. The Common Core en Español also presents a new opportunity for the leadership of students, parents, teachers, and school administrators to recognize the link between cognitive development and language, and to embrace the responsibility for transforming our educational system so that it is responsive to the needs of a multilingual and multicultural 21st-century citizenry.

District Level

Implementation of the Common Core en Español at the district level will require special attention to pacing guides and curriculum maps. A clear vertical articulation of Spanish-specific augmentation standards, along with ongoing capacity building and collaboration through the establishment of professional learning communities, is essential for effective implementation. This includes professional development dedicated to the study of Spanish-specific language and foundational skills, strategic and intentional teaching of linguistic transfer and formative writing assessment, and cross-linguistic analysis of oral and written language production.

Teacher Education

The CCSS reforms also affect university teacher education programs because their credential programs prepare pre-service teacher candidates for the increased academic rigor through innovative and refocused pedagogy, as articulated in the Common Core en Español. The beginning phase of teacher education reform to meet the increased professional demands that teachers face has begun with providing university faculty with the research and knowledge base that underpin the CCSS and Common Core en Español. Project CORE, a collaborative project between the SDCOE and San Diego State University, provided leadership and funding to engage university faculty in workshops and guided syllabi revision and alignment to ensure that credential program courses address the CCSS.

Implementation Challenges and Opportunities

A significant challenge is the development of resources necessary to sustain the instructional rigor demanded by the Common Core en Español. While the Common Core en Español does not have the ample funding allocation that the CCSS has, it has field experts ready to develop and engage in product development, and a growing and enthusiastic following among parents, educators, policymakers, and legislators. University faculty who teach curriculum and methods courses in teacher education programs need to be brought on board because the CCSS reforms are significant, although many faculty see the Common Core en Español and the California English Language Development Standards (2012) as a much welcomed return to effective second language and literacy pedagogy.

The most important challenge to overcome, as well as the most exciting opportunity for dual language educators, is the development of summative and formative assessments that provide the structure for accountability, rigor, and instructional decision making needed for the promise of biliteracy to be realized.

4.11 What are the roles of bilingual education teachers and bilingual content classes in Common Core State Standards implementation?

■ *Sandra Butvilofsky, Susan Hopewell, and Kathy Escamilla*

The role of the bilingual teacher and the schools and districts in which he or she teaches is to ensure that biliteracy and bilingualism are the end goals for students, despite the fact that the Common Core State Standards (CCSS) and the assessments that measure them are limited to English only. Students' abilities to analyze, infer, give evidence, and expand academic discourse (skills valued within the CCSS) are expanded through the development of bilingualism and biliteracy, and as such should be measured in two languages.

To ensure that emergent bilingual (EB) learners reach the English language arts (ELA) CCSS, bilingual language arts need to include both Spanish and English literacy instruction, wherein connections between Spanish and English are made explicit to students, and where instruction on speaking, listening, reading, writing, and metalanguage is emphasized in both languages. This holistic approach to planning, organizing, and delivering instruction ensures a comprehensive and coordinated literacy experience for EB learners. This coordinated experience is called the holistic biliteracy framework; it is an essential construct to Literacy Squared, a research-based and research-tested program (Escamilla et al., 2014). Regardless of bilingual program type (e.g., one-way and two-way bilingual models, maintenance and early-exit programs), the intent of bilingual and biliteracy instruction is to focus on coordinating instruction across environments so that what is learned in one language will aid learning in the other and is not duplicative. In essence, time allocations matter less than time utilization within each language environment. The CCSS provide a window into what students need to accomplish; however, they lack the pedagogy. Within Spanish–English bilingual programs for EBs, we suggest that the cognitive "lifting" occur in the Spanish and that the information presented and skills and language learned in the additional language (English) be intentionally and purposefully built on this foundation. In other words, bilingual teachers should begin their planning for Spanish instruction and then plan carefully how to complement, supplement, and develop English.

Research has consistently shown the benefits of bilingual literacy instruction, as opposed to English-only instruction for EB learners. EB learners come into schools with home language resources that should be nurtured and developed alongside their additional language. As such, bilingual teachers and content classes need to take into consideration all of the linguistic skills and knowledge that are distributed across languages. This consideration requires a holistic understanding of bilingualism and biliteracy, in that the distribution of skills and knowledge between languages are mutually reinforcing. They can be developed simultaneously to achieve the CCSS, especially in ELA, in which the expectations are for learners to master specific standards in reading, writing, speaking, listening, and language.

A major critique of the CCSS is its monolingual and monocultural English focus, for both instruction and assessing students' learning. While current bilingual teachers are bound by the mandates of the CCSS, they should not rely solely on English-only instruction to help them meet those mandates. While teachers can plan for effective biliteracy instruction to meet the demands of the language arts CCSS, it is more important that the English-only assessment systems are supplemented with assessments that can be used to measure EB learners' biliteracy achievement, and that this be done in a way that ensures instruction matches assessment. Instead, we recommend that bilingual teachers collect a body of evidence that includes both languages in the EB learners' linguistic repertoire, even if the teacher does not have knowledge of the students' non-English languages. Collecting evidence in a holistic manner provides insight into the totality of what EB learners know.

■ *Kate Seltzer and Susana Ibarra Johnson*

There is no question that language plays a huge role in the CCSS. The CCSS require *all* students to read complex informational texts, write in a variety of genres, and use oral language to present their ideas and perspectives across all subject areas (Brisk & Proctor, 2012). If these tasks present a challenge to an English-speaking student, they are an even taller order for EBs learning in a new language. For these students to find academic success, bilingual content-area teachers must develop engaging, culturally sustaining units that align with standards *and* move students toward biliteracy.

Though the CCSS necessitate that all teachers become teachers of literacy, bilingual educators have the opportunity and ability to teach students in both the language(s) they know and the language they are learning in school. As teachers design standards-aligned units, they must keep several factors in mind. First, they must ensure that they teach content in ways that are comprehensible and engaging. Second, they must understand students' languaging in both the home *and* new languages and consider how the unit will move them towards biliteracy. According to Hornberger (2004), bilingual teachers can best facilitate this movement by enabling students to draw from *all* of their languages. She writes, "the more their learning contexts. . .allow learners and users to draw from across the whole of each and every [linguistic] continuum, the greater are the chances for their full biliterate development and expression" (p.158). This accommodation for flexible, dynamic languaging is what García (2009a) and others call "translanguaging." Thus, when bilingual teachers plan units that ask students to draw from *all* of their languages at *all* times, they help them meet academic standards and progress in their command of all their languages. The following examples illustrate this kind of planning in action:

- A grade 5 dual language teacher taught a science unit about the solar system. One of the objectives was to write a response that developed a topic with facts, definitions, and concrete details (ELA-Literacy.W.5.2b). To scaffold this objective, students used a graphic organizer called *una tabla de proceso*. They worked on *la tabla* throughout the writing process, using both English and Spanish flexibly. This tool helped students access content and practice writing in a more fluid way. Though their final responses were written in English, students used this bilingual tool to formulate and organize their ideas about new content in two languages.
- A grade 8 bilingual math teacher led her department in designing a geometry unit. Part of the unit required students to use informal arguments to establish facts about certain geometric concepts (Math.Content.8.G.C.5). She used the New and Home Language Arts progressions to set expectations for students at different levels of proficiency in both languages. For example, students who were "entering" proficiency in English but who were "expanding" it in Spanish wrote topic sentences in English but supported and expanded their arguments in Spanish. Students in general education *and* bilingual math classrooms benefited from this focus on content-area literacy.

- A social studies teacher designed a grade 12 unit on being active, critical citizens. He timed this unit with local elections in the city. As students immersed themselves in the politics, they worked in groups to design fact sheets that would inform the community and encourage people to vote (ELA-Literacy.RH.11–12.9). Students framed the issues in ways that benefited their diverse audiences and wrote fact sheets in English, Haitian Creole, and French.

Examples such as these show how bilingual content-area teachers can develop engaging, culturally sustaining units that align with standards *and* move students towards biliteracy.

4.12 Why and how must the roles of the English as a second language teacher and class change under Common Core State Standards implementation?

■ *Diane Staehr Fenner*

As a former English as a second language (ESL) teacher who now supports ESL and content teachers in implementing the Common Core State Standards (CCSS), this question has been driving much of my recent work. I am also not the only one asking the question. In fact, the Teaching English to Speakers of Other Languages (TESOL) International Association recently convened a group of teachers, administrators, researchers, policymakers, and thought leaders around the role of the ESL teacher during the implementation of the Common Core. I helped facilitate the convening and also wrote the report in collaboration with TESOL. Major findings recognized that ESL teachers' expertise is often misunderstood, sometimes relegating them to a lower status within the classroom or school. Because of the new demands of the Common Core and their emphasis on academic language, ESL teachers' roles must now shift to those of collaborators, advocates, and experts (TESOL, 2013).

Developing English as a Second Language Teachers' Leadership Skills

For ESL teachers to move into more prominent roles within the CCSS framework, administrators must provide vehicles for them to develop their leadership voices and have a greater impact on policy decisions that affect English language learners (ELLs) in their schools. Some ways I've been working with districts to develop ESL teachers' leadership skills have included meeting with ESL teachers to brainstorm the expertise they possess and also ways they can use this expertise to work with content teachers on CCSS implementation. I help them set goals and develop talking points to use in certain scenarios they encounter with content teachers. Then, I bring in content teachers and set up a space for them to draw on ESL teachers' skill sets in collaboratively planning instruction of academic language and content within the CCSS framework. This cycle is ideally repeated on an ongoing basis with the support of administrators.

English as a Second Language Teachers as Collaborators, Advocates, and Experts

One way for ESL teachers to collaborate with content teachers and advocate for ELLs is to create an individual plan that contains goals for each ELL, maps goals to specific instructional supports, and drives instruction across the content areas (Staehr Fenner, 2014). Teachers can meet on a regular basis to set goals and update the individual plan. The individual plan for ELLs can contain distinct elements within the Common Core framework that are outlined in the following table (Staehr Fenner, 2013a).

Role of the English as a Second Language Class

Because there are currently so many program models that offer ELLs linguistic support, the role of the ESL class within the CCSS framework will initially depend, to some degree, on the model that's in place. However, educators must examine what works with the current ELL program model and what does not support ELLs within the CCSS framework. Educators should advocate to change the role of the ESL class in their context if necessary so that ELLs are given the best support they can receive to experience success with CCSS-based instruction.

Individual English Learner Plan and Considerations for Common Core State Standards–Based Instruction

Element of Individual English Learner Plan	Considerations in Planning Common Core State Standards–based Instruction
The demands of the CCSS in the EL's grade level	• What the CCSS require for ELs to do in ELA and mathematics • Types of tasks assigned for homework and assessments
Which ELP/D standards guide instruction	• Share ELP/D standards with content teachers
Which ELP/D assessment ELs take and what scores mean	• Share ELP/D assessments and scores to set objectives
Kinds of scaffolds to support ELs in CCSS	• Sample strategies for scaffolding ELs' instruction depending on CCSS demands and ELP level • Decide on scaffolds together
Student objectives • Content • Language • Learning	• Consider which objectives are achievable in content areas with scaffolding and support

CCSS, Common Core State Standards; EL, English learner; ELA, English language arts; ELP/D, English language proficiency/development.

4.13 What should English as a second language or English language development curriculum and instruction look like relative to the Common Core State Standards?

- *Nancy Commins*

Emergent bilinguals (EBs), not only need to "learn English," they also need to learn the content of the school curriculum using a full range of language and literacy skills. Providing for the variety of quality learning and assessment opportunities students deserve requires schoolwide planning that addresses bilingual learners' need for both explicit instruction in their second language and the delivery of instruction in all subject areas that is comprehensible and interactive (Miramontes, Nadeau, & Commins, 2011). English as a second language (ESL)/English language development (ELD) time is when second language learners can accelerate their learning and work on aspects of language and literacy particular to their needs and proficiency levels, without competition from fluent native speakers.

Building Language Repertoires

Snow (1992) suggests that students can only demonstrate those language skills that they have had a chance to acquire and practice. Without formal instructional experiences with the kinds of complex tasks characteristic of both the Common Core State Standards (CCSS) and the New Generation Science Standards (NGSS), students' language repertoires run the risk of centering mainly on social interaction.

During ESL/ELD periods learners should engage in a range of communicative and academic tasks that build on the resources they bring in their primary language and across their linguistic repertoires. To maximize students' potential to succeed, assessment and instruction should be based on the language and interaction competencies students need to participate fully in the academic curriculum.

Content and Language Connection

To capture the interconnection of language and content, think of using a camera with a zoom lens to take a picture of friends in a beautiful landscape. If you zoom in on the people, the landscape provides the backdrop. If you focus on the landscape your friends are still in view. It is the same with teaching language and content. While both are always in the picture, there are instructional moments when each should be the focus. During ESL/ELD time, the lens zooms in on language and the content is the backdrop.

All teachers should be able to focus their lens and identify the *language demand* of their instruction and the aspects of *language structure* and *function* that are salient for a particular unit or topic. In addition, all teachers should incorporate hands-on interactive activities that are scaffolded to make them more comprehensible and accessible and intentionally build students' language proficiency.

The focus on language in ELD is more than being "language sensitive" (e.g., posting language objectives or a list of vocabulary words). It means providing sufficient support and practice for students to develop the discourse skills they need to function in academic registers. However, a language classroom that concentrates only on discrete skills or grammar in isolation is counterproductive. Too narrow a focus reduces students' opportunities to build the linguistic schema surrounding the concepts and the interactional skills that they will be held accountable for knowing and using in their content classrooms.

Teacher/School Collaborations

The goal during dedicated ESL/ELD times is to connect the language students develop to ongoing activities during grade-level or content-area instruction. Formal structures for communication and coplanning need to be established so that language acquisiton and content specialists can support each other to make the connections and devise assessments that allow students to demonstrate what they know and can do.

One of the strengths of working from common standards is that the language demands inherent in a particular content area (e.g. algebra, U.S. history, botany) will be similar across schools and districts. This means that work done to identify language demands, create language supports, and devise appropriate assessments in one school can be shared widely with content and language teachers in others.

Advocacy in Common Core State Standards Implementation

4.14 Why is there a need for advocacy for English language learners/emergent bilinguals?

■ *Diane Staehr Fenner*

The Common Core State Standards (CCSS) were not created with the specific strengths and unique challenges that English language learners (ELLs) present in mind. Because ELLs were not at the forefront of the conversation when the CCSS were written, they must now be a crucial part of the process during the standards' implementation. All ELL educators must speak up on their students' behalf so that these students are positioned to achieve within the CCSS framework. To that end, everyone—content teachers, English as a second language (ESL) teachers, and administrators—must advocate for them and share the responsibility of supporting ELLs' success within the CCSS.

Much like scaffolding instruction for ELLs—or providing a temporary, "just right" amount of instructional support for them on a case-by-case basis—educators also need to scaffold their advocacy efforts for ELLs in the Common Core (Staehr Fenner, 2014). Educators need to know each ELL's background to develop a CCSS advocacy plan for every student. Advocacy for ELLs should also be temporary; the goal of advocating for ELLs is to develop their own and their families' advocacy skills so that they are able to advocate for themselves.

Common Core for English Learners Equity Audit

I created the Common Core for English Learners (EL) Equity Audit (see following table) as a tool to begin conversations and build collaboration around ways to ensure that ELs have a place at the table when it comes to implementing the Common Core. The Equity Audit helps educators develop an action plan to advocate on behalf of ELs and their families, who may have not yet fully developed their own advocacy skills. Many schools and school districts have found this tool helpful in prioritizing their ELL Common Core advocacy efforts and in determining next steps.

Where to Begin

While it would be ideal for schools and districts to embrace the notion of advocating for ELLs within the CCSS framework, advocacy for ELLs can also begin at the classroom level. All teachers of ELLs can work within their own *sphere of influence* to ensure that ELLs are provided the support they need to be successful within the CCSS (Staehr Fenner, 2013b). In international relations, a sphere of influence is a spatial region or conceptual division over which a state or organization has significant cultural, economic, military, or political influence. In education, educators each work within a sphere of influence where they have the power to create an equitable environment for ELLs.

Common Core for English Learners Equity Audit

Consideration	Questions to Ask: To What Degree	Actions
Role of ESL teacher	Are ESL teachers working as experts, advocates, and consultants? Are they effectively collaborating with general education teachers in implementing the CCSS?	
Instructional materials and curriculum	Are CCSS-based instructional materials and curriculum appropriate for ELs?	
Professional development	Does professional development focus on preparing *all* teachers to implement the CCSS for ELs?	
Assessment	Are teachers aware of the demands of CCSS assessments for ELs? Do they adjust instruction accordingly?	
EL parent outreach	Are EL parents aware of implications of the CCSS and CCSS-aligned assessments?	
Teacher evaluation	Is teacher evaluation for all teachers inclusive of ELs accessing the CCSS?	

That space might be at the classroom, grade, or district level. Once educators have experienced success advocating within their spheres, they can expand them to reach more educators and ELLs.

■ *Stephen Krashen*

There is a problem with ELLs/emergent bilinguals (henceforth ELLs), but it is not the problem that is typically stated in the media. And there is a solution, but it is very different from the one that is currently being offered by the Common Core. In fact, the Common Core promises to make things much worlse for ELLs, and for all students in public schools today.

According to Uro and Barrio (2013), there are two big problems for ELLs:

1. ELLs aren't as proficient as fluent English speakers: Test results show "wide gaps in reading and mathematics between ELLs and non-ELLs . . . and that only 5% to 6% of ELLs score at or above proficient on grade 4 reading tests in several cities" (p. 100).

   This kind of comment shows an astonishing lack of understanding of what an ELL is. If the results did not show gaps between ELLs and non-ELLs, the ELLs would not *be* ELLs. Also, if an ELL scores at or above proficient, that ELL should not be classified as such. If 5% of a group of ELLs score at or above proficient, that 5% have been misclassified.

2. The Great Cities reports that ". . . .trend lines suggest that ELLs have not made meaningful progress academically between 2005 and 2011" (p. 100).

   This second "problem" is equally irrelevant. We would not expect ELLs as a group to "improve"; when ELLs make sufficient progress, they are reclassified as non-ELLs. The group average test score should stay about the same.

There are, however, real problems for ELLs:

1. We are not using the best pedagogy—study after study has informed us that comprehension-based methods are far superior to skill-based methods for second language and literacy development, but much instruction remains skill-based. In addition, despite overwhelming evidence, we have not taken advantage of education in the first language, a powerful means of accelerating literacy development and making second language input more comprehensible (Crawford & Krashen, 2007).

2. A large percentage of ELLs live in poverty (Batalova, 2006; Crawford, 1997). Poverty means inadquate diets, inadequate health care, and little access to books; all of these have a devastating effect on school performance. The best teaching in the world will not help if students are hungry, ill, and have no access to reading material.

The Common Core will do nothing to solve these problems, and will do a lot to make things worse. The Common Core language standards are in general hostile to a comprehension approach to language development (Krashen, 2013), and the Common Core approach for ELLs is to force students to deal with demanding and difficult nonfiction texts to promote earlier mastery of "academic language" (Maxwell, 2012).

There is no evidence that making reading harder produces better results, and plenty of evidence that the route to academic language includes a great deal of self-selected, recreational reading, which now is nearly impossible to include in the current version of the Common Core (Krashen, 2013).

For standards to be enforced we must have tests, and the Common Core testing demands are incredible; they will insist on more testing than we have ever seen on this planet. The U.S. Department of Education asserts that we will have testing at all grade levels in all subjects, interim tests, and maybe even pretests in the fall to measure improvement through the academic year (Krashen, 2013). The tests will be administered online, an untested plan that will cost billions. They will demand more and more taxpayer money as computers become obsolete, and as new "advances" in technology are developed (Krashen & Ohanian, 2011), draining money from projects and approaches that would actually help students.

The Common Core, a product of the business world, not professional educators, is such an extreme and misguided proposal that we cannot even discuss implementation. We can only discuss resistance.

4.15 In what ways does educating English language learners/emergent bilinguals entail advocacy by school administrators and educators?

■ *Salvador Gabaldón*

As publicly funded institutions, public schools at times implement policies that are based on political or ideological considerations rather than pedagogical ones. With that understanding, all parents should be prepared to advocate for their children and to protect them from policies, practices, or circumstances they judge to be contrary to their children's best interests. This is particularly true with issues relating to the education of English language learners (ELLs)/emergent bilinguals (EBs); yet the parents of such children face tremendous obstacles that can undermine their ability to advocate appropriately. First, they are often unable to communicate in the language of the school, and securing a district's interpreter services—if and when available—can be a challenge. Secondly, given their unfamiliarity with the U.S. public school system, parents may feel too intimidated to intervene effectively. Finally, whether documented or undocumented, their legal status often precludes them from advocating through the ballot box. Consequently, school administrators and educators have a special responsibility to advocate on their behalf.

The most basic form of advocacy involves promoting the use of effective, research-based instructional strategies in your school and district, and then sharing accurate and positive information with the public about the way ELL programs support student achievement. Misinformation and misunderstanding about such programs can mislead the public into perceiving ELLs/EBs as a problem rather than a resource for their schools. Administrators and teachers should take every opportunity to highlight demonstration projects and artistic performances by these students, underscoring the positive contributions they make to the schools and to the community at large. Schools should regularly invite parents, school board members, the media, local elected officials, and local business and community groups to attend such activities.

One of the central principles behind the Common Core State Standards (CCSS) is that all students must be held to the same high expectations. The theory is that higher expectations for all will lead to higher achievement levels for all. ELLs/EBs will now more frequently engage in the reading, discussion, and production of complex texts, and will be assessed with the same technology-based instruments used for mainstream students. Some proponents of the CCSS expect the new standards to reduce the achievement gap between ELLs and other students. While everyone would agree that it is important to have high expectations for all students, many educators are concerned that having the *same* high expectations for all students may be developmentally inappropriate. Because the new standards were never field-tested, educators must be watchful to see whether the CCSS only widen the achievement gap. They must also be prepared to advocate for professional development that addresses instructional strategies specifically intended to help ELLs meet the heightened expectations. Finally, educators must advocate for ways to monitor, revise, and adjust the standards as needed. This is a crucial task because no mechanism currently exists for implementing any changes to the standards. High expectations alone will not produce academic gains; they must be supported with appropriate resources and institutional flexibility.

What are some specific examples of advocacy efforts that have improved the schooling of ELLs/EBs? Rigid, one-size-fits-all policies relating to the education of ELLs are not a new phenomenon. Since 1998 several states have implemented policies that devalue the native language skills of ELLs. Yet even in the most extreme cases, educators have been able to successfully advocate on behalf of ELLs. In Arizona, for example, teachers in the Tucson Unified School District convinced the governing board to adopt a Native Language Bill of Rights, specifying the rights of ELL students to use their native language in school as they acquire English. In 2012, when the governing board adopted a desegregation plan that gave additional resources to advanced learning experiences (ALEs) classes, such as GATE, advanced placement, and international baccalaureate, teachers successfully advocated for granting ALE status to dual language classes as well.

4.16 In what ways does educating English language learners/emergent bilinguals entail advocacy by scholars and linguists?

■ *Lilia Bartolomé*

The greatest goal of education should be to create social structures based on justice, equity, and equality. Any time language scholars work with, teach about, or study student populations that are underserved by schools and other social institutions, they must resist making a living off these groups without also attempting to advocate on their behalf. Advocacy becomes pivotal in school contexts where native languages are outlawed and ever-increasing numbers of English language learners (ELLs) struggle to meet academic standards and pass standardized tests in a language they have not yet mastered.

For example, in my immigrant parent work I incorporate advocacy when I provide the parents with information to help them understand that schools often unintentionally underserve poor and linguistic minority students, unless parents actively and consistently intervene on their behalf and work to increase their children's chances of academic success. In addition to sharing school district drop-out data as a strategy for awakening them into action, I also introduce parents to mandates such as English-only policy, Common Core State Standards (CCSS) standards, and standardized assessments, and explain how these tools can adversely affect their children. I describe the public outcry, particularly from affluent majority parents and an increasing number of school districts, about the controversial way the CCSS were developed and imposed on public schools to help them understand that they too can protest the "one-size-fits-all" standards and call for challenging yet pedagogically sound and linguistically appropriate schooling for their children.

It is important to note that I do not present the CCSS as a reified construct that must be implemented unquestioningly. The parents I work with quickly comprehend the political aspects of education and schools as an unbalanced system that requires their constant monitoring and involvement to ensure that their children receive as high-quality an education as possible in school. Although most of these parents are economically and politically disempowered and have few influential connections, their optimism and high level of hope never fail to astound and inspire me.

Despite the limits of their English language fluency and prior schooling, I have found these parents to be intelligent and politically pragmatic. While they recognize the importance of national standards and want their children to be proficient in English as quickly as possible, they recognize that the standards and tests are not attuned to their children's current academic progress because many are struggling to achieve basic English proficiency. While parents bemoan their limited ability to help their children with academic and English language assignments, they are quick to learn how to mindfully prepare their children at home despite constraints on their time and economic situations. They also begin to develop plans to work with school educators to better serve their children.

These parents look to me and my staff for assistance, and I eagerly put myself at their service and use my knowledge and networks to get them the information and assistance they want and need. Offering this kind of service requires me to work on behalf of ELLs and their parents whenever possible and by any means necessary, with the goal of moving school personnel to look beyond ELLs' temporary language barriers and to imagine them as the future leaders who Fuentes (1999) describes, "as the young teachers of their own and others; they are the new business people rapidly growing and diversifying U.S. services and production; they are the new doctors and lawyers and architects and biologists and politicians; they are the new singers and actors and dancers and stage directors and painters and musicians enriching U.S. culture with contrast, diversity, and generosity" (p. 15).

DISCUSSION QUESTIONS

After reading this chapter, engage in dialogue with peer educators, including school principals, other administrators and supervisors, teachers of different subjects, specialists in different areas, paraprofessionals, and parents/community members to discuss support systems for ELLs/EBs. Here are some questions to reflect on individually, with a colleague, or ideally, as part of a professional learning community at your school. If you are in a school, the members of this group would comprise the school's ELL/EB leadership team, whose responsibility it is to collectively make the decisions that affect the education of ELLs/EBs.

1. What is the potential for collaborative leadership like that suggested by Hunt and Kleyn (see 4.6b) and described by Gil and Sylvan (see 4.7) to determine how "top-down" policies like NCLB or the CCSS should be implemented in ways that are most beneficial for ELLs/EBs in your school's context? To what extent is the leadership of local schools actually collaborative, drawing on the expertise of ESL and bilingual teachers in making decisions that pertain to ELLs/EBs? If your school leadership is not collaborative, write three steps describing how such collaboration could be fostered.

2. Write a list of all of the school, city, and or state policies in place that affect the instruction of ELLs/EBs in your area. Are there language education policies, such as regulations regarding which educational program(s) should be offered to ELLs/EBs and in what language(s)? Are there assessment policies that influence how ELLs/EBs are taught? If so, add these to your list. Then evaluate to what extent, if any, these policies support the home language practices and cultures of ELLs/EBs. If your evaluation uncovers shortcomings, in what ways can you advocate for the needs of ELLs/EBs (e.g., through partnerships between educators and parents)?

3. A strong theme in the responses in this chapter is that the use of students' home languages in instruction, particularly through bilingual education, does not run counter to the CCSS. Instead, it is made clear that embracing students' home language practices are necessary for ensuring that ELLs/EBs meet the new standards. Locate three examples of this argument in the chapter. Do you agree or disagree with this assertion?

4. De Jong and Gort (see 4.3) argue that "Because the CCSS do not highlight students' home language resources and the role they play in ensuring equal access to quality education, educators who work with EBs must articulate a language policy for their school(s) that explicitly takes a *language-as-resource* orientation." Do you agree or disagree with this statement? Why? What would a language policy look like in your school? Would it embrace a language-as-resource orientation, building on the students' home language practices and their cultures?

TOPICS FOR REFLECTION AND ACTION

The following statements are organized around the big ideas of the chapter. Read through them and indicate the extent to which each applies to your community and your school. After you complete the survey, discuss your responses with your team. Then write down one to three reflection points that have emerged from your discussions. Finally, identify one to three concrete actions that you/your team can take.

DK don't know   1 strongly disagree   2 disagree   3 agree   4 strongly agree

SCHOOL LANGUAGE POLICY						
1. My school or context has a clear and consistent schoolwide language policy in place that all of the administrators, teachers, staff, parents, and children understand and have agreed on, and that they support equally.	DK	1	2	3	4	
2. Key constituents in my school, including ESL and/or bilingual education teachers, parents, and community members, have a strong say in which language(s) will be taught to ELLs/EBs in school and for what purposes.	DK	1	2	3	4	
3. Regardless of the program model(s) in place, the languages and cultures of the emergent bilinguals in my school or context are embraced as positive resources.	DK	1	2	3	4	
4. Regardless of the program model(s) in place, the languages and cultures of the ELLs/EBs in my school or context are embraced as positive resources used in instruction as a daily part of classroom interaction.	DK	1	2	3	4	
5. Regardless of the program model(s) in place, the languages and cultures of the ELLs/EBs in my school or context are nurtured and developed to the greatest extent possible.	DK	1	2	3	4	
6. My school fosters an ecology of multilingualism, wherein the entire range of language practices of *all* children and families are evident in the school's textual landscape (e.g., in signs throughout the school, texts in the library, and classrooms) and in the interactions of all members of the school community.	DK	1	2	3	4	
Knowledge Base						
7. I am familiar with all of the policies that affect the education of ELLs/EBs in my setting.	DK	1	2	3	4	
8. I have a clear understanding about different language education programming options for ELLs/EBs in my school or setting, and about the long-term effects of each program choice on their lifelong language practices and future opportunities.	DK	1	2	3	4	
9. The administrators in my setting have received the prior preparation and support that they need to adopt and implement educational policies and develop programming to best educate ELLs/EBs in my context.	DK	1	2	3	4	
10. The teachers in my setting have received the prior preparation and support that they need to implement educational policies and develop programming to best educate ELLs/EBs in my context.	DK	1	2	3	4	
CCSS Implementation in Schools						
11. My school's language policy and vision for the education of ELLs/EBs anchors us and guides how we implement the CCSS.	DK	1	2	3	4	

SCHOOL LANGUAGE POLICY *cont.*					
12. The curriculum we are using to ensure students attain the CCSS was developed for ELLs/EBs and is appropriate for them.	DK	1	2	3	4
13. The curriculum we are using to ensure students attain the CCSS is available in the languages of the ELLs/EBs in my school.	DK	1	2	3	4
14. The curriculum we are using to ensure students attain the CCSS is consistent with the educational program model(s) we have adopted for ELLs/EBs.	DK	1	2	3	4
15. Leadership in my school or context is collaborative.	DK	1	2	3	4
16. All key constituents (e.g., ESL or bilingual education professionals, parents of ELLs/EBs, community members) had a say in determining how the CCSS would be implemented for EBs in my school or context.	DK	1	2	3	4
17. I feel I have the support I need to implement the CCSS well for the ELLs/EBs with whom I work.	DK	1	2	3	4
18. I see myself as an advocate for ELLs/EBs, keeping their needs at the forefront of my decision making and reaching out to others to ensure they do the same.	DK	1	2	3	4

Reflection:

Action Steps:

Chapter **5**

Teaching and Learning

The relationship between teaching and learning is a complicated process that has been explored by educators and researchers for a long time. As educators, we know we cannot "make" students learn. On the other hand, we know educators' roles in learning are critical. So what is their role? How can we support English language learners' (ELLs')/emergent bilinguals' (EBs') learning in meaningful and relevant ways and create pathways for them toward academic achievement? This chapter has captured the thoughts and experiences of educators from various backgrounds, including administrators and teacher educators, to answer these questions in the context of Common Core State Standards (CCSS).

ELLs/emergent bilinguals are the fastest-growing student group in U.S. schools. Given the increased emphasis on standards and accountability, it is imperative that we provide teachers with the knowledge, skills, and practices needed to help this group participate in meaningful ways in grade-level curricula, while also acquiring the language that supports their participation. Historically, the academic performance of ELLs/EBs has lagged behind that of other subgroups. In 1968, the Bilingual Education Act marked the first time the unique educational needs of ELLs/EBs were formally recognized through the funding of bilingual education programs. In 1974, *Lau v. Nichols* made equitable educational outcomes for ELLs/EBs even more visible within the civil rights agenda by requiring full access to education through specialized supports for language learning, instead of simply using the same curricula and instructional approaches as for monolinguals. Since that time, we have seen legislation for and against bilingual education, learned that home language instruction is a key component of effective education for ELLs/EBs, adopted high standards and accountability requirements, and witnessed the enduring opportunity gap for these students in U.S. schools. The current college- and career-readiness standards do not supplant the No Child Left Behind (NCLB) Act from 2001; instead they sustain the law's requirements that schools show ELLs'/EBs' growth in English language proficiency (ELP) and academic achievement in reading and mathematics. For ELLs/EBs to meet academic achievement expectations, they need to develop language skills and practices. Therefore, they need to be able to understand and express thoughts, ideas, and information orally and in writing across various contexts, including academic contexts that use language in ways specific to a particular context. They also need to demonstrate mastery of subject-area knowledge, skills, and practices (August & Shanahan, 2006).

Chapter 5 has been organized to include discussions of both language and content teaching and learning. The first section examines the language demands of college- and career- readiness standards, such as the CCSS and the Next Generation Science Standards (NGSS). We invited language and content experts to provide a richer understanding of the language practices that schooling demands. The second section discusses literacy and multiliteracy development across content areas. While literacy across content areas is not a new concept, the CCSS have highlighted its importance through the secondary grades.

One of the past pitfalls in the education of ELLs/EBs has been changing the cognitive or the content expectations of the particular grade-level content standards as a way to "differentiate" instruction. However, language differentiation does not require modifying the cognitive expectations or the content; instead, it involves designing the process and language involved in different elements in the environment to allow students to achieve the targeted content and cognitive engagement. This may mean adding supports, encouraging different interactions, and creating a rich environment that supports language processing and use. In the third section, authors discuss how language and literacy are used and developed for disciplinary purposes.

Responses in this chapter consider the role of language in teaching and learning in the CCSS and set the stage for the professional learning for educators who need to align their instruction and assessment to these standards. Authors in this chapter provide valuable information on the language demands of the college- and career-readiness standards, literacy development, and the use of various resources, including bilingual methods, to engage ELLs/EBs meaningfully in learning across the various content areas. However, this chapter only scratches the surface of what can and should be done to help these students experience academic success. We hope these ideas inspire deeper conversations among educators, and even new ideas of their own. Rather than picking strategies or interventions, we hope the reader can think about the larger approaches offered in this chapter and adopt ideologies that can nurture various strategies and open pedagogical possibilities for educators.

Content-Area Language Demands

5.1 What are the language demands for English language arts in the Common Core State Standards?

■ *Diane August and Timothy Shanahan*

Uses and purposes for language in the English language arts (ELA) Common Core State Standards (CCSS). The CCSS require that, beginning with grade 2, students learn to negotiate the linguistic demands of grade-level texts. Past standards emphasized skills alone, but ignored students' levels of linguistic proficiency. Requiring that students read texts in English will be challenging for English language learners (ELLs), partially because they know fewer vocabulary words than native speakers of English. Research indicates that to fully comprehend text the reader must know at least 95% of the words in it (Hirsch, 2003). Additionally, the grammatical complexity of compound and complex sentences pose challenges for students whose first language is not English, and reference chains or cohesive links (such as the use of pronouns and synonyms) can be difficult for English learners to negotiate (Bae, 2001). For example, consider this sentence: "When Mary Lennox was sent to Misselthwaite Manor to live with her uncle, everyone said she was the most disagreeable-looking child ever seen." To comprehend the sentence, ELLs will have to know that "her," "she," and "the most-disagreeable looking child ever seen" refer to Mary.

Challenges and opportunities for ELLs/emergent bilinguals (EBs) participating in CCSS-aligned (English) language arts curriculum and instruction. There are challenges and opportunities for ELLs participating in CCSS-aligned instruction. The opportunity for ELLs is that they are expected to meet the same ELA standards as their English-proficient classmates. This helps ensure that they will receive instruction aimed at developing both their literacy and language proficiency skills and that the skills they are taught are grade-level appropriate. It also means they will be asked to read and think about content and ideas that are consistent with their intellectual abilities. However, the text-complexity demands of the CCSS are likely to mean that many ELLs will be asked to read texts at least two grade levels above their instructional reading levels. To make instruction effective, ELLs will need appropriate scaffolding to allow them to read such texts. Because of the time requirements of such supports, students may be limited in how much text they are able to read. This is a big issue because it is through the wide reading of a comprehensible text that students acquire both the language and content-area knowledge necessary for reading and understanding ever more complex texts. Teachers will need to balance reading opportunities that allow students to engage texts of sufficient difficulty with those that allow them to read more extensively. Another issue is that the CCSS discourage the provision of much background information; students are to determine the meaning of a text through close reading alone. However, many ELLs lack the background knowledge assumed by the authors of the text or that would be needed to make sense of an English text. Teachers will have to balance these needs with the demands of close reading to serve these students effectively.

■ *Lily Wong Fillmore and Rebecca Blum Martinez*

The language demands for Common Core ELA are, or should be, within the reach of native or fluent non-native speakers during each grade or grade band in reading, writing, speaking, listening, and learning, if they are to handle the literacy and learning demands of college and career by the time they have completed grade 12. Language development is far from complete at age 5 or 6. A 5-year-old child is said to have a "mental lexicon" of around 16,000 words on average (Carey, 1978), whereas the average 17-year-old high school student is said to have around 80,000 (Miller & Gildea, 1987)—a fourfold increase over 12 years. To manage that, children would have to learn about 14 new words each day between ages 5 and 17. Even more crucially, they would also have to learn enough about the grammatical workings of academic language to deal with the literacy demands of high school level reading and writing tasks. The only way that students can attain the levels of language and literacy proficiency required for college and the work world is by reading materials that provide access to such skills, level by level.

Built in to the Common Core ELA standards is a "staircase of complexity" and language demands, so that at each grade level students are expected to work with materials that are more demanding in content and language than in those used the year before. We find, for example, in texts offered as exemplars for materials to be used in kindergarten and grade 1, stories written as simple narratives with dialogues between characters:

> Frog was in his garden. Toad came walking by. "What a fine garden you have, Frog," he said. "Yes," said Frog. "It is very nice, but it was hard work." "I wish I had a garden," said Toad. (Lobel, 1971, p. 18)

Such language, while not precisely the same as spoken language, is not greatly different from it, and is therefore an appropriate step up for native speakers of English who are proficient in the spoken registers of the language but not in the written ones they encounter in school.

But what about English learners (ELs)? How appropriate are the Common Core's language demands for students who are not yet fully proficient in the language they are reading, writing, and learning in? Shouldn't the language demands be dialed down and set at students' English proficiency levels rather than at their grade level? How appropriate are materials aligned to the Common Core for ELs?

These are reasonable questions for educators to ask—and yet, as difficult to believe as it might at first seem, the greater language demands of the Common Core ELA are precisely what ELs need if they are to gain the English proficiency required for full literacy development. Consider this: when ELs are provided, year after year, with materials geared to their English proficiency level and are given reading and writing tasks that are different from those their English-proficient classmates are working on, how do they ever gain the advanced literacy skills needed for progress in school? Many, if not most, simply do not (Valdés, 2001). We need only to look at the growing ranks of long-term English learners (LTELs) to see what can happen to ELs after six or more years of instruction based on materials that are said to be aligned to their English proficiency levels (Menken & Kleyn, 2010; Olsen, 2010).

ELLs do require special attention, materials, and instructional treatment in school when they are brand new to English. They need the specialized instructional support of teachers who can help them gain a hand-hold in English by use of specially designed instructional materials that get them beyond the starting point where nothing makes sense. And while individuals vary in how rapidly they learn a new language, all students will make some progress after a year of such support, and are at a different place than they were when they started. But at what point are the students deemed to be far enough along in English to be able to handle the language demands of Common Core–aligned materials and instruction? And how do they get there?

The answer? They need to be working with such materials as soon as possible—not when they achieve an advanced level of English proficiency, as many educators believe—but as soon as they get beyond the earliest stages of proficiency. They do not—or are highly unlikely to—catch up with their age-mates in a Common Core–aligned curriculum if they are not provided early access to grade-level appropriate texts within a year or a year and a half of support in English. ELs would be lost working on such materials, of course, without appropriate and sufficient instructional support from teachers who are ready to work with them on the content and the language. In fact, they can hardly advance beyond the intermediate level without such access and support. The longer students are kept from the materials their age-mates are working with, the further behind they get. The language demands of materials in the early years of school are just an easy step up from spoken language, as we have seen with the excerpt from Lobel's *Frog and Toad*.

But as students progress upward in the grades, the language demands of the texts and tasks they are given rise accordingly. By grades 4–5, students who are fully proficient in English, whether as a native or second language, should be reading stories written in the richly descriptive and figurative resources used by skilled writers of narratives and informational texts that would have been too difficult for them at an earlier age. An excerpt from the prologue to Babbitt's (1975) *Tuck Everlasting* suggests that language demands must rise steeply from year to year to prepare students for a text like this one by grades 4 or 5:

> The first week of August hangs at the very top of summer, the top of the live-long year, like the highest seat of a Ferris wheel when it pauses in its turning. The weeks that come before are only a climb from a balmy spring, and those that follow a drop to the chill of autumn, but the first week of August is motionless, and hot. (Common Core story exemplar for grades 4–5, see Appendix B)

The excerpt describes the story's setting at a particular time of the year, the beginning of August, with changes in temperature just before (a climb from a balmy spring) and after that moment (a drop to the chill of autumn), bracketing the atmosphere of the place when the story begins. The words used in the text are not necessarily difficult or unusual, but to fully appreciate the writer's purpose in so describing the setting, the reader would have to reach beyond the literal meanings of words and phrases and access their figurative meanings, evoking a world in which time, space, and movement are conflated into a singular place where time seems to stand still. The Ferris wheel as a metaphor for time (seasonal changes and cycles) and for life itself (the seasons between birth and death) is evoked in the prologue. The reader is invited to consider the seat at the highest point of the wheel—that fleeting instant when it appears to pause after rising within the curve, and just before it begins to descend on the outer curve. It is illusory, of course. The rotation of the wheel is constant, but the suspended seats swing to remain in a horizontal position as each reaches the apex. The only time a seat can remain at the top for longer than that is when the wheel is stopped for riders to disembark and embark.

But of what benefit are texts like *Tuck Everlasting* to ELs? It's fiction—just a story, after all. Wouldn't a less demanding text—say an adaptation designed for ELs, be better for developing independent reading skills and English? Actually, no. ELs are no different than other students in their need to work with beautifully written texts. They may require more teacher support to get at the writer's intentions, but the benefit they derive from having worked with a beautifully crafted text is the same for them as it would be for anyone else.

What is particularly beneficial for ELs is inclusion in discussions of the use, not just of vocabulary in such materials, but of the imagery evoked by the writer's choices of words, metaphors, and tropes, and of what they signify. These are cultural—they figure in the background knowledge that readers are expected to bring to the act of reading. The ones that figure in literature are mostly learned through reading, but only if the materials make use of such language, and the reader notices and considers their significance in the light of the text at hand.

For example, the Ferris wheel is a frequently used trope in story and poetry, and indeed in discussions of life in general, at least in 20th-century American culture. It is probably unfamiliar to many young readers, or they may not know what it is called. In this regard, ELs are not so different from some of their classmates. Readers who have read this story and been invited to think about the use and meaning of the metaphor in this excerpt will have gained a bit of background knowledge that might be useful when reading another text in which a wheel, Ferris or otherwise, figures and does not refer to an actual wheel. All readers need to learn when the language used in a text is to be understood more or less literally, and when it is being used to enlist the reader to relate their knowledge and experience of one conceptual domain (seasonal changes in a calendric cycle) to another domain (changes over the course of the life cycle). Experiences in dealing with language that evokes sensory, emotional, and conceptual frames of reference (as in *Tuck Everlasting*) are necessary for getting ELs to full proficiency in English. They will not get as much out of it as will students who are fully proficient in English, but they will learn a lot more than they would working with simplified texts that provide none of the challenges or opportunities that this one does.

What they learn is that difficult material, with a little extra effort and some help from teachers, is within their reach. ELs who are given only materials that they can read by themselves with little effort or help sometimes become complacent, and come to believe that they are competent enough in English and with their reading skills. They seldom realize that the super-simplified materials they have been getting in school are pitched at a considerably lower level than they should be, given their age and grade level. It comes as a surprise when they are eventually mainstreamed that they are not as capable of making sense of things as they had been led to believe.

The question of language demand in language arts materials must also be considered when children are in dual language or bilingual programs. For ELs fortunate enough to be in such a program, literacy development can progress in the primary language, unhindered or slowed down by the need to learn the language from scratch, as is the case in English. But here too, care must be taken in selecting materials with attention to their potential for stimulating language development. Just because students are native speakers of a language does not mean they are "home free" in that language, as argued previously. For ELs who are fortunate enough to be in bilingual or dual language programs where literacy development is fostered in both languages, reading materials can, and should be, selected for clarity, effective communication of ideas and information, and the beautiful use of language that can inspire young students to read more.

An example of such writing can be seen in *El cuento-historia de los gatos,* a historical novelette written for young readers by Agustín Cadena. The story is about a band of cats living in Mexico City during the 1910 revolution. In the following excerpt, the cat's ability to see in the dark is contrasted with the human's difficulty to see without light:

> Ciertamente lo que para el ojo humano resulta un abismo insondable de color negro, para el gato es una luminosidad encarnada que envuelve las cosas como un agua roja en una ciudad sumergida. Y los seres que pueblan esto que nosotros llamamos oscuridad, abandonando sus colore diurnos, se convierten en figuras líquidas e irradiantes.

To understand the information contained in complex texts such as this one, students must be able to track the information that is presented in complex sentences and follow the connections that are made between sentences and paragraphs. This requires that students pay attention to the ways in which information is presented—the structures used, the words and phrases that alert the reader to changes, and the cohesive devices that allow a text to hang together. As Annette Maestas, a teacher in the Albuquerque Public Schools, tells her students, "You have to become language detectives."

And, although vocabulary is a necessary aspect of learning and using more sophisticated language in more complex texts, secondary and tertiary meanings and suffixes and prefixes that can be used to fit one's needs is critical, as in the case of *insondable* and *luminosidad encarnada.* Here, too, students need support from teachers to handle the language demand of a text like this one. How might a teacher such as Maestas work with such a text? She would select a couple of sentences to go over with the students each day as were the two sentences frow the preceding extract.

These two lovely sentences were chosen for their complexity and their beauty, and as an example of the kinds of language demands that the CCSS place on bilingual students. In this text, students must be able to connect the comparisons made in previous sentences about the vision of humans and cats to the sentences presented here. By introducing the first sentence with "*ciertamente*" (certainly), the author is affirming the differences between human and feline vision. But this only makes sense in light of the previous comparisons. *Lo que,* the compound relative pronoun introducing the first clause is another link to previous sentences and refers to the cats' ability to see in the dark, described before. The frame "*lo que para x. . .para x. . .*" allows the author to compare "*el ojo humano*" (human vision) in the first clause to that of cats, "*para el gato*" in the next clause. This kind of construction is one that students will encounter frequently in other texts and in other genres. Pointing out these kinds of constructions to students allows them to notice the ways in which comparisons can be made by others, and by themselves. Moreover, by placing *lo que* at the beginning of the sentence, the "unfathomable black abyss" of human vision is fronted so that the end focus of the sentence, and what remains in the mind of the reader, is on the beautiful description of how cats see the world; "a ruby afterglow surrounding everything like the red water of a submerged city."

■ *George Bunch*

The CCSS in ELA and disciplinary literacy call for all students, including ELLs/EBs, to read and analyze complex texts, to construct oral and written arguments using evidence, to collaborate with others in discussing and debating ideas, and to demonstrate their ability to craft language to accomplish all of the above. The language demands facing students in the process of developing English as an additional language are particularly salient (Bunch, Kibler, & Pimentel, 2012):

- The standards call on students to *read and comprehend literature and informational texts of increasing complexity*. This requires ELLs to process "intricate, complicated, and often obscure linguistic and cultural features accurately while trying to comprehend content, and while remaining distant from it to assess the content's value and accuracy" (Bernhardt, 2011, p. 19).
- To meet the standards, students must *write different text types* (arguments, informative and explanatory reports, narratives)—*and to use writing to synthesize knowledge gained through research*. This requires ELLs to use their developing proficiency in English, reading skills, and knowledge of writing conventions to articulate questions, seek evidence, evaluate claims, advance their own arguments, and "craft" language for different audiences and purposes to communicate all of the above.
- Through *engaging in speaking and listening*, the standards require students to work collaboratively, to understand multiple perspectives, and to present ideas. To do so, ELLs must use their developing oral English comprehension and production abilities to engage with the ideas of others, demonstrate their understanding, and articulate their own arguments—both in ongoing interactions with peers and teachers and in more formal presentations.
- To engage in the practices just outlined, students are called on by the standards to *draw on conventions of standard English as well as to "appreciate that language is at least as much a matter of craft as of rules"* (CCSS ELA standards, p. 25). Meeting the standards requires students to choose language and conventions to achieve particular functions and rhetorical effects and to develop grammatical structures, vocabulary, and written and oral conventions for use as meaning-making resources.

Of course, with challenges come opportunities. Instruction must be designed to support all students in meeting these challenges, rather than attempting to shield ELLs from them (Bunch, Kibler, & Pimentel, 2012; Kibler, Walqui, & Bunch, 2014). In envisioning, enacting, and evaluating support for ELLs, whether in mainstream settings or in interventions designed specifically for ELLs, what is the extent to which instruction for ELLs includes opportunities for them to engage in the previously discussed practices? Rather than separating ELLs from opportunities to participate in these practices until they are deemed to have achieved a particular level of control of discrete features of English, scaffolding can allow ELLs with imperfect, still-developing English language proficiency to begin to participate meaningfully in the practices called for by the standards, providing opportunities for language and literacy development in the process.

This is *not* to argue for a "sink or swim" approach, whereby ELLs are asked to engage in these practices without support. To apprentice ELLs into the language, literacy, and disciplinary practices called for by the new standards, instruction must (1) capitalize on students' existing resources, including home language and literacy practices, developing proficiency in English, and background knowledge, interests, and motivations (Brisk & Proctor, 2012); and (2) embed scaffolding that is carefully conceived, planned, and enacted (Schleppegrell & O'Halloran, 2011; Walqui, 2006; Walqui & van Lier, 2010). A publicly available ELA unit (Walqui, Koelsch, & Schmida, 2012) developed by the *Understanding Language* initiative and videos from its piloting (Chope, 2013) demonstrate how affordances for language and literacy development, including attention to language forms and conventions, can be embedded through apprenticeship into the kinds of practices called for by the new standards. This approach stands in contrast to traditional notions of language instruction that see teaching linguistic forms and features as prerequisites to—and disembodied from—the central practices called for by the standards (Valdés, Kibler, & Walqui, 2014).

We don't have time to wait to educate an entire generation of ELLs until their English proficiency is deemed "ready" to begin to engage in core disciplinary practices. Negotiating meaning, interacting with others, reading and writing challenging and meaningful texts, and engaging in the other practices the standards demand are precisely the conditions, *with support*, under which ELLs will develop the language and literacy necessary to meet increasingly demanding standards in ELA and across the curriculum.

5.2 What are the language demands of the Common Core State Standards for mathematics?

■ *Judit Moschkovich*

The Common Core State Standards for Mathematics (CCSSM; National Governors Association Center for Best Practices & Council of Chief State School Officers, 2010) call for a shift in teaching mathematics. In particular, the eight standards for mathematical practice described in the CCSS require that students actively engage in mathematical practices such as reasoning abstractly, constructing arguments, and attending to precision (National Governors' Association Center for Best Practices, 2010). This new emphasis on mathematical practices places language demands on students; opportunities to participate in those eight mathematical practices involve language in multiple ways. Students will need to learn not only how to think and reason mathematically but also to use language (and other symbol systems) to communicate—talk, listen, read, and write—about mathematics. Instruction as envisioned in the CCSS is expected to provide students opportunities to communicate about mathematical ideas as they engage in these mathematical practices. Students will need to learn to use multiple representations (not only numbers but also pictures, diagrams, charts, models, etc.) and participate in mathematical discussions (in a variety of structures, including teacher-led, whole class, small group, pairs, and student presentations).

Before focusing on language demands, it is important to first align mathematics instruction with the CCSS and current research on effective mathematics teaching. First and foremost, mathematics instruction aligned with the CCSS means teaching mathematics for understanding (Hiebert & Grouws, 2007) and keeping tasks at a high cognitive demand (American Educational Research Association, 2006). When the focus is on understanding, students actively use and connect multiple representations, develop meaning for symbols, and have opportunities to share and refine their explanations, conjectures, reasoning, justifications, and arguments. These research-based recommendations and the new emphasis in the CCSS on mathematical practices require that teachers include mathematical discussions in their lessons—discussions that involve mathematical objects, focus on mathematical content, and are aimed at a mathematical point. Teachers need to provide opportunities for students to construct, share, discuss, and refine their mathematical ideas, solutions to problems, reasoning, conjectures, explanations, and arguments. Student participation in mathematical discussions is important for all students, and *essential* for English language learners (ELLs) to learn both content and language. Instruction aligned with the CCSS should thus include student participation in mathematical discussions (for five ways of orchestrating such discussions, see Smith & Stein, 2011).

One strategy that teachers can use to engage students in standards-based math practices and support mathematical discussions is to build on student language resources during mathematical discussions to support ELLs in meeting the language demands of the CCSS. How can teachers build on students' language resources in ways that help ELLs meet the demands of the CCSS? Teachers can build on these language resources in multiple ways. In particular, teachers can build on student resources and focus on three of the CCSS mathematical practices (MP): reasoning abstractly and quantitatively (MP #2), constructing viable arguments and critiquing the reasoning of others (MP #3), and attending to precision (MP #6). Recommended strategies include revoicing student contributions using more formal ways of talking (Chapin, O'Connor, & Anderson, 2003; Moschkovich, 1999), asking for clarification (Moschkovich, 1999), and probing a student's thinking (Herbel-Eisenmann, Steele, & Cirillo, 2013).

Teachers may wonder, however, if ELLs/emergent bilinguals (EBs) can participate in mathematical discussions before they learn English. Yes, they can. Research has provided examples of classrooms where students who are learning English or are EBs participate in mathematical discussions (e.g., Khisty, 1995; Khisty & Chval, 2002; Moschkovich, 1999, 2007, 2011). This research has also provided examples that examine the *language resources* these students bring to mathematics discussions and how ELLs express mathematical ideas in emerging—and sometimes imperfect—language, instead of focusing on challenges. ELL students use a variety of language resources to communicate mathematical ideas: their first language; everyday language; and mathematical practices, gestures, and objects (Moschkovich, 2011).

A second strategy teachers can use is to consider the full spectrum of academic mathematical language when designing lessons. We can all agree that mathematics instruction for ELLs needs to provide students opportunities to develop and use academic language in mathematics, or mathematical discourse. It is almost common sense that "mathematical discourse," "academic language," and "language resources" are important for ELLs. However, these phrases can have many meanings and some interpretations mislead us to reduce the complexity of language. For example, we could imagine that these three phrases refer principally to vocabulary. Although learning the multiple meanings of words is important, mathematical discourse involves much more than using individual words, phrases, or technical vocabulary. Mathematical discourse also involves multiple representations (e.g., objects, pictures, words, symbols, tables, graphs), modes (e.g., oral, written, receptive, expressive), types of written and oral texts (e.g., textbooks, word problems, student explanations, teacher explanations), kinds of talk (e.g., exploratory and expository), and audiences (e.g., presentations to teacher, to peers, by teacher, by peers) (Moschkovich, 2013). When designing mathematics instruction that supports mathematical discussions and builds on student language resources, it is crucial to go beyond words and vocabulary and, instead, support students in engaging in the full spectrum of academic communication in mathematics.

5.3 What are the language demands for science in the Next Generation Science Standards? How do they relate to the literacy standards for science in the Common Core State Standards?

- *Okhee Lee and Lorena Llosa*

The Next Generation Science Standards (NGSS) offer a vision of science learning and teaching that seamlessly blends science and engineering practices, crosscutting concepts, and disciplinary core ideas to form a portrait of comprehensive science knowledge. The eight science and engineering practices are as follows:

1. Ask questions (for science) and define problems (for engineering)
2. Develop and use models
3. Plan and carry out investigations
4. Analyze and interpret data
5. Use mathematics and computational thinking

6. Construct explanations (for science) and design solutions (for engineering)
7. Engage in argument from evidence
8. Obtain, evaluate, and communicate information

These science and engineering practices are language intensive and require students to engage in classroom science discourse. For example, students must read and write, as well as view and represent visually, as they develop their models and explanations. They must speak and listen as they present their ideas or make reasoned arguments based on evidence. Science and engineering practices offer rich opportunities and demands for language learning at the same time as they promote science learning. Hence, these practices merit special attention in science classrooms that include English language learners (ELLs).

The literacy demands for science in the Common Core State Standards (CCSS) directly align with the NGSS in three major ways. First, both the CCSS and NGSS make explicit connections between English language arts (ELA)/literacy and science. The CCSS address science literacy in terms of reading, writing, listening, speaking, and language. The CCSS focus on literacy in content areas is a departure from traditional standards for ELA, reading, and writing. In a similar manner, the NGSS make direct connections to the CCSS (see NGSS Appendix M, Connections to CCSS-Literacy in Science and Technical Subjects). Second, the CCSS and NGSS share a common emphasis on disciplinary practices and classroom discourse. For example, the CCSS highlight that students "comprehend as well as critique" and "value evidence" (p. 7). The NGSS also highlight that students "engage in argument from evidence (science and engineering practice 7)." This focus on argument from evidence is also highlighted in the CCSS for mathematics. Finally, the CCSS and NGSS share a common emphasis on language, including language functions (e.g., explanation, argument) and text complexity, in addition to vocabulary and conventions.

As the CCSS and NGSS, or indeed any academically rigorous approach, are language intensive, science teachers need to recognize and meet increased language demands while capitalizing on language learning opportunities for all students, especially ELLs/emergent bilinguals. An important role of science teachers is to encourage and support language use and development in the service of making sense of science. When supported appropriately, most ELLs are capable of learning subjects such as science through their emerging language and of comprehending and communicating sophisticated language functions using less-than-perfect English. They *can do* a number of things using whatever level of English they have and can participate in science and engineering practices. By engaging in such practices, moreover, they grow in both science knowledge and language proficiency (i.e., capacity to do more with language). Through the CCSS and NGSS, teachers and students engage in "doing" science and engineering and "using" language during their interactions.

5.4 What are the language demands for social studies in the Common Core State Standards?

■ *Robin Liten-Tejada*

While Virginia has not adopted the Common Core, we have our own demanding Standards of Learning (SOL), with similar challenges for English language learners (ELLs). In Arlington Public Schools, we recognize the importance of explicitly teaching our ELLs the academic language necessary to comprehend and communicate content knowledge required by the SOL.

Content standards indicate the knowledge students will be able to demonstrate, but educators of ELLs also need to determine what vocabulary and language structures students will utilize to communicate that knowledge, and to incorporate practice in those structures within their lessons. For example, analyzing and explaining cause and effect is a common academic task in social studies. After reading a text, a typical classroom activity would be to list the causes and corresponding results in a chart; however that does not ensure that students can actually communicate the relationships using appropriate academic vocabulary and syntax. Following that cause-and-effect chart, a variety of scaffolds and structured language activities will help students comprehend and communicate those relationships, such as the use of colors to visually denote relationships in a sentence, sentence frames, manipulatives, and moving from oral language to written language, as students develop the ability to communicate an academic message.

A method that I have found particularly effective for teaching students how to analyze and communicate cause and effect (as well as other language structures) is the following:

- I make colored sentence strips of the causes and effects from the lesson, using two different colors, such as red for the cause and blue for the effect. I cut up commas, periods, and pronouns that may be needed, along with the appropriate signal words. (See the following figure and imagine the different colors.)
- I share with students the academic vocabulary, that is, the signal words we use to describe cause/effect relationships—because, since, so, therefore, as a result, consequently, thus.
- I present a simple cause/effect sentence to analyze how the sentences are formed (focus on syntax), including the punctuation. We then review how the sentences are constructed using frames.

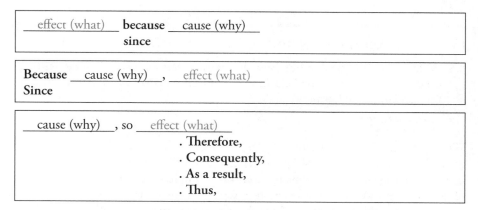

- I then give student partners a packet of the cut-up causes and results from the lesson. They work together to match up the appropriate cause/effect pairs, and then insert the various signal words and punctuation while reading the resulting sentences aloud with their partners.
- After the oral practice, students individually write the variety of cause/effect sentences that they formed.
- From there, we expand to the discourse level where students work on an essay describing the causes and results of the topic at hand. At this point, we would reinforce the key aspects of essay writing to include an introduction with a thesis statement, supporting details and evidence using the sentence structures we just practiced, and a conclusion.

With this lesson, students have experienced firsthand how language is used in describing cause-and-effect relationships. They will then have the tools to identify causes and results in further readings. As a follow up, students should be asked to identify the signal words in other texts and to highlight the causes and results in separate colors, comparing and justifying their thoughts with a partner.

This lesson provides one strategy for integrating content instruction with language development while moving ELLs from the vocabulary level, to syntax, to discourse in building academic language proficiency (Zwiers, 2008). Without a structured language practice like this that incorporates an explicit focus on key vocabulary and syntax, hands-on experience in manipulating the language, and oral language development, ELLs will struggle to acquire and express the knowledge demanded by challenging standards.

Content-Area Literacy and Multiliteracy Development

5.5 What is the relationship between literacy and language development? How do different views of this relationship influence instructional approaches for English language learners?

■ *Mariana Castro*

When planning for the education of English language learners (ELLs), their educators are faced with the decision of how to approach literacy instruction. Some educators include language and literacy instruction within English language arts (ELA). Others place language and literacy instruction in separate content areas (e.g., ELA and structured English immersion [SEI], English language development [ELD], English as a second language [ESL]). However, regardless of programming, most educators have a tough time differentiating between language and literacy instruction. One of the reasons for this difficulty is that the two areas are interrelated. Language, for instance, may be strictly thought of as the vehicle to mediate learning and to communicate ideas, concepts, and information, a view that permeates school life. However, while language is used in mathematics, science, social studies, and other academic areas in school, in language arts, it is not only used; it is also part of the content being learned. In the same way, literacy—being able to read and interact with text—is also critical across content areas, as well as the subject of study in language arts.

The definition of literacy has also evolved over the last few decades to include the set of practices that students need to participate meaningfully in local and global economies and cultures, thus broadening the definition of text. Instead of literacy, some scholars recognize multiple literacies (Street, 1995). College- and career-readiness standards, like the Common Core State Standards (CCSS), take these perspectives into account and have set expectations for literacy across content areas. While views of literacy that focus on reading emphasize the development of phonemic awareness, phonics, fluency, guided oral reading, vocabulary knowledge, and reading development (National Reading Panel, 2000), the CCSS move the scope of ELA from an emphasis on skills toward a focus on the practices needed to interact with the text and the world. When literacy views included only an emphasis on skills, it was easier for educators to see the difference between reading and having the language to understand the text. However, with the expansion of scope in literacy instruction and the ideology behind multiple literacies, it has become harder to differentiate what constitutes language and what constitutes literacy. While this is an interesting and challenging debate for scholars, for educators it constitutes an increased challenge in deciding how to meet the needs of ELLs.

Instructionally, we know that teaching phonics like "cat, fat, sat" to ELLs is useless if they do not know what "cat," "fat," or "sat" means. We also know that teaching language outside of a context is less effective than in meaningful contexts (Brown, 2007; García, 2005; García & Hamayan, 2006; Halliday & Hasan, 1989). Rather than teaching lists of words and grammatical structures, addressing language instruction while teaching children how to read text and connect it to themselves and the world is a way to teach language explicitly, while retaining a context in which to teach it.

5.6 How does the perspective on initial literacy found in the Common Core State Standards differ from previous views?

■ *Diane August and Timothy Shanahan*

The Common Core State Standards (CCSS) continue to emphasize the dual importance of both foundational skills and language/comprehension learning in beginning literacy development. Research demonstrates that young children must develop phonological awareness, knowledge of the alphabet, concepts of print, and phonics and oral reading fluency skills (National Early Literacy Panel, 2008; National Institute of Child Health and Human Development, 2000). It also shows that ongoing reading comprehension growth depends on students' early oral language development (National Early Literacy Panel, 2008). Accordingly the CCSS establish learning goals in each of these skills in reading, writing, speaking, listening, and language. Research shows that these skills are equally important in the literacy development of English language learners (ELLs) (August & Shanahan, 2006).

While the perspectives on preliteracy and early literacy development embodied by the CCSS do not differ substantially from previous views on the early goals of literacy development, it is important to remember that the CCSS only establish learning goals, they do not dictate the instructional methods or approaches to be used to teach early literacy. Research indicates that explicit phonological awareness, phonics, and oral reading fluency instruction, shared-reading interventions, and explicit efforts to teach language are the most effective methods for developing these skills in young children (National Early Literacy Panel, 2008; National Institute of Child Health and Human Development, 2000). These same methods are effective for ELLs but need to take into consideration the skills and knowledge ELLs have acquired in their home language. Knowledge and skills acquired in students' home languages can transfer to English (Dressler & Kamil, 2006). High-quality programming that uses students' home languages as well as English is as effective—or more effective—than programs that use only English to teach literacy (Francis, Lesaux, & August, 2006). Additionally, to be most effective, content delivered in English should be scaffolded to ensure it is comprehensible to ELLs (August & Shanahan, 2006). Both parents and teachers can play an important role in supporting and teaching early literacy and language skills. Parents of ELLs should be encouraged to provide support in their home languages and in English, if they are English proficient.

5.7 How does the perspective on literacy in the elementary and secondary grades in the English language arts standards differ from previous views?

■ *Carole Edelsky*

Beginning around 1970, some U.S. schools (and many more in Canada and the United Kingdom) offered English language arts (ELA) instruction that fit the view of language (oral and written) as learned through use with others who show you how it works and what it's for. Students read real books, both fiction and nonfiction. They wrote for a wide range of purposes. They received help to improve as readers and writers in reading/writing workshops. Teachers in those schools formed a grassroots effort to pass their teaching methods on to other educators.

But a corporate-backed conservative backlash extinguished this effort and took us back to teaching the language arts as a list of out-of-context skills. In this backward-for-the-future move, culminating most recently in the Common Core State Standards (CCSS), what gets taught has little to do with how people read and write in real life (Bozakis, Burns, & Hall, 2014). The ELA standards in the Common Core view literacy as a set of separate skills (e.g., seeing phonetic analysis as separate from comprehension) to be learned—even used—in linear order (e.g., "getting" the sounds, then the words, and, finally, the sentence) and detached from sociocultural contexts.

In such a situation, how do we support English language learners (ELLs)/emergent bilinguals (EBs)? Here are four places to start:

1. Remember that if authentic literacy is the desired end, it must also be the means. Students should do what readers and writers do in the world. Writers don't write from a prompt. Readers don't read to answer questions at the end of a chapter. Kids in school need to read. For real. A lot. Yes, students need coaching. But more than anything, they need to be doing the real thing. If they rarely read—for real—it is hard for them to learn to read. What encourages reading? Opportunities to self-select what to read simply for one's own purposes, and time to do the reading. Class time filled with reading exercises deprives kids of time to read (and therefore time to learn to read) (Krashen, 2013).
2. Plan for inquiry. Inquiry encourages engagement, and engagement itself—intellectual and social—supports learning for ELLs. Inquiry projects are characterized by first-hand investigation of compelling issues, collaboration with peers, and help from teachers on how to gather and analyze data and present results to relevant audiences (e.g., especially outside school audiences, thus creating greater urgency to use conventional spelling). Students of all ages can do inquiry projects on any topic, including language. (Who switches from Spanish to English? When? What devices do different people use to switch topics? What "rules" about writing are violated in published works?)
3. Tryouts promote growth without pressure. Trying out multiple beginnings in a written draft or trying different authors' ways of using two languages in a story for various effects—just to experiment, not to get a grade—is a meaningful way to pay atten-

tion to how certain grammatical forms produce different effects. Drama—students enacting other students' stories, role plays, readers' theater, shadow plays—lets students try out another character's voice and thus helps reduce the fear of betraying self or culture (e.g., it's OK to try out sounding "standard" and possibly pretentious when it's only "an act").

4. Bringing students' lives into the curriculum helps those whose communities, traditions, and languages are often invisible in school. Learning demands predicting and understanding (Smith, 1975), and cultural and linguistic familiarity makes it easier to predict and understand. Linking students' lives to curriculum includes using neighborhoods as "laboratories"; teaching reading in the dominant language; reading and writing the community's own texts; and asking students to explicitly discuss how a textbook chapter, news article, test item, school assignment, or school board policy connects (or doesn't) with their lives.

In other words, support for ELLs in all grades means giving them the richest, most meaningful, most authentic educational experiences possible.

5.8 How can grades 6–12 language arts teachers support literacy development in history/social studies, science, and technical subjects for English language learners/emergent bilinguals?

■ *Michael F. Graves*

Scaffolding English Language Learners' Comprehension of Text

With the Common Core State Standards' (CCSS) emphasis on the use of challenging text for all students, including English language learners (ELLs), it becomes increasingly important for all content teachers to have tools that fully prepare their ELLs to read the assigned texts. The most comprehensive, versatile, and easily implemented tool for fostering comprehension of individual texts that I have worked with is the scaffolded reading experience (SRE). The SRE approach is grounded in the concept of scaffolding—providing learners with temporary support that allows them to complete a task that they could not complete independently—and in the belief that every reading experience should be one in which the reader comprehends the text, has a positive reading experience, and is successful in understanding and learning from the text. The SRE framework presents teachers with a set of prereading, during reading, and postreading options from which they select those activities that will lead a particular group of students to success with a particular text. A model of the framework is shown in the following figure. A list of possible prereading, during reading, and postreading activities follows the figure.

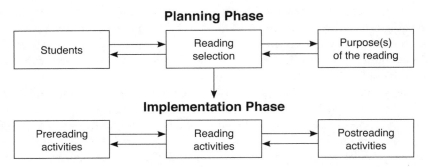

Two phases of a scaffolded reading experience.

Possible Components of a Scaffolded Reading Experience

Prereading Activities

Motivating
Activating or building background knowledge
Providing text-specific knowledge
Relating the reading to students' lives
Preteaching vocabulary
Preteaching concepts
Prequestioning, predicting, and direction setting
Suggesting strategies
Using students' native languages
Engaging students, families, and the community as resources

Reading Activities

Silent reading
Reading to students
Supported reading
Oral reading by students
Modifying the text
Using students' native languages
Engaging students, families, and the community as resources

Postreading Activities

Questioning
Discussion
Building connections
Writing
Drama
Artistic, graphic, and nonverbal activities
Application and outreach activities

Using students' native languages
Engaging students, families, and the community as resources

As shown in the figure, the teacher begins by considering the students who will be reading the text, the text itself, and what the reader is expected to gain from the reading. Based on these three factors, he or she creates a set of prereading, during reading, and postreading activities that will help this group of readers succeed with this text. Importantly, the goal is neither to use as few activities as possible nor as many activities as possible. Instead, the goal is to create and use just those activities that will ensure this particular group of students achieves the goals for the reading.

Suppose, for example, that a group of intermediate level ELLs are about to read the first chapter in Freedman's *Eleanor Roosevelt*, a biography written for middle grade students. The SRE for this chapter might include the following activities.

Prereading

Motivating—perhaps stressing that Roosevelt was one of the most amazing and influential women in U.S. politics
Building background knowledge—about Eleanor Roosevelt and the times she lived through
Vocabulary—both content-specific academic vocabulary and general academic vocabulary

During Reading

Reading to students—The teacher reads the first two pages aloud to the class.
Supported reading—Students are given a series of questions to answer in pairs as they read the chapter.

Postreading

Questioning—Pairs form groups of four and reach consensus on responses to the during-reading questions.
Discussion—The class as a whole discusses both the during reading questions and other questions the teacher or the class bring up.
Building connections—The teacher situates Eleanor Roosevelt and her life in the broader context of 20th-century U.S. history.

Of course, this is only one of myriad possibilities for an SRE. With other students, other texts, or other purposes, an SRE would be very different. Also, while the SRE approach is a simple and straightforward one, this has been a very brief introduction to the procedure. See Fitzgerald and Graves (2004, 2005), Graves and Fitzgerald (2009), and Graves and Graves (2003) for a much fuller explanation of SREs, many sample activities, and some complete SREs.

5.9 How can bilingual curriculum and instruction support emergent bilingual students' content, language, and literacy learning relative to the Common Core State Standards?

■ *Kathy Escamilla, Susan Hopewell, and Sandra Butvilofsky*

Historically, effective bilingual instruction for emergent bilingual (EB) learners (no matter the program type) has included well-defined language allocations. In fact, bilingual programming is often defined by the amount of time allocated to the use of a language other than English (LOTE) for instructional purposes. Consider, for example, how dual language programs use language proportions to describe themselves (e.g., 90:10; 50:50). Research is definitive that student outcomes in English, especially in reading, are greater when students have access to well-defined bilingual curriculum and language support that capitalizes on all of the linguistic resources of the students (August & Shanahan, 2006). Simply allocating a percentage of time to one language or the other, however, is not enough.

For the past decade, we have developed and tested a Spanish–English biliteracy model in which the literacy block is conceptualized holistically, beginning in kindergarten. What takes place in one language is directly and explicitly connected to what happens in the other. Students are held accountable to use what they know and can do in one language while developing language and literacy in the other. The following figure illustrates this holistic framework.

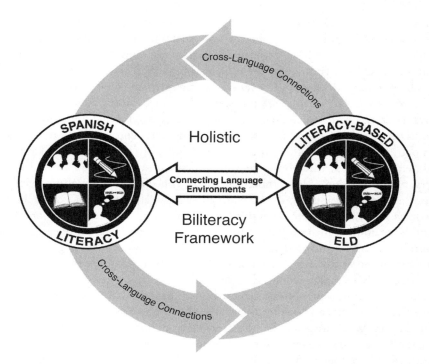

Holistic biliteracy framework. (Reprinted with permission from Escamilla, K., Hopewell, S., Butvilofsky, S., Sparrow, W., Soltero-González, L., Ruiz-Figueroa, O., & Escamilla, M. [2014]. *Biliteracy from the start: Literacy Squared in action.* Philadelphia: Caslon. © Caslon, Inc.)

Within the holistic biliteracy framework, time is allocated to the development of reading, writing, oracy, and metalanguage in both Spanish and English. Language environments are connected through shared exploration of themes, genres, comprehension strategies, oracy structures, bilingual texts, and so forth. Students' metalinguistic awareness is developed as teachers help them to critically examine oral and written texts within and across languages.

A commitment to holistic planning and assessment rejects the reductionist idea that parallel monolingualism results in greater language and literacy outcomes. In fact, within our model, even though the majority of students are simultaneous bilinguals, we find that their proficiency in Spanish literacy often surpasses their English literacy proficiency. Therefore, we ask teachers to choose English language reading texts based on students' Spanish language reading scores. Underlying this guideline is the theoretical supposition that the Spanish language score is likely more indicative of the reading skills and behaviors a student has mastered, while the English language reading score is more indicative of language proficiency levels. Using Spanish language outcomes to inform English literacy instruction results in students' earlier exposure to more complex and rigorous texts. A decade of data collection confirms that holistic planning and assessment accelerates English language literacy while maintaining Spanish language literacy.

One strategy that we have found to be particularly powerful in creating holistic connections across environments for students in grades 3 and up is called *así se dice* (that's how you say it). At first glance it seems extremely simple; yet, when strategically integrated into literacy instruction, purposefully planned, and structured to be collaborative, *así se dice* results in students gaining great insights into the similarities and differences between Spanish and English. *Así se dice* asks students to engage in translating from one language to the other for the express purpose of thinking and talking about the intersection of culture and language. Students quickly become astute language observers who develop a deep understanding of concepts, a thorough knowledge of culture, a precise use of vocabulary, a willingness to collaborate and negotiate, and the knowledge of how and when to consult outside references. The richness of *así se dice* is not in the creation of the translation, but in the discussion in which students are asked to justify and defend their language choices. We have seen students argue adamantly over whether the words "told," "commanded," or "demanded" were more appropriate. Sometimes, it is a simple sentence that can lead to the most sophisticated discussions. Consider, for example, the common translation of the idiom "*Caras vemos, corazones no sabemos*" as "Don't judge a book by its cover." At first glance, this seems like a reasonable interpretation. When we share that the deeper cultural meaning in Spanish is negative while the English idiom implies something positive, however, it becomes inadequate. In a search to keep the meaning, groups often land on more nuanced translations such as "wolf in sheep's clothing" or "All that glitters isn't gold." (For more on *así se dice* see Escamilla et al., 2014). Again, the power is in the discussion, the creation of the argument, and the ability to justify choices—all skills important in the Common Core State Standards (CCSS).

■ *Kate Seltzer and Susana Ibarra Johnson*

Sailing a ship toward its destination requires tacking either windward, crosswind, downwind, or directly into the upwind, resulting in a course that appears to be a zig-zag pattern. Like a ship captain's, a bilingual teacher's compass always points north—toward the goal of biliteracy. However, along the journey are important targets like standards, teaching and learning goals, and the development of language and literacy for academic purposes. These targets require educators to "zig zag," making decisions that help students grow and find success. For example, when Sandra, a grade 3 two-way bilingual teacher, began to teach from her thematic unit on understanding connections among U.S. historical events and people (New Mexico Public Education Department, 2009), she began by reading the book *Pink y Say* (Polacco, 1994). The goal of the activity—literature circles—was to describe the characters in the story (National Governors' Association for Best Practices 2010, ELA-Literacy.RL.3.3). Sandra knew that her students would have many connections to the story and the history, but would need to use *both* Spanish and English to describe and expand on those connections. Thus, much like a sailor might adjust to a change in the wind, when a student departed from the text Sandra adjusted and created a teachable moment. The adjustment resulted in a connection to the present and created a deeper understanding of the conditions during Lincoln's presidency, a topic explored within the unit:

Teacher (T): What do you think about the story *Pink y Say* that took place during the Civil War?

Student 1 (S1): The best part was when Pink told Say to touch him *porque el toco a* Abraham Lincoln.

T: Why?

S1: Because Abraham Lincoln *era muy popular cuando él era* president. Like Obama right now, *verdad*. The president is popular.

T: Well, it all depends. Do you think Abraham Lincoln *era popular* with all Americans? What about those living in the south?

S2: Well, the textbook said that he was one of the greatest presidents and especially liked by *nuestra gente*.

T: *Bueno*, Lincoln won the 1860 election with 39% percent of the popular vote—the lowest in history—and took office with seven southern states leaving the union. I believe, as most do, that Abraham Lincoln was our greatest president, as history has shown, but during his life he was far from being our most popular president.

This classroom example represents a moment in which Sandra realized she had to change her course of action during and after the activity to support students, and thus adjusted her bilingual curriculum. During the activity she joined students "upwind," by navigating the discussion questions with them and using translanguaging, or moment-to-moment interactions among participants using their entire linguistic repertoire to make meaning and learn (García, 2011). This pivotal moment—which could *only* have occurred through the flexible use of both Spanish and English—changed the direction of the unit, making it more relevant and "real" for students. After this conversation, Sandra added a comparison between Lincoln and Obama and a project in which students took on the role of Obama and wrote speeches about Lincoln's influence on his presidency to the unit. Though the unit's path often varied based on students' authentic questions and ideas, Sandra kept her compass fixed on the larger goals—reading and comprehending texts, writing descriptive essays, expressing ideas, and understanding other perspectives through collaborative and translanguaging. As teachers navigate the seemingly troubled waters of standards-based education, it is important that they keep their compasses pointed north towards biliteracy and shift with the tides of students' languages and inquiries.

■ *Silvia Dorta-Duque de Reyes and Jill Kerper Mora*

A bilingual curriculum enables EB students to continue to develop their primary language and second language literacy through rigorous and equitable instruction in two languages. It offers bilingual learners intellectually challenging and motivating instructional context. Bilingual learners can then avail themselves of their primary language literacy skills and content knowledge to inform their second language and content knowledge development.

A bilingual curriculum includes teaching for transfer, where teachers plan instruction explicitly and strategically for transfer and prompt student metacognition as they engage students in metalinguistic analysis rather than assuming this cross-linguistic "transfer" will take place independently of instruction. Time allocated for explicit teaching of skill transfer may vary according to grade levels and program type.

A well-planned, comprehensive assessment cycle that includes analysis of the development and correlation between the primary and second language is crucial to the achievement of biliteracy. The Common Core en Español, developed by the San Diego County Office of Education in collaboration with the Council of Chief State School Officers and the California Department of Education, provides a strong foundation for bilingual teachers to teach for biliteracy.

Teacher leaders are moving forward by studying the Common Core en Español, paying explicit attention to the Spanish-specific standards at their grade levels. They are developing lessons and teacher-created resources to engage in academically challenging Spanish language and literacy learning using Spanish as the medium of instruction for significant portions of content-area instruction. Teachers are placing special emphasis on the alignment of texts, tasks, and standards, ensuring the selection of high-quality literature and informational text in Spanish to promote meaningful discussions, in-depth learning, and proficient writing.

Schools within San Diego and throughout California are already implementing Common Core en Español. Teachers, coaches, coordinators and district administrators are collaborating to develop pacing plans, instructional units, and performance tasks aligned to Common Core en Español.

Teachers come together for professional development (PD) conducted in Spanish. In grade-level groups, they select and analyze text for critical close reading. They also formulate text-dependent questions that increase in depth and complexity, and create engaging prompts and tasks for collaborative conversations.

Attention is also being given to the correlation among the English language arts standards, the English language development standards, and the Common Core en Español. Careful and strategic planning for preteaching, teaching, and review of skills and concepts across language standards ensures bilingual learners the instructional conditions that maximize initial learning in primary language, transfer of skills, and access to rigorous second language development—resulting in proficient biliteracy and high levels of academic achievement.

An effort to develop formative writing assessment tasks in Spanish aligned to the rigor and format of the Smarter Balanced writing assessments in English is a high priority. The development of these formative writing assessments in Spanish is a long-term endeavor that needs district- and site-level support and is implemented in phases: a development phase, a pilot phase, districtwide and school-level implementation, and sustainability. Districts committed to biliteracy as an outcome of their instructional program understand how formative writing assessments will increase instructional rigor, program effectiveness, and accountability.

5.10 How can teachers use Big Questions to meet the expectations of the Common Core State Standards?

■ *Lorrie Stoops Verplaetse*

Doug Bowman, a middle-school bilingual language arts teacher in New Haven, CT, has been preparing his English learners (ELs) to meet Common Core expectations long before the Common Core State Standards (CCSS) existed. Many of these expectations, such as to obtain information from texts and generate thoughtful responses by analyzing, evaluating, or justifying, are transferable to disciplines other than language arts. Doug's dialogic instructional practices result in a language-rich classroom where students engage with the topic in extended utterances; take subsequent turns at speaking—not waiting for the teacher to comment; and respond frequently to high-cognitive, open-ended questions in pairs, small groups, full-class discussions, and written tasks.

Such accomplishments do not come easily to his students. An ethnographic study of his teaching practices revealed that he apprenticed his students in a months-long process that included an abundance of open-ended, high-cognitive, thematically relevant Big Questions (Wiggins & McTighe, 2005); multiple, highly structured, small-group experiences to prepare them for full-class activities; and ample opportunities for students to practice academic language accompanied by the modeled language needed to do so. One wouldn't know by his demanding language expectations that his students were immigrants who had been in the country less than 30 months.

Early in the school year, he modeled his expectations for an interactive classroom. He bombarded his students with Big Questions (six in 35 minutes), for example, "Why did Carmen feel lonely? Think about your own experiences." "How does that relate to 'finding your own place' (the unit's main theme)?" At first, students were reluctant to respond. So, he scaffolded their participation, following up with yes/no questions: "Do you want to forget about being Mexican?" Or, after an extended period of silence, he modeled a desired answer to his Big Question. In so doing, he modeled not only the language required for the discussion, but also his dialogic expectations.

These expectations were also present in class drills and written assignments. In his oral, full-class vocabulary drills, he followed up simple student responses with "Why?" or "Give me an example." Thus, he created more opportunities for students to practice extended, academic language. Bowman's big, thematic questions were also found in weekly quizzes. Supplementing the publisher's multiple-choice questions, Doug asked students to respond to two to three interpretive statements/questions, such as, "Compare and contrast yourself to Carmen." and "Why do you think the story . . .is part of a unit called 'Finding Your Own Place?'" Each answer required "at least 40 words."

This teacher recognized the need for abundant opportunities to practice using academic language. He created frequent, very short, highly structured, small-group activities; before each, he modeled both language and process. Every activity provided another opportunity for students to practice their responses to Big Questions before engaging in full-class discussions.

Each week, students produced more talk in response to the teacher's Big Questions. Students began to help each other with their turns at talking. Those unable to express full ideas in English were allowed to speak in Spanish. By the year's end, students were speaking in full sentences, justifying their answers, and responding to each other's ideas.

Exemplifying Walqui and van Lier's (2010) concept of "amplifying," not "simplifying," Bowman consistently modeled high expectations for students, accompanied by modeled language and process. Students responded by meeting his dialogic expectations.

5.11 How can educators connect the content and language expectations in standards like the Common Core with the experiences of English language learners/emergent bilinguals in and out of school?

■ *Marylin Low*

Language is a resource by which students are learning to be, think, and do.

Language and content are always already inherently connected. Central to any school learning is language; hence, learning and learning in language at school are a simultaneous endeavor. The question becomes not how to connect them, but how to make their connection more explicit for learners, especially those who are learning in a language that is not their first language (L1). For example, when students are judged on a composition they write (e.g., why shark fishing should be banned), the teacher reads and assesses the content using the evidence of the wording. The connection, then, is how wording makes meaning. Focusing on language use that is meaning-based, relevant to the learners, and in a familiar context is key.

English learners (ELs) and emergent bilinguals (EBs) require significant language resources to make meaning in English. The Common Core State Standards (CCSS) for English language arts (ELA) make high demands of language knowledge and use. This includes academic and technical vocabulary, grammar, and knowledge of how second language (L2) sentences and texts work. Take the notion of comparison. We compare in English across the curriculum regularly and use certain words and phrases that signal comparison (e.g., similar to, alike, different). Recently where I work in the Pacific islands, students were comparing different types of ecosystems on their own low island (an atoll). Graphic organizers visually mapped the comparison of three types of environments: coral reefs, coastal shoreline, and lagoon. Students were provided English support through vocabulary and sentence frames but continued to struggle. The teacher explained the language of comparison in the L1. Once they understood linguistically, they were able to transfer conceptual and linguistic knowledge to English—a process that strengthened understanding in and of both languages. Teachers that learn how to identify and attend to features of language, such as in the preceding example, can integrate this into all aspects of their teaching. It is a daunting task as most content teachers shy away from teaching language, even though they are inherently using language to teach.

One benefit of the CCSS for ELA is the strong emphasis on language and literacy, especially across the curriculum in later grades when foundational knowledge and purposes of language and literacy expand and communication becomes more complex. It is guided by mainland ideals and designed for English speakers, however, and often supported by curricular materials unfamiliar to ELs and EBs. While the CCSS are designed to foster high-achieving students who can compete globally (in English), what may have been left out of this discussion is the value of bilingual brains.

In contexts where English is the dominant language of the community and L1 teachers are not readily available, we have promoted the use of the L1 by negotiating L1 goals with family and students; by helping bilingual students develop supportive contacts with other bilingual (or monolingual) users of their L1; and, by developing ways of assessing students' progress that take account of linguistic and cultural knowledge of, and skills in, the L1. These conditions establish strong, positive relationships and interactions among teachers, students, and families that promote literacy learning; build on students' languages, cultures, and identities; and raise teachers' awareness of the cultural and linguistic capital these students and their families bring to school.

In the Pacific, oral and visual literacies dominate outside of school. Witnessing how students engage with learning when permitted to extend their literacy practices through the visual and oral is impressive. Slam poetry has become an expressive form of resistance and argumentation that is as powerful as any print-oriented essay.

In a current literacy and numeracy assessment project in the Pacific, we reaffirm that family literacy practices matter. Students who have a literate sibling, have books at home (in L1 and/or English), and someone who reads with them have demonstrated better literacy outcomes in both the vernacular and English than those students who do not.

This takes us back to the promise of achieving high outcomes for literacy learning, as expected in the CCSS. Embracing the L1 resources given to us by the children we teach would be a good place to start.

Languages and Literacies for Disciplinary Purposes

5.12 How can language arts teachers meet the challenge and expectations of language arts in the Common Core State Standards when working with English language learners/emergent bilinguals?

■ *Patricia Velasco*

There is no doubt that the Common Core State Standards (CCSS) era posits challenges that revolve around two paradigms: mastery of content-area expectations and academic language. Mastery of content is reflected in how a student examines questions, looks at multiple issues, and finds a variety of ways to solve problems. For emergent and proficient bilinguals, content-area mastery in the CCSS era will allow them to demonstrate their knowledge through performance tasks and projects while they develop language for academic purposes.

One of the key features of academic language is vocabulary knowledge, which also has a strong impact on reading comprehension. In bilingual classrooms, word knowledge has taken the form of cognate teaching. The focus of this section is to present innovative ways of interconnecting Spanish and English that go beyond teaching cognates to foster vocabulary growth. In the CCSS, it is specifically addressed in anchor standard 4 for reading literature and informational texts: Interpret words and phrases as they are used in a text, including determining technical, connotative, and figurative meanings, and analyze how specific word choices shape meaning or tone.

Taking standard 4 as a baseline, this discussion focuses on how vocabulary in Spanish–English classrooms can interconnect languages with the purpose of fostering "word consciousness" (Graves & Watts-Taffe, 2009). Word consciousness refers to fostering metacognition of words, as well as motivation and interest in students to pursue knowing more words and more about them.

Vocabulary Knowledge in Bilingual Settings

In bilingual Spanish–English classrooms, working with cognates has already opened the door for interconnecting languages. However, there are two related areas that have remained unexplored by classroom instruction: false cognates and interlexical homographs. False cognates are words that are similar in form but have divergent meanings. An example of a false cognate is abogado (lawyer), which can be confused with avocado (aguacate). Interlexical homographs share one graphemic form and two distinct meanings. For example, in Spanish, *ten* is a command (take it) and, in English, a number (10).

New Pedagogical Practices in Language Arts Classrooms

Here, false cognates and interlexical homographs are presented within a vignette or question that contextualizes the words. The process for implementing these vignettes is quite simple. The teacher and the students read the text and subsequently open it for discussion, as shown in the following examples.

False Cognates

In Spanish *embarazada* (pregnant); in English *embarrassed* (ashamed)

> Can you think of a reason of why a woman who is *embarazada* would feel *embarrassed*?

Interlexical Homographs

In Spanish *once* (number 11); in English *once* (one time)

> *Once* there was a dog named Sputnik. One day Sputnik was looking sad and had no energy. Sputnik's owner, Ms. Morales, took him to the vet. The vet recommended some pills to give Sputnik energy. When Ms. Morales got the pills, the recommendation for the dosage said: take *once* a day. So, she gave him *once* pills in a day. How do you think Sputnik felt?

In Spanish *pie* (foot); in English *pie* (a sort of cake)

> How do you think that a *pie* made of *pies* would taste?

These exercises are not exclusive to Spanish–English language arts. Math vocabulary also opens a wide array of possibilities.

In Spanish *resta* (subtraction); in English *rest* (relax)

> Can you *rest* when you are doing a *resta*?

In Spanish *adición* (sum); in English *addiction* (dependence)

> Should you go to the doctor if you have an *addiction* to *adiciones*?

Understanding these bilingual texts requires inductive reasoning, moving from a specific observation—determining the language and meaning the words have in the text—to forming a more specific definition of each word.

Conclusions

These are examples of new pedagogical practices that emphasize the interplay among languages. These practices have the potential of actively using emergent bilinguals' (EBs) vocabulary resources to establish connections among the languages, create mnemonic (memory) devices, understand subtleties in word meanings, and develop an overall sense of word consciousness in both languages. The most important element in this practice is captured in the word *interplay.* Connecting languages allows students to play and experiment *with* language as they learn *about* language. Most importantly, it can give them a sense of joy.

■ *Amanda Kibler*

The CCSS for English language arts (ELA) and literacy in history/social studies, science, and technical subjects offer EB English language learners (ELLs) new possibilities for learning, and these students' language arts teachers are key to helping them make the most of these opportunities. This discussion focuses specifically on such issues in primarily English-medium language arts classrooms.

Understanding the standards' new emphases is an important first step in developing responsive and scaffolded curricula and instruction that support EB ELL students and stay true to the standards' expectations. As my colleagues and I have described elsewhere, the standards differ from many previous state-level versions by requiring students to

- Engage with complex texts to build knowledge across the curriculum.
- Use evidence to analyze, inform, and argue.
- Work collaboratively, understand multiple perspectives, and present ideas.
- Use and develop linguistic resources to do all of the above (Bunch, Kibler, Pimentel, 2014).

These are ambitious goals for *all* students, and superficial changes to pedagogy will be insufficient to ensure students' success, especially that of EB ELL students, who are still acquiring the linguistic knowledge and practices necessary to engage with the standards. More dramatic changes are necessary.

Teachers can benefit from critically examining their assumptions about language acquisition, instruction, and curriculum, and the relationships among them. Building on work completed for *Understanding Language*, my colleagues and I suggest that there are at least three possible "reconceptualizations" that would benefit teachers (Kibler, Walqui, & Bunch, 2014):

1. Understand language acquisition as a process of apprenticeship that takes place in social contexts rather than as an individual process.
2. Conceptualize pedagogical activities as those that scaffold students' development and increase autonomy rather than as "help" provided to students primarily so that they can "get the job done."
3. Engage students in reading complex, amplified texts rather than simple or simplified ones.

These ways of thinking have implications for how teachers conceptualize their students, select teaching materials, plan instruction, and engage with learners during in-the-moment teaching.

Such notions are valuable across all content areas, but language arts teachers are uniquely positioned to create learning opportunities that are particularly beneficial for EB ELL students. Language arts teachers can critically approach language and literacy, showing students that language can be seen as a matter of *creation*, not obedience. For example, teachers can draw on authors' creative uses of language—in which different varieties of English or different languages are employed to achieve very particular effects—to help students see their own use of multiple languages and language varieties in new ways. Teachers can also discuss fiction and nonfiction texts in terms of authorial choices, which depend on the audiences for whom they are writing and the purposes they wish to achieve rather than simple adherence to rules or conventions. As teachers revise what "language arts" are, critical literacy skills can be usefully applied, not only to written texts but a range of oral, visual, and multimedia texts as well, texts that are increasingly important for students to comprehend, analyze, and produce. (Such skills are also transferrable in many ways across languages and apply directly to texts that EB ELL students read and write both inside and outside of school.)

Such efforts, however, cannot take place in a vacuum. The introduction of the CCSS reminds us all that the language and literacy development of EB ELL students has to be a schoolwide responsibility. Teachers across subject areas (including English as a second language teachers), along with their administrators, must work together to understand the CCSS and thoughtfully implement them throughout the school day so that students from all language backgrounds are able to achieve the goals set out for them in the new standards.

5.13 How can math teachers meet the challenge and expectations generated by the Common Core State Standards when working with English language learners/emergent bilinguals?

- *Sylvia Celedón-Pattichis*

With the current demands on teachers to meet the Common Core State Standards (CCSS) in mathematics, there is a need for teachers to serve as advocates for all students, especially emergent bilinguals (EBs). Ramirez and Celedón-Pattichis (2012) provide the following guiding principles for teachers to engage EBs in rigorous mathematics, as well as in mathematics discourse communities (MDCs) that talk mathematics (Willey, 2010). In addition, they provide teacher actions that can support mathematics learning at different stages of English language development (ELD). Consider the following principles:

1. *Challenging mathematical tasks.* Students at all ELD levels need challenging mathematical tasks, made accessible through supports that clarify their understanding of

the task. Although the tasks may be the same for all levels of language development, the teacher actions required for students to gain access to them and communicate their understanding often differ at each stage.

2. *Linguistically sensitive social environment.* The best mathematical learning occurs in a linguistically sensitive social environment that takes into consideration linguistic demands and discourse elements (Chval & Chávez, 2011/2012; Chval & Khisty, 2009) and is characterized by ongoing, teacher-supported, quality interactions that include all forms of communication between teachers and students and between students and students.

3. *Support for learning English while learning mathematics.* Facility with the English language is acquired when English language learners (ELLs) learn mathematics through effective instructional practices, including support structures that scaffold students' language development, engage students in MDCs, make mathematics content linguistically comprehensible to them, and assess progress in reaching predetermined linguistic and mathematical goals.

4. *Mathematical tools and modeling as resources.* Mathematical tools and mathematical modeling provide a resource for ELLs to engage in mathematics and communicate their mathematical understanding, and are essential in developing a community that enhances discourse.

5. *Cultural and linguistic differences as intellectual resources.* Students' cultural and linguistic differences in the mathematics community should be viewed as intellectual resources rather than deficits and should be used in the classroom to connect to prior knowledge and to create a community whose members value one another's ways of engaging in mathematics.

All of these principles are critical when working with EBs. The third principle, support for learning English while learning mathematics, is particularly important, and it requires that teachers not only include mathematics content objectives but also integrate language objectives (Echevarría, Vogt, & Short, 2013) that go beyond covering vocabulary (Moschkovich, 2012). These principles can be achieved by offering students opportunities to engage in challenging problem-solving tasks that also develop speaking, listening, reading, writing, and representation. These language domains are prioritized in bilingual education and overlap with other content areas. However, representation is unique to mathematics in that there are multimodal approaches to representing and communicating solutions to mathematical problems (Chval & Khisty, 2009). Teachers can encourage students to use oral, pictorial, symbolic, and written representations of their solutions. For example, the CCSS for mathematics emphasize the importance of developing base-10 thinking in a grade 1 classroom (Celedón-Pattichis & Musanti, 2013). Teachers can support EBs in developing base-10 thinking by including the following content and language objectives, respectively: "Students will solve problems related to base-10 thinking" and "Students will explain, compare, and justify solutions using multimodal representations (i.e., writing, illustrations, symbols, and algorithms)." Teachers can use a box of 10 crayons and pose problems such as, "There are

Base-10 Thinking Problems Using Corn Tortilla Factory Context

You have 3 bags of tortillas and 4 extra tortillas.	Draw the bags and the extra tortillas.	Write a number sentence.	Write your solution using words to explain your thinking.
	|10||10||10| | | | |	$10 + 10 + 10 + 4 = 34$	*I have three bags of tortillas. That is the same as thirty. I also have 4 extra tortillas. Thirty plus four is the same as thirty-four.*

From Celedón-Pattichis, S., & Musanti, S. I. (2013). "Let's suppose that. . .": Developing base-10 thinking. In M. Gottlieb & G. Ernst-Slavit (Eds.), *Academic language in diverse classrooms: Mathematics, grades K–2: Promoting content and language learning* (pp. 87–128). Thousand Oaks, CA: Corwin.

3 boxes of crayons. How many crayons are there in total?" They then extend the task to include problems such as, "There are 5 (or 11 to make the problem a bit more challenging) boxes of crayons and 8 extra crayons. How many are there in total?"

As shown in the table, teachers drew from students' familiar context of a corn tortilla factory in the neighborhood to support them in illustrating the total number of tortillas (assuming there are 10 in each bag)—if there are 3 bags of tortillas and 4 extra tortillas—writing a number sentence and explaining their solution in writing.

In the following figure, a teacher drew from students' native language to support EBs in the beginning stages of ELD to demonstrate that students understood the concept of base-10 thinking. The use of the native language is critical in determining how to bridge mathematical language and concept development. How EBs' native languages are positioned in the classroom plays a key role in students' engagement with mathematical tasks (Turner & Celedón-Pattichis, 2011).

Lee:	¿Cómo lo sabes? Escríbelo con palabras y números.
Tú tienes ___5___ cajas de crayolas y ___3___ crayolas sueltas. ¿Cuántas crayolas tienes en total? ___83___	Porque veo 10. Yo conte de 10 cajas Y si hay de 8 de crayolas Y 3 sueltas en total son 83. $10+10+10+10+10+10+3=83+10+10$

Example of base-10 thinking task in Spanish. (From Celedón-Pattichis, S., & Musanti, S. I. (2013). "Let's suppose that . . .": Developing base-10 thinking. In M. Gottlieb & G. Ernst-Slavit (Eds.), *Academic language in diverse classrooms: Mathematics, grades K–2: Promoting content and language learning* (pp. 87–128). Thousand Oaks, CA: Corwin.)

In summary, teachers determine the classroom norms that are set for EBs to engage in MDCs from the beginning of the school year. Supporting EBs in meeting content and language objectives and clarifying and extending their mathematical thinking will be critical to advance their education.

■ *Kristina Robertson*

Keeping Math Content Challenging While Building Academic Language for English Language Learners

"Mrs. Robertson, can I be the guest teacher Friday? And can I use your clipboard?" Elizabeth, one of my grade 4 ELL students, was excited to teach the class about fractions. It had been a long journey for my students to get to this point and I was very proud of them because they had taken on math challenges while also working on developing their language skills. When this group of nine struggling ELL students was assigned to me I was overwhelmed and, frankly, a little scared. Thankfully, I was confident I could plan for their language development needs and I just needed to stay a day or two ahead of them on math content—or so I thought. I soon realized I needed a better grounding in math standards to understand the essence of the language demands of certain tasks. I also needed to get to know my students well and understand what might motivate them into "productive struggle" within this content. Finally, as a language teacher, I knew they had to focus on producing academic language within math context.

I began by reviewing the math curriculum materials to locate the standards for each unit. The standard and key math vocabulary (there was a lot!) was listed, but I knew my students needed to be able to speak like mathematicians and that wasn't in the book. I needed to determine what a mathematician would "sound like" when discussing or answering a math problem. To prepare, I wrote the standards as questions. For example, "Compare two fractions with different numerators and different denominators." became "Which fraction is larger? Which fraction is smaller? In what ways can you compare two fractions using numerator and denominator?" I then developed language exemplars for each question to guide my modeling of the language of math. Possible language exemplars included the following:

- X fraction is larger because the denominator is the same and the numerator is larger.
- X fraction is smaller because the denominator is the same and the numerator is smaller.
- You can compare different fractions by finding a common denominator for both fractions by multiplying the two denominators or finding the lowest common denominator. Next you multiply the numerator by that same multiplier.

In addition to the content and language preparation, getting to know my students and sharing my belief in their abilities was extremely important to the work we would be doing. On our first day I gave them a math perception survey I had devised. They ranked themselves regarding interest, frustration, and problem-solving perseverance in math. All nine reported overwhelmingly negative feelings regarding math. I shared my own math frustrations (which surprised them) and then switched topics to discuss their career dreams. Students wanted to be businessmen, teachers, professional sports players, and major fashion designers. I asked, "Do you think you will need math skills in your career?" They all begrudgingly answered "yes." We talked about the fact that they didn't need to know all areas of math, but that they had to be problem solvers and understand basic concepts. We made a pact that we would help each other work on this together.

I made it clear that an important part of our work was producing math language by discussing math problems and the rationale for the solution. I expected them to question and clarify if they weren't sure of something, and they needed to use technical vocabulary and sound like a "professor" in their responses. I modeled the math concept and "professor" language and provided supports such as sentence frames and scaffolded activities to provide them time to process and practice the math concept. Students worked in small groups to solve problems and I observed them interacting while problem solving. I assisted when students were confused, and I encouraged them to use academic language to question, clarify, and explain their problem-solving process. Sometimes the groups were very noisy and there were heated debates with students jumping to the whiteboard to show their own process to the solution. Soon our guest teacher program was born. Students began volunteering to be the guest teacher and were thrilled to get to use my clipboard for their lesson plans (for some reason the clipboard fascinated them). For example, when Elizabeth was the guest teacher, I met with her to discuss her lesson plan. She needed to have a lesson objective and together we identified the academic language she would model as she demonstrated the math concept. She also needed to include assessment problems for her peers to work on in small groups. Eventually all students could "talk like a professor" about math and took on leadership roles within the learning community to challenge themselves. I had solid evidence of their learning every day and when students were weak in an area or not putting forth their best efforts, others helped them or challenged them to show their thinking. My best moment was when one of my more sullen participants beamed at me and said, "I feel smart!"

On reflection, I can see connections between my math class and Common Core math standards, which require students to "Make sense of problems and persevere." and "Look for and express consistency in repeated reasoning." In my classroom there was exposure to technical math vocabulary, problem-solving procedures, and use of negotiating and explaining language. The students actively engaged in problem solving after observing modeling of the process and language of math. They definitely showed perseverance as they took on new tasks and held each other accountable for their learning.

I believe the students gained a greater awareness of academic language and how it is used within different content, for example, constructing arguments and explaining their reasoning. The students began to reflect on the "best ways" to say things to get their point across, and we discussed language within a variety of contexts. I openly shared with them that my goal for them was to use academic language as much as possible throughout the day because if they didn't say it in school, it wasn't likely they would say it anywhere else. I wanted them to be prepared to speak their minds eloquently wherever they went.

5.14 What types of resources can mathematics teachers use to meaningfully engage English language learners/emergent bilinguals with the language demands of the Common Core State Standards?

■ *Holly Hansen-Thomas*

Resources that mathematics teachers can use to help their students be successful with the intense language demands of the Common Core run the gamut from English as a second language training and knowledge of cultural differences in math, to the multiple curricular frameworks and bilingual mathematical materials developed with English language learners (ELLs) in mind, to the professional organizations that serve math teachers of bilingual students (e.g., *TODOS*, http://www.todos-math.org). Employing *all* useful resources will contribute positively to ELLs' success in math. Arguably, classroom discourse is one of the most important resources that teachers can draw on to meaningfully engage ELLs in mathematics classrooms.

With respect to classroom discourse, there are a number of useful tools teachers should employ to promote precision and argumentation, two critical components of the CCSS in math. *Cognates*, *collocations*, and *sentence frames* can be used to facilitate student language use, development, and importantly, interaction, in math class.

Vocabulary is one important part of academic language and classroom discourse. Using *cognates*, words that have a shared origin and are often spelled similarly across languages (English, and usually Latin or Greek in the case of math), can be useful for

ELLs in their development of lexical knowledge. However, these cousin words must be taught explicitly, otherwise these "clues" may, to use a common English idiom, "be Greek to them." Attending to important *collocations*, or groups of words that occur together frequently, can benefit students by providing structure, clarity, and independence (Daloğlu & Tarhan, 2005). Learning expressions like "multiply by ___ to get ___" or "3 times 3 equals ___," or even oral expressions for written formulas such as "the perimeter of a rectangle is ___ (p = 2l + 2w)" helps students use academic language fluidly and autonomously.

Like collocations, partially scripted linguistic scaffolds, *sentence stems*, can be used to promote discussion and clarity of concepts. Also called *accountable talk stems*, scaffolds such as "one thing I observed is___," or "I think this is ___ because ___" can help students talk (and indeed write) like mathematicians. Stems provide just enough help for language learners to start a discussion and promote interaction.

They can be in the form of sentences such as

- I think the answer was ___
- My strategy was ___
- I used the operation of ___
- I can prove my thinking by ___

Or these starters can be presented as questions, as in "How did you solve the problem?" or "What was your strategy?"

Similarly, definitions and concepts can be presented with sentence stem hints, as one grade 6 math teacher in Texas regularly does. She announces, "Percent means ___ " and her students oblige her by shouting, "___ out of a hundred!" Her use of this common stem facilitates their ability to "get" the definition of percent and to be able to use it in classroom discourse.

Having accessible sentence stems will help ELLs to be more independent in their use and development of academic mathematical language. They will also help ELLs to make the important connections between the oral language used in classroom activities and the more abstract, and often less accessible, language from texts, such as word problems on tests.

Finally, it is important not only to provide the scaffolds ELLs need to engage fully and meaningfully, but also to *draw attention to* and *model* these supports so that students have the skill and training to use them appropriately. It is great when math teachers post important mnemonics and handy tools on the walls, but it is fundamental that the teachers remember to point these out at appropriate times.

5.15 What types of resources can science teachers use to engage English language learners/emergent bilinguals with the language demands of the Next Generation Science Standards?

■ *Juliet Langman*

A range of resources exist for science teachers working with English language learners (ELLs), including materials for students (e.g., bilingual dictionaries and native language textbooks), and materials for teachers (e.g., lesson plan outlines that provide ideas for adapting lessons to meet the needs of diverse students). One key resource most under the control of teachers is the method of verbal delivery in class. Science teachers are accustomed to thinking in precise terms about the processes of science. Taking the idea of precision in science and applying it to how language is used in explanations is a great way to begin to orient teaching to support learning. One myth about science is that, because it is "hands on"—either teachers demonstrating and/or students doing—ELLs will be able to it learn easily. Participating in procedures—following along—can be done with little language. However, because our Next Generation Science Standards (NGSS)–aligned objectives include supporting students' abilities to demonstrate understanding through explanation, modeling and scaffolding precise language is essential.

Let's unpack *language precision* as a resource that teachers can use with their demonstrations. Modeling language precision is a good first step in introducing ELLs to the language of science. (The next step will be to have students display their linguistic knowledge in oral or written form.) In the case of demonstrations, the idea is to show *and* tell in precise ways.

Here's an example:

> "Next you're gonna want to trim this and expose that."

What is this teacher demonstrating? Let me give a bit more language.

Example—Take Two

> "Try to trim the yellow stuff off as best you can; you see that spongy tough thing like a spaghetti noodle coming out the back. It is very tough if you feel it, so don't cut that optic nerve. With your scissors, get all the extra stuff off and try to expose that noodle as best you can."

What is this teacher demonstrating? With the clue, "optic nerve," its likely part of an eye dissection lab. If the students were able to carry out the task of "cutting the yellow stuff off," would they be able to tell you what they are doing, in a way that would demonstrate their understanding of dissection or the eye? How can you make the language accompanying the actions in the demonstration more precise, without losing the conversational style?

As a trick, imagine reminding a colleague over the phone or in the dark how to demonstrate this part of the dissection. Say it out loud, and then read on.

Example—Take Three

Try to use your scissors to trim **the fat**, that is, *the yellow stuff*, as best you can. When you do, you will see the **optic nerve**. The **optic nerve** is here (pointing), that *spongy tough thing like a spaghetti noodle* coming out the back of the eye. That material is very tough, feel it like this with your scissors, that is your **optic nerve**. Once you have trimmed all **the fat** and **muscle** off the sheep's eye, you should have a perfect **spherical** or *round* **eyeball** with an **optic nerve** coming out the back.

What does this third example do in terms of precise language? What does the example suggest about your delivery of lessons? A few ideas are outlined here:

- Employ academic terms.
- Repeat academic terms often, to help fix the terms in the students' minds.
- Combine academic terms with social terms that serve as clues or explanations of those terms.
- Summarize processes and results at the end.
- Encourage students to employ similar types of precise language in oral and written reports.

■ *Gilberto Lobo*

This piece was created from an interview that Mariana Castro conducted with Mr. Lobo, a bilingual grade 6 science in Spanish teacher in New Mexico. Mr. Lobo has been a teacher for 18 years and his work with bilingual students in science has been recognized at local and state levels (e.g., Outstanding Science Teacher Award in 2004; Dual Language Education New Mexico Teacher of the Year in 2009; and Soleado feature, winter, 2009). Throughout the interview, Mr. Lobo talked about his students and presented a counter-narrative to that of standardized education. In his counter-narrative, he proposed a student-centered and democratic education model, where standards are a tool to guide instruction, not the center of instruction. Teaching science, like all teaching, according to Mr. Lobo, is about connecting personally, culturally, and emotionally with students.

Mr. Lobo's student-centered approach starts from the beginning of the year and before he begins teaching science. Mr. Lobo has participated in the community where he teaches and has developed connections with many of the families of his students and with the community itself. Once school starts, he tries to connect personally with each individual student and to nurture connections among students. Mr. Lobo's intent is to create a community of learners in his classroom. To this end, during the first couple of weeks of the school year, Mr. Lobo spends a lot of time learning about and from his students. He engages them in activities that require them to work together and think critically, skills that, according to Mr. Lobo, are essential in both science and life. Through these activities, he believes that his students not only learn to work as part of a team, but also to observe, negotiate, and problem solve. These activities also allow opportunities for students to build a sense of community. Through all these activities, language is the vehicle for communication and dialogue, and this is a critical component for bilingual students who need multiple opportunities to use language in authentic and relevant ways.

Mr. Lobo's approach to teaching bilingual students also includes certain aspects of democratic education; specifically, facilitating students' conversations about what they want to learn in class. He tells students that the classroom belongs to them. Then he asserts this idea by having them create classroom norms, taking their concerns and interests seriously throughout the year, and letting them select areas of study that interest them. Throughout the year, Mr. Lobo continues to collect data from students through the use of consensograms, a qualitative tool to collect information about individuals' perceptions. Rather than using standards to prioritize learning, Mr. Lobo shifts the focus of his instruction from standards-centered to student-centered.

In this era of standards and accountability, Mr. Lobo provides an example of how to bring the focus back to students and how to engage them in a democratic approach to education that turns many of his students toward lifelong learning. Mr. Lobo shared how many of his students continue to visit and write, even after they graduate from the district. However, it is important to highlight that his approach does not prevent him from using standards as a tool, and that his students have shown growth in learning both content and language, but as he likes to say, that is secondary. What he considers primary are "respeto, mente positive, y ganas (respect, positive attitude, and effort)."

5.16 How can educators meet the challenge and expectations of social studies in the Common Core State Standards when working with English language learners/emergent bilinguals?

■ *Lorena Mancilla*

Social studies offers students a well-rounded education because it gives them opportunities to develop as global citizens and apply critical thinking skills as they engage with a variety of social issues. This key area of study is rich with opportunities for teachers to incorporate students' languages and cultures as learning resources. For emergent bilinguals (EBs), the ability to make connections to home, school, and community experiences not only mediates their learning of new content, but also mediates their language development (Collier, 1995; Escamilla & Hopewell, 2010; García, 2005; Goldenberg & Coleman, 2010; González, Moll, & Amanti, 2005; Nieto, 2008). Creating pathways for students to make such connections can be achieved in a variety of ways. For instance, comparing historical events in the curriculum to historical or current events in students' home countries or the United States allows students to draw from their personal experiences. Introducing primary and secondary sources in students' home languages not only exposes students to multiple text types, but also allows them to use their home language. Incorporating various forms of media, such as technology, can help students develop global perspectives on issues because technology allows them to connect with people from around the world.

For example, in one middle-school social studies classroom, a teacher working with Latino EBs helped her students connect to the topic of the Cold War by drawing on students' experiences and home language. The Spanish news network frequently featured stories on Cuba–U.S. relations. Students were exposed to these current events at home and in their communities and were interested in learning more about them. By introducing this topic in the classroom during the Cold War unit, the teacher helped students develop an understanding of communism that then facilitated their ability to discuss relations between the U.S. and USSR during the Cold War. This experience not only taught students that concepts in social studies can be applied in today's world, but it also validated the knowledge and experiences they brought from home.

When designing learning experiences for social studies using the Common Core State Standards (CCSS), educators will notice the emphasis on the identification of key ideas and details, the integration of knowledge and ideas, and a specific focus on craft and structure. In the preceding paragraphs, I identified a few examples of how to facilitate connections between content and students' experiences. However, for EBs, educators must also plan functional and communicative opportunities for meaningful language use. Expanding on the strategies suggested previously, students using technology or other sources of media in their home language to help them connect to the concepts in class, can then synthesize this information and report on it in English. This synthesis can be achieved by crafting scaffolded activities and planning for meaningful peer interaction. Thus, this approach provides EBs with opportunities to think critically about both content and language use.

From the language development perspective, we also need to connect the targets identified from the CCSS to English language development (ELD) and Spanish language development (SLD) standards to scaffold EBs' language development based on the information we have about their linguistic abilities. In other words, the strategies used to provide EBs access to the content, is only half the work; we must also include language development standards to continue to scaffold EBs' language development.

The preceding considerations should also be taken into account when working with younger EBs. For example, when learning about communities, students in a grade 1 classroom can gather information from primary sources, such as interviews with community workers, or compare communities by analyzing various artifacts. Such experiences provide EBs at various ELD levels with opportunities to engage in content-related discussions. This does not mean that the English they will use will be native-like or proficient under a particular scale, but it does mean that, regardless of their language proficiency, they can still engage in meaningful ways. And, just like older EBs, younger EBs are developing English in addition to other language(s). Educators teaching social studies can create learning environments that engage students with critical thinking and meaningful language use that are applicable in other areas, yet customizable to their individual students.

5.17 How can teachers use English and Spanish language development standards to scaffold and support English language learners/emergent bilinguals in content and language development classes?

■ *Mariana Castro*

When English language learner (ELL)/emergent bilingual (EB) students enter our schools, they need support acquiring the language of school, whether that language is their home language, English, or both. After all, no one is born speaking the language of school, or academic language, as some educators call it. While we know that there is no single way in which all children learn language, educators of ELL/EB students have long struggled to balance language and content instruction, as well as to decide how and what language to teach.

In this piece, I will show some ways for educators to use the World-class Instructional Design and Assessment (WIDA) standards for English language development (ELD) or Spanish language development (SLD) to identify (1) ways to differentiate language to provide access to the content, and (2) language targets and objectives to guide ELL/EB students' language development. In other words, I will attempt to explain the dual use of WIDA ELD and SLD standards in "breaking down" language barriers while "building" language skills. While this may seem double the work, this is exactly the work we are asking our ELL/EB students to do when they come into our classrooms, that is, to learn content and English simultaneously.

The WIDA language standards were created to be used with content standards like the Common Core State Standards (CCSS), the Next Generation Science Standards (NGSS), and other college- and career-readiness standards. The rationale behind this is that research has shown us that learning language in context is better than learning it in isolation (Genesee, 1994; Grabe & Stoller, 1997; Lightbown & Spada, 2011; Snow, 2001). The following table includes the WIDA ELD standards. The standards reflect the expectations of how students should use and process language to communicate ideas, concepts, and information in the context of content instruction. The WIDA SLD standards are similar in format. It is important to recognize that these are not *content* standards, but rather, standards about the *language* of the content. The use of the WIDA language standards in instruction and assessment requires not only that educators use the standards themselves, but that they use the elements of the framework in which they exist.

WIDA English Language Development Standards

ELD Standard	Definition
1	English language learners **communicate** for social and **instructional** purposes within the school setting
2	English language learners **communicate** information, ideas and concepts necessary for academic success in the content area of **language arts**
3	English language learners **communicate** information, ideas and concepts necessary for academic success in the content area of **mathematics**
4	English language learners **communicate** information, ideas and concepts necessary for academic success in the content area of **science**
5	English language learners **communicate** information, ideas and concepts necessary for academic success in the content area of **social studies**

Courtesy of WIDA Consortium.

As you can see from the following figure, the standards interact with WIDA's performance definitions. These performance definitions describe the language features students typically use and process across various levels of language development. While these levels help guide instruction because they make thinking of language more concrete, it is important to remind educators that proficiency is not a static concept. Students' proficiency varies depending on the context and on many other factors. Thinking about levels is a convention that helps to show language development over time.

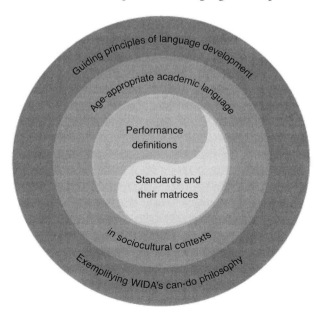

WIDA's standards framework. (Courtesy of WIDA Consortium.)

These standards matrices provide specific examples of how the WIDA standards connect with the content and what students may be able to do within the context of that content. They are organized by grade level and by language domain (listening, speaking, reading, and writing) to provide the most specific examples of language performance. These matrices help to differentiate language for students at various stages of language development so that they can participate in instruction. The strands can also help educators plan for possible targets in language instruction by looking at what students are expected to do at higher levels of language proficiency. The following table is an example of a strand, or scaffolded continuum, showing language expectations in speaking for students studying electricity and magnets in grade 3. Note the connection to the content standard and the description of the context.

ELD Standard 4: Language of Science

EXAMPLE TOPIC: Electricity and Magnets

CONNECTION: *Next Generation Science Standards, Physical Sciences, Forces and Interactions PS2-3, PS2-4 (Grade 3).* Ask questions to determine cause and effect relationships of electric or magnetic interactions between two objects not in contact with each other. Define a simple design problem that can be solved by applying scientific ideas about magnets.

EXAMPLE CONTEXT FOR LANGUAGE USE: Students discuss their observations and draw conclusions about the outcomes of electricity and magnetism experiments in small groups to practice designing their own experiments.

COGNITIVE FUNCTIONS: Students at all levels of English language proficiency *Analyze* experimental observations.

	Level 1 Entering	Level 2 Emerging	Level 3 Developing	Level 4 Expanding	Level 5 Bridging
SPEAKING	State reasons for outcomes of experiments on electricity using illustrations or realia and teacher guidance (e.g., "electricity goes", "electricity stops" when circuit is open or closed)	State reasons for outcomes of experiments on electricity using illustrations or realia, oral sentence starters, and teacher guidance (e.g., "The bulb turned on because . . .", "The balloons attracted/repelled because . . .")	Explain outcomes of experiments on electricity using illustrations and oral sentence frames	Explain in detail outcomes of experiments on electricity using illustrations or realia and word/phrase banks	Explain in detail outcomes of experiments on electricity using illustrations or realia

Level 6—Reading

TOPIC-RELATED LANGUAGE: Students at all levels of English language proficiency interact with grade-level words and expressions, such as: turn on, turn off, static electricity, charge, attract, repel, open/closed circuit

Courtesy of WIDA Consortium.

From the preceding example, you can see that while the language is scaffolded, the intention is to keep the cognitive demand and the content the same. What changes is the language used to demonstrate analysis of the observations. While a fluent speaker may be able to explain in detail the outcomes of the experiment, a student who speaks at the emergent level in English would state reasons for those outcomes. While the task is very similar, the linguistic demand involved in explaining is different from that in stating reasons. Using the same strand, a language educator could plan for instruction of the student speaking at the emerging level targeting the next level, which offers the example of explaining using sentence frames to scaffold the language development.

The SLD standards have a similar format, so that bilingual educators are able to work on similar language purposes even though the language features in each language may be different. In addition to providing consistency, such practice offers opportunities to engage in metalinguistic dialog with students about how different languages accomplish a common purpose through different language conventions, forms, structures and, of course, vocabulary.

The use of language standards, then, can provide opportunities for educators to engage all students in the content of college- and career-readiness standards, such as the CCSS and NGSS, by offering ways of differentiating language and scaffolding its development. While the use of ELD and SLD standards provide guidance on functional uses of language and the performance definitions provide general ideas of the language features appropriate for each level of language proficiency, these resources are too general to provide everyday guidance. Instead, they provide examples of possible paths, with the hope that as educators become more comfortable with these examples, they can begin to make their own decisions on language targets for their language instruction, as well as on how to differentiate the language of instruction and assessment to provide access to the content based on their own knowledge of their students and the content they teach.

DISCUSSION QUESTIONS

After reading this chapter, engage in dialogue with peer educators, including school principals, other administrators and supervisors, teachers of different subjects, specialists in different areas, paraprofessionals, and parents/community members to discuss how to engage ELLs/EBs in core content-area instruction. Here are some questions to reflect on individually, with a colleague, or ideally, as part of a professional learning community at your school. If you are in a school, the members of this group would comprise the school's ELL/EB leadership team, whose responsibility it is to collectively make the decisions that affect the education of ELLs/EBs.

1. How do you support ELLs'/EBs' access to standards-based content? What resources exist to support you in your role? What additional resources could help you achieve your goals?

2. Survey strategies used among your colleagues to provide access for ELLs/EBs to the content and language expectations in the CCSS. How do these strategies compare

to those offered by the various authors in this chapter? Do the strategies used maintain the challenge and expectations in the standards? How so? Do they take into account the specific cultural and linguistic needs of ELLs/EBs? How so?

3. How do you and your colleagues focus your instruction on ELLs'/EBs' language and literacy development across the content areas, moving toward the linguistic and literacy expectations outlined in the CCSS, the NGSS, and/or other college- and career-readiness standards? How do you monitor ELLs'/EBs' language growth in these various areas? How do you set language goals, targets, and/or objectives for your ELLs/EBs?

4. How are content-area teachers supported in aligning the curriculum to standards? How do content and language educators collaborate to ensure that language instruction corresponds to the content expectations in the CCSS, the NGSS, and/or other college- and career-readiness standards? How can you advocate for support and resources in these areas?

   • If your context includes bilingual education programming for ELLs/EBs: What does content instruction look like? How is alignment of content to curriculum created across the two languages? How are language goals for both languages related to each other and how do they correspond to the content? What opportunities exist to explore metalinguistic, cross-linguistic, and translanguage practices with ELLs/EBs?

   • If your context does not include bilingual education programming for ELLs/EBs: How can home language be used a support for ELLs/EBs? How are ELLs'/EBs' languages and cultures recognized as an asset in teaching and learning?

TOPICS FOR REFLECTION AND ACTION

The following statements are organized around the big ideas of the chapter. Read through them and indicate the extent to which each applies to your community and your school. After you complete the survey, discuss your responses with your team. Then write down one to three reflection points that have emerged from your discussions. Finally, identify one to three concrete actions that you/your team can take.

DK don't know 1 strongly disagree 2 disagree 3 agree 4 strongly agree

LANGUAGE DEMANDS OF THE CONTENT AREAS					
1. The educators in my school (district) are aware of the language demands that the CCSS and NGSS present for ELL/EB students.	DK	1	2	3	4
2. The administrators in my school (district) have (or are in the process of implementing) a plan to support the language demands of the CCSS and the NGSS that ELL/EB students face.	DK	1	2	3	4
Literacy and Multiliteracy Development across the Content Areas					
3. Early childhood practitioners and administrators in my school (organization or district) understand and support the development of early literacy of our dual language learners.	DK	1	2	3	4

LANGUAGE DEMANDS OF THE CONTENT AREAS *cont.*					
4. Educators in elementary and secondary grades in my school (district) understand and are ready to implement the literacy perspective found within ELA in the CCSS.	DK	1	2	3	4
4.1 (Subsequent statement, if you chose 3 *or* 4 for question 4.) Educators in elementary and secondary grades in my school (district) are knowledgeable and feel comfortable in creating pathways for ELL/EB students to meet the literacy expectations found within ELA in the CCSS.	DK	1	2	3	4
5. The grades 6–12 ELA educators in my school (district) support the literacy development of EBs/ELLs in history/social studies, science, and technical subjects.	DK	1	2	3	4
6. Educators and administrators in my school (district) recognize the role of the home language of ELL/EB students in their linguistic and literacy development and academic success.	DK	1	2	3	4
7. My school (district) provides opportunities for ELL/EB students to develop their languages and literacies through bilingual education programs, methods, or supports.	DK	1	2	3	4
7.1 (Subsequent statement, if you chose 3 *or* 4 for question 7.) My school (district) provides an appropriate amount and variety of materials, resources, and supports in ELL/EB students' home language (e.g., staff allocation, library books, content textbooks).	DK	1	2	3	4
7.2 (Subsequent statement, if you chose 3 *or* 4 for question 7.) The materials, resources, and supports in ELL/EB students' home language help ELL/EB students meet the demands and content of the CCSS.	DK	1	2	3	4
7.3 (Subsequent statement, if you chose 3 *or* 4 for question 7.) Bilingual instruction in my school (district) is designed taking into account content and language development standards for each of the languages that are included in our bilingual program to ensure language development in each of those languages.	DK	1	2	3	4
Languages and Literacies for Disciplinary Purposes					
8. Educators and administrators in my school (district) understand and support the development of both the language and literacy of our ELL/EB students.	DK	1	2	3	4
9. Educators across the various content areas understand the importance of developing language and literacy in those areas to help ELL/EB students be successful.	DK	1	2	3	4
10. Educators in my school (district) engage in instructional practices that provide access for all students, and maintain the challenge and expectations of the CCSS for ELL/EB students.	DK	1	2	3	4
11. Educators in my school (district) use and integrate the CCSS and English language development (or proficiency) standards to scaffold ELLs'/EBs' development of academic language in addition to engaging with the content.	DK	1	2	3	4
12. Our school and district have created tools or provided guidance on how to align or integrate content and language development standards.	DK	1	2	3	4

Language Demands of the Content Areas *cont.*

Reflection:

Action Steps:

6

Professional Learning

R esearch has shown a positive relationship between professional learning opportunities provided to educators and improvement in their students' academic achievement. Meaningful and engaging pedagogy and professional learning communities (PLCs) among staff have also been identified as significant conditions for students' academic success. However, professional development (PD) opportunities specifically related to the academic success of English language learners (ELLs)/emergent bilinguals (EBs) are greatly needed. ELLs/EBs have the double challenge of learning the same content as their peers while also acquiring the language of instruction. Their success, then, is directly related to their educators' ability to support both endeavors: learning the content and acquiring the language(s) of instruction. While professional teacher organizations have begun to address the needs of ELLs/EBs through the publication of resources to support students' access to content information, knowledge, and concepts (e.g., National Council of Teachers of English, National Council of Teachers of Mathematics), the role of the English as a second language (ESL) or bilingual educator is not always understood, and in many schools their role is limited to tutoring or reteaching content.

Leveraging the linguistic resources that students bring into the classroom requires a deeper understanding of the linguistic factors that students need to be successful academically. It also requires pedagogical practices that leverage and expand students' language practices while also supporting the learning of concepts, ideas, and information related to academic content. We see an increased interest in the discussion of linguistic factors in ELLs' schooling in educational and applied linguistics literature and in educational assessment literature. Unfortunately, however, we do not see focused and sustained attention to professional learning opportunities for all in-service teachers to ensure that they know how to teach the ELLs/EBs in their classes. In the new era of college- and career-readiness standards, in-service teachers need opportunities for professional learning as much as pre-service teachers. Ongoing and on-the-job professional learning opportunities for teachers are one of the ways administrators can achieve sustainability and build local capacity.

While the need for PD is great, high-quality, research-based professional learning related to ELLs/EBs is not always readily available. One-time workshops or short-term assistance are abundant, but so is the research that shows that these learning opportunities do not achieve local sustainability. One of the reasons for this is that the type of PD needed to affect teacher practice and, ultimately, student academic achievement requires a lot of time for educators to meet, dialogue, and connect with each other. Designing education systems where the teachers of ELLs/EBs (whether general education or ESL/bilingual educators) have ample time to grow, share, and collaborate with others is of critical importance in making this happen. Along the same lines, support and PD for administrators, so that they have the knowledge and understanding necessary to make these decisions about educating ELLs/EBs, is even more critical.

An important goal of this chapter is stimulating conversation and action about how to best prepare all teachers and administrators to educate all students, particularly ELLs/EBs, in the context of the Common Core State Standards (CCSS) and Next Generation Science Standards (NGSS). An important theme is that ELLs/EBs are everyone's responsibility, not just the responsibility of the ESL teacher—who has traditionally worked in isolation. The first section examines the changing role of ESL educators in schools, with attention to how ESL specialists can more effectively work with K–12 generalists, content teachers, literacy specialists, and bilingual educators. The second section considers what is involved in the complex job of planning for the professional learning of all in-service K–12 teachers and administrators who work with ELLs/EBs— including long-term ELLs and ELLs with learning disabilities—to meet the academic and language demands of the CCSS and NGSS. This is an enormous challenge, and one that preK–12 systems need to do strategically. The chapter concludes with discussions of what it means to prepare and evaluate K–12 teachers who have ELLs/EBs in their classes. This chapter, with its focused attention to local context, reminds us that, just as there is no one-size-fits-all approach to instructing ELLs/EBs, there is no one type of PD that will quickly solve this complex and exciting challenge. We encourage readers to engage in critical conversations and action relating to professional learning in their school and community contexts.

Shifting Roles of English as a Second Language Educators

6.1 How can English as a second language teachers/specialists engage English language learners/emergent bilinguals in the Common Core State Standards and Next Generation Science Standards?

■ *Don Hones*

On a bright autumn afternoon, teacher Traci V. is outside on the grounds of Lincoln Elementary School with 20 prekindergarten children, the majority of whom are native Hmong speakers. The children are on a nature walk, with frequent stops to pick up red, green, and golden leaves that litter the ground. With leaves in hand, the children re-enter their classroom, where they listen to Traci's clear, friendly voice, repeat the parts of the leaf, and practice color words. Then each child works on some leaf-inspired art with found objects, paper, markers, and glue. Traci circulates between the tables, and children gravitate towards her, sometimes with questions, sometimes with a shoe to be tied, sometimes proudly displaying a beautiful drawing.

That was sixteen years and many standards ago. Today, Traci works at a different elementary school. She has no room of her own. Much of her day is spent working quietly in the back of various classrooms with one or two refugee children from Iraq, Burma, or the Congo. A few times each day, she will take a newcomer out to the hall-way to practice some oral language or reading and writing strategies. With one or two teachers she has developed a co-teaching relationship. In these cases, Traci will help design curriculum units, and will teach parts of the unit to the whole class, the majority native English speakers as well as the non-native English speakers present. An experienced, talented teacher, Traci wheels her teaching cart through the halls, finding ways to support the 40 non-native English speakers spread among a dozen classrooms. As a professional, Traci is being marginalized, much as the students she serves have been and continue to be marginalized within the public schools.

For English as a second language (ESL) teachers and specialists, who have tradition-ally been the first line of support for English language learners (ELLs), the Common Core State Standards (CCSS) offer the challenge of remaining relevant: How does such a professional fit into the model of the "push-in" classroom, so popular at the moment, a model that asks one professional to work, often unobtrusively, in the class-room of another? How do ESL professionals continue to feel like teachers when they are placed in situations where, to the untrained eye, they appear more like teacher's aides? How much will other teachers in a school be willing to learn from such a profes-sional who does not seem to fit the image of what a teacher is supposed to be?

ESL teachers and specialists have much more to offer than just one-on-one instruc-tion whispered in the back of a room. To truly contribute to the academic success of ELLs and emergent bilingual (EB) students, ESL professionals need opportunities to utilize all of their skills and knowledge in the service of the whole school. Such profes-sionals need to be fully supported by school administration and staff in the following roles:

- True co-teachers. Full collaboration in curriculum development and teaching will benefit all students in the classroom, not just the ELLs.
- Professional development (PD) specialists in second language acquisition. Administrators would be wise to utilize the knowledge base of ESL teachers in schoolwide initiatives for curricular and instructional reform that highlights interaction with academic content, language, and culture.
- Cultural mediators. ESL teachers, and especially bilingual specialists can have special relationships with immigrant and refugee families and communities. ESL professionals can help lead programs that share about the educational system and learn from the immigrant families and communities. As funds of knowledge research has shown, such programs can lead to curricular innovation that supports the Common Core by drawing on the knowledge base of immigrant communities (González, Moll, & Amanti, 2005).

For the CCSS to have a lasting value, all educational professionals must be willing to learn from the children, youth, and families they are serving. ESL teachers are in a unique position to mediate such an exchange. To do so, they must be supported in roles that truly challenge them as professionals.

- *Joanne Marino*

The CCSS and the Next Generation Science Standards (NGSS) provide an unprecedented opportunity for ESL teachers and specialists to engage ELLs/EBs in these and all content standards. In their roles as resource teachers and as purveyors of language learning strategies, ESL specialists guide content teachers on how to create engaging classroom environments for all students. They show how to modify the norms of student interaction and clarify how language manifests itself in its different domains (listening, speaking, reading, writing). Moreover, ESL teachers demystify academic language development by helping content teachers learn how to provide access to content concepts, including thinking that academic oracy supports reading, writing, and content comprehension. This collaboration results in ELLs meeting the CCSS and NGSS, regardless of their language proficiency level.

For example, in Molly Poston's biology class, ESL Specialist Deborah Wilkes guided Poston to enunciate, increase wait time, and make use of gestures, pictures, and realia. As students examined the structure and function of carbohydrates, they used all four language domains. During class, students explained pretaught vocabulary and differentiated between the tier 2 words "discuss" and "distinguish." Students worked in pairs, receiving different, actual foods to examine. With this, as well as the text, their notes, and a word wall, they engaged in academic conversation with higher-level thinking to determine connections between the foods. They formulated decisions, provided evidence and justifications, completed a graphic organizer, and presented the analysis to the class. The teacher monitored the students' conversations, eliciting elaboration and clarification.

To engage grade 3 ELLs, ESL Specialist Karen Solis focused on the standards for mathematical practice and the Common Core speaking and listening anchor standards. Solis modeled constructive conversations to build comprehension and collaboration, and developed a student friendly rubric to illustrate how students fortify and negotiate ideas. She supported ELLs with conversation prompt/response cards. Prompts included questions such as, "How else can we show this?" "What symbols can we use?" "What method is most useful and why?" Response cards included sentence starters such as, "Maybe we can use ___; Symbols we could write are ___; Another way to show this is ___." In this way. students built language functions as they increased mathematical understanding through discussion of math solutions, approaches, and reasoning.

Engaging students with complex texts, close reading, and output activities that use content language are major features of the CCSS. ESL specialists, as experts in second language acquisition, can model the use of reading comprehension strategies to deconstruct a text and summarize it through a teacher read aloud/think aloud. Mark Hildreth, an ESL/language arts instructor, teaches his middle school ELLs to visualize, generate questions, and identify text structure (e.g., cause and effect, compare/contrast, problem–solution, sequence) as he models. He demonstrates reading as an active process. After teacher modeling, students partner read, alternately reading sentence by sentence and summarizing together after each paragraph. In this way, teachers build reading skills by guiding students to focus on content, structure, and passage vocabulary as well as pronunciation, fluency, intonation, and inflection.

After 10–15 minutes of partner reading, students anchor content knowledge and build literacy skills. Hildreth's students complete I charts where they clarify the reading by identifying new vocabulary and summarizing the selection. They then respond to the reading by connecting it to the world, themselves, or another text.

In their various roles, ESL teachers and specialists engage ELLs in the CCSS and NGSS by sharing their knowledge of language domains, language learning strategies, and second language acquisition. They engage ELLs by using collaborative skills to support colleagues and students. They complement the CCSS by providing the intervention methods necessary to support all students' learning and meeting the CCSS and NGSS.

6.2 What does effective collaboration between content and English as a second language teachers/specialists look like?

■ *Trish Morita-Mullaney*

A collaborative relationship between content and English as a second language (ESL) teachers must be reciprocal, strategic, and coherent.

Reciprocal or reciprocity. The relationship with the ESL specialist and the classroom/content area teacher must foster conditions of *reciprocity*: A shared and distributive leadership for ESL students in areas of instruction, curriculum, and assessment (Bell & Baecher, 2012; Brooks, Adams, & Morita-Mullaney, 2010). The specialist and the teacher must be equally regarded in this professional partnership, ensuring that each educator has a sense of confidence and security in their roles to realize a genuine partnership (Creese, 2002).

Strategic and formal. Being strategic and formal guides the ESL–mainstream teacher partnership. Formalizing and scheduling time together is paramount for planning instruction and assessment. School administrators must ensure that time is devoted to planning within the pre-existing structure for grade/content-area team meetings and that the ESL staff is intentionally scheduled with a venue for contribution. Because ESL teachers often serve multiple teams, it is important that these team meetings are staggered. If meetings are held after school, one team meets on Monday, another on Tuesday, and so forth. This structure allows for the ESL teacher to be available for most team meetings, so their contribution is anticipated and valued.

Coherence. Coherence refers to clarity about the structure and content of collaboration. A schedule for collaboration may be well conceived and staggered, but intentional affirmation about each teachers' expertise is a necessary condition for coherence. Arkoudis' (2006) research shows that when an ambiguous relationship between ESL teachers and mainstream teachers exists, ESL educators are perceived as strategy "suggesters" and are marginalized within the teacher/specialist relationship (Creese, 2002).

Coherent collaboration calls for a reconceptualization of the ESL and mainstream teachers' roles of augmenting content by using appropriate English language learner (ELL) strategies. The merit of coherence is the improvement of each teacher's instruction and is regarded as an authentic means of professional development (PD). Further, adults modeling collaboration fosters a more collegial learning environment for all children.

Horizontal and vertical structures ensure that expertise is fostered within mainstream and ESL teams. Horizontal coherence references coordination among grade/content areas within academic content standards. ESL teachers are a part of this horizontal arrangement because they are familiar with ESL standards and can contribute to strategies that are language specific and provide appropriate instructional scaffolding for the ESL students during instruction of content standards. Vertical coherence attends to building the expertise of ESL educators. A regularly scheduled meeting at the building and/or district level offers opportunities for ESL teachers to continually improve and where their confidence and security are affirmed (Arkoudis, 2006; Creese, 2002).

What Perspectives Do English as a Second Language Teachers/Specialists Bring to Planning, Curriculum, and Instruction?

Planning. Because ESL teachers have worked within diverse contexts, they are familiar with the academic content standards for a grade/content area and likely have appropriate instructional strategies and scaffolds for supporting academic language learning. ESL teachers typically teach multiple grade and content areas and understand specific expectations, making them aware of necessary scope and sequence between various levels and related content. Working with multiple teachers makes them astute at coordinating and mapping complex master schedules for maximizing instructional and collaborative time.

Curriculum and instruction. Arkoudis (2006) challenges the perception that ESL teachers only offer strategies, which differs from the content expertise of the mainstream teacher. ESL teachers have specific training in English language development (ELD) and this knowledge, along with coordinating strategies, should be regarded as content. This ESL content knowledge and pedagogy can offer supporting curriculum that amplifies the content-area curriculum. Acknowledgement of these skills contributes to a relationship of reciprocity where each teacher values their respective skill sets.

■ *Margot Downs*

> I am proud of the presentation with my group because it help me practice with my English, speaking in public, and it help me learn what a simple machine is. Next time I speak a little louder because some people can't hear well when I speak.
>
> —Trinh, grade 8

Recorded on a self-reflection form, Trinh's comment shines light on how even the smallest collaborative efforts between educators can offer ELLs authentic opportunities to engage with academic language and build positive peer relationships. Like many teachers, my first collaborative teaching experience started small. Over a series of lunch conversations, a grade 8 science teacher and I discovered we shared a common vision of success for ELLs.

Guided by research, we knew effective models of academic language instruction required engaging ELLs and their native-English-speaking peers in age-appropriate academic content with scaffolding (Hammond & Gibbons, 2005). Our collaboration began by making assessments more linguistically accessible and identifying science language to preteach during my ESL support class. I valued the scientific knowledge of my colleague and she valued my ability to make that knowledge more accessible to our students. With small successes (and some setbacks), we became more intentional in our approach. Even though we communicated well, using a planning protocol made our conversations more efficient and effective with our limited planning time. By thoughtfully engaging all students and their various cultural and linguistic backgrounds, we aspired to create a more cohesive learning community. Unfortunately, when teaching assignments changed the following year, the collaboration ended. A formal structure would have enabled us to sustain our learning and extend it to other interested colleagues.

With the number of school-aged ELLs increasing across the nation, collaboration between ESL teachers/specialists and general education teachers is becoming an essential component of school culture. Collaboration often develops as a teacher-driven initiative to share accountability for ELLs' academic achievement and ELD, and can take many forms, from co-planning to co-teaching. A formal collaborative process, including a collective commitment from administrators, teachers, and parents, can help ensure success and sustainability (Horwitz et al., 2009). Now is the perfect opportunity to bring ESL teachers/specialists and general education teachers together to discuss the adoption of the Common Core State Standards (CCSS), their implication on curriculum development, and the increased academic language demands placed on students.

ESL teachers/specialists offer expertise in accessing the cultural and linguistic assets of students, analyzing the academic language demands of instructional tasks, identifying appropriate instructional supports to make content comprehensible, and integrating strategies to promote student engagement with academic language.

Just as we expect students to collaborate effectively in our classes, students need to see us model collaborative relationships with our colleagues. To ensure a successful collaborative environment, a formal process needs to include opportunities for educators to

- Understand the rationale for collaboration
- Articulate demographic trends and related instructional challenges and opportunities
- Acknowledge that all teachers and staff are valuable members of a learning community and contribute to student achievement
- Adopt protocols to increase optimum use of planning time
- Apply new learning strategies in manageable increments with administrative support
- Observe collaborative instruction and share successful practices
- Integrate language and culture components into content-specific PD
- Engage all students and families in collaborative initiatives
- Reflect on instructional practices to gauge impact on student learning.

Honigsfeld and Dove (2010) offer an extensive analysis of collaboration models and resources on implementing collaborative strategies in the context of English language teaching.

The CCCS compel us to move beyond instructional models that either isolate ELLs and ESL teachers/specialists from general education programs or leave ELLs and general education teachers unsupported. While the implementation of a formal collaborative process may seem overwhelming, it allows us to tap into the much richer collective knowledge base of educators who together can improve language and learning opportunities for ELLs.

■ *John Hilliard and Margo Gottlieb*

With the national rollout of the CCSS comes a unique opportunity for K–12 educators. Recently, there has been a push for general education teachers, who have traditionally focused on content delivery, and teachers of English learners (ELs) and emergent bilinguals (EBs), whose primary focus has been on the students' language development, to collaborate as equals to strengthen each others' instructional skill sets. With standards-based collaboration envisioned across the planning of curriculum, assessment, and instruction, we also have begun to see a more equitable distribution of instructional responsibility for educating language learners. In addition, language considerations for all learners are being infused into general education content instruction.

The focus of this teacher collaboration should center on the natural "crosswalks" between content standards, illustrated by the CCSS and Next Generation Science Standards (NGSS), and language development standards. The following table is a side-by-side comparison of the features of the CCSS and the World-class Instructional Design

Comparing Common Core State Standards and WIDA English Language Development Standards

Common Core State Standards	Aspect of Comparison	WIDA Language Development Standards
YES (vertical) ↑ grade	Presence of scaffolds	YES (horizontal) → prof. level
YES	Topics	YES
L, S, R, & W in language arts standards	Language domains	L, S, R, & W in each standard
★ YES	Academic language	★ YES
YES (grades 6–12)	Cross-content literacy	YES (K–12)
Individual grade K–8 HS 9–10, 11–12 clusters	Grade-level organization	Individual grade K–8 HS 9–10, 11–12 clusters
NO	Instructional supports	YES

and Assessment (WIDA) English language development standards. The shared aspects are ready-made channels for content and language educators to begin to develop a common language and exchange instructional assessment strategies. The primary crosswalk between the two sets of standards is the use of academic language to promote learning.

Changing the Education Equation

Historically, EL/EB instructors have not participated alongside their colleagues in conversations around curriculum and assessment. Often their strengths in the areas of language development and instructional strategies for second language learners have not been considered in the discussion of effective content instruction. With the implementation of the CCSS and their emphasis on academic language development for all students, this professional inequity is equalizing. Teachers with ESL backgrounds and bilingual/multicultural education bring a strong understanding of the importance of academic language use in sociocultural contexts that has served to elevate their professional status and has placed them in leadership roles.

Academic Language Use: The Anchor for Collaboration

Teachers and school leaders bring different perspectives to their understanding of what academic language means and how it is used. Content educators have traditionally seen their primary instructional responsibility as the transfer of content-area concepts and skills to their students. For this reason, they have tended to view academic language use as an implicit part of instruction and have not considered it separately from content knowledge and skills. This perspective has allowed many content educators to make assumptions about their students' abilities to manage the language demands of specific content. It has also created confusion in distinguishing between the challenges that their students have with academic language use within a content area and their students' ability to process the concepts and skills associated with that content.

In contrast, language educators bring a rich understanding of the role that language and culture play in accessing grade-level content. Their instructional emphasis has been on language development and they have been trained to parse out the language demands of specific content, to make these demands explicit, and to offer their students specific supports to access the content. By having content and language educators share their perspectives and instructional assets around academic language use, they create an anchor for future collaboration.

Reaching consensus on the definition of grade-level academic expectations that are referenced to both content and language standards strengthens the bond among teachers and serves as an impetus for ongoing collaboration.

6.3 How can administrators leverage the expertise of English as a second language and bilingual teachers to support English as a second language/ emergent bilingual student learning?

■ *Lydia Stack*

To implement the Common Core State Standards (CCSS) successfully, administrators need to become familiar with English as a second language (ESL) professionals and bolster their possibly new roles in supporting content instructors. Following are some specific ways for administrators to consider as they plan for implementation of the CCSS.

Changing ESL instruction. Administrators need to know that the way ESL professionals teach English has changed. Language can no longer be taught in isolation (e.g., vocabulary, structures, and functions). The focus should be on language as action or language in use so that English learners (ELs) can meet the rigorous content and language development standards of the CCSS. Beyond the language for everyday needs, instruction must emphasize the use of academic language necessary for understanding and communicating disciplinary concepts and knowledge. ESL instruction should be aligned to the grade-level content being taught and ESL students should be supported to accomplish the CCSS standards within the lessons. ESL teachers should be encouraged to share the responsibility for supporting ELs as they learn to talk and write about the concepts and knowledge they are exposed to in the content classes, that is, language arts, mathematics, science, and social science. When evaluating the ESL teacher, administrators should look for scaffolding of grade-level content and language production.

Culture and language of ESL students. ESL professionals can help administrators establish an inclusive school that values the students' home language and culture. ESL professionals usually know about the culture and language of the students they teach and can help make an inclusive school a reality by sharing cultural information with classroom teachers. In addition, their knowledge can be helpful when working with parents. They know what new immigrant parents should understand about the school, graduation requirements, rules and regulations, and the best ways to communicate that information to parents. For example, a small utility knife is a tool most high school students in other countries carry to school; however, it is considered a weapon in most U.S. schools. Helping parents and students bridge these sorts of cultural differences is a role the ESL professional can play.

Teaching strategies that scaffold learning for ELs. ESL professionals can be a tremendous resource for classroom teachers. They have knowledge of many teaching strategies that teachers can use to scaffold grade-level content. In addition to forms such as graphic organizers, ESL professionals can help teachers select language to emphasize in their lessons. They can help design rubrics to measure language and content understanding. They have valuable information on what works for different proficiency levels and they can help teachers with just the right scaffolding—that is, ways to differentiate for different English proficiency levels based on state language development standards.

How the Roles of English as a Second Language Professionals Must Change

In establishing the roles of ESL professionals in the CCSS era the focus should be on language and content instruction that empowers all students, especially ELs, to meet the grade-level standards in the various content areas and the language development standards.

Resource role. ESL professionals with their expertise in language and learning can be a resource for school staff in the following areas:

- Expanding professional libraries in language and literacy topics
- Providing professional development (PD) concerning the language needs of ELs
- Participating in professional learning communities advocating for ELs
- Modeling tasks for promoting classroom interaction
- Coaching strategies that make content accessible for ELs
- Training paraprofessionals

Collaborator role. In the CCSS era, collaboration between ESL professionals and content-area teachers seems the most promising approach. ESL professionals can be a vital support to classroom teachers as they design lessons for the CCSS in all content areas. ESL teachers should not work in isolation. They need to form collaborative relationships, including co-teaching structures, with classroom teachers. Co-teaching relationships between ESL professionals and content-area teachers must be clearly defined, with the focus on coherent instruction for ELs that promotes English language proficiency and content-area knowledge. ESL professionals should not be seen as classroom aides for ELs while the content-area teachers focus on the mainstream students. There should be shared responsibilities across all aspects of instruction—planning, delivery, grouping, and assessment—and how these responsibilities are distributed should be clearly defined in advance. The ESL professional brings expert knowledge of language in use, while the content-area teacher is grounded in the disciplinary knowledge, and their joint challenge is to make the content accessible to all students, especially ELs.

■ *Wilma Valero*

Muchos yo en un nosotros. . . .Affirming and investing in our students' plurality. How can we develop learning environments that promote and affirm our students' language and culture and at the same time meet the high academic and linguistic expectations of this competitive global society? More than ever, educators are facing the challenge of facilitating a learning environment where students claim ownership of their learning and where delivery of instruction is in the modality reflective of students' lives. Furthermore, as educators, we are well aware that the foundational blocks of a solid learning community stem from the development of caring and nurturing relationships. This begins with recognizing and validating the cultural and linguistic fabric of the community we serve. We cannot afford to stay in silos anymore; our sense of urgency must focus on building bridges of equity and social justice, empowering our students with the rigor and relevance of linguistically and culturally responsive standards-based instruction.

The complexity of delivering excitement and joy within the teaching and learning process in our schools starts at the crucial moment where collaborative teams of EL and general education teachers plan and strategically design student-centered learning environments. This environment doesn't refer only to the physical space, but rather to the holistic framework of a learning community that is inclusive and reflective of our students' languages and cultures.

This involves the intentional design of curricular programs that are collaboratively developed, while keeping in mind our target audiences. Language and cultural identity are purposely embedded within the district's instructional programs. Students' bilingualism is considered a high commodity, a valuable asset and not a disability. Active integration and participation of ELs and English-dominant students is expected and highly valued not only in the classrooms but also in the school, setting the tone of our district's culture. Opportunities to develop bilingualism and biliteracy skills are strategically planned within the collaborative effort of the district's ELL and curriculum and instruction departments. Standards-based instruction is at the center stage.

We create effective instructional tools that support and enhance learning at the district level. Language of instruction allocation by grade level must be established, as well as a grade-level curriculum-alignment plan that integrates the district's curricular expectations for all students. Content-based thematic units serve as a means of teaching language and content skills. This method integrates content under the umbrella of high-interest themes to engage students. The classroom learning environment purposely displays linguistic spaces that are well-established, reflecting the academic rigor of content and language where both English and the target language are valued. These linguistic spaces are facilitated by the teachers; however, they are generated by students through strategically planned interactive activities.

Students' work samples are displayed to reflect the progression of learning and pride in the journey. The target language isn't circumscribed only to the classroom, but is also validated through use on school walls and in daily messages. Authentic, high-interest literacy, mirroring students' demographics, is available and aligned to standards and content areas. Teacher teams work in collaboration, while EL practitioners share their expertise with colleagues—developing consistency and coherence and differentiating instruction based on students' strengths and areas of improvement. This collaboration must be embedded in effective teacher practices that promote and encourage deep conversations about serving all students within the lenses of equity and social justice.

Planning for Professional Learning

6.4 What should educational leaders consider when creating a vision for professional learning relative to the Common Core State Standards and Next Generation Science Standards and the needs of English language learners/emergent bilinguals?

■ *Christy Reveles*

Working successfully with college- and career-readiness (CCR) standards and creating a vision for professional learning for educators that meets the needs of English language learners (ELLs)/emergent bilinguals (EBs) requires several important considerations: (1) educator needs and wants relative to ELL teaching and learning; (2) a pedagogical framework that supports ELLs' academic and language development; and (3) a learning initiative design with supports to ensure sustained transference to classroom practice. Given that the majority of U.S. teachers do not share the same cultural and linguistic backgrounds as their ELL students, these learning design components have special significance when situated within an ELL-focused context for professional learning.

CCR standards ask educators to structure learning in ways (such as fostering students' speaking and listening skills and their ability to elaborate, explain, and critically engage with informational texts) that were not required in previous content standards. Ensuring that ELLs have equitable access to master these standards will likely require that educators implement different ways of teaching and assessing. Thus, it is imperative that a vision for educator professional learning focuses not only on the academic and language development of ELLs but also on the unique learning needs of the educators. In planning a vision for professional learning, it is important to consider the educators' knowledge of language development, their readiness for change, their cultural competence, and their motivation for working with ELLs. By assessing the educators' knowledge and dispositions up front, learning can be better differentiated for their unique learning needs related to working effectively with ELLs.

CCR standards offer challenging expectations for what students should know and be able to do; however, standards are not sufficient unto themselves as the "content" for professional learning. What is not addressed within the standards is a framework for instructional practices, or pedagogy, especially with ELLs in mind. A grounded, research-based pedagogical framework can empower ELL teachers to facilitate standards-based learning in meaningful and challenging ways. For example, in the five standards for effective pedagogy (Dalton, 2008), ELLs' learning is facilitated by educators who (1) collaborate with students in their learning and foster collaborative classrooms; (2) develop language and literacy across the curriculum; (3) make learning meaningful with direct connections to students' experiences, cultural context, and community; (4) challenge students to think critically; and, most importantly, (5) mediate learning and language development through instructional conversations between teacher and students. Within this framework, educators provide differentiated assistance and opportunities for ELLs to elaborate, explain, solve problems, and develop academic language. Moreover, this model can help educators understand the language demands within different academic content areas and how they can mediate learning to develop students' academic language across the curriculum. This pedagogy honors ELLs, building on their background, language, and culture as strengths rather than deficits, while challenging students to achieve high standards.

Finally, it is also important to consider the "andragogy" (or model) for adult learning as it relates to supporting ELL educators. Effective educator professional learning includes a variety of formats, including face-to-face workshops, technology-supported learning, and job-embedded practices, such as coaching, action research, lesson study, and professional learning communities (PLCs). Having regular opportunities for educators to work with each other in teams and with ELL specialists to reflect on their practice, share ideas, collaborate, and problem solve together as professionals provides a supportive environment to implement new practices with students. Professional learning works when educators can apply their newly learned skills and successfully sustain them over time in their daily work with students. With a special focus on supporting ELLs to meet the demands of CCR standards, educational leaders can help by creating and sustaining a culture of continuous learning for both adults and students within the school.

■ *Cathy Fox*

To be successful in meeting the needs of ELLs and EBs within the Common Core State Standards (CCSS) and the Next Generation Science Standards (NGSS), administrators and educational leaders need to ensure that they are planning for language development, as well as content. In creating a vision for professional learning, administrators need to think in terms of providing a basic understanding of second language acquisition for *all* educators. Building on this base, administrators and educational leaders can engage school and district educators in looking at data and examining school practice to determine next steps for professional learning.

During my tenure at Central Falls School Disctict I have had some phenomenal professional development (PD). In Rhode Island, we have been using the World-class Instructional Design and Assessment (WIDA) English language development (ELD) standards for ten years and I have had extensive PD from WIDA. The WIDA ELD standards provide a context for me to plan for the language domains of reading, writing, speaking, and listening that students need to access the content I am teaching. It is essential for administrators and educational leaders to consider PD for educators in the ELD standards. *All* teachers need to consider themselves language *and* content teachers if they want their ELLs to be successful with the CCSS and the NGSS.

Another aspect to consider when planning for professional learning for school and district educators is training in SIOP (sheltered instruction observation protocol). The SIOP protocol is a research-based instructional model for teaching ELLs from the Center for Applied Linguistics. SIOP consists of eight interrelated components with 30 different features. It provides a framework for teaching ELLs that ensures both language and content goals are met with each lesson. The training I received in SIOP has shaped the approach I use in my classroom each day and is invaluable to me as an ELL teacher.

Administrators and teachers also need to assess student achievement and look at program effectiveness, using reliable data sources. Three years ago my school was part of a WIDA pilot for LADDER.[1] It is one of the most powerful PD experiences I have had. It brings together school-level personnel and helps them form a team whose focus is ELLs' academic success. The team goes through a cycle of stages, and in the process makes data-informed decisions affecting programming and instruction for ELLs. Using the WIDA ACCESS for ELLs Growth Reports, individual schools can look at the growth of their students compared to all the students taking ACCESS across the country. In my school we have focused on the writing domain because our students were making less than average growth in that area. We have developed interim assessments and use the writing rubric from WIDA MODEL to calibrate scores and measure students' progress. These monthly meetings are powerful professional learning opportunities that help us focus our instruction and share strategies to improve our ELLs' writing skills. In the process of looking at student work and discussing instructional strategies, teachers have formed a PLC.

The CCSS call for students to participate in academic conversations and rigorous content acquisition. Our ELLs/EBs are capable of engaging in academic language and tackling higher cognitive levels with the proper scaffolds when instruction is aligned with their ELD levels. Therefore, when administrators are creating a vision for professional learning for educators, they must first consider providing a clear understanding of second language acquisition for *all* teachers. With this common vision, educators can then look at the data and determine next steps for planning and evaluating best practice for *including all* of our students.

---

[1] WIDA LADDER for language learners. Retrieved from http://ladder.wceruw.org

6.5 What professional learning opportunities should be available for teachers who are implementing the new standards in classrooms with English language learners/emergent bilinguals?

■ *Aída Walqui*

Teachers are key to the future of students and their communities. Because teaching takes place against a continuously changing societal background, it stands to reason that to perform their work judiciously and effectively, teachers must be supported as they develop their expertise in the face of new societal demands.

What Do Teachers Learn?

The development of teacher expertise—knowledge and the ability to use it effectively in specific contexts—comprises the coherent growth of six key dimensions:

1. *Vision* (of their students and of learning and teaching)
2. *Motivation* (the reasons, incentives, and emotions that give meaning to teachers' actions)
3. *Knowledge* (comprehensive, domain-encompassing subject matter knowledge; pedagogical knowledge; knowledge of students; knowledge of language as action; knowledge of second language acquisition; pedagogical subject-matter knowledge)
4. *Reflection* (recollective, interactive, anticipatory)
5. *Context* (classroom, school, societal, and how to navigate them to create optimal learning opportunities for the specific students in a class)
6. *Practice* (elegantly enacting it all together in class).

These dimensions and the evolution of teacher expertise should be continuously refined through a lifetime of reflective, supported practice.

How Do Teachers Learn?

At the moment of graduation from teacher education programs, teachers are novices in need of opportunities to grow through situated learning. To be effective, these opportunities need to form part of a coherent portfolio of development intended to increase their knowledge and the ability to transform it into effective practice for the students they serve. Teacher learning should engage them in activity with peers; introduce them to practices; and increasingly solidify, extend, and refine these practices and the theories that give them sense and meaning.

During professional development (PD) sessions, for example, lessons can be modeled (teachers work as if they were students). Then the experience is used as an anchor for the development of teacher knowledge, vision, and reflection (teachers work as teachers). In this example, discussion of how the specific learning arrangements that were modeled work leads to readings and discussions on pedagogical theory and the reasons why they work. In this sequence, emphasis is placed on the lesson as a whole, on leading students through expert guidance from activity centered on ideas, processes, and language to knowledge and skills they did not possess before the lesson started.

Carefully designed lessons and planned and purposeful articulation among activities are very different from teaching teachers strategies—piecemeal pedagogical ideas without an understanding of when, why, and in which sequences they might work.

Teachers could then be invited to visit a peer in action, or to view a video of that peer teaching. The focus for the ensuing reflection can vary from an emphasis on elements of quality teaching studied (academic rigor, high challenge/high levels of support, quality interactions, and so forth),[1] to concentrating on specific exchanges and discussing (a) what they show about student development, and (b) what they signal for future development (and teacher planning and action).

The opportunity to observe colleagues in successful pedagogical action strengthens teachers' vision of their students' potential and provides a local setting for the development of their professional capital, thus establishing schools as centers of inquiry. Reflecting on how teachers give up (or struggle to give up) old conceptions of second language development, disciplinary practices, and pedagogy can be very productive once a safe, collegial environment has been established. Equally important, these activities are highly motivating for teachers and strengthen their knowledge, resolve, and energy for becoming increasingly accomplished teachers.

Sometimes work within the portfolio of teacher opportunities to enhance their learning can take place within discipline or grade-level teams. At other times, it is important that all the teachers in a school meet to renew their commitment to the education of English language learners (ELLs) and all other students around a single vision of excellence, toward which multiple, consistent paths can be designed.

When should these professional learning opportunities take place? How can we pay for them? School schedules and activities need to be reorganized to provide teachers with consistent opportunities to grow on the job, and these opportunities should be offered to educators as professional rights (that include responsibilities). Needless to say, this implementation would be costly. In reality, however, it is much more costly to society not to offer these opportunities to all teachers in all schools, especially in schools where ELLs remain underserved.

6.6 What do teachers need to understand about the challenges that the Common Core State Standards and Next Generation Science Standards present for long-term English language learners/emergent bilinguals?

■ *Kate Menken and Tatyana Kleyn*

While the Common Core State Standards (CCSS) seek national uniformity in student learning, they fail to recognize the diversity among U.S. students. Not only are emergent bilinguals (EBs) entirely absent from any discussion within the CCSS themselves, in school these students are also often misperceived as a monolithic group. The reality is far more complex in that there is great variation in home language practices, prior

---

[1]See, for example, Walqui & van Lier (2010), chapter 4, for principles of quality teaching with English learners.

schooling experiences, culture, and identity, to name but a few variables. This means that students arrive in school at all different points along a continuum of language and literacy practices. Schools at the secondary level are best prepared to educate those students who arrive with high levels of literacy in their home language, when in fact there are many students who arrive at the earlier stages of academic language and literacy learning both in English and in their home languages.

Our focus is on students referred to as "long-term English language learners" (LTELLs) in U.S. schools. As opposed to new arrivals, these students have attended U.S. schools for seven or more years, and remain entitled to receive language support services such as English as a second language (ESL) and/or bilingual education programming, according to their performances on English language proficiency assessments. While there are no national estimates, LTELLs currently comprise about 12% of all EBs in Chicago, 13% in New York City, 23% in Colorado, and 50% in certain California districts (Gwynne, Pareja, Erlich, & Allensworth, 2012; New York City Department of Education, 2013; Olsen, 2010).

Students labeled as LTELLs have received inconsistent U.S. schooling, moving between ESL, bilingual, and/or monolingual classrooms without language supports, or have moved back and forth between the United States and their families' countries of origin (Menken & Kleyn, 2010). As a result, these students have not had the opportunity to develop high levels of language and literacy for academic purposes either in their home language or English. While LTELLs are characterized by complex and dynamic bilingual language practices, regularly moving between English and their home languages, these language practices are typically marginalized in schools where they are deemed low performing on traditional measures of student performance (Menken, 2013).

As U.S. schools work to implement the CCSS in schools serving EBs, decisions about implementation need to be driven by who the students are and by their educational needs. In the following sections we identify effective strategies for meeting the needs of students labeled LTELLs. Note, however, that no one strategy will suffice outside of a well thought-out program that incorporates explicit literacy instruction, home language development, and a coherent schoolwide language policy.

Differentiating Programming and Bilingual Instruction

LTELLs typically have high levels of language for social purposes and therefore should not attend ESL classes geared toward new arrivals; nor should they attend foreign language courses where their home language practices are deemed incorrect. Instead, LTELLs need consistent programming in which instruction (a) is bilingual, using language dynamically and flexibly; (b) focuses on literacy development; and (c) explicitly values, builds on, and extends students' complex language and literacy practices in English and their home languages.

Activating Prior Knowledge

Students labeled as LTELL come to school with a range of backgrounds and experiences across languages, cultures, and countries. When teachers take time to learn about students' interests and build on their knowledge, learning becomes more meaningful and relevant. This is especially important for LTELLs, who are often disengaged from school and see it as separate from and even oppositional to who they are and how they identify.

Oral Language Development

LTELLs do not have issues in expressing themselves but they may not be versed in using more formal "academic" registers. Asking students to use oral language in debates, to role play, or to discuss concepts in English and their home language allows them to be more aware of how and why they are using language and offers a natural segue into other literacies without devaluing their home languages and literacy practices.

Attention to Vocabulary

LTELLs tend to rely on basic or high frequency words orally and in writing. Therefore, instruction that focuses on building a broader academic lexicon and engages students' language resources flexibly is important. This can be done through the use of a thesaurus to identify precise language, discussion of bilingual cognates that are both high and low frequency, and creation of bilingual word walls.

Active Read-Alouds

Although less common in secondary school, read-alouds offer students the space to follow along in their own texts as the teacher models reading, while answering questions posed by the teacher and asking their own questions too. For instance, the teacher is able to provide students a focused approach to the reading, scaffold their understanding through questioning, and clarify explicit strategies that readers use. This structure scaffolds texts and makes the reading process accessible and interesting to all students.

6.7   What do teachers need to understand about the challenges that the Common Core State Standards and Next Generation Science Standards present for students with interrupted formal education?

- *Suzanna McNamara and Annie Smith*

In answering this question, we draw on our work developing the New York State (NYS) Students with Interrupted Formal Education (SIFE) Curriculum (2013–2015) to design Common Core–aligned curricula targeted to the unique instructional needs of SIFE with the lowest levels of home language literacy. This project is an offshoot of a larger initiative called *Bridges*, a one-year, four-subject academic program for low-literacy SIFE entering high school as newcomers. The goals of the SIFE curricula are to target: *foundational literacy*, *academic conceptual knowledge*, and *academic ways of thinking and using language* so that low-literacy SIFE (LL SIFE) can meaningfully participate in grade-level curricula.

Students with Interrupted Formal Education Characteristics

It is important to understand the heterogeneity of the SIFE population (see the following figure). Our work has focused on the LL SIFE subgroup of SIFE. Decisions about which CCSS to target, and how to embed the CCSS in curriculum and instruction, first requires an understanding of the nuances among SIFE, a population often assumed to be homogeneous.

In New York, SIFE are defined as English language learners (ELLs) who are at least two years below grade level in home language literacy and math skills, as a result of interrupted or inconsistent schooling (New York State Education Department, 2014). Although students entering grade 9 with grade 7 home language literacy skills are considered SIFE, these SIFE are *already* readers and writers in their home languages and are able to transfer their reading skills to the new language. In our experience, many students at this level *can* participate in content classes with appropriate scaffolds.

By contrast, LL SIFE are at or below grade 3 literacy in their home language, meaning they are not yet fluent readers in any language and do not independently use text as a resource to build new knowledge. Their levels of literacy include emergent, early, and transitional.[1] Emergent and early readers have had little to no exposure to print in the

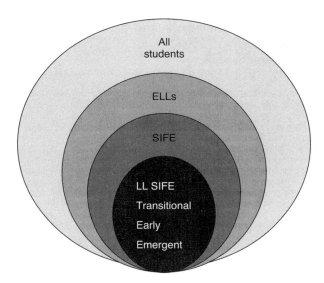

Graphic representation of the heterogeneous SIFE population.

---

[1]We use the terms "emergent" and "transitional" to refer to the developmental literacy levels of students in their home languages. These are not to be confused with the same terms used by the NYS Bilingual Common Core Progressions, which refer to English language proficiency levels.

home country or may have some alphabetic skills, but little to no reading comprehension or writing skills. They are learning to go to school, perhaps for the first time, and most importantly—they are learning to read *for the first time in a language they do not speak.*

LL SIFE require curricula and intensive, daily instruction that targets all of the CCSS foundational skills, typically reserved for early elementary students. These include orientation to print, the concept of print carrying meaning, how to track print on a page, connecting sound-symbol relationships, blending sounds to read words, segmenting sounds to spell, and instantly recognizing a large number of sight words. In most cases, these students must develop these skills in a language they do not yet know, which poses great challenges for students and teachers. LL SIFE, therefore, face the greatest challenges in accessing curricula and meeting the CCSS at the secondary level.

LL SIFE with transitional literacy have grade 2 or 3 home language literacy levels. They understand that print carries meaning, can often decode, and can recognize some sight words. These students can track print, hold a pencil, and write basic texts. Students near grade 3 levels of home language literacy bring many foundational skills that transfer to English. While they cannot yet read and write to learn in the home language, they are on the cusp.

Common Core State Standards Challenges
for Students with Interrupted Formal Education

The Common Core State Standards (CCSS) articulate rigorous grade-level standards for *all* students including ELLs/emergent bilinguals (EBs). The emphasis on rigor and quality teaching for all students is imperative; even more so for secondary SIFE who must gain *foundational literacy, academic conceptual knowledge, and academic ways of thinking and using language* in a few years.

The CCSS pivot on six pedagogical shifts that direct instruction for all students. These shifts are predicated on students' ability to access and acquire grade-appropriate academic language. A closer look at two of the shifts reveals the challenge that attaining the CCSS poses for LL SIFE.

- Shift 2: Knowledge in the disciplines *demands that students build knowledge about the world through* **text**, *rather than through the teacher or activities.*
- Shift 3: Staircase of complexity *demands that students read the central, grade-appropriate text around which instruction is centered.*

Each of these shifts makes evident the emphasis on acquiring knowledge through grade-level text. This stance assumes that all students have the skills necessary to use text to learn and acquire knowledge. It implies that students have levels of literacy in their home language(s) that transfer to English and allow them to access and analyze text at close to grade level. In this scenario, students make use of their literacy and academic conceptual knowledge and ways of thinking to build both language and content knowledge. It is a process of leveraging and transferring what they have already developed in the home context to the context of the U.S. classroom. Clearly this scenario characterizes students with a very different profile than the LL SIFE who arrive in secondary classrooms throughout the United States.

Curricula that meet the needs of LL SIFE must build academic conceptual knowledge across the disciplines and teach students to read and write, so that they can use text as a learning resource. A standards-based, grade-level curriculum without these components risks disenfranchising LL SIFE who are unable to participate in the classroom discourse and build academic identities. In many circumstances, this leads to educational foreclosure; LL SIFE sitting in secondary classrooms without engaging meaningfully with the curricula often drop out.

Teacher Understanding of Common Core State Standards and Implications for Low-Literacy Students with Interrupted Formal Education

> Students advancing through the grades are expected to meet each year's grade-specific standards, retain or further develop skills and understandings mastered in preceding grades, and work steadily toward meeting the more general expectations described by the CCR standards.[2]

The college- and career-readiness (CCR) goals of the CCSS give students thirteen years (K–12) to progress vertically up each standard. The grade-level articulation of any standard assumes that students have mastered that standard in earlier grades. The articulation of a given standard in the early grades contains the building blocks for meeting the demands of that standard in the higher grades. The standards assume that students are meeting the increasingly complex cognitive demands of each standard with increasingly complex text.

These assumptions may hold true for many U.S. students, but not for LL SIFE. The LL SIFE for whom our curricula are designed have not had the academic instruction necessary to master the subskills articulated at the lower grade levels. As a result, LL SIFE come to secondary classrooms not having developed key foundational academic skills expected from early elementary standards. A closer look at one standard reveals the challenges.

Reading for Information standard 2 (RI.2) requires students to: Determine *central ideas* or *themes* of a text, *analyze* their development, and *summarize* the key supporting details and ideas.

According to this standard, a student in grade 9 must be able to determine a central idea in a grade 9 text, analyze its development throughout the text, discuss how it is shaped by details, and provide a summary. ELLs with grade-level literacy in the home language, strong academic conceptual knowledge, and academic ways of thinking and using language *can* meet these standards, with appropriate scaffolds (see 2.15b for further information about Common Core progressions). These students transfer many skills from the home country academic context to U.S. secondary classrooms.

---

[2]Retrieved from http://www.corestandards.org/ELA-Literacy/introduction/key-design-consideration/

Component of Grade 9 Standard	Subskills Required for Proficiency in this Standard
Determine a central idea	• Identify topic in text • Identify key details • Use details to articulate a central idea
Analyze the development of central idea throughout the text (how it emerges and is shaped by details)	• Identify text structure • Understand the relationship between text structure and central idea
Provide a summary	• Distinguish fact from opinion • Determine importance

The table unpacks three main components of the grade 9 standard to reveal the subskills that lay beneath. LL SIFE most likely have not mastered these subskills in the home context before arriving in a grade 9 U.S. classroom.

Before students can approach RI.2 in grade 9, they must learn these subskills. Students must know how to identify the topic of a text before determining a central idea. They must be able to identify text structure before analyzing the development of a central idea in text. They must be able to distinguish fact from opinion, as well as more important from less important information before providing a summary. They must understand how the relationship between text structure, key ideas, and details supports comprehension. Above all, students must reach a certain threshold of literacy to grapple with ideas in text they read on their own. Students who have not yet developed foundational literacy skills in any language expend all of their cognitive resources on deciphering words, with limited resources remaining for comprehension.

Curriculm Designed for Low-Literacy Students with Interrupted Formal Education in the Context of Common Core State Standards

Curricula and instruction for LL SIFE must strategically target these building blocks of grade-level standards. Students need explicit instruction and repeated opportunities to apply these skills to increasingly complex text. LL SIFE need to engage with the skills using both read-aloud text and text they can read on their own. We designed our curriculum to serve these purposes.

The goals of the SIFE curriculum are to target the three major "cracks in the foundation" for LL SIFE: *foundational literacy, academic conceptual knowledge*, and *academic ways of thinking and using language* so that they can meaningfully participate in grade-level curricula.

The NYS Curriculum Project focuses on the development of two courses for SIFE in both middle and high school. The two courses, English language arts (ELA)[3] and foundational language and literacy (FLL), comprise a three-strand model to accelerate

---

[3]The SIFE ELA class is assumed to be multilingual, with limited if any resources for teaching students to read and write in the home language. If schools have an ELA class where there is a shared home language, then it is highly recommended that schools develop a learning-to-read component in the home language.

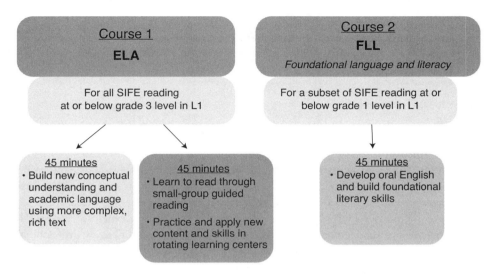

Three strands of the NYS SIFE curriculum.

learning for the lowest-level SIFE in secondary schools. The figure illustrates the three curriculum strands and goals: *ELA part 1, ELA part 2,* and *FLL.*

This unique design for secondary schools reflects our beliefs about what SIFE need to progress up the CCSS ladders of complexity. The integration of the three strands builds skills that support students to *learn to read and write* and *read and write to learn.* All students must learn to read and write, but only when students can *use* academic language and literacy as tools for acquiring new knowledge can they fully participate in school and society.

The goal is for all students to meet grade-level standards with grade-level texts. However, because of the mismatch between the knowledge and skills that LL SIFE bring from their home contexts and the demands of U.S. classrooms, instruction must cut across a wider scope of knowledge and skills. While moving students *toward* grade-level standards, instructers must consider where students are now and what they need *next.* This requires *scooping under* the K–12 progressions for each standard, and teaching the building blocks that will support students in eventually meeting the grade-level standard.

There are chasms, rather than small gaps, between the demands of grade-level CCSS and LL SIFE *literacy levels, academic conceptual knowledge,* and *academic ways of thinking and using language* skills on entry into U.S. middle and high school classrooms. The goal must be to work *toward* the grade-level standards, while providing explicit instruction and practice in the subskills, ensuring that students are exposed to rich academic conceptual knowledge along the way.

6.8 What do teachers need to understand about the challenges that the Common Core State Standards and Next Generation Science Standards present for English language learners/emergent bilinguals with learning disabilities?

■ *Erin Arango Escalante and Anna Halverson*

Introduction

As the majority of states shift to the Common Core State Standards (CCSS) and Next Generation Science Standards (NGSS) to better prepare K–12 students for college and career readiness, teachers of students who are English language learners (ELLs), with and without disabilities, might be wondering, "What does this mean for us?" The following figure provides a framework for understanding standards as one piece of a puzzle focusing on academic success of ELLs with complex needs. We hope it provides a space for educators to consider multiple components necessary to ensure academic success. All components—standards; research; federal, state, and local laws and policies; professional development (PD); and family and community participation—must be viewed from the content and language perspectives, which are illustrated using black and shades of gray. The outer circle symbolizes "unchangeable" elements, meaning these elements are relatively stable, and unlikely to be altered by those who work closely with ELLs with disabilities. The inner Venn diagram includes overlapping elements that directly affect those who work closely with this population. In the center of the diagram, where the sections meet, lies the result of all components working in harmony: joint planning and collaborative instructional practices. When developing individualized education plans (IEPs) for this population, administrators, special education teachers, general education teachers, language specialists, related service providers, and parents must collaborate, communicate, plan, and, ultimately, learn from each other to effectively facilitate student content and language learning.

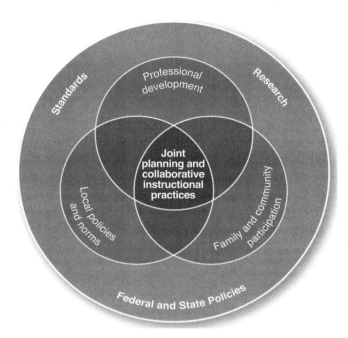

Framework for understanding standards.

Standards

Thinking of content and language standards as teaching tools can help guide educators when planning curriculum, instruction, and assessment for ELLs with disabilities. In every state, no matter what content standards are currently in use for ELLs with disabilities, it is vital that language standards are in place as well. The World-class Instructional Design and Assessment (WIDA) language standards were developed with content standards in mind. When content and language standards are used in conjunction with developmentally appropriate modifications based on individual student needs, practitioners are able to appropriately support, instruct, and assess ELLs with disabilities. The use of both content and language standards is essential to elicit the language needed for students to access grade-level content and be prepared for postsecondary options.

Research

The identification and implementation of evidenced-based practices (EBP) are major tenets of both the Individuals with Disabilities Act (IDEA) and No Child Left Behind (NCLB) Act. The effective use of EBP has and will continue to transform the field of special education, improving the quality and equity of services provided. When teaching ELLs with disabilities, the number of variables can make the use of EBP difficult for administrators and educators. Because of the complex needs of this population, EBP must be used in conjunction with the professional wisdom of special education practitioners and knowledge and expertise of language specialists.

Policy

Current federal policies guiding practices for ELL students with disabilities are IDEA and NCLB. Policies at state and local levels vary and are often separated for ELLs and students with disabilities. As the figure illustrates, it is important to consider laws, statutes, and policies for both ELLs and students with disabilities when making educational decisions. Refer to the National Association of State Directors of Special Education policy report for a breakdown of state policies and issues surrounding ELLs with disabilities (Keller-Allen, 2006). For information on current state practices and their policy implications, see Findings on Special Education LEP [Limited English Proficient] Students (Zehler, Fleischman, Hopstock, Pendzick, & Stephenson, 2003).

Professional Development

Both formal PD programs and less formal forums for communication and collaboration can be valuable tools for ensuring effective instruction for ELLs with disabilities. When general, special, and English as a second language (ESL)/bilingual teachers; administrators; and support staff participate in programming related to the success of ELLs with disabilities (e.g., culturally and linguistically sensitive teaching, behavior management methods, accommodations), the likelihood of student success increases. For a detailed analysis of how some states are facilitating communication and collaboration between special education and ELL staff, see the policy report from the National Association of State Directors of Special Education (Keller-Allen, 2006).

Family and Community Participation

While practitioners are able to share experiences and expertise related to ELLs with disabilities during formal and informal PD opportunities, families have a similar opportunity during IEP team meetings. Including families' perspectives, cultural values, knowledge, and experiences is essential for ensuring the academic and linguistic success of their children. Collaborative educational planning must include families.

When language and content standards, research, and policies are considered; PD opportunities are utilized; and families are respected IEP team members, the results are comprehensive, annual IEPs; collaborative instructional practices; and, ultimately, success in meeting individualized educational goals for each student identified as an ELL who also has a disability.

Preparing and Supporting Educators

6.9 How should pre-service education programs prepare educators to meet the needs of English language learners/emergent bilinguals relative to Common Core State Standards and Next Generation Science Standards curriculua?

■ *Nancy Commins and Diep Nguyen*

The wide diversity of students based on language, culture, and class that teachers are likely to meet in their classrooms is the new "norm" in public schools (Commins & Miramontes, 2005). Consequently, linguistic and cultural competence must be central to the preparation of *all* teachers, regardless of their particular content area, intended grade level, or field of specialization.

Educators must ensure that their instruction is focused on, and driven by, students' needs. In the case of English language learners (ELLs) and emergent bilinguals (EBs), while the Common Core State Standards (CCSS) and Next Generation Science Standards (NGSS) provide frameworks on which to build curriculum, day-to-day lessons and experiences, during which students access that curriculum, must take into account their language proficiency levels and build on the sociocultural assets that they bring from home.

We are guided by the assumption that effective teachers are reflective professionals who recognize the work of teaching as a political endeavor. The education of ELLs/EBs cannot be separated from the larger issues surrounding immigration and national language policy. Educators can either perpetuate or counteract external societal forces.

If all students are to meet the increasingly complex challenges of schooling, their teachers need both a transformative mindset and particular skills to actively engage in a cycle of teaching, learning, assessment, reflection, and revision in diverse environments. Understanding of language development and cultural identity must move from the periphery to the center of teacher preparation curricula.

Linguistically and culturally competent pre-service teachers need to learn how to do the following:

● Focus on equity and create a climate of belonging for all students
● Design and implement instructional activities to account for language and cultural demand
● Plan collaboratively for shared responsibility in instruction and flexible grouping
● Become familiar with learners' prior language and literacy experiences and development to build language proficiencies for students
● Use appropriate assessment to monitor student growth and create meaning-based instruction
● Develop and implement lessons that integrate both language and content goals
● Implement learning activities that are interactive and cognitively challenging
● Advocate for equitable education for all students and serve as catalysts for change in schools

- Practice reflection and continuous improvement as a teaching professional
- Organize instruction that is built on all the linguistic resources and skills that students bring to the classroom

We propose a framework for the preparation of all teachers that addresses the knowledge, skills, and dispositions that are necessary for candidates in the current context. The framework encompasses three areas:

1. Ideological clarity regarding multilingualism, translanguaging, and cross-cultural competence
2. Teaching practice embedded in constructivist learning theory and expressed through pedagogical competence
3. A skill set to address multilingualism and language development in and out of the classroom.

Course- and fieldwork should be organized to allow students to critically examine their beliefs, develop professional dispositions, acquire discipline-specific knowledge (the what), and develop pedagogical skills (the how). Programs must also provide candidates opportunities to apply their learning in authentic/diverse settings.

Effective programs will prepare all teacher candidates to understand that schooling is a process of identity development and that students' home language is fundamental to their identity. Such programs view diversity as a resource and take an additive approach to bilingualism, seeing it as an asset for all students. For teachers who will be bilingual or English as a second language (ESL) specialists, additional coursework related to the structure of English, biliteracy development, and second language methodologies should be included.

Given the need to develop these skills we propose the following organizing principles for teacher preparation programs related specifically to linguistic diversity. All programs must do the following:

- Facilitate teachers' systemic and critical examination of their own and others' assumptions about culture, power, privilege, and difference
- Provide teachers with the knowledge and skills that allow them to see themselves as language facilitators and cultural mediators
- Allow teachers to explore the demographics and resources of the communities in which they will work
- Provide opportunities to collaborate with others (peers, school staff, families) toward a common goal that benefits students
- Provide experiences that allow pre-service teachers to consider multiple perspectives and multiple voices, including their own
- Infuse a critical stance that allows for multiple perspectives to be explored in every content area

The exact ways that different institutions incorporate these principles into courses and fieldwork will necessarily vary based on the nature of the institution and local contexts.

6.10 What are some considerations when evaluating the educators of English language learners/emergent bilinguals?

■ *H. Gary Cook and Mariana Castro*

Recently, there have been a lot of conversations at the national level about ways to evaluate teacher effectiveness in supporting the academic success of their students, including English language learners (ELLs)/emergent bilinguals (EBs). In contrast to accountability based on school, district, and state assessment scores, the calculation of teachers' contribution to ELLs'/EBs' academic success is a much more complex issue. Despite the higher degree of sophistication of various approaches schools and districts are considering, there are still many concerns about establishing a relationship between teacher effectiveness and the academic success of ELLs/EBs. In this piece, we explore areas of concern related to the use of summative test data in the evaluation of educators of ELLs/EBs and explore ideas on alternative approaches to supporting the education of ELLs/EBs.

Among the various methods that have been considered to evaluate teacher effectiveness, value-added models (VAMs) offer some advantages. These methods are an improvement over comparing across classrooms and teachers or progress measures that compare a teacher's student scores from one year to another year. The main reason is that VAMs examine teachers' contribution in terms of growth, that is, they compare their students' scores in a given year to the scores of those same students in previous school years and to the scores of other students in the same grade level (Hanushek & Rivkin, 2010). However, these advantages also have limitations. VAM calculations include a teacher's students for a particular year, which result in data from a relatively small number of students; this can lead to dramatic year-to-year fluctuations. This is because of the methodology and the nature of the data, not because of teacher effectiveness. In general, no single teacher can be credited or blamed for the success or failure of students. It is unrealistic to assume that other educators who interact with students on a daily basis do not influence students' learning. Also, as students change teachers year to year, it is impossible to calculate how much of their learning is affected by previous educators. For ELLs/EBs, this reality is exacerbated because they interact with more than one educator to ensure they get the linguistic support they need to have access to grade-level, standards-based academic content.

While the flexible structure of VAMs allows including multiple teacher effects and conditioning student outcomes on previous achievement, introducing additional layers of complexity increases the burden on necessary assumptions, and more importantly, the requirements on data quality. Based on these issues, the research community cautions against heavy reliance on student test scores for high-stakes decisions (Baker et al., 2010; Braun, Chudowsky, & Koenig, 2010; Educational Testing Service's Policy Information Center, 2005; McCaffrey, Koretz, Lockwood, & Hamilton, 2003). If state policy requires the use of test scores for teacher accountability—either academic achievement or language proficiency tests—the proportion of such scores used should be small (Sahakyan, 2012). Administrators should collect other types of data to broaden the educational portrait of ELLs/EBs. Some of these data include teacher observations, portfolios of student work, and educators' professional development (PD) plans. Using a wider range of data, in addition to test scores, can provide a broader perspective on the specific strengths and opportunities for professional growth for educators and can inform the specific needs of ELLs/EBs.

For schools and educators to be effective in meeting the needs of ELLs/EBs, we need to shift the practice of looking at "end-of-the-game" data to more dynamic practices of planning, collecting, analyzing, and making decisions based on "during-the-game" data. Designing PD for educators of ELLs/EBs must begin with committing to a vision and to standards for the education of these children (Loucks-Horsley, Love, Stiles, Mundry, & Hewson, 2003). Summative data, then, become additional *input* in the design of professional learning for educators and *not* the springboard or basis for it. In addition to committing to a vision and setting standards for professional growth and to using data, professional learning plans should acknowledge the context and resources in which ELLs/EBs and their educators learn and interact.

6.11 How can teacher evaluation systems be used as springboards for professional learning?

■ *Diane Staehr Fenner and Ayanna Cooper*

Race to the Top demands multiple ways of measuring teacher performance with an emphasis on student growth (U.S. Department of Education, 2010). The primary tools for measuring teacher quality include teacher observations and student test scores (Jones, Buzick, & Turkan, 2013). To that end, numerous states and districts have adopted the Danielson or Marzano teacher evaluation frameworks. While these frameworks have certainly brought attention to teacher evaluation, they tend to fall short in one noteworthy area—teachers' abilities to effectively teach English language learners (ELLs) or students with disabilities (SwDs) receives minimal focus (Jones, Buzick, & Turkan, 2013). The limited extent to which current teacher evaluations address the most vulnerable population of students, ELLs and SwDs, is a concern for the validity of evaluation systems.

Inclusive Framework, Evaluation Questions, and Look-Fors

To address the need to include ELLs and SwDs, the American Federation of Teachers (AFT) worked with five districts each in New York and Rhode Island to develop and pilot inclusive teacher evaluation practices. This work was guided by four evidence-based principles in the evaluation of teachers focused on the inclusion of all learners in general education classrooms (August, Salend, Staehr Fenner, & Kozik, 2012). Staehr Fenner, Kozik, and Cooper (2015) have refined the four principles that complement both the Danielson and Marzano frameworks to support successful inclusive practice (see the following table).

Alignment between Danielson, Marzano, and Shared Values Teacher Evaluation Frameworks

Danielson Domain	Marzano Domain	EL/SwD Shared Values Principle
Planning and preparation	Classroom practices and strategies	Committing to equal access for all learners
Classroom environment	Planning and preparing	Preparing to support diverse learners
Instruction	Reflecting on teaching	Reflective teaching using evidence-based strategies
Professional responsibilities	Collegiality and professionalism	Building a culture of collaboration and community

In the following table, we briefly define each shared values principle and provide one sample question and look-for for evaluators to determine the inclusiveness of all ELL teachers' practices. This is not an exhaustive list of questions or look-fors.

Shared Values Principle, Description, Sample Question, and Sample Look-For

Shared Value Principle	Description	Sample Question for Teachers of ELLs	Sample Look-For for Evaluators
Committing to equal access for all learners	All teachers adhere to the laws and precedents set in numerous court decisions regarding full and equal access to public education for ELLs. Preobservation conversation includes adaptations observer can expect to see and lesson plans that include theoretical and evidence-based practices.	Can teachers articulate a vision and a commitment to educating *all* students, including ELLs?	Demonstrating understanding of the CCSS, curriculum, English language proficiency and development, and assessments for the CCSS and language standards.
Preparing to support diverse learners	All teachers articulate multiple ways that ELLs will be engaged in the lesson, how the information provided during the lesson will be represented, and how ELLs will express the learning that they have achieved.	How are support systems such as preferral strategies, response-to-intervention, ESL programs, and first and second language support programs implemented in the classroom and school?	Describing high expectations for ELLs that demonstrate an understanding of how English language proficiency level and other background variables determine the type of instructional scaffolding needed.
Reflective teaching using evidence-based strategies	All teachers provide instruction that is individualized, student-centered, varied, appropriately challenging, standards-based, and grounded in evidence-based practice.	How are language-rich, culturally responsive, flexibly grouped, student-initiated, and authentic and relevant learning experiences manifested for ELLs in the classroom?	Using visuals, graphic organizers, first language materials, and supports (e.g., sentence frames) that are supported by learning objectives.
Building a culture of collaboration and community	All teachers build professional relationships, communicate with, and connect to ELLs' families, culture, and community. All teachers support the academic, social, and emotional growth of ELLs. Co-teaching can be described, as can relationships with paraprofessionals and related service providers.	How are supports, such as ELL scheduling arrangements, parent and professional conferences, and resources for professional development and planning utilized?	Reflecting on teaching, maintaining required and appropriate records to document ELLs' language growth, and effectively communicating with ELL families.

Conclusion

During this time of great change, we must empower all ELL teachers to have deeper knowledge of each of their students. We must support them to develop professionally to provide an equitable education for ELLs.

DISCUSSION QUESTIONS

After reading this chapter, engage in dialogue with peer educators, including school principals, other administrators and supervisors, teachers of different subjects, specialists in different areas, paraprofessionals, and parents/community members to discuss effective professional learning for all educators who are responsible for educating ELLs/EBs in the context of the CCSS and accountability requirements. Here are some questions to reflect on individually, with a colleague, or ideally, as part of a professional learning community at your school. If you are in a school, the members of this group would comprise the school's ELL/EB leadership team, whose responsibility it is to collectively make the decisions that affect the education of ELLs/EBs.

1. What new ideas or thoughts emerged for you in this chapter? What is one that you could put in practice right away? What others might you work on in the future? What resources do you need to do so?

2. What view does your school/organization have on professional learning? How is this view enacted? What changes could improve current professional learning at your site?

3. How are professional learning needs identified? How are they met? How is the learning of ELLs/EBs included in the professional learning at your school? How are ESL/bilingual educators included in professional learning opportunities offered at your school?

4. Engage in dialogue with your colleagues, including administrators, teachers, specialists, and paraprofessionals, to discuss support systems for ELLs/EBs and their educators. What opportunities or structures exist at your site to collaborate with others? How can these be leveraged to enhance the instruction of ELLs/EBs? How are these opportunities supported through existing structures or by administrators?

5. What relationships do you and your school, district, or organization have with institutes of higher education? Are they reciprocal? How do these relationships support the preparation or ongoing professional learning of educators who work with ELLs/EBs in the area?

6. How are ELLs/EBs with diverse needs (e.g., LTELLs, ELLs with disabilities, and SIFE who are also ELLs/EBs) served at your school or district? Is there a sense of shared responsibility for their education? Is there consistent support across environments, grades, and buildings? How do educators receive support for working with these students?

TOPICS FOR REFLECTION AND ACTION

The following statements are organized around the big ideas of the chapter. Read through them and indicate the extent to which each applies to your community and your school. After you complete the survey, discuss your responses with your team. Then write down one to three reflection points that have emerged from your discussions. Finally, identify one to three concrete actions that you/your team can take.

DK don't know   1 strongly disagree   2 disagree   3 agree   4 strongly agree

SHIFTING ROLES OF ESL EDUCATORS					
1. The ESL teachers/specialists in my school (district) are part of the planning for the implementation of the CCSS in our educational program.	DK	1	2	3	4
2. The ESL teachers/specialists in my school (district) collaborate with other educators in the implementation of the CCSS in our educational program, sharing effective practices on how to help ELL/EB students be successful.	DK	1	2	3	4
3. Administrators in my school (district) encourage all educators to see themselves as language teachers and to take responsibility or play a role in the education of ELL/EB students.	DK	1	2	3	4
4. Administrators in my school (district) leverage the expertise of ESL teachers/specialists to build capacity and sustainability related to effective educational practices in working with ELL/EB students (e.g., through opportunities to co-plan, collaborate, coach, and mentor).	DK	1	2	3	4
Planning for Professional Learning					
5. Professional learning opportunities in my school (district) include topics related to effective practices and resources for working with ELL/EB students on CCSS–aligned instruction.	DK	1	2	3	4
6. Professional learning opportunities in my school (district) are available for all teachers, including ESL teachers/specialists.	DK	1	2	3	4
6.1 (Subsequent statement, if you choose 3 *or* 4 for question 6.) These professional learning opportunities include topics specific and relevant to the work of ESL teachers/specialists.	DK	1	2	3	4
6.2 (Subsequent statement, if you choose 3 *or* 4 for question 6.) These professional learning opportunities include opportunities to coconstruct new knowledge and codevelop new practices with general education teachers and other specialists.	DK	1	2	3	4
7. All educators in my school (district), including ESL teachers and specialists, receive professional learning opportunities or support with a focus on supporting ELL/EB students from diverse backgrounds, abilities, and experiences—for example, SIFE, LTELLs, and students with disabilities.	DK	1	2	3	4
Preparing and Supporting Educators					
8. My school (district) collaborates with universities, colleges, and other institutions of higher education to ensure pre-service teachers receive the tools and resources that will help them be ready to teach ELL/EB students within the context of the CCSS.	DK	1	2	3	4

SHIFTING ROLES OF ESL EDUCATORS *cont.*					
9. My school (district) collaborates with institutions of higher education and other organizations to build the expertise and capacity of in-service teachers and help them teach ELL/EB students within the context of the CCSS.	DK	1	2	3	4
10. Educators in my school (district) engage in instructional practices that provide access, and yet maintain the challenge and expectations of the CCSS for ELL/EB students.	DK	1	2	3	4
11. Administrators in my school (district) see evaluation systems as an opportunity to align professional learning to the needs of educators, especially in relation to teaching ELL/EB students within the context of the CCSS.	DK	1	2	3	4
12. Administrators in my school (district) create plans for professional learning using a clear vision of what the education of ELL/EB students within the context of the CCSS should look like, and take into consideration other factors, which include, but are not limited to, educator evaluation systems.	DK	1	2	3	4

Reflection:

Action Steps:

Chapter 7

Assessment and Accountability

Assessment is and will remain a cornerstone of standards-based education reform in U.S. schools, as it is about to become the driving force behind the Common Core State Standards (CCSS). In the 2014–2015 school year (as this book goes to press), the United States will move forward into the assessment phase of CCSS implementation. The federal education policy of 2001, entitled No Child Left Behind (NCLB), required the assessment of all students, including emergent bilinguals (EBs), to ensure that these students were learning the English language and acquiring the academic content standards that had been set under the law. This resulted in the use of high-stakes tests, for instance to determine students' grade promotion and/or high school graduation, and as a way for the federal government to evaluate states, school districts, schools, and teachers.

The high-stakes tests used to evaluate EBs' content knowledge are typically the same tests as those given to English monolinguals and administered in English only, with a set of test accommodations intended to erase the impact of language proficiency on test results. Whether or not this erasure of difference is even possible is a lingering question of serious concern. The testing of EBs has remained a particularly controversial component of federal policy mandates, with some maintaining that the testing of these students is necessary to ensure their needs are not overlooked and others arguing that their inclusion in state testing has proven to be more harmful than helpful. The concerns arise because EBs across the United States typically underperform in comparison to their peers, and are more likely to be punished as a result (e.g., by being retained in grade and/or barred from receiving a high school diploma). As schools begin assessing student attainment of the CCSS, the practice of high-stakes testing will remain as a lasting legacy of NCLB. As noted previously, the CCSS have not altogether replaced NCLB; while the previous standards and assessments are being replaced with new ones, the two policies otherwise work in tandem.

Two state consortia, the Partnership for Assessment of Readiness for College and Careers (PARCC) and the Smarter Balanced Assessment Consortium (SBAC), received federal grants of approximately $185 million each to develop new CCSS–aligned assessments. At present, PARCC has 9 member states plus the District of Columbia, and SBAC has 17 member states. Remaining states are undecided, using assessments of their own, and/or are not CCSS members. CCSS assessment approaches currently being developed by individual states and by these two state consortia continue to operate under the same accommodations paradigm as that of NCLB, for instance by relying on extended time, bilingual glossaries, and instructions read aloud to remove the impact of language on EBs' test scores. While psychometricians continue working to develop better measures that truly will level the playing field between EBs and their English monolingual peers, the effectiveness of this approach is debatable. Also questionable is what effect the emphasis on testing will ultimately have on student learning of the CCSS, and whether test-based accountability is an effective means of ensuring real learning rather than "teaching to the test."

Amidst many uncertainties, what is clear is that the testing industry stands to gain a great deal from the CCSS. PARCC and SBAC will contract with testing companies to publish and score the tests. This is a lucrative prospect for a company that wins the contract of one of the consortia, given the large numbers of tests and students involved and promises unprecedented earnings for the U.S. testing industry. Most states that develop their own assessments of the CCSS will also likely contract with testing companies to publish and score the tests. In addition, given that extremely high stakes are attached to these test scores, schools will be under great pressure to adopt the curricula most aligned to the tests, such as those on offer by the very companies publishing the tests.

This chapter delves into the many issues raised by the assessment of EBs with regard to their attainment of the CCSS and with testing still serving as the foundation on which accountability systems rely. This chapter deepens our understanding of issues raised in Chapter 1, weighing the overall effect of the latest education reforms on U.S. schooling for EBs because it is in the testing of the CCSS that actual results are demanded; in this way, assessment is "where the rubber meets the road." The first group of questions in this chapter set the current assessment and accountability landscape by looking at both the rationale and the impact of previous test-driven reforms, addressing lingering questions and concerns. Given that assessment of the CCSS is just beginning nationally, the chapter next previews what can be expected from this phase of implementation and how to use the data that will be generated. What is striking about the responses in this chapter is how the experts all highlight tremendous complexity in the assessment of EBs, and the reality that current testing instruments are too limited to do all that current policies require of them. The final section looks toward the future by identifying ways to improve assessment and accountability for EBs and highlighting promising practices, such as translanguaging, now being field tested.

Goals and Challenges

7.1 Why has the federal government emphasized assessment and accountability in recent education reforms?

■ *Holly Yettick*

When President George W. Bush signed the federal No Child Left Behind (NCLB) Act in 2002, the legislation was viewed as a veritable diner menu of education policy that offered something that nearly everyone could stomach, regardless of political party.

Then-Education Secretary Rod Paige summed up the Republican view when he praised the way in which the law treated federal spending as an "investment" that gave the federal government the "leverage to demand results" (Robelen, 2002). Accountability measures became the financial statement. Test scores were to be the net income that demonstrated whether or not the investment had yielded results. For many Democrats, a more appealing aspect of the law was its emphasis on assessing that *all* groups of students were making progress, not just the average child. "[T]he law demands that all children must benefit—black or white, immigrant or native-born, rich or poor, disabled or not," now-deceased Democratic Senator Edward M. Kennedy of Massachusetts wrote in 2008. "Before its enactment, only a handful of states monitored the achievement of every group of students in their schools. Today, all 50 states must do that." Although Democrats and Republicans might have had different motives when they supported the law, in the end their efforts at consensus resulted in a focus on holding educators accountable by assessing all children, including English learners (ELs).

This means that, under Title I of the Act, schools must assess the progress of multiple subgroups, including ELs, in the core academic subjects of reading, math, and science. Title III of the Act also requires educators to track emerging bilinguals' (EBs) progress toward English proficiency. In line with the law's emphasis on accountability, schools, districts, and states face consequences if they consistently miss subject-specific or language proficiency targets. In complying with these measures, educators face several practical challenges. One problem is that reading, math, and science tests that are written in English may reflect a child's language proficiency rather than his or her knowledge of these subjects. Additionally, if the child participates in a transitional bilingual or dual language immersion program, English exams do not provide the child with an opportunity to demonstrate proficiency in the language of instruction. Some states have responded to this challenge by making at least some of the tests available in languages other than English. However, in many areas, educators have reacted by immersing students in English as quickly as possible (Gándara & Hopkins, 2010; Menken & Solorza, 2014; Zehr, 2007). A downside of this response is that a large body of research suggests that bilingual instruction and bilingualism have many benefits (McCabe et al., 2013).

Another problem is that, unlike subgroups based on race, ethnicity, or socioeconomic status, the EL category is, by definition, a classification for those who have not yet reached proficiency. Once proficiency is attained, the student is removed from the category. Some states have addressed this issue by attaining federal waivers that permit them to combine ELs into a category with other subgroups, creating so-called "super-subgroups" (Klein, 2014). As a result, average improvements may help compensate for the challenges inherent in the EL category. A drawback of this approach is that it may mask problems for ELs (Lyons, 2014). Another more promising solution has been to obtain federal waivers that emphasize academic growth targets that compare children with peers whose past test scores are similar.

Title III English proficiency exams may also be administered one-on-one, multiple times per year. This is challenging because it can be time-consuming and costly, yet Title III funds cannot be used to offset testing-related expenses. Federal officials have suggested that, given the low levels of per-pupil funding attached to the program, districts and states need to be covering the cost of instructing and monitoring ELs rather than expecting Title III to pick up the tab. "There is very little funding in this program," a U.S. Department of Education official said in 2013. "It's the cherry on top of your cake. It is restrictive because there's very little funding. It is designed to be a supplemental program. . . .If the district is clear about the core program they don't [have problems] understanding how to supplement it" (Buechner Institute for Governance, 2013, p. 64).

■ *Monty Neill*

Test-Based Accountability Fails English Language Learners

NCLB has failed to improve student achievement or close gaps among student subgroups. This failure is particularly striking for English language learners (ELLs) (Guisbond, Neill, & Schaeffer, 2012). Unfortunately, the new Common Core tests will perpetuate, not solve, the problem (FairTest, 2013).

NCLB requires annual reading and math testing in grades 3–8 and once in high school. That federal mandate alone forced the average state to more than double the number of standardized exams it administered. The idea was that by requiring 100% "proficiency" by 2014, schools would act to improve outcomes, particularly for low-scoring groups of students such as ELLs.

Each year under NCLB, growing numbers of schools failed to make "adequate yearly progress" (AYP) and faced escalating sanctions. Seeking to boost scores and avoid punishment, schools often narrowed curriculum, reduced time on nontested subjects, and even turned reading and math into little more than test prep programs. Low-scoring classrooms, in particular, were flooded with "interim" tests as a means to gauge progress toward the end-of-year exams and to control teachers' practice. Some districts now administer more than 30 tests annually in some grades.

NCLB's improvement strategy has failed, even as gauged by reading and math scores on the National Assessment of Educational Progress (NAEP). In general, progress on NAEP reading and math exams in grades 4, 8, and 12 slowed or halted for almost every demographic group, including ELLs, since NCLB was implemented.

The most striking example is grade 4 reading. ELLs gained 12 points on NAEP from 1998–2003, before NCLB took effect, but only one more point from 2003–2013

(National Assessment of Educational Progress, 2013).The score gap with non-ELLs closed 8 points before NCLB, but widened 4 points afterward. Since 2003, grade 8 reading and grades 4 and 8 math gaps have widened by 2–4 points. Learning outcomes actually declined for 17-year-old ELLs: from 2004–2013, reading scores fell 7 points while math dropped 9.

Despite this abysmal record, NCLB proponents have "doubled down" on test-based accountability, most recently by embracing the Common Core State Standards (CCSS). The Obama Administration's decision to use Race to the Top stimulus funds and Department of Education waivers to revise the accountability structure means that the more than 40 participating states must intervene only in their lowest performing schools. Schools with large percentages of ELLs are likely to be heavily represented. States also must use student scores as a "significant part" of evaluating *all* teachers and principals. This will greatly increase the number of required exams and ratchet up pressure on teachers to teach to the test.

CCSS assessments will not change the fundamental test-and-punish framework. In fact, the new exams are designed to be even more difficult. When New York installed a temporary Common Core test in 2013, scores plummeted, with only 3% of ELLs scoring proficient in reading (*New York Times*, 2013).

Proponents tout the CCSS exams as a major improvement over existing tests. However, they will remain largely multiple choice, with some open-ended questions, and a few short performance tasks. The new tests will have very limited capacity to evaluate how well students grasp concepts or can apply their knowledge.

The Forum on Educational Accountability (2011), which I chair, is one group that has proposed a very different approach to assessment and accountability, including for ELLs. U.S. policy must shift in three key ways:

1. Stop high-stakes uses of standardized tests.
2. Reduce the number of standardized exams and the time and money spent on them.
3. Replace reliance on standardized tests with multiple forms of evidence of student learning.

7.2 What are the aims of data-driven instruction, and what are its limitations?

■ *Julie Marsh*

Data-driven instruction refers to a process of systematically collecting and analyzing various types of data—such as test results, student work, attendance and other behavioral data, observations of instruction, course enrollment patterns—to guide practice. Advocates argue that student learning will improve if teachers use data to reflect on, plan, and alter their instruction. While educators have long argued the value of formative assessment results guiding practice, in recent years, federal and state accountability policies have focused on state and district interim assessments as major drivers in the movement to promote data-driven instruction in the United States. Teachers are expected to use these test results to measure student progress toward standards and to adjust instruction (e.g., lesson planning, grouping and differentiation strategies, identification of topics requiring more attention) to meet the needs of individual students, including English learners (ELs). Given the new instructional demands of the Common Core State Standards (CCSS), results from CCSS-aligned assessments will likely play an important role in the ongoing call for data-driven instruction in the coming years.

Recent scholarship points to the potential for data to change classroom instruction (e.g., Nelson, Slavit, & Deuel, 2012). These studies show that, in some instances, student learning data can substantively shape teachers' practice. However, research also indicates that educators often use data in simplistic ways that do not significantly alter instruction (e.g., Ikemoto & Marsh, 2007). Studies find that teachers often respond to data by reteaching content, identifying particular students for out-of-class support, and making other procedural changes to practice. Still others have documented teachers responding to test results by teaching test-taking skills or "gaming" the system (e.g., focusing on the "bubble kids," students who are close to proficient on the test), which may yield short-term improvements in achievement but not necessarily the deeper learning intended by those promoting data-driven instruction.

Several factors contribute to these mixed effects (Marsh, 2012). First, data properties contribute greatly to teachers' patterns of use. When data are not perceived to be timely, accurate, aligned with what is being taught, or providing insight into student's conceptual understanding, they are generally not used to improve instruction. Second, time matters. Without significant time set aside to analyze data, reflect on the causes of observed results, and determine action steps, the data are not likely to spur intended change and improvement. Third, research indicates that teachers often lack adequate skills and knowledge to formulate questions, interpret results, and develop instructional responses, and that school leaders play a critical role in facilitating support, providing a safe environment to examine data, and ensuring productive use of data.

These factors suggest that to be effective, future systems promoting data use must first and foremost ensure that the data are credible and valid. This will be particularly important for the new Common Core–aligned interim and formative assessments being developed. If teachers do not view them as providing accurate measures of what they are now being asked to teach and what their students know and understand, then these assessment results may not spur deeper reflection and adjustments to practice as intended. Second, accountability systems and leaders need to provide consistent messages about the purposes of the various assessments. Assessments used for summative judgments with consequences may work against the formative, learning goals of data-driven instruction, leading to the strategic behaviors well documented in the literature on test-based accountability. Finally, investments are needed to build teacher capacity to use data. Research indicates that time and opportunities to collaboratively discuss and develop responses to data, as well as high-quality coaching focused on adjusting practice, can assist this process. Pre-service training could also place greater attention on building these skills and knowledge.

7.3 What have been the benefits and drawbacks of testing and accountability for English language learners/emergent bilinguals under No Child Left Behind, and what are their implications under the Common Core State Standards?

■ *Kate Menken*

In this response, I clarify why the requirements of No Child Left Behind (NCLB) still hold true, and some of the ways that the Common Core State Standards (CCSS) support and amplify the three most problematic aspects of NCLB mandates for emergent bilinguals (EBs). The CCSS are a state-led initiative whose development included governors and state education commissioners from 48 states and the District of Columbia under the leadership of the National Governors Association Center for Best Practices and the Council of Chief State School Officers. Because the CCSS are a state initiative, albeit with national reach, they do not supplant the requirements of current federal education policy. What this means is that as states and school systems work to implement and now assess the CCSS, they still have to contend with the assessment and accountability requirements of NCLB, the federal education policy that was passed into law by Congress in 2001. Specifically, NCLB requires that EBs are tested annually in English, math, and English language proficiency, and show continual gains in these areas as a means for the federal government to ensure that states, school districts, and individual schools are held accountable for student growth. Schools failing to make required performance gains face sanctions, such as closure or restructuring, over time.

This system of accountability has been particularly damaging for EBs. The problem, which has by now been widely documented, is that language proficiency hinders student performance on assessments administered in English, which means that such tests become language proficiency exams for EBs even when they are intended to measure academic content knowledge (Menken, 2008). Accordingly, each year since NCLB was passed into law, there has remained a wide achievement gap, anywhere from 20–50 percentage points, in all states between EBs and their monolingual peers—in spite of states using testing accommodations, such as extended time or bilingual dictionaries, in an effort to "level the playing field" between EBs and English monolinguals. EBs disproportionately face punishment, for instance by being barred from high school graduation or grade promotion, for failing these high-stakes exams. The schools that serve large numbers of EBs are also far more likely to face sanctions under NCLB, and far more of these schools than others have closed in the years since NCLB was passed into law.

Because the assessment and accountability mandates of NCLB will fundamentally remain unchanged under the CCSS, so too will the troubling consequences for EBs and the schools that serve them. While educational policies oftentimes do work in opposition, particularly when developed and adopted by differing entities (e.g., state vs. city policy or district vs. individual school), there are several ways that the CCSS will only intensify several of the more problematic aspects of NCLB for EBs.

Of these problematic aspects, the following are the three gravest mistakes made by NCLB for EBs that the CCSS are repeating:

1. Like NCLB, the CCSS propagate an English-only orientation, threatening pedagogy and programming that use students' home languages in instruction (García & Flores, 2013). One of the main mechanisms for this orientation is through English-only testing, which undermines and threatens bilingual education programs because educators and administrators match the language of instruction to the language of the tests in an effort to increase test scores (Menken, 2008; Menken & Solorza, 2014).
2. EBs are again at the periphery of the CCSS, with a mere 2.5-page afterthought discussion of these students in the original Common Core standards document, leaving states and various organizations scrambling to incorporate EBs into implementation efforts. This has meant that very few considerations have been made for EBs.
3. The CCSS assessment approaches currently being developed by individual states and by two state consortia (Partnership for Assessment of Readiness for College and Careers and the Smarter Balanced Assessment Consortium) continue to rely on the same accommodations that have already proven ineffective and detrimental for EBs under NCLB, leaving these students disproportionately likely to fail high-stakes tests and face the resulting consequences (Menken, 2008; Solórzano, 2008).

High-stakes tests always pose a threat to standards-based education reform because educators are pressured to teach to the tests rather than to the standards, rendering the standards themselves irrelevant. To avoid this, a major educational decision should never be made based on the results of a single test score, particularly for EBs. Instead, these students need to be evaluated based on multiple measures, such as portfolios with a range of samples of student work, formative teacher assessments, and teacher evaluations, to garner a more holistic understanding of what an EB knows and is able to do. Likewise, the standards should be assessed multilingually rather than monolingually, as a means to promulgate support for multilingualism on one hand, and, more pragmatically, to gain a more accurate picture of EBs' content knowledge on the other. Moreover, EBs need to be at the center of current and future efforts to implement the CCSS, which cannot simply be taken at face value. Instead, these standards need to be negotiated, resisted, and/or modified when implemented for EBs.

7.4 What are the challenges of test-based accountability for English language learners/emergent bilinguals?

- *Ronald W. Solórzano*

As the educational community prepares for the implementation of the Common Core State Standards (CCSS), issues persist regarding how content standards in general, and these standards in particular, will affect emergent bilinguals (EBs)/English language learners (ELLs).[1] In part, these issues relate to the nature of the standards, and whether

---

[1] The terms emergent bilinguals and English language learners are used interchangeably with the understanding that emergent bilingual is an empowering label while English language learner may be viewed as a deficit label—but is still widely used.

they represent the background knowledge and experiences of ELLs (Solórzano, 2012), and the uses of related high-stakes CCSS assessments. In the latter case, these tests likely will be used in high-stakes contexts and will play a vital role in determining state-wide school academic rating systems (academic performance indexes). They could also have repercussions for teachers (value-added models), administrators (failing school policies), and students (instructional assignments, tracking, retention, and graduation) (Solórzano, 2008).

A central issue with high-stakes testing for EBs is that these tests are not developed with them in mind. They are developed for native-English-speaking students relative to language and content. English language proficiency (ELP) is assumed because these tests are intended to evaluate students' content-area knowledge, not ELP. Accommodations, while helpful, only serve to verify the mismatch between test and test-taker. This mismatch is prompted by variations in ELP (and native language literacy levels); lack of familiarity with the test construct and test administration; mismatch between test items and sociocultural experiences, references, and background; and "opportunity to learn" the content area assessed (especially in cases where ELLs are segregated in English language development instruction with low redesignation rates). While accommodations for ELLs are meant to "reduce construct irrelevant variance because of language," and some appear encouraging (e.g., simplified English and English dictionaries and glossaries), their effectiveness in high-stakes testing, especially for low-level English-proficient ELLs, is uncertain or minimal. This being said, in high-stakes tests, language proficiency should not be an issue—only content knowledge.

An additional validity concern related to instruction—and of paramount importance to teachers, parents, and administrators—centers around the aforementioned "opportunity to learn" the content area at grade level.[2] Because ELLs are often placed in remedial (e.g., structured English immersion) programs, grade-level content knowledge in English is often delayed, if ever achieved. Each content area (e.g., history, math) has a unique vocabulary and related concepts (e.g., registers) that require special attention. For instance, math has a special vocabulary that includes ". . .technical terms, symbolic expressions, and terms with multiple meanings" that ELLs need to grasp in addition to the English language (Roberson & Summerlin, 2005). Teachers have to ensure that EBs are receiving this specialized instruction in each content area if they are to be successful on these tests.

Another testing issue concerns *when* EBs are ready to take CCSS-related tests. A reliable assessment of readiness in *academic* English is necessary for the test to be valid. Most school districts address this concern by giving an English proficiency test to determine English fluency as a criterion for testing in English. However, in many cases, these English proficiency tests do not predict success on English content-area tests. These tests rarely evaluate the academic or content-based vocabulary knowledge of ELLs; therefore they are poor predictors of achievement and lead to inappropriate and false predictions of ELLs' academic levels or program placement.

---

[2]This assumes that the content is worth learning. This brief review will not address the quality of the CCSS content.

Because of misguided statewide propositions and state/federal regulations, teachers have been prevented from offering effective instruction to EBs. Instead of developing the cognitive potential of these students, teachers have been required to teach primarily in the English language. This presents a major challenge to teachers. However, progressive educators and administrators have sought statewide waivers, when necessary, so they can offer native language instruction in the content areas while providing English language development instruction to promote second language learning. In this way, students can realize their true potential to become biliterate.

Assessing Student Attainment of the Common Core State Standards and Making Meaning of the Results

7.5 What new (summative) assessments are being designed under the Common Core State Standards, and how are English language learners/emergent bilinguals to be included? What are test accommodations and which, if any, are most effective for emergent bilinguals?

- *Jamal Abedi*

New Summative Assessments Based on the Common Core State Standards and English Language Learner Accessibility

Two consortia, Partnership for Assessment of Readiness of College and Careers (PARCC) and the Smarter Balanced Assessment Consortium (SBAC), that are supported by the Race to the Top (RTT) initiative are developing assessments in English language arts (ELA) and mathematics for their member states. Both consortia are in the process of developing systems that provide valid, reliable, and fair assessments that are aligned to the Common Core State Standards (CCSS) in ELA/literacy and mathematics for grades 3–8 and 11 for all students. Both consortia aim to make their assessments accessible for subgroups of students, such as English language learners (ELLs) and students with disabilities, by incorporating accommodations and accessibility features that are both effective and valid.

I am focusing my attention on the linguistic accessibility for ELL students. This aspect of assessment is of paramount importance because the CCSS in both ELA/literacy and mathematics are more linguistically demanding than many of the existing state content standards. While the focal construct in ELA/literacy is language, in mathematics language that is not directly related to the focal construct (i.e., mathematics) may be a source of construct-irrelevant variance and may seriously affect the validity of test outcomes. For example, the CCSS require all students to be highly proficient in verbal and written language to "discuss," "elaborate," "explain," and "describe" concepts and content in mathematics (CCSS Initiative, 2012b). Therefore, lack of general English proficiency may affect student performance in content areas like mathematics, where language is not the target of measurement.

To elaborate on the concept of linguistic accessibility, we first need to distinguish between language that is related to the focal construct (construct-relevant) and language that is unrelated to the construct (construct-irrelevant). Both consortia have incorporated language-based accommodations and accessibility features into the item development and field-testing process to control for sources of unnecessary linguistic complexities in their assessments, particularly in mathematics assessments.

However, it must be noted that many of the accommodations used for ELL students may be ineffective in making assessments more accessible (e.g., see Abedi, 2012), because they may not provide the type of linguistic support that ELL students need to present their content knowledge (e.g., in mathematics). Therefore, the RTT consortia tried to identify accommodations that are effective in making content-based assessments more linguistically accessible for ELL students, without altering the focal construct. Following is a summary of the study SBAC conducted to identify accommodations and accessibility features that can be used to provide reliable and valid assessments for ELL students controlling for sources of linguistic complexities that are considered irrelevant to the assessments.

The study reviewed the accommodation literature for ELL students and identified accommodations that both are effective in making assessments more accessible for ELL students and provide reliable and valid results (Abedi & Ewers, 2013). Some of these accommodations were labeled as "accessibility features" that can be used for all students, including ELLs. These features can be considered as "good practice" in test development. For example, English or bilingual glossaries were recommended as accessibility features, as long as they do not provide definitions or elaboration on content-related terms. Another example of accessibility features is a "linguistically revised" version of an assessment in which test items are revised to reduce or eliminate unnecessary linguistic complexities. On the other hand, accommodations such as "read-aloud test items in reading" were not recommended as accommodations to use for ELL students because evidence suggests that they may alter the focal construct.

In summary, the new generation of assessments under development by the two RTT consortia is designed to be more accessible to ELL students. The assessments incorporate accommodations and accessibility features that reduce the impact of construct-irrelevant variance because of cultural and linguistic biases.

■ *Jamie Schissel*

The summative assessments being designed under the CCSS have introduced new approaches for testing EBs but also utilize previous practices of test accommodations. In new approaches, the testing consortia—PARCC and SBAC—have designed features to increase access for all students. These features are either embedded in computer-based delivery or external resources. Features common on both tests include spell checking, using computer notepads, or having scratch paper available. Other supports, or test accommodations, need to be preassigned based on individual need and previous use in the classroom and are targeted at the needs of EBs and students with disabilities.

Test accommodations are designed to make tests more accessible to EB students but not to alter an assessment that was developed for and piloted on targeted test takers. However, the definition of targeted test takers is problematic because such test takers are, for the most part, monolingual. The PARCC and SBAC assessments continue to use test accommodations that require EB students to perform based on the monolingual norm assumed by the assessments. This practice raises questions of validity, given that EBs are not monolingual.

Further complicating test accommodation use is the concern that any accomodation could provide an unfair advantage by altering what information or skills the assessment measures. For EBs who are offered the opportunity to use their home languages as an accommodation, this means selectively excluding the use of other languages. For example, bilingual translation glossaries are only available for content-unrelated words. The purpose of this is to prevent EB students from directly using other languages when it may help them understand English content words.

In terms of more problematic accommodations, PARCC offers the translation of directions into a language other than English, which provides few benefits for EBs who may not understand the content of the test item. PARCC also offers an English-only scribe or test-to-speech accommodation, which is more commonly used for students with disabilities. The use of English-only scribe accommodations that mirror practices for students with disabilities disregard previous scribe accommodations used for EBs, where responses were translated into English. PARCC, therefore, provides an accommodation that conflates EBs' needs with students with disabilities.

Of the current accommodations offered by the testing consortia, the translation dictionaries described previously have proven to be effective for EBs, if they also used this strategy during instruction. In a more promising direction, SBAC offers a bilingual Spanish and English assessment and has plans for additional bilingual assessments. PARCC is making provisions for bilingual assessments, but will charge states for that test version. These bilingual assessments are available for mathematics, with ELA remaining English only. Bilingual assessments have been shown to be beneficial for EBs but are usually recommended for students who received bilingual instruction. Within the SBAC translation framework, they offer guidelines for developing assessment for diverse linguistic communities. They point out, however, that the feasibility of developing such assessments is dependent on a large, stable population of EBs who will use the assessment.

Additional guidelines similar to the SBAC translation framework build on the perspective that EB student language practices are the standard and could be used in the future to foster emergent bilingualism in all students. Dynamic assessments that provide bilingual scaffolds to demonstrate what students can do with and without support may provide a more accurate picture not only of students' content knowledge, but also their growing bilingualism (Flores & Schissel, 2014; Logan-Terry & Wright, 2010). Cumulative, holistic assessments such as portfolios may allow for students' bilingualism to be incorporated and recognized as an advantage. The challenges are great, yet developing assessments that appropriately meet the linguistic needs of EBs is essential to recognize and develop the bilingualism already present in classrooms.

7.6 How is English language proficiency assessed under the Common Core State Standards, and how can we use these data to inform and improve instruction?

■ *Kenji Hakuta*

Two consortia of states are developing the next generation of English language proficiency (ELP) tests—World-class Instructional Design and Assessment (WIDA) and ELPA21. In addition, several states with large English learner (EL) populations are developing their own tests (California, New York, and Texas) that that correspond to college- and career-ready standards. Because the assessments are under various stages of development, one can only make general assertions.

First, the assessments will follow the paths that are being charted by the Common Core State Standards (CCSS) assessments (Partnership for the Assessment of Readiness for College and Careers [PARCC] and Smarter Balanced Assessment Consortium [SBAC]) in being primarily computer administered. There are several differences, however, from the CCSS assessments. First, neither PARCC nor SBAC will provide assessments of student listening and speaking, whereas ELP assessments must (by law) assess and report on speaking and listening and be held accountable to meeting targets in these areas, in addition to reading and writing. Also, the CCSS assessments start at grade 3, whereas the highest use of the ELP assessments will be in the lower grades down to kindergarten. Therefore, the appropriateness of computer-administered assessments in the earliest grade levels comes into question.

Second, the assessments will gravitate more toward competencies that correspond to the Common Core. Documents such as the English Language Proficiency Development Framework, developed and released by the Council of Chief State Schools Officers (2012), will be influential in determining what standards are assessed. It is highly likely, therefore, that the language that supports the practices of the CCSS—such as finding evidence in text and explaining mathematical reasoning—will be salient in the new tests.

Third, the CCSS assessments themselves will hopefully provide additional information about student ELP progress. Reading and writing items in those tests that align to specific ELP standards might be tagged and used later for tracking the continued progress of reclassified ELs who are no longer administered the ELP assessment. At the same time, such an overlap may eventually lead to better coordination of the content and ELP assessment programs, so that information from both is taken into account. A step in this direction has already been taken; SBAC has tagged all of their assessment items for language complexity, which should enable statistical analysis of items to see how ELs navigate the complexities of language contained in the CCSS assessments. This is a research agenda for now, but hopefully will lead to better assessment systems in future iterations.

■ *Tim Boals*

The CCSS make the role of language in teaching and assessing content more explicit by adding listening and speaking standards to the expected components of reading and writing in an English language arts (ELA) curriculum, and by emphasizing key language functions like argumentation, explanation, and discussion in the other core academic subjects. This is now part and parcel of what students must do to demonstrate content knowledge. The CCSS thus raise the bar for language and subject matter that all students, and English language learners (ELLs) in particular, must reach within school accountability systems. Gone are the days when, for example, language didn't seem relevant to performance in a mathematics class. Language is integral to successful participation in every aspect of schooling.

While the basic purposes of identification; placement for support; progress monitoring of listening, speaking, reading, and writing domains; and, finally, overall English proficiency attainment continue to be the prominent reasons why we use ELP assessments, the CCSS have influenced how ELP assessments are designed. They have also influenced how the results are interpreted because language growth and attainment *are defined within the context of school success.*

Current ELP assessments are markedly different from the more generic conversational English tested 15 years ago. The context for what is tested and how is now found in school classroom settings, which allows for assessment of the specific language needed to perform in core content-area classes like science or mathematics. Item and test development are far more rigorous because tests are equated in ways that provide meaningful comparisons of student scores over time. ELP assessments are aligned to ELP standards and, to ensure matching of language and content, ELP standards now correspond to (are linked to) the CCSS. Thus, the newest wave of ELP assessments, as part of aligned standards and accountability systems, give us better information about English development related to and driven by the need to meet grade-level content-area expectations.

When properly linked to grade-level standards, assessments can have a positive effect on teaching and learning. This idea of "washback" encourages changes in curriculum that, in this case, move us away from remedial models emphasizing basic skills and toward content- and language-rich classrooms that accelerate learning. This is key for ELLs because they must acquire sufficient English language and literacy skills to participate in an academic setting, while simultaneously learning new, challenging content guided by the CCSS. ELP assessments are designed to foster "washback" that positively influences the way teachers construct their daily instruction and assessment (Cheng, Watanabe, & Curtis, 2004).

We face both challenges and opportunities in today's high-stakes context relative to assessing English proficiency. Better assessments that are situated within standards-based systems offer the prospect of better information to guide teachers' instruction. But better information must be accompanied by appropriate, long-term professional development that affects the entire school if we are to systemically change instructional practices. Results of ELP assessments must be not only valid and reliable, but transparent and accessible to all constituents, from federal and state policymakers to local educators, parents, and students. Only then will these assessments play their intended role in this era of CCSS.

■ *Ayanna Cooper*

When schools engage in data-driven discussions about student performance, they need to explicitly identify which students are ELs. They also need to include ELP and English language development (ELD) assessment data. Oftentimes, schools collect and analyze formal and informal data about student performance, but there is no mention of ELs and no inclusion of ELP/ELD data. Without including this critical information, data-driven discussions will never be complete.

For example, I visited a school to facilitate professional learning about ELs. The assistant principal invited me to see their data room with extensive graphs displaying student performance. They had student data charted in ways that showed students either performing above, at, or below grade level. The teachers met periodically to move students from one area to another as they made progress. I remember noticing the students who were performing below grade level. I asked if any of those students were ELs. The assistant principal didn't know. We discussed the need to make EL data easily accessible and useful to all teachers and administrators. The principal agreed that their data collection methods needed to be more balanced, comprehensive, and inclusive.

It is important to remember that ELP/ELD data should not be used in isolation. For a more complete picture, educators can use portfolios that include evidence of student content learning and language development collected from multiple sources over time. The portfolios might include content-area work samples, student self-assessments, and samples of work (e.g., an essay) performed in the home language, in addition to evidence of ELD. Portfolios are a powerful way to show how students are progressing academically and how they are developing oral and written English for academic purposes over time. The portfolio data provide an important complement to the state-mandated ELP/ELD data.

Educators should also look at ELD/ELP assessment data in the context of the learning opportunities the school provides for ELs. Data-driven discussions need to include, for example, information about the English language program model (e.g., bilingual, English-medium) implemented in the district/school and how much time students spend in ELD instruction. These discussions should also consider general education teachers' qualifications (e.g., coursework, PD, evaluations) to work with ELs and any additional resources that the school has put in place to support student learning. Information about staffing is especially important in areas that rely on itinerant teachers.

Educators are beginning to understand that language development occurs all day, not at a particular time or day of the week. All teachers who have ELs in their classes are language teachers and all teachers need to know how to analyze and use ELD/ELP data. Providing more opportunities for *all* teachers to become proficient in analyzing ELD/ELP data will strengthen data-driven discussions. By approaching ELD/ELP data holistically, in context, and with prior knowledge about how and why the data are used, educators will be better prepared to inform and improve instruction.

When working with administrators and teachers I pose a number of questions to help prepare them for data-focused meetings. Here is a sample of those questions:

- Is the goal of the ELD/ELP data analysis to have a discussion or to make a decision? These are two very different goals.
- Are all those involved knowledgeable about ELD/ELP data in general? If not, professional development many be needed before hand.
- Are students and/or parents to be included in the data sessions?
- How often are the meetings occurring?
- What pieces of evidence are being evaluated?
- What criteria (e.g., rubrics, benchmarks, exit-criteria, scores) are being used to evaluate the evidence?
- What happens when the data show conflicting information?
- What do you hope to accomplish?
- What kinds of follow-up meetings are planned?

7.7 How can we use home language assessment data to inform and improve instruction for all English language learners/emergent bilinguals, and why is this important relative to the Common Core State Standards?

■ *Kathy Escamilla*

To respond to this question, I must first say that I will be using the term home language*s* rather than home language. An increasing number of students are simultaneous bilingual children who come from homes where both English and another language are spoken, read, and written. It is important that we acknowledge that exposure to two languages from birth is the "new normal." To illustrate, the number of elementary school aged–simultaneous bilingual children is now estimated to be around 77% (Capp, Fix, Murray, Ost, Passel, & Herwantoro, 2005). For that reason, if schools and assessment programs are to understand the "new normal" they must develop assessment systems that evaluate emerging bilingualism and biliteracy, and not simply emergent English. In this regard, I would argue that it is essential that home languages are assessed for emergent bilinguals (EBs).

With regard to how assessments in home languages fit into the Common Core State Standards (CCSS), it is no secret that the CCSS have a monolingual English focus, both in the content of the standards and in the creation of the high-stakes testing programs to assess the attainment of the standards. However, while the CCSS summative assessment system may be limited to English, there is no reason why teachers, schools, and districts cannot use assessment data from students' home languages for formative purposes, particularly in schools and districts where bilingual and dual language programs will continue to be implemented. In the Literacy Squared program, we have created empirically based biliterate reading and writing trajectories, benchmarks, and zones that offer concrete biliteracy targets and anticipated outcomes for students in Spanish and English (Escamilla et al., 2014).

As most of the nation moves toward the monolingual high-stakes testing system that is the core of the CCSS, it will be increasingly important for districts and schools implementing bilingual and dual language instruction to document children's progress in two languages and to continue to document the potential of biliteracy. In the Literacy Squared model, we encourage teachers to use children's Spanish reading levels to guide their decision making for English literacy instruction because Spanish reading levels are frequently higher than English reading levels.

Finally, it is axiomatic that improved accountability systems are needed for all children, most especially for emerging bilingual children. To this point, however, I would argue that improved accountability should not be limited to testing and assessment. Accountability systems must include opportunities to learn the standards. For emerging bilingual children, all responsible parties (state and federal governments, school districts, schools, and teachers) must ensure that children have the following:

- Safe and nurturing environments in which to learn
- Adequate books and learning materials
- Teachers who are well prepared to teach diverse learners
- Ongoing professional development for their teachers
- A clearly articulated curriculum that is specifically tailored to meet the needs of emerging bilingual children

In short, improving accountability systems must take into account a multitude of factors related to improving schooling. The current hyperfocus on accountability as limited to testing will not likely improve schooling for any child, especially emerging bilinguals.

7.8 How can we use Common Core State Standards content assessment data to inform and improve instruction?

■ *Laura Ascenzi-Moreno*

After testing "season," school administrators and teachers are left with an abundance of student data that they are expected to use for underpinning and improving instruction. However, the task of using the data as the catalyst and foundation for instructional improvement is far from simple, especially when the data at hand are from the assessments of emergent bilingual (EB) students. First and foremost, assessing EB students and ensuring that the data are accurate is a complicated task because *monolingual* assessments fail to capture the entirety of emergent *bilingual* students' knowledge base (García, 2009a). Furthermore, because content assessments attempt to assess knowledge of a given topic through language, it is nearly impossible to discover if EB students' results are because of their level of content knowledge or their language abilities. Lastly, large-scale exams, such as the ones used to measure students' acquisition of skills and understandings as spelled out by the Common Core State Standards (CCSS), produce summative data that present a cumulative snapshot of student learning for a particular year and, therefore, awkwardly serve as a tool to truly inform instruction at the day-to-day level.

Despite these very real challenges, there are some promising venues for the use of large-scale assessment data to affect the instruction and, ultimately, learning of EB students. In my qualitative research of how teachers of EB students use data from large-scale exams, a small group of teachers laid out proposals to *inject* student input into the process of analyzing large-scale assessment data. Data from tests based on the CCSS will yield similar types of data for teachers and administrators to the tests that preceded this latest reform effort.

In my work with teachers and administrators I have observed "data day," when teachers work individually with students to interpret test results and help students set goals. This promising practice has the potential to alter the process of analyzing large-scale assessment data for teachers because it allows the flow between test data and students to be *dynamic*. In other words, instead of administrators and teachers using data to make inferences about students and group them, without their input, through this process, students are able to provide information to teachers and administrators about their unique experiences with assessment. Therefore, instead of using testing data to label, group, and evaluate students, students are given a voice and agency in the analysis of their assessment performance. Students can explain and describe their experiences and thought process while taking the exam, and in this way illuminate for teachers the undeniable interplay between the test and student abilities. This process can be particularly revealing for EB students who encounter both content and language challenges in exams. This process is important instructionally because it allows the test data to be used accurately. When student input is not set along-side the test data, there is a danger that the instructional plans resulting from the analysis of test data (such as groups) do not truly address students' academic needs. Following are two recommendations, or directions, for school leaders to explore to ensure that the data from tests based on the CCSS are analyzed and used in ways that improve instruction:

1. Institute a "data day" with students. This allows students to convey their test-taking experience on many levels. It allows them to provide teachers and administrators a window into their emotional and academic experience in taking the exam. Although it would be ideal to meet with all students, as a start, it would be valuable to do a post-test interview with a select group of students. Ask them questions such as, "What parts of the test did you feel prepared for?" "Why?" "What portions of the test were tricky?" "Why?" The responses and examples that students provide have the potential to provide teachers with valuable information about how students applied or did not apply what they learned to the testing environment. In addition, students' input would provide teachers with a perspective of what testing skills students need to build, separate from the academic skills students need help with.
2. Institute a study group for teachers to analyze test questions. When test results are reported to teachers, skills are often pegged to specific test questions. However, for

EB students, the language of tests sometimes poses challenges in addition to the content of the questions. Thus, it is important for teachers to sit down with copies of the test to examine test questions from the angle of experts in the diverse needs of their EB students. "In what ways does the wording of test questions pose difficulty for EB students?" "Does this question assess the skill it is linked to, or would it assess other skills as well?" When teachers are given the responsibility to analyze tests, they learn in ways that directly affect the instruction they can provide to their EB students.

Teachers and school administrators have a pivotal role in ensuring that data from large-scale assessments are used appropriately, meaningfully, and critically to spur instruction. School staff must be aware about how current assessments may not capture EBs' skills and abilities, and the ways in which analysis of assessment data can be modified to better inform instruction for EB students. Furthermore, it is critical that school staff feels empowered to engage in schoolwide practices that allow the results from CCSS-based exams to be analyzed from the perspective of EB students so that instruction is appropriate to their needs.

7.9 What is the value of formative classroom-based assessments by teachers relative to the Common Core State Standards?

■ *Margo Gottlieb*

With the adoption of the Common Core State Standards (CCSS) by the majority of states has come a cry for equalizing the use of different forms of assessment to create a balanced system. Nowhere are data from multiple measures more relevant and more important than in schools where assessment for formative purposes reigns. Crafted by teachers thinking about each and every one of their students, formative assessment strategies are individualized and internal to the functioning of classrooms.

Formative classroom assessment falls within the spectrum of instructional assessment. Its primary purpose is threefold:

1. To allow students opportunities to reflect on their learning in systematic ways
2. To encourage teachers to provide real-time descriptive feedback to their students on specified learning targets and objectives based on standards-referenced evidence
3. To inspire teachers to use evidence from their students to adjust their instructional practices

There is a range of thinking on what constitutes assessment for formative purposes and how the data are used. It spans from the use of any assessment that improves instructional decisions (William, 2011), to a set of continuous instructional *practices* associated with assessment *for* learning (Stiggins, 2005), to a planned *process* integral to instruction (Heritage, 2010; Moss & Brookhart, 2009; Popham, 2008), and finally, to a comprehensive *system* grounded in the classroom (Frey & Fisher, 2011; Marzano, 2010). What is undeniable about these formative assessment approaches is their value for improving teaching and learning, especially for students challenged by school (Black

& William, 1998). Given the strong research base, data from formative classroom assessment are not only worthwhile but invaluable for everyday decision making.

Benefits of Formative Assessment Use at the Classroom Level

Classroom assessment used on a formative basis is a powerful tool for teaching and learning. In classrooms where it is the norm, a partnership of trust between teachers and students is built. As a result, the classroom culture revolves around a shared understanding of expectations that are integrated into daily activities and tasks.

The value of structured descriptive feedback, the mainstay of formative classroom assessment, is that students

- Understand their performance in relation to a set of preset (ideally, mutually agreed on) criteria for success
- Build intrinsic motivation to learn and gradually take responsibility for learning
- Realize the purpose for and the usefulness of learning
- Engage in self-reflection and self-assessment
- Exchange information on meeting outcomes during peer assessment
- Have opportunities to use their home languages as instructional resources during academic conversations.

Formative classroom assessment is equally valuable for teachers. Data collected on a formative basis allow teachers to

- Apply the criteria for success in giving students criterion-referenced feedback; consider formative assessment data as the class norm in lieu of relying on giving grades based on a 100-point system
- Plan differentiated instruction for students' achievement and language development lesson by lesson
- Respond in real time to individual student performance, interests, and needs
- Document student performance day by day, week by week
- Examine their personal instructional practices and make adjustments
- Facilitate educational decision making minute by minute.

College- and career-readiness standards have elevated accountability for educational outcomes to unforeseen levels and the new generation of consortia-led achievement testing is more high-stakes than ever. We need to counteract this trend with its heavy reliance on annual results and insist on using data internal to the everyday functioning of classrooms. Classroom assessment built around formative practices acknowledges the professional accountability of teachers, allows teachers and students to have a voice, and offers greater opportunities for classrooms to be more student-centered places to learn.

■ *Margaret Heritage*

No two English language learners (ELLs)/emergent bilinguals (EBs) are the same, and so the way they acquire language will not be the same either. These students do not move up a "ladder" of language learning in lockstep. Rather, ELLs/EBs develop their language capacity from their own starting points and in their own timeframe as they engage in content-area learning. This recognition is fundamental to the practice of formative assessment, which, when effectively implemented, can provide the necessary guidance to teachers and students to support individual students' ongoing language learning.

The purpose of formative assessment is to assist learning while it is in development, not to gauge student achievement at the end of a period of learning; that is the role of assessment for summative purposes. Formative assessment encompasses a set of practices that have been shown to improve student learning (Black, Harrison, Lee, Marshall, & William, 2003). These practices center on the notion of feedback (Sadler, 1989). More specifically, in his seminal model, Sadler conceived of formative assessment as a feedback loop to close the gap between a student's current learning status and desired learning goals. He made clear that information itself is not feedback, but only becomes feedback when it is actively used "to alter the gap" (Sadler, 1989, p. 121).

When this model of formative assessment is applied to the learning of ELLs/EBs, teachers collect evidence from what their students say or write in the context of subject-matter learning, minute by minute, day by day. Teachers interpret the evidence in relation to the lesson-sized learning goals, derived from standards, that identify the concepts to be learned and the language through which the concepts are learned and sustained. Once interpreted, the evidence then becomes information that teachers can use to engage in contingent pedagogy. In other words, teachers are able make informed decisions about what kind of instructional response, including feedback to the students, will help advance language and content learning toward the desired learning goals. In Sadler's terms, the teacher's response is intended to "alter the gap."

At the same time, when students are clear about what their learning entails, they can engage in self-assessment, monitoring how their language learning is progressing and collaborating with their teacher to make decisions about how they can advance. Similarly, peers can provide each other with constructive feedback that can result in deepening the feedback giver's and the feedback receiver's awareness of language.

Unlike the end-of-the year assessments for the purposes of accountability, formative assessment is integral to teaching and learning, and therefore is within the purview of teachers only. As the new assessments of the CCSS are implemented, policymakers and administrators will need to embrace formative assessment, not as a finer-grained test within an accountability system, but as a set of practices indigenous to the teaching and learning process. The overall priority of assessment-based accountability systems must be that they do not inhibit or diminish teachers' formative assessment practices. If they do, the documented power of formative assessment to enable learning for ELLs/EBs will not be realized.

■ *Barbara Marler*

How Can We Use English Proficiency Assessment Data to Inform and Improve Instruction?

"Accountability is not only about measuring student learning, but actually improving it" (Darling-Hammond, 2004, p. 1078). How can educators use data collected around English proficiency to go beyond mere measurement and move to informing and improving instruction?

Formative assessments can be the answer to that question. Formative assessments yield data that give us a freeze-frame glimpse into students' English language proficiency at a particular moment in time. Given that formative assessments are not considered "high-stakes," feedback to students is typically qualitative, rather than a numeric score—and the turnaround time is fast. Formative assessments often provide timely information students need to adjust their own learning practices. These assessments also help educators to ascertain what students are learning, how students are learning, and how well instruction is working. A collection of formative assessments can indicate the rate, breadth, and depth of the progression of students' learning and the impact of instruction over longer periods of time.

When formative assessments are designed to be implemented districtwide, the results can be used to inform and influence instruction at a program level. Results collected from across the district can help guide decision making about standards-based instruction for English learners, determine appropriate pacing and differentiation at different grade levels and at different language proficiency levels, guide the purchase of instructional and supplemental materials, influence the design of additional formative assessments, and signal the types of professional development that are warranted.

When designed for implementation at the school level or at a particular grade level, the results from formative assessments can bring learning and instruction into even sharper focus. The results from these assessments can help educators focus on individual students, a small group, or a grade level. Teachers can analyze a student's developing English proficiency, the gaps that might be present in his or her English acquisition, and the slight or small advances each student is making in each language domain. Teachers can compile this information to create a profile for one student, small groups, or even grade-level groups. In turn, teachers can use information gleaned from analysis of formative assessment results to make adjustments to instruction in a timely way; to craft lesson plans that specifically provide necessary reteaching; and to plan for scaffolding or extension and enrichment in a one-on-one, small-group, or large-group format. When teachers come together to evaluate students' formative assessments using a common rubric, they not only increase the group's level of inter-rater reliability, they also typically engage in an informal professional development session where they share strategies, activities, and materials that they have found to be successful.

When formative assessments are designed to be performance-based, their power and utility increases. Performance-based assessments add another dimension to the mix so that not only are we assessing what students' know, but we are also assessing their ability to apply what they know to given situations (Abedi, 2010). When we measure language proficiency and application of that language proficiency in a given situation, we are addressing the full complexity of the language acquisition process more completely.

Improving Assessment and Accountability

7.10 How can districts and schools balance their assessment and accountability systems for English language learners/emergent bilinguals in inclusive and comprehensive ways?

■ *Diep Nguyen*

Since 2001, student assessment has been elevated to the top priority for schools and is used as the major vehicle to keep schools accountable for student achievement. In a recent analysis of the impact of the educational policies derived from No Child Left Behind (NCLB) on emergent bilinguals (EBs), Hopkins, Thompson, Linquanti, Hakuta, and August (2013) indicated that current policies regarding school accountability with respect to EBs' achievement are built on faulty information gathered from flawed and invalid assessments. They suggested that the implementation of an accountability system for EBs needs to be more nuanced and multidimensional, with special attention paid to the relationship between English language development, time in the school system, and academic progress.

BASIC Model

The BASIC (balanced assessment and accountability system that is inclusive and comprehensive) model, created by Gottlieb and Nguyen (2007), is a comprehensive framework for selecting and using multiple assessments that yield relevant information to support teaching and learning in the classroom while meeting both internal and external accountability demands. Its major features include the following:

- The system is balanced in its inclusion of assessments implemented at the classroom, school, district, program, and state levels to measure both growth and achievement.
- Special emphasis is placed on measuring both language development and academic attainment. The relationship between language development and academic attainment is clearly delineated, resulting in more valid and reliable information about EBs' performance.
- Multiple assessments—closely aligned with learning standards, goals, and benchmarks—are used to provide robust information on EBs' performance in each major learning area.
- The collection of data is contextualized, using historical and program information to frame decision making regarding the collection, analysis, and use of assessment data.
- The system of assessment is built by consensus and collaboration among teachers and administrators, with the primary purpose of supporting classroom teaching and learning.

- The system is dynamic, evolving over time, and adjusting to current students' needs and external accountability demands.
- Assessment information and data, both formative and summative, are systematically collected on each EB student from multiple sources throughout the year.

Pivotal Portfolio

The systemic collection of essential student assessment information is organized into the *pivotal portfolio*. This pivotal portfolio is kept during each EB student's entire time of participation in the language program and is used to inform critical decisions regarding the student's program of study. Teachers and other professionals use information from the pivotal portfolio on a regular basis to monitor student progress, make important instructional decisions for individual and groups of students, and make program improvements.

Common assessments are the building blocks of the pivotal portfolio. Teachers collaborate to create, adopt, or adapt common assessments based on program goals and students' needs. When making decisions about adopting or selecting common assessments, teachers may want to take inventories of all the assessments that are currently implemented in their classroom and school.

Common assessments should provide informative about students' growth in critical learning areas such as oral language development, literacy development, and academic learning in core-content subjects. Data collected through common assessment should be complementary and not duplicate information that can already be gained in standardized test results and other idiosyncratic assessment practice by individual teachers.

In *Assessment and Accountability in Language Education Programs*, Gottlieb and Nguyen (2007) provided case studies of three bilingual teachers who implemented the pivotal portfolio. They used common assessments and utilized the information gathered to make various instructional decisions.

To begin implementing the BASIC model, schools and districts may want to consider forming teams of teachers to do the following:

- Conduct an inventory of all assessments undertaken throughout the year in the school or district.
- Evaluate each assessment regarding the degree of cultural loading and linguistic demands that will affect the performance of EBs and, consequently, the validity and fairness of the assessment when used with this group of students (Rhodes, Ochoa, & Ortiz, 2005).
- Determine for each assessment the extent to which the information is useful and accessible for your teachers to monitor their EBs' learning and inform their instruction.
- Establish a global assessment plan for all the EBs in the school by determining what data/information teachers need to best monitor student learning and plan their instruction in key areas.
- Undergo a process of eliminating, selecting, adopting, and adapting a set of common assessments for key learning areas based on program goals and learning expectations.

Select common assessments that can serve the dual purposes of informing classroom instruction and providing evidence for accountability. Eliminate assessments that yield poor information. Encourage teachers to create curriculum-based, common assessments that provide them with rich information about their students' learning.

- Detail the specifics of the assessment plan, keeping in mind the balance between assessment and instruction, and integrating as much assessment as possible with instruction.
- Based on the common assessments selected, create a prototype pivotal portfolio that can be implemented with every student in the program or school.
- Provide professional development for teachers to implement gradually each component of the pivotal portfolio.
- Review your assessment plan every two years and make changes based on new accountability demands and the relevancy and utility of assessment information gathered and used by teachers.

In the current assessment environment, teachers are often overwhelmed by data that are irrelevant to their teaching priorities or their EBs' learning needs. Through the implementation of the pivotal portfolio, administrators can skillfully lighten the testing burden for EBs and encourage the use of a balanced system of assessment and accountability that allows teachers to collect only necessary assessment data and use all the assessment information that they have to encourage EBs to learn.

7.11 How might a translanguaging approach in assessment make tests fairer and more valid for English language learners/emergent bilinguals?

■ *Guillermo Solano-Flores*

In the context of classroom-based assessment, translanguaging practice addresses the fact that emergent bilinguals' (EBs') language practices are complex, interrelated, and multifaceted (García, 2009a and b) and support students' knowledge construction (Soltero-González, Escamilla, & Hopewell, 2012). These practices are consistent with the view of assessment as a communication process (Ruiz-Primo, Solano-Flores, & Li, 2014). Both teachers and students use their linguistic resources in full by using their home (L1) and second (L2) languages to ask and respond to questions. This should be the case especially for informal formative assessment—in which teachers gather information about their students' learning through multiple, unplanned social interactions (Ruiz-Primo, 2010).

In the context of large-scale assessment, several test administration and test development approaches can be characterized as consistent with the notion of translanguaging (see, e.g., Solano-Flores, 2012; Solano-Flores & Li, 2006, 2013; Solano-Flores & Trumbull, 2008). Because they have different sets of advantages and limitations, the approaches should be used in combination to ensure fairer and more valid assessment for EBs.

Test Administration Approaches

Testing EBs with items worded in L1 and L2 in combination. This "code-switching" approach is no more effective than any other blanket approach where all EBs are tested in one language. Because linguistic features of items reflect their writers' idiosyncrasies, bias resulting from using two languages may be equivalent to that of using only one language in the wording of items.

Testing EBs with some items in L1 and other items in L2. This approach does not produce any more valid measures of academic achievement for EBs than testing them only in their L1 or L2.

Testing EBs with bilingual, side-by-side formats. While popular, this strategy assumes the test taker has sophisticated metalinguistic skills (e.g., the ability to identify a term not understood in the L2 and locate it in the L1 version). In addition, bilingual formats increase tremendously the reading demands of items.

Administering the same set of items in two languages but at different times. This approach addresses two facts: First, EBs have different strengths and weaknesses in their L1 and L2. Second, even within the same broad linguistic group, some EB subgroups perform better in the L1 and others perform better in the L2. This approach can inform decisions concerning the language in which a given group of EBs should be tested.

Test Development Approaches

Test translation into EBs' L1. This is the first approach that comes to mind as a translanguaging approach. However, its effectiveness is threatened by testing policies that fail to properly address the dynamic nature of bilingualism (García & Wei, 2014) and improper implementation of translation procedures. In addition, testing in the L1 does not necessarily favor EBs with a schooling history mostly in the L2.

Accessibility tools. Recent advances made by the Smarter Balanced Assessment Consortium take advantage of current information technology to provide EBs with stacked translations and glossaries as accessibility tools (Chia, 2014). However, information technology has yet to allow automatic and dependable interpretation of students' responses in either the L1 or L2.

Concurrent test development. In this approach, the two language versions of a test are developed simultaneously and the wording of items is negotiated across languages. While effective in ensuring item equivalence across language (Solano-Flores, Trumbull, & Nelson-Barber, 2002), this approach may be costly and time consuming.

Statistical representation of EBs. This approach ensures the participation of EBs on all pilot stages during the process of test development in which student understanding of the wording of items is probed and refined. A large spectrum of linguistic issues that affect the validity of test items could be identified by simply including EBs in pilot student samples, even if tests are to be administered only in English (Solano-Flores, 2008). Unfortunately, this simple and promising approach is rarely used by test developers.

■ *Alexis Lopez, Danielle A. Guzman-Orth, and Sultan Turkan*

Translanguaging is a commonly used pedagogical approach in bilingual classrooms, where students are presented with opportunities to actively learn and strategically participate using all their languages as resources, depending on their communicative needs (Baker, 2001; García, 2009b; García, Flores, & Woodley, 2012). Translanguaging may create a more equitable classroom environment for all EB students because it encourages students to use their entire linguistic repertoire flexibly to learn academic content and language. While useful for all, translanguaging might be particularly relevant for a special subgroup of English learners (ELs)—late arrivals to U.S. schools who have had content instruction in their home countries but who are still in the process of developing academic language skills in English. Extending translanguaging from classroom instruction to assessment is timely, especially in the current era of the Common Core State Standards (CCSS). The CCSS are intended to promote "higher, deeper" opportunities for all students to demonstrate their knowledge. However, EBs may not always be able to do so, considering the heavy language demands implicit in CCSS-based assessments. Hence, we posit two reasons for using translanguaging in assessment contexts.

First, translanguaging offers EB students the opportunity to demonstrate what they know and can do in a content domain, even if their English language skills are not fully developed. By minimizing potential language barriers and allowing bilinguals to draw on their home language(s), translanguaging resources have the potential to allow EB students to complete next generation assessment tasks that measure the use of higher-order thinking skills. Our research demonstrates a way to provide these test takers with multiple translanguaging resources delivered via a computer-based test platform to promote bilingual autonomy so that they could use these practices whenever needed. Resources include the opportunity to see or hear an item in both the home language and English, and the opportunity to write or say responses in either language or both. Using translanguaging resources, middle school bilingual students' responses to CCSS-based mathematics content items showed they tried answering some of the questions in English but soon switched to Spanish. For example, one student explained that he read a problem in English first, but would then read it in Spanish to make sure he understood it correctly. Another student switched to Spanish because he did not understand a concept (least common multiple) in English. The idea is not to separate languages, as has been done in the past to assess the content knowledge of bilingual students, but to allow students to utilize their entire linguistic repertoire by fluidly moving from one language to another to demonstrate their content knowledge during the test-taking experience.

Secondly, incorporating translanguaging opportunities into a traditionally monolingual context suggests a way forward to create fairer assessments for EB students by facilitating the integration of both content knowledge and emerging language proficiencies (including the language of mathematics). For example, one student chose to express reasoning using a combination of language and numbers "141 dividido 5 = 28.2" and then only numbers for the next step "28.2 × 8 = 225.6." Translanguaging in this instance is likely because the student understood the mathematical procedures necessary to obtain the correct answer but may not have learned the culturally specific mathematical operator to fully communicate meaning. The division sign (" / " or " ÷ ") is not a universally used symbol; other countries may use symbols like "∟" to divide numbers. From an educator perspective, this instance suggests explicit instruction may be needed in this specific area.

EB students face the double challenge of learning content knowledge through the second language they are still developing. As a result, their second language proficiency might be a threat to validly measuring content knowledge in a monolingual assessment context. Translanguaging may provide a fair, ethical assessment procedure to minimize EBs' risk of being placed at a disadvantage by potential language barriers.

DISCUSSION QUESTIONS

After reading this chapter, engage in dialogue with peer educators, including policy-makers, administrators, teachers, specialists, and paraprofessionals to discuss the assessment of ELLs/EBs. Here are some questions to reflect on individually, with a colleague, or ideally, as part of a professional learning community at your school.

1. Consider all of the assessments used in your school or by schools in your area, and make a list. Rank these in order from those with highest stakes for ELLs/EBs to those with the lowest stakes and discuss what you find. Reflect on your list and consider these questions: How are the results from each of these tests used for ELLs/EBs? Are these uses *valid* (i.e., are the assessments being used as was originally intended), and are the results meaningful? If you have identified validity concerns, what can be done to make improvements?

2. No Child Left Behind emphasizes testing/assessment of ELLs/EBs in English—why has this been criticized? Do you have personal experience with this? If so, please offer an example for discussion.

3. How can we maximize our analyses of assessment data (as recommended in question 7.8) and also balance the current reliance on annual assessment results with data internal to the everyday functioning of classrooms (as per 7.9)? Specifically, how can we ensure that schools develop and use formative classroom assessments in addition to the summative assessments already in place, and ensure that both are used to inform the instruction of ELLs/EBs schoolwide?

4. What are dynamic assessments and translanguaging practices in assessment (see 7.5b and 7.11), and how might these promising approaches be incorporated into your school's and state's current assessments?

TOPICS FOR REFLECTION AND ACTION

The following statements are organized around the big ideas of the chapter. Read through them and indicate the extent to which each applies to your community and your school. After you complete the survey, discuss your responses with your team. Then write down one to three reflection points that have emerged from your discussions. Finally, identify one to three concrete actions that you/your team can take.

DK don't know   1 strongly disagree   2 disagree   3 agree   4 strongly agree

ASSESSMENT AND ACCOUNTABILITY					
1. The statewide assessments currently used to evaluate ELLs/EBs in my school/setting are valid, appropriate, and fair.	DK	1	2	3	4
2. The uses of student performance results on statewide tests for accountability purposes are valid, appropriate, and fair for ELLs/EBs and their teachers.	DK	1	2	3	4
3. The statewide assessments currently used to evaluate ELLs/EBs in my school or setting are available in the language(s) spoken by the ELLs/EBs in my building.	DK	1	2	3	4
4. In my school or setting, teachers make the best possible use of data generated by the state's summative assessments to inform their instruction of ELLs/EBs.	DK	1	2	3	4
5. The classroom-based, formative assessments used in my school or setting are valid, appropriate, and fair for ELLs/EBs.	DK	1	2	3	4
6. The classroom-based, formative assessments used in my school or setting are available and offered in the language(s) spoken by the ELLs/EBs in my building.	DK	1	2	3	4
7. In my school or setting, teachers make the best possible use of the data generated by classroom-based, formative assessments to inform their instruction of ELLs/EBs.	DK	1	2	3	4
Knowledge Base					
8. I am knowledgeable about all of the assessments ELLs/EBs take in my school or setting, including both state assessments and classroom-based assessments.	DK	1	2	3	4
9. I understand how ELLs/EBs' test scores in my school or setting are used.	DK	1	2	3	4
10. I know which test accommodations are permitted for ELLs/EBs in my state, and how to provide them during test administration.	DK	1	2	3	4
11. I understand the challenges of test-based accountability for ELLs/EBs.	DK	1	2	3	4
Perceptions of Testing and Accountability					
12. In my school or setting, teachers of ELLs/EBs teach to the test.	DK	1	2	3	4
13. Test accommodations are used appropriately for ELLs/EBs in my school or setting.	DK	1	2	3	4
14. Test accommodations for ELLs/EBs are sufficient for these students.	DK	1	2	3	4
15. Overall, the inclusion of ELLs/EBs in high-stakes testing has been beneficial for these students in my school or setting.	DK	1	2	3	4

Reflection:

Action Steps:

References

Abedi, J. (2010). *Performance assessments for English language learners.* Stanford, CA: Stanford University, Center for Opportunity Policy in Education.

Abedi, J. (2012). Validity issues in designing accommodations. In G. Fulcher & F. Davidson (Eds.), *Routledge handbook of language testing.* London: Routledge, Taylor & Francis.

Abedi, J., & Ewers, N. (2013). *Accommodations for English language learners and students with disabilities: A research-based decision algorithm.* Smarter Balanced Assessment Consortium. Retrieved from http://www.smarterbalanced.org/wordpress/wp-content/uploads/2012/08/Accomodations-for-under-represented-students.pdf

Adesope, O. O., Lavin, T., Thompson, T., & Ungerleider, C. (2010). A systematic review and meta-analysis of the cognitive correlates of bilingualism. *Review of Educational Research, 80,* 207–245.

Alberti, S. (2012/2013). Making the shifts. *Educational Leadership, 70*(4), 24–27.

Alonzo, A., & Gotwals, A. (Eds.). (2012). *Learning progressions in science: Current challenges and future directions.* Rotterdam, the Netherlands: Sense.

American Educational Research Association. (2006). Do the math: Cognitive demand makes a difference. *Research Points, 4*(2), 1–4.

Arkoudis, S. (2006). Negotiating the rough ground between ESL and mainstream teachers. *International Journal of Bilingual Education, 9,* 415–433.

Artiles, A. J., & Harry, B. (2004). *Addressing culturally and linguistically diverse student overrepresentation in special education: Guidelines for parents.* NCCRESt Practitioner Brief Series. Retrieved from http://www.nccrest.org/

August, D., & Hakuta, K. (1997). *Improving schooling for language minority children: A research agenda.* Washington, DC: National Academy Press.

August, D., Salend, S., Staehr Fenner, D., & Kozik, P. (2012). *The evaluation of educators in effective schools and classrooms for all learners.* AFT-NYSUT-RIFTHP Educator Evaluation for Excellence in Teaching and Learning (E3TL) Consortium Issue Brief. Retrieved from http://connectingthedots.aft.org/sites/aft/files/documents/i3_Grant-ELL-SWD_Working_Group-Shared_Values_Paper-FINAL-7-3-12.pdf

August, D., & Shanahan, T. (2006). *Developing literacy in second-language learners: Report of the national literacy panel on language-minority children and youth.* Mahwah, NJ: Erlbaum.

Babbitt, N. (1975). *Tuck everlasting.* New York: Farrar, Straus, and Giroux.

Bae, J. (2001). Cohesion and coherence in children's written English: Immersion and English-only classes. *Issues in Applied Linguistics, 12,* 51–88.

Bailey, A. L., & Heritage, M. (2010). *English language proficiency assessment foundations: External judgments of adequacy.* Evaluating the Validity of English Language Proficiency Assessments (EVEA) Project. Retrieved from http://www.eveaproject.com.

Bailey, A. L., & Heritage, M. (2014). The role of language learning progressions in improved instruction and assessment of English language learners. *TESOL Quarterly, 48*(3), 480–506.

Bailey, A. L., & Orellana, M. F. (2015). Adolescent development and everyday language practices: Implications for the academic literacy of multilingual learners. In D. Molle, E. Sato, T. Boals, & C. D. Hedgspeth (Eds.), *Multilingual learners and academic literacies: Sociocultural contexts of literacy development in adolescents* (pp. 53–74). New York: Routledge.

Bailey, A. L., Reynolds Kelly, K., Heritage, M., Jones, B., & Blackstock-Bernstein, A. (2013). *Creation and study of prototype dynamic language learning progressions and development of the DRGON system: Pilot phase report—revised.* Los Angeles: University of California, Dynamic Language Learning Progressions Project.

Baker, C. (2001). *Foundations of bilingual education and bilingualism* (3rd ed.). Clevedon, UK: Multilingual Matters.

Baker, E. L., Barton, P. E., Darling-Hammond, L., Haertel, E., Ladd, H. F., Linn, R. L., . . . Shepard, L. A. (2010). *Problems with the use of student test scores to evaluate teachers.* Economic Policy Institute Briefing Paper #278. Washington, DC. Retrieved from http://www.epi.org/publications/entry/bp278

Baquedano-López, P., Alexander, R. A., & Hernandez, S. J. (2013). Equity issues in parental and community involvement in schools: What teacher educators need to know. *Review of Research in Education, 37*(1), 149–182.

Batalova, J. (2006). *Spotlight on limited English proficient students in the United States.* Migration Information Source. Retrieved from http://www.migrationinformation.org/usfocus/display.cfm?ID=373

Beeman, K., & Urow, C. (2013). *Teaching for biliteracy: Strengthening bridges between langauges.* Philadelphia: Caslon.

Bell, A., & Baecher, L. (2012). Points on a continuum: ESL teachers reporting on collaboration. *TESOL, 3*(3), 488–515.

Bergen, B. K. (2012). *The new science of how the mind makes meaning.* New York: Basic Books.

Bernhardt, E. B. (2011). *Understanding advanced second-language reading.* New York: Routledge.

Bialystok, E. (2011). Reshaping the mind: The benefits of bilingualism. *Canadian Journal of Experimental Psychology/Revue canadienne de psychologie expérimentale, 65*(4), 229.

Black, P., Harrison, C., Lee, C., Marshall, B., & Wiliam, D. (2003). *Assessment for learning: Putting it into practice.* New York: Open University Press.

Black, P. & Wiliam, D. (1998). Assessment and classroom learning. *Assessment in Education: Principles, Policy & Practice, 5,* 7–74.

Blommaert, J. (2010). *The sociolinguistics of globalization.* Cambridge, UK: Cambridge University Press.

Bozakis, S., Burns, L., & Hall, L. (2014). Literacy reform and Common Core State Standards: Recycling the autonomous model. *Language Arts 91*(4), 223–235.

Braun, H., Chudowsky, N., & Koenig, J. (Eds.). (2010). *Getting value out of value-added: Report of a workshop.* Washington, DC: National Research Council, Committee on Value-Added Methodology for Instructional Improvement, Program Evaluation, and Accountability.

Brice Heath, S. (1983). *Ways with words.* Cambridge, UK: Cambridge University Press.

Brisk, M. E. (2005). *Bilingual education.* In E. Hinkel (Ed.), *Handbook of research in second language teaching and learning.* Mahwah, NJ: Erlbaum.

Brisk, M. E. (2006). *Bilingual education: From compensatory to quality schooling* (2nd ed.). Mahwah, NJ: Erlbaum.

Brisk, M. E., & Proctor, P. C. (2012). *Challenges and supports for English language learners in bilingual programs.* Paper presented at the Understanding Language Conference, Stanford, CA. Retrieved from http://ell.stanford.edu/papers/policy

Brooks, K., Adams, S., & Morita-Mullaney, T. (2010). Creating inclusive communitites for ELL students: Transforming school principals' perspectives. *Theory into Practice, 49*(2), 145–151.

Brown, H. D. (2007). *Teaching by principles: An interactive approach to language pedagogy* (3rd ed.). White Plains, NY: Pearson.

Buechner Institute for Governance. (2013). *Reauthorizing ESEA: A view from the West: Balancing federal priorities and local control in Colorado.* Denver: University of Colorado, School of Public Affairs.

Bunch, G. C. (2006). "Academic English" in the 7th grade: Broadening the lens, expanding access. *Journal of English for Academic Purposes, 5*(4), 284–301.

Bunch, G. C. (2013). Pedagogical language knowledge: Preparing mainstream teachers for English learners in the New Standards era. *Review of Educational Research, 37,* 298–341.

Bunch, G. C., Kibler, A. K., & Pimentel, S. (2012). *Realizing opportunities for English learners in the common core English language arts and disciplinary literacy standards.* Paper presented at the Understanding Language Conference, Stanford, CA. Retrieved from http://ell.stanford.edu/papers/practice

Bunch, G., Kibler, A. K., & Pimentel, S. (2014). Shared responsibility: Realizing opportunities for English learners in the Common Core English Language Arts and Disciplinary Literacy Standards. In L. Minaya-Rowe (Ed.), *Effective educational programs, practices, and policies for English learners* (pp. 1–28). Charlotte, NC: Information Age.

California Department of Education (2014). *English Language Arts/English Language Development Framework.* Sacramento, CA: Author.

California English Language Development Standards. (2012). Retrieved from http://www.cde.ca.gov/sp/el/er/eldstandards.asp

Canagarajah, A. S. (2013). *Translingual practice: Global Englishes and cosmopolitan relations.* Abingdon, UK: Routledge.

Capp, R., Fix, M., Murray, J., Ost, J., Passel, J. S., & Herwantoro, S. (2005). *The new demography of America's schools: Immigration and the No Child Left Behind Act.* Washington, DC: Urban Institute.

Carey, S. (1978). The child as word learner. In J. Bresnan, G. Miller, & M. Halle (Eds.), *Linguistic theory and psychological reality* (pp. 264–293). Cambridge, MA: MIT Press.

Celedón-Pattichis, S., & Musanti, S. I. (2013). "Let's suppose that. . .": Developing base-10 thinking. In M. Gottlieb & G. Ernst-Slavit (Eds.), *Academic language in diverse classrooms: Mathematics, grades K–2: Promoting content and language learning* (pp. 87–128). Thousand Oaks, CA: Corwin.

Chang, F., Crawford, G., Early, D., Bryant, D., Howes, C., Burchinal, M., . . . Pinata, R. (2007). Spanish-speaking children's social and language development in prekindergarten classrooms. *Early Education and Development, 18,* 243–269.

Chapin, S. C., O'Connor, C., & Anderson, N. C. (2003). *Classroom discussions: Using math talk to help students learn, grades K–6* (2nd ed.). Sausalito, CA: Math Solutions.

Cheng, L., Watanabe, Y., & Curtis, A. (Eds). (2004). *Washback in language testing: Research contexts and methods,* Mahwah, NJ: Erlbaum.

Chia, M. (2014). *English language learners, test resources.* Smarter Balanced Assessment Consortium.

Chope, J. (2013). Video series playlist: English language learners [Six-part video series]. Available from https://www.teachingchannel.org/blog/2013/10/25/video-playlist-ell-instruction/

Chval, K., & Chávez, O. (2011/2012). Informing practice: Designing mathematics lessons for English language learners. *Teaching Mathematics in Middle School, 17*(5), 261–265.

Chval, K. B., & Khisty, L. (2009). Latino students, writing, and mathematics: A case study of successful teaching and learning. In R. Barwell (Ed.), *Multilingualism in mathematics classrooms: Global perspectives* (pp. 128–144). Clevedon, UK: Multilingual Matters.

Collier, V. P. (1995). Acquiring a second language for school. *Directions in Language & Education, 1*(4), 1–10.

Commins, N. L., & Miramontes, O. B. (2005). *Linguistic diversity and teaching.* Mahwah, NJ: Erlbaum.

Common Core State Standard Initiative. (2012a). *Morphemes represented in English orthography. Examples of derivational suffixes in English.* Retrieved from http://www.corestandards.org/assets/Appendix_A.pdf

Common Core State Standards Initiative. (2012b). *The standards.* Retrieved from http://www.corestandards.org/the-standards.

Common Core State Standards Initiative. (2012c). *Students who are college and career ready in reading, writing, speaking, listening, and language.* Retrieved from www.corestandards.org/ELA-Literacy/introduction/students-who-are-collegeand-career-ready-in-reading-writing-speaking-listening-language

Common Core State Standards Initiative. (2015). *English language arts standards: College and career readiness anchor standards for language.* Retrieved from http://www.corestandards.org/ELA-Literacy/CCRA/L

Confrey, J., & Maloney, A. (2010). The construction, refinement, and early validation of the equipartitioning learning trajectory. *ISLS, 1,* 968–975.

Cook, H. G., Linquanti, R., Chinen, M., & Jung, H. (2012). *National evaluation of Title III implementation supplemental report: Exploring approaches to setting English language proficiency and performance criteria and monitoring English learner progress.* Washington, DC: U.S. Department of Education. Retrieved from http://www2.ed.gov/rschstat/eval/title-iii/implementation-supplemental-report.html

Cook, H. G., & MacDonald, R. (2014). *Reference performance level descriptors: Outcome of a national working session on defining an "English proficient" performance standard.* Washington, DC: Council of Chief State School Officers.

Corcoran, T., Mosher, F. A., & Rogat, A. (2009). *Learning progressions in science: An evidence-based approach to reform of teaching* (CPRE Research Report 63). New York: Consortium for Policy Research in Education, Center on Continuous Instructional Improvement, Teachers College, Columbia University.

Corson, D. (1999). *Language policies in schools. A resource for teachers and administrators.* Mahwah, NJ: Erlbaum.

Council of Chief State School Officers. (2012). *Framework for English language proficiency development standards corresponding to the Common Core State Standards and the Next Generation Science Standards.* Washington, DC: CCSSO.

Crawford, J. (1997). *Best evidence: Research foundations of the Bilingual Education Act.* Washington, DC: National Clearinghouse for Bilingual Education. Retrieved from http://www.ncela.gwu.edu/ncbepubs/reports/bestevidence/index.htm#Contents

Crawford, J., & Krashen, S. (2007). *English learners in American classrooms.* New York: Scholastic.

Creese, J. (2002). The discursive construction of power in teacher partnerships: Language and subject specialists in mainstream schools. *TESOL Quarterly, 36,* 597–616.

Cruz, M. (2004). Can English language learners acquire academic English? *English Journal, 93*(4), 14–17.

Cuban, L. (1998). How schools change reforms. *Teachers College Record, 99*(3), 453–477.

Cummins, J. (1981). The role of primary language development in promoting educational success for language minority students. In C. S. D. of E. Office of Bilingual Bicultural Education (Ed.), *Schooling and language minority students: A theoretical framework* (pp. 3–49). Los Angeles: California State University, Evaluation Dissemination and Assessment Center.

Cummins, J. (1986). Empowering minority students: A framework for intervention. *Harvard Educational Review, 56,* 18–36.

Cummins, J. (1991). Interdependence of first- and second-language proficiency in bilingual children. In E. Bialystok (Ed.), *Language processing in bilingual children* (pp. 70–89). Cambridge, UK: Cambridge University Press.

Cummins, J. (1999). Alternative paradigms in bilingual education research: Does theory have a place? *Educational Researcher, 28*(7), 26–32, 41.

Cummins, J., & Corson, D. (Eds.). (1997). *Bilingual education.* Dordrecht, the Netherlands: Kluwer.

Cummins, J., & Man, Y. F. E. (2007). Academic language: What is it and how do we acquire it? In J. Cummins & C. Davison (Eds.), *International handbook of English language teaching* (vol. 2, pp. 797–810). Norwell, MA: Springer.

Daloğlu, A., & Tarhan, M. (2005). Reducing learning burden in academic vocabulary development. *EFLIS Newsletter, 5*(1), 1–4.

Dalton, S. S. (2008). *Five standards for effective teaching: How to succeed with all learners.* San Francisco: Wiley & Sons.

Danielson, C. (2007). *Enhancing professional practice: A framework for teaching* (2nd ed.). Alexandria, VA: Association for Supervision and Curriculum Development.

Darling-Hammond, L. (2004). Standards, accountability, and school reform. *Teachers College Record, 106*(6), 1047–1085.

Darling-Hammond, L. (2007). Race, inequality and educational accountability: The irony of "No Child Left Behind." *Race, Ethnicity and Education, 10*(3), 245–260.

DeCapua, A., & Marshall, H. W. (2011). Reaching ELLs at risk: Instruction for students with limited or interrupted formal education. *Preventing School Failure, 55*(1), 35–41.

de Jong, E. J. (2012). *Foundations for multilingualism in school: From principles to practice.* Philadelphia: Caslon.

Delpit, L. (2006). *Other people's children: Cultural conflict in the classroom.* New York: New Press.

Dewey, J. (1916). *Democracy and education: An introduction to the philosophy of education.* Mineola, NY: Dover.

Dressler, C., & Kamil, M. L. (2006). First- and second-language literacy. In D. August & T. Shanahan (Eds.), *Developing literacy in second-language learners: Report of the National Literacy Panel on language-minority children and youth.* Mahwah, NJ: Erlbaum.

Duschl, R. A., Schweingruber, H. A., & Shouse, A. W. (Eds.). (2007). *Taking science to school: Learning and teaching science in grades K–8.* Washington, DC: National Academies Press.

Echevarría, J., Vogt, M., & Short, D. J. (2013). *Making content comprehensible for English learners: The SIOP model* (4th ed.). New York: Pearson.

Educational Testing Service's Policy Information Center. (2005). *A primer on value-added models, Educational Testing Service Policy Perspective.* Princeton, NJ: Author. Retrieved from http://www.ets.org/Media/Research/pdf/PICVAM.pdf

Elbow, P. (2012). *Vernacular eloquence: What speech can bring to writing.* New York: Oxford University Press.

Escamilla, K. (2012, October). *Academic literacy development in adolescent English language learners' schooling begins before adolescence: The case of Manuel.* Paper presented at the Sociocultural Contexts of Academic Literacy Development for Adolescent English Language Learners (WIDA/WestEd), Madison, WI.

Escamilla, K., & Hopewell, S. (2010). Transitions to biliteracy: Creating positive academic trajectories for emerging bilinguals in the United States. In J. Petrovic (Ed.), *International perspectives on bilingual education: Policy, practice, controversy*. Charlotte, NC: Information Age.

Escamilla, K., Hopewell, S., Butvilofsky, S., Sparrow, W., Soltero-González, L., Ruiz-Figueroa, O., & Escamilla, M. (2014). *Biliteracy from the start: Literacy Squared in action*. Philadelphia: Caslon.

Espinosa, L. (2010). *Getting it right for young children with diverse backgrounds: Applying research to improve practice*. Upper Saddle River, NJ: Pearson.

Fairbairn, S., & Jones-Vo, S. (2010). *Differentiating instruction and assessment for English language learners: A guide for K-12 teachers*. Philadelphia: Caslon.

FairTest. (2013). *Common Core assessment myths and realities*. Retrieved from http://fairtest.org/common-core-assessments-factsheet

Faltis, C. (2013). Language, language development and teaching English to emergent bilingual users: Challenging the common knowledge theory in teacher education and K–12 school settings. *AMAE Journal, 7*(2), 18–29.

Fenner, D. S. (2014). *Advocating for English learners: A guide for educators*. Thousand Oaks, CA: Corwin.

Fitzgerald, J., & Graves, M. F. (2004). *Scaffolding reading experiences for English-language learners*. Norwood, MA: Christopher-Gordon.

Fitzgerald, J., & Graves, M. F. (2005). Reading supports for all. *Educational Leadership, 62*(4), 68–71. Retrieved from http://www.ascd.org/publications/educational-leadership/dec04/vol62/num04/Reading-Supports-for-All.aspx

Flores, N., & Schissel, J. L. (2014). Dynamic bilingualism as the norm: Envisioning a heteroglossic approach to standards-based reform. *TESOL Quarterly, (48)*3, 454–479.

Forum on Educational Accountability. (2011). 2011 recommendations for improving ESEA/NCLB [Summary]. Retrieved from www.edaccountability.org

Francis, D., Lesaux, N., & August, D. (2006). Language instruction. In D. August & T. Shanahan (Eds.), *Developing literacy in second-language learners: Report of the National Literacy Panel on language-minority children and youth* (pp. 365–413). Mahwah, NJ: Erlbaum.

Freeman, Y. S., Freeman, D. E., & Mercuri, S. P. (2005). *Dual language essentials for teachers and administrators*. Portsmouth, NH: Heinemann.

Frey, N., & Fisher, D. (2011). *The formative assessment action plan: Practical steps to more successful teaching and learning*. Alexandria, VA: ASCD.

Fuentes, C. (1999). Introduction. In E. J. Olmos, L. Ybarra, & M. Monterrey (Eds.), *Americanos: Latino life in the United States*. Boston: Little Brown.

Fullan, M. (2011) *Choosing the wrong drivers for whole system reform, Center for Strategic Education*. Retrieved from http://www.michaelfullan.ca/media/13501655630.pdf

Funk, A. (2012). *The languages of New York State: A CUNY-NYSIEB guide for educators*. New York: CUNY-NYSIEB, Graduate Center, City University of New York. Retrieved from http://www.nysieb.ws.gc.cuny.edu/files/2012/07/NYSLanguageProfiles.pdf

Gándara, P., & Hopkins, M. (Eds.). (2010). *Forbidden language: English learners and restrictive language policies*. New York: Teachers College Press.

Gándara, P., Rumberger, R., Maxwell-Jolly, J., & Callahan, R. (2003). English learners in California schools: Unequal resources, unequal outcomes. *Education Policy Analysis Archives, 11*(36), 1–52.

García, E. E. (2005). *Teaching and learning in two languages: Bilingualism and schooling in the United States*. New York: Teachers College Press.

García, E. E., & Hamayan, E. (2006). What is the role of culture in language learning? In E. Hamayan & R. Freeman Field (Eds.), *English language learners at school: A guide for administrators* (pp. 61–64). Philadelphia: Caslon.

García, O. (2009a). *Bilingual education in the 21st century: A global perspective*. Malden, MA: Wiley-Blackwell.

García, O. (2009b). Education, multilingualism and translanguaging in the 21st century. In A. Mohanty, M. Panda, R. Phillipson, & T. Skutnabb-Kangas (Eds.), *Multilingual education for social justice: Globalising the local* (pp. 128–145). New Delhi: Orient Blackswan.

García, O. (2011). From language garden to sustainable languaging: Bilingual education in a global world. *NABE Perspectives*, 1–9.

García, O., & Bartlett, L. (2007). A speech community model of bilingual education: Educating Latino newcomers in the USA. *International Journal of Bilingual Education and Bilingualism, 10*(1), 1–25.

García, O., & Flores, N. (2013). Multilingualism and common core state standards in the US. In S. May (Ed.), *The multilingual turn: Implications for SLA, TESOL, and bilingual education*. New York: Routledge.

García, O., Flores, N., & Woodley, H. (2012). Transgressing monolingualism and bilingual dualities: Translanguaging pedagogies. In Y. Androula (Ed.), *Harnessing linguistic variation to improve education* (pp. 45–76). Bern: Peter Lang.

García, O., Ibarra Johnson, S., & Seltzer, K. (in preparation). *The translanguaging classroom*. Philiadelphia: Caslon.

García, O., & Kleifgen, J. A. (2010). *Educating emergent bilinguals: Policies, programs, and practices for English language learners*. New York: Teachers College Press.

García, O., & Menken, K. (2015). Cultivating an ecology of multilingualism in schools: Building interindividuality of voices and ideologies. In B. Spolsky, O. Inbar, & M. Tannenbaum (Eds.), *Challenges for language education and policy: Making space for people* (pp. 95–108). New York: Routledge.

García, O., & Wei, L. (2014). *Translanguaging: Language, bilingualism, and education*. Hampshire, UK: Palgrave Macmillan.

Gass, S. (2013). *Second language acquisition* (4th ed.). New York: Routledge.

Gee, J. P. (1992/2014). *The social mind*. Champaign–Urbana, IL: Common Ground.

Gee, J. P. (2000). Identity as an analytic lens for research in education. *Review of Research in Education, 25*, 99–125.

Gee, J. P. (2001). Forward. In T. M. Kalmar (Ed.), *Illegal alphabets: Latino migrants crossing the linguistic border* (pp. i–iv).

Gee, J. P. (2004). *Situated learning and language: A critique of traditional schooling*. London: Routledge.

Gee, J. P. (2014). *An introduction to discourse analysis: Theory and method* (4th ed.). London: Routledge.

Genesee, F. (1994). *Integrating language and content: Lessons from immersion*. Educational Practice Report #11. Santa Cruz: University of California, National Center for Research on Cultural Diversity and Second Language Learning.

Genesee, F., Lindholm-Leary, K., Saunders, W., & Christian, D. (2006). *Educating English language learners: A synthesis of research evidence*. New York: Cambridge University Press.

Gewertz, C. (2014). Common Core at four: Sizing up the enterprise. *Education Week, 33*(29), s4–s6.

Gold, N. (2006). *Successful bilingual schools: Six effective programs in California*. San Diego: San Diego County Office of Education. Retrieved from www.californianstogether.org/docs/download.aspx?fileId=23

Gold, E., Simon, E., & Brown, C. (2002). *The education organizing indicators framework: A user's guide. Strong neighborhoods, strong schools*. Chicago: Cross City Campaign for Urban School Reform.

Goldenberg, C. (2013). Unlocking the research on English learners: What we know—and don't yet know—about effective instruction. *American Educator*, 4–38. Retrieved from http://www.aft.org/pdfs/americaneducator/summer2013/Goldenberg.pdf

Goldenberg, C., & Coleman, R. (2010). *Promoting academic achievement among English learners: A guide to the research*. Thousand Oaks, CA: Corwin.

Gomez, L., Freeman, D., & Freeman, Y. (Eds.). (2010). Dual language education: A promising 50-50 model. *Bilingual Research Journal, 29*, 145–164.

González, N., Moll, L. C., & Amanti, C. (2005). *Funds of knowledge: Theorizing practices in households, communities and classrooms*. Mahwah, NJ: Erlbaum.

Gottlieb, M., & Ernst-Slavitz, G. (2014). *Academic language in diverse classrooms: Promoting content and language learning*. Thousand Oaks, CA: Corwin.

Gottlieb, M., & Nguyen, D. (2007). *Assessment and accountability in language education programs*. Philadelphia: Caslon.

Grabe, W., & Stoller, F. L. (1997). Content-based instruction: Research foundations. In M. A. Snow, & D. M. Brinton (Eds.), *The content-based classroom: Perspectives on integrating language and content* (pp. 5–21). New York: Longman.

Graves, M., & Watts-Taffe, S. (2009). Fostering word conciousness. In M. Graves (Ed.), *Essential readings in vocabulary instruction* (pp. 114–123). Newark, DE: International Reading Association.

Graves, M. F., & Fitzgerald, J. (2009). Implementing scaffolding reading experiences in diverse classrooms. In J. Coppola & E. Primas (Eds.), *Language, literacy, and learning in multilingual classrooms: Research to practice* (pp. 121–139). Newark, DE: International Reading Association. Retrieved from http://www.learner.org/workshops/readingk2/support/ScaffoldingReadingExp.1.pdf

Graves, M. F., & Graves, B. B. (Eds.). (2003). What is a scaffolded reading experience? In *Scaffolding reading experiences: Designs for student success*. Norwood, MA: Christopher-Gordon. Retrieved from http://www.onlinereadingresources.com/sre/SRECha_2.pdf

Grosjean, F. (1989). Neurolinguists, beware! The bilingual is not two monolinguals in one person. *Brain and Language, 36*, 3–15.

Guisbond, L., Neill, M., and Schaeffer, B. (2012). NCLB's lost decade for educational progress: What can we learn from this policy failure? Retrieved from http://fairtest.org/NCLB-lost-decade-report-home

Gwynne, J., Pareja, A., Ehrlich, S., & Allensworth, E. (2012). *What matters for staying on-track and graduating in Chicago public schools: A focus on English language learners*. Chicago: University of Chicago, Consortium on Chicago School Research.

Haas, M. (1992). *Institutional racism: The case of Hawai'i*. Westport, CN: Praeger.

Hakuta, K. (2011). Educating language minority students and affirming their equal rights: Research and practical perspectives. Seventh Annual Brown Lecture in Education Research. *Educational Researcher, 20*, 1–12.

Halliday, M. A. K. (1993). Towards a language-based theory of learning. *Linguistics and Education, 5*, 93–116.

Halliday, M. A. K., & Hasan, R. (1989). *Language, context, and text*. Oxford, UK: Oxford University Press.

Hammond, J., & Gibbons, P. (2005). Putting scaffolding to work: The contribution of scaffolding in articulating ESL education. *Prospect Special Issue, 20*(1), 6–30.

Han, Y.-C. (2012). From survivors to leaders: Stages of immigrant parent involvement. In E.G. Kugler (Ed.), *Innovative voices in education: Engaging diverse communities* (ch 12). Lanham, MD: Rowman & Littlefield.

Hanushek, E. A., & Rivkin, S. G. (2010). Generalizations about the use of value-added measures of teacher quality. *American Economic Review, 100*(2), 267–271.

Harry, B., & Klingner, J. (2014). The construction of family identity: Stereotypes and cultural capital. In B. Harry & J. Klingner (Eds.), *Why are so many minority students in special education? Understanding race and disability in schools* (2nd ed., pp. 78–98). New York: Teachers College Press.

Heitin, L. (2014). Common-assessment groups differ on accommodations. *Education Week, 33*(29), s30–s33.

Henderson, A. T., Mapp, K. L. Johnson, V. R., & Davies, D. (2007). *Beyond the bake sale: The essential guide to family-school partnerships*. New York: New Press.

Herbel-Eisenmann, B., Steele, M., & Cirillo, M. (2013). Developing teacher discourse moves: A framework for professional development. *Mathematics Teacher Educator, 1*(2).

Heritage, M. (2008). *Learning progressions: Supporting instruction and formative assessment*. Washington, DC: Council of Chief State School Officers. Retrieved from www.ccsso.org/content/PDFs/FAST%20Learning%20Progressions.pdf

Heritage, M. (2010). *Formative assessment: Making it happen in the classroom*. Thousand Oaks, CA: Corwin.

Hiebert, J., & Grouws, D. A. (2007). *Effective teaching for the development of skill and conceptual understanding of number: What is most effective?* (Effective Instruction Brief). Reston, VA: National Council of Teachers of Mathematics. Retrieved from http://www.nctm .org/uploadedFiles/Research_News_and_Advocacy/ Research/Clips_and_Briefs/Research_brief_01_-_ Effective_Teaching.pdf

Hirsch, E. D. (2003). Reading comprehension requires knowledge—of words and the world: Scientific insights into the fourth-grade slump and the nation's stagnant comprehension scores. *American Educator, 38*(1), 13–29, 44–45.

Honigsfeld, A., & Dove, M. G. (2010). *Collaboration and co-teaching: Strategies for English learners.* Thousand Oaks, CA: Corwin Press.

Hopkins, M., Thompson, K., Linquanti, R., Hakuta, K., & August, D. (2013). Fully accounting for English learner performance: A key issue in ESEA reauthorization. *Educational Researcher, 42*(2).

Hornberger, N. H. (2004). The continua of biliteracy and the bilingual educator: Educational linguistics in practice. *International Journal of Bilingual Education and Bilingualism, 7*(2–3), 155–171.

Horwitz, A. R., Uro, G., Price-Baugh, R., Simon, C., Uzzell, R., Lewis, S., & Casserly, M. (2009). *Succeeding with English language learners. Lessons learned from the Great City School.* Washington DC: Council of Great City Schools.

Howard, E. R., & Sugarman, J. (2007). *Realizing the vision of two-way immersion. Fostering effective programs and classrooms.* Washington, DC: Center for Applied Linguistics and Delta Systems.

Hunt, V. (2011). Learning from success stories: Leadership structures that support dual language programs over time in New York City. *International Journal of Bilingual Education and Bilingualism, 14*(2), 187–206.

Ikemoto, G. S., & Marsh, J. A. (2007). Cutting through the "data-driven" mantra: Different conceptions of data-driven decision making. *Yearbook of the National Society for the Study of Education, 106*(1).

Immigration Reform and Control Act. (1986). Retrieved from http://thomas.loc.gov/cgi-bin/bdquery/z?d099 :SN01200:@@@L&summ2=m&%7CTOM:/bss/ d099query.html

Johnson, E. J., & Johnson, D. C. (2014). Language policy and bilingual education in Arizona and Washington State. *International Journal of Bilingual Education and Bilingualism, 18*(1), 92–112.

Jones, N., Buzick, H., & Turkan, S. (2013). Students with disabilities and English learners in measures of educator effectiveness. *Educational Researcher, 42*, 234–241.

Katz, C. (2011, October). *Superman, tiger mother: Aspiration management and the child as waste.* Diane Middlebrook and Carl Djerassi Professorship Lecture, Jesus College, University of Cambridge, Cambridge, UK.

Keller-Allen, C. (2006). *English language learners with disabilities: Identification and other state policies and issues.* Alexandria, VA: National Association of State Directors of Special Education.

Khisty, L. (1995). Making inequality: Issues of language and meanings in mathematics teaching with Hispanic students. In W. Secada, E. Fennema, & L. Byrd Adajian (Eds.), *New directions for equity in mathematics education* (pp. 279–297). New York: Cambridge University Press.

Khisty, L., & Chval, K. (2002). Pedagogic discourse and equity in mathematics: When teachers' talk matters. *Mathematics Education Research Journal, 14*(3), 154–168.

Kibler, A. K., Walqui, A., & Bunch, G. C. (2014). Transformational opportunities: Language and literacy for English language learners in the Common Core era in the United States. *TESOL Journal, 10.*

King, K., & Fogle, L. (2006). Raising bilingual children: Common parental concerns and current research. Washington, DC: Center for Applied Linguistics. Retrieved from http://www.cal.org/resources/digest/ raising-bilingual-children.html

Klein, A. (2014). Miller and minority lawmakers: NCLB waivers hinder educational equity. *Education Week.* Retrieved from http://blogs.edweek.org/edweek/campaign -k12/2014/02/miller_and_minority_lawmakers_ .html?qs=English+learners+subgroup+No+Child +Left+Behind

Kloss, H. (1998). *The American bilingual tradition.* McHenry, IL: Center for Applied Linguistics & Delta Systems.

Kohn, A. (1998, April). Only for my kid: How privileged parents undermine school reform. *Phi Delta Kappan,* 569–577.

Kramsch, C. (2014). Teaching foreign languages in an era of globalization: An introduction. *The Modern Language Journal, 98*(1), 296–311.

Krashen, S. (1982). *Principles and practice in second language acquisition.* Oxford, UK: Pergamon Press.

Krashen, S. (2013). Access to books and time to read versus the Common Core State Standards and tests. *English Journal, 103*(2), 21–29.

Krashen, S., & Ohanian, S. (2011, April 8). High tech testing on the way: A 21st century boondoggle? *Living in Dialogue.* Retrieved from http://blogs.edweek .org/teachers/living-dialogue/2011/04/high_tech _testing_on_the_way_a.html

Kriteman, R., & Tabet-Cubero, E. (2014). Sheltered instruction revisited: Ensuring access to content, language, and community. *Soleado: Promising Practices from the Field, 7*(1).

Kroskrity, P. V. (2004). Language ideologies. In *A companion to linguistic anthropology* (pp. 496–517). Retrieved from http://roozbehhormozi.persiangig.com/ document/duranti,%20a%20-%20a%20companion %20to%20linguistic%20anthropology.pdf#page=516

Lawrence Lightfoot, S. (2004). *The essential conversation: What parents and teachers can learn from each other.* New York: Random House.

Levenson, E., Tsamir, P., & Tirosh, D. (2010). Mathematically based and practically based explanations in the elementary school: Teachers' preferences. *Journal of Mathematics Teacher Education, 13*(4), 345–369.

Lightbown, P., & Spada, N. (2011). *How languages are learned* (3rd ed.). Oxford, UK: Oxford University Press.

Lindholm-Leary, K. J. (2001). *Dual language education.* Clevedon, UK: Multilingual Matters.

Linquanti, R., & Bailey, A. L. (2014). *Reprising the home language survey: Summary of a national working session on policies, practices, and tools for identifying potential English learners.* Washington, DC: Council of Chief State School Officers.

Linquanti, R., & Cook, G. (2013). *Toward a "common definition of English learner": Guidance for states and state assessment consortia in defining and addressing policy and technical issues and options.* Washington, DC: Council of Chief State School Officers.

Lippi-Green, R. (2012). *English with an accent* (2nd ed.). New York: Routledge.

Lobel, A. (1971). *Frog and toad together.* New York: HarperCollins.

Logan-Terry, A., & Wright, L. (2010). Making thinking visible: An analysis of English language learners' interactions with access-based science assessment items. *AccELLerate!, 2*(4), 11–14.

Long, M. (1983). Does second language instruction make a difference? A review of research. *TESOL Quarterly, 17,* 359–382.

Los Angeles Unified School District. (2010). *Guidelines for Implementation of the LAUSD Biliteracy Awards.* Retrieved from http://sealofbiliteracy.org/sites/default/files/resource_docs/LAUSDReferenceGuide.pdf

Loucks-Horsley, S., Love, N., Stiles, K. E., Mundry, S., & Hewson, P. W. (2003). *Designing professional development for teachers of science and mathematics.* Thousand Oaks, CA: Corwin.

Lyons, J. (2014). The promise of equal and effective education for emerging bilingual students in the Obama administration. Boulder, CO: BUENO National Policy Center.

Manger, T., Soule, H., & Wesolowski, K. (2011). *P21 Common Core toolkit: A guide to aligning the Common Core State Standards with the Framework for 21st Century Skills.* Retrieved from www.p21.org/storage/documents/P21CommonCoreToolkit.pdf

Mapp, K. L. (2012). *Title I and parent involvement: Lessons from the past, recommendations for the future.* Washington, DC: Center for American Progress.

Marsh, J. A. (2012). Interventions promoting educators' use of data: Research insights and gaps. *Teachers College Record, 114*(11).

Marzano, R. (2010). *Formative assessment and standards-based grading: Classroom strategies that work.* Bloomington, IN: Marzano Research Institute.

Maxwell, L. (2012, April 23). Language demands to grow for ELLs under new standards. *Education Week.* Retrieved from http://www.edweek.org/ew/articles/2012/04/25/29cs-ell.h31.html

McCabe, A., Tamis-LeMonda, C., Bornstein, M., Cates, C., Golinko, R., Guerra, A., . . . Song, L. (2013). Multilingual children: Beyond myths and toward best practices. *Social Policy Report, 27*(4), 3–36.

McCaffrey, D. F., Koretz, D, Lockwood, J. R., & Hamilton, L. S. (2003). *Evaluating value-added models for teacher accountability.* Santa Monica, CA: RAND Corporation.

McField, G. (Ed.). (2013). *The miseducation of English learners: A tale of three states and lessons to be learned.* Charlotte, NC: Information Age.

Menken, K. (2008). *English learners left behind: Standardized testing as language policy.* Clevedon, UK: Multilingual Matters.

Menken, K. (2010). No Child Left Behind and English language learners: The challenges and consequences of high-stakes testing. *Theory into Practice, 49*(2), 121–128.

Menken, K. (2013). Emergent bilingual students in secondary school: Along the academic language and literacy continuum. *Language Teaching, 46*(4), 438–476.

Menken, K., & Kleyn, T. (2010). The long-term impact of subtractive schooling in the educational experiences of secondary English language learners. *International Journal of Bilingual Education and Bilingualism, 13*(4), 399–417.

Menken, K., & García, O. (Eds.). (2010). *Negotiating language policies in schools: Educators as policymakers.* New York: Routledge.

Menken, K., & Solorza, C. (2014). No child left bilingual: Accountability and the elimination of bilingual education programs in New York City schools. *Educational Policy, 28*(1), 96–125.

Michael, A., Andrade, N., & Bartlett, L. (2007). Figuring "success" in a bilingual high school. *Urban Review, 39,* 167–189.

Miller, G. A., & Gildea, P. M. (1987). How children learn words. *Scientific American, 257*(3), 94–99.

Miramontes, O. B., Nadeau, A., & Commins, N. L. (2011) *Restructuring schools for linguistic diversity: Linking decision making to effective programs.* New York: Teachers College Press.

Morales, A., & Hansen, W. E. (2005). Language brokering: An integrative review of the literature. *Hispanic Journal of Behavioral Sciences, 27*(4), 471–503.

Moschkovich, J. N. (1999). Supporting the participation of English language learners in mathematical discussions. *For the Learning of Mathematics, 19*(1), 11–19.

Moschkovich, J. N. (2007). Beyond words to mathematical content: Assessing English learners in the mathematics classroom. In A. Schoenfeld (Ed.), *Assessing mathematical proficiency* (pp. 345–352). New York, NY: Cambridge University Press.

Moschkovich, J. N. (2011). Supporting mathematical reasoning and sense making for English Learners. In M. Strutchens & J. Quander (Eds.), *Focus in high school mathematics: Fostering reasoning and sense making for all students* (pp. 17–36). Reston, VA: National Council of Teachers of Mathematics.

Moschkovich, J. N. (2012, January). *Mathematics, the common core, and language: Recommendations for mathematics instruction for ELs aligned with the common core.* Paper presented at the Understanding Language Conference, Stanford University, Stanford, CA.

Moschkovich, J. N. (2013). Principles and guidelines for equitable mathematics teaching practices and materials for English language learners. *Journal of Urban Mathematics Education, 6*(1), 45–57.

Mosher, F. A. (2011, September). The role of learning progressions in standards-based education reform. *Consortium for Policy Research in Education: Policy Briefs,* 1–16.

Moss, C. M., & Brookhart, S. M. (2009). *Advancing formative assessment in every classroom: A guide for instructional leaders.* Alexandria, VA: ASCD.

Moss, P. A., Pullin, D. C., Gee, J. P., & Haertel, E. H. (Eds.). (2007). *Assessment, equity, and opportunity to learn.* Cambridge, UK: Cambridge University Press.

National Assessment of Educational Progress. (2013). Retrieved from http://www.nationsreportcard.gov/. I calculated all the NAEP numbers from NAEP Main and Long-Term Trend reports.

National Association for the Education of Young Children (NAEYC). (1995a). *Responding to linguistic and cultural diversity recommendations for effective early childhood education.* Position Statement of the National Association for the Education of Young Children. Washington, DC: National Association for the Education of Young Children.

National Association for the Education of Young Children (NAEYC). (1995b). *School readiness.* Position Statement of the National Association for the Education of Young Children. Washington, DC: National Association for the Education of Young Children.

National Early Literacy Panel. (2008). *Developing early literacy: Report of the National Early Literacy Panel.* Washington, DC: National Institute for Literacy.

National Education Association (2011). *Preparing 21st century students for a global society: An educator's guide to the "four Cs."* Retrieved from http://www.nea.org/assets/docs/A-Guide-to-Four-Cs.pdf

National Governors' Association Center for Best Practices & Council of Chief State School Officers. (2010). *Common Core State Standards for mathematics.* Washington, DC: Authors.

National Institute of Child Health and Human Development. (2000). *Report of the National Reading Panel: Teaching children to read: An evidence-based assessment of the scientific research literature on reading and its implications for reading instruction.* (NIH #00-4769). Washington, DC: U.S. Government Printing Office.

National Reading Panel. (2000). *Teaching children to read: An evidence-based assessment of the scientific research literature on reading and its implications for reading instruction.* Retrieved from http:// http://www.nichd.nih.gov/research/supported/Pages/nrp.aspx/

National Research Council. (2011). *Allocating federal funds for state programs for English language learners.* Panel to review alternative sources for the limited English proficiency allocation formula under Title III, Part A., Elementary and Secondary Education Act, Committee on National Statistics and Board Testing and Assessment. Washington, DC: National Academies Press.

Nelson, T. H., Slavit, D., & Deuel, A. (2012). Two dimensions of an inquiry stance toward student-learning data. *Teachers College Record, 114*(8), 1–42.

Nero, S., & Ahmad, D. (2014). *Vernaculars in the classroom: Paradoxes, pedagogy, possibilities* (Routledge Research in Education). Oxford, UK: Taylor & Francis Group.

New Mexico Public Education Department (2009). *New Mexico social studies standards.* Santa Fe: Author. Retrieved from http://www.ped.state.nm.us/standards/

New York City Department of Education, Office of ELLs. (2013). *2013 demographic data report.* New York: Author.

New York State Bilingual Common Core Initiative. (2014). Retrieved from http://www.engageny.org/resource/new-york-state-bilingual-common-core-initiative

New York State Department of Education, Office of Bilingual Education and World Languages. (2004). *The teaching of language arts to limited English proficient/English language learners: Learning standards for native language arts.* Albany, NY: Author.

New York State Department of Education. (2014). *Proposed addition of subparts 154-1 and 154-2 of the Commissioner's Regulations.* Memorandum to P–12 Education Committee 9/11/14. Albany, NY: Author. Retrieved from http://www.regents.nysed.gov/meetings/2014/September2014/914p12a3.pdf

New York Times. (2013, August 7). New York's Common Core test scores. (Editorial.) Retrieved from http://www.nytimes.com/2013/08/08/opinion/new-yorks-common-core-test-scores.html

Nieto, S. (2008). *Affirming diversity: The sociopolitical context of multicultural education* (5th ed.). New York: Allyn & Bacon.

No Child Left Behind (NCLB) Act (2001). Pub. L. No. 107-110, § 115, Stat. 142.

Norris, J. & Ortega, L. (2000). Effectiveness of L2 instruction: A research synthesis and quantitative meta-analysis. *Language Learning, 50,* 417–528.

Olivas, M. (2012). *No undocumented child left behind: Plyler v. Doe and the education of undocumented schoolchildren.* New York: NYU Press.

Olivos, E. M., Jiménez-Castellanos, O., & Ochoa, A. M. (Eds.) (2011). Critical voices in bicultural parent engagement: A framework for transformation. In *Bicultural parent engagement: Advocacy and empowerment* (pp. 1–17). New York: Teachers College Press.

Olsen, L. (2010). *Reparable harm: Fulfilling the unkept promise of educational opportunity for California's long term English learners.* Long Beach, CA: Californians Together.

Olsen, L., & Spiegel-Coleman, S. (2010, July 11). A skill not a weakness—A skill, not a weakness. *Los Angeles Times.*

Orellana, M. F. (2009). *Translating childhoods: Immigrant youth, language and culture.* New Brunswick, NJ: Rutgers University Press.

Ortiz, A., & Artiles, A. J. (2010). Meeting the needs of English Language Learners with disabilities: A linguistically and culturally responsive model. In G. Li & P. Edwards (Eds.), *Best practices in ELL instruction* (pp. 247–272). New York: Guilford.

Parrish, T. B., Linquanti, R., Merickel, A., Quick, H., Laird, J., & Esra, P. (2002). *Effects of the implementation of Proposition 227 on the education of English learners, K–12, Year 2 Report.* San Francisco: WestED.

Pennycook, A. (2010). *Language as a local practice.* London: Routledge.

Phelan, P., Davidson, A. L., & Yu, H. C. (1998). *Adolescents' worlds: Negotiating family, peers, and school.* New York: Teachers College Press.

Polacco, P. (1994). *Pink y Say.* New York: Philomel.

Popham, W. J. (2008). *Transformative assessment.* Alexandria, VA: ASCD.

Potowski, K. (2013, July). *U.S. Spanish: Some useful linguistic facts for teachers.* Presentation at the Teaching for Biliteracy Summer Institute, Chicago, IL.

Ramirez, N., & Celedón-Pattichis, S. (2012). Understanding second language development and implications for the mathematics classroom. In S. Celedón-Pattichis & N. Ramirez (Eds.), *Beyond good teaching: Advancing mathematics education for ELLs* (pp. 19–37). Reston, VA: National Council of Teachers of Mathematics.

Rasmussen, M. (2008). *Assessment and accountability: An exploration of teachers' practices in assessing English language proficiency* (Doctoral dissertation). Grand Forks: University of North Dakota. Retrieved from http://books.google.com/books/about/Assessment_and_Accountability_An_Explora.html?id=CFD8-gKtlFMC

Ready, D. D., & Wright, D. L. (2011). Accuracy and inaccuracy in teachers' perceptions of young children's cognitive abilities: The role of child background and classroom context. *American Educational Research Journal, 48*(2), 335–360.

Rhodes, R. L., Ochoa, S. H., & Ortiz, S. O. (2005). *Assessing culturally and linguistically diverse students: A practical guide.* New York: Guilford.

Robelen, E. (2002). ESEA to boost federal role in education. *Education Week, 1,* 28–29, 31. Retrieved from http://www.edweek.org/ew/articles/2002/01/09/16esea.h21.html?qs=No_Child_Left_Behind

Roberson, S., & Summerlin, J. (2005). *Mathematics and English language learners in high school: A review of the literature.* Retrieved from http://www.tsusmell.org/resources/mell-resources.htm

Rodela, K. (2013). Latino families and parent involvement in Oregon: Current issues and models (White paper). Corvallis, OR: Center for Latin@ Studies and Engagement, Oregon State University. Retrieved from http://liberalarts.oregonstate.edu/sites/default/files/latino_families_and_parent_involvement_in_oregon_schools_2013.pdf

Rodriguez, D., Carrasquillo, A., & Lee, K. S. (2014). *The bilingual advantage: Promoting academic development, biliteracy, and native language in the classroom.* New York: Teachers College Press.

Ruiz, R. (1984). Orientations in language planning. *NABE Journal 7*(2), 15–24.

Ruiz-Primo, M. A. (2010). Developing and evaluating measures of formative assessment practice (DEMFAP): Theoretical and methodological approach (Internal document). Denver: University of Colorado, Laboratory of Educational Assessment, Research, and Innovation (LEARN).

Ruiz-Primo, M. A., Solano-Flores, G., & Li, M. (2014). Formative assessment as a process of interaction through language: A framework for the inclusion of English language learners. In P. Colbert, C. Wyatt-Smith, & V. Klenowski (Eds.), *The enabling power of assessment* (pp. 265–282). Heidelberg: Springer-Verlag.

Rumsey, A. (1990). Wording, meaning, and linguistic ideology. *American Anthropologist, 92*(2), 346–361.

Retrieved from http://onlinelibrary.wiley.com/doi/10.1525/aa.1990.92.2.02a00060/full

Sadler, D. R. (1989). Formative assessment and the design of instructional strategies. *Instructional Science, 18,* 119–144.

Sahakyan, N. (2012). *Evaluating ELL teacher effectiveness using value-added models and ACCESS for ELLs.* Retrieved from https://www.wida.us/downloadLibrary.aspx

Sawchuk, S. (2014). Vision, reality collide in common-core tests. *Education Week, 33*(29), s8, s10, s12.

Schleppegrell, M. J., & O'Halloran, C. L. (2011). Teaching academic language in L2 secondary settings. *Annual Review of Applied Linguistics, 31,* 3–18.

Shannon, S. M. (2011). Parent engagement and equity in dual language programs. In E. M. Olivos, O. Jiménez-Castellanos, & A. M. Ochoa (Eds.), *Critical voices in bicultural parent engagement: Operationalizing advocacy and empowerment* (pp. 83–102). New York: Teachers College Press.

Smith, F. (1975). *Comprehension and learning: A conceptual framework for teachers.* New York: Holt McDougal.

Smith, M. S., & Stein, M. K. (2011). Five practices for orchestrating productive mathematics discussions. Reston, VA: National Council of Teachers of Mathematics.

Snow, C. E. (1992). Perspectives on second language development: Implications for bilingual education. *Educational Researcher, 21*(2).

Snow, M. A. (2001). Content-based and immersion models for second and foreign language teaching. In M. Celce-Murcia (Ed.), *Teaching English as a second or foreign language* (3rd ed., pp. 303–318). Boston: Heinle & Heinle.

Snow, M. A., Met, M., & Genesee, F. (1989). A conceptual framework for the integration of language and content in second/foreign language instruction. *TESOL Quarterly, 23*(2), 201–217.

Solano-Flores, G. (2008). Who is given tests in what language by whom, when, and where? The need for probabilistic views of language in the testing of English language learners. *Educational Researcher, 37*(4), 189–199.

Solano-Flores, G. (2012). *Translation accommodations framework for testing English language learners in mathematics.* Developed for Smarter Balanced Assessment Consortium (SBAC). Retrieved from http://www.smarterbalanced.org/wordpress/wp-content/uploads/2012/09/Translation-Accommodations-Framework-for-Testing-ELL-Math.pdf

Solano-Flores, G., & Li, M. (2006). The use of generalizability (G) theory in the testing of linguistic minorities. *Educational Measurement: Issues and Practice 25*(1), 13–22.

Solano-Flores, G., & Li, M. (2013). Generalizability theory and the fair and valid assessment of linguistic minorities. *Educational Research and Evaluation, 19*(2-3), 245–263.

Solano-Flores, G., & Trumbull, E. (2008). In what language should English language learners be tested? In R. J. Kopriva (Ed.), *Improving testing for English language learners* (pp. 169–200). New York: Routledge.

Solano-Flores, G., Trumbull, E., & Nelson-Barber, S. (2002). Concurrent development of dual language assessments: An alternative to translating tests for linguistic minorities. *International Journal of Testing, 2*(2), 107–129.

Solórzano, R. (2008). High stakes testing: Issues, implications, and remedies for English language learners. *Review of Educational Research, 78*(2), 260–329.

Solórzano, R. W. (2012). English language learners (ELLs) and subject area tests. In C. A. Chapelle (Ed.), *Encyclopedia of applied linguistics.* Oxford, UK: Wiley-Blackwell.

Soltero-González, L., Escamilla, K., & Hopewell, S. (2012). Changing teachers' perceptions about the writing abilities of emerging bilingual students: Towards a holistic bilingual perspective on writing assessment. *International Journal of Bilingual Education and Bilingualism, 15*(1), 71–94. Retrieved from http://www.tandfonline.com/doi/abs/10.1080/13670050.2011.604712

Staehr Fenner, D. (2013a). *Your role in the CCSS: Advocacy action items* (Part 2). Retrieved from http://blog.colorincolorado.org/2013/12/05/your-role-in-the-ccss-advocacy-action-items-part-2/

Staehr Fenner, D. (2013b). *Your role in the CCSS: Advocating for ELLs* (Part 1). Retrieved from http://blog.colorincolorado.org/2013/11/26/your-role-in-the-common-core-advocating-for-ells/

Staehr Fenner, D. (2014). *Advocating for English learners: A guide for educators.* Thousand Oaks, CA: Corwin.

Staehr Fenner, D., Kozik, P., & Cooper, C. (2015). *Evaluating ALL teachers of English learners and students with disabilities: Supporting great teaching.* Thousand Oaks, CA: Corwin.

Steedle, J. T., & Shavelson, R. J. (2009). Supporting valid interpretations of learning progression level diagnoses. *Journal of Research in Science Teaching, 46,* 699–715.

Stiggins, R. J. (2005). From formative assessment to assessment for learning: A path to success in standards-based schools. *Phi Delta Kappan 87*(4), 324–328.

Street, B. (1995). *Social literacies: Critical approaches to literacy in development, ethnography, and education.* London: Longman.

Swanson, C. B. (2009). *Perspectives on a population: English language learners in American schools.* Bethesda, MD: Editorial Projects in Education. Retrieved from http://www.edweek.org/go/copies

Sztajn, P., Confrey, J., Wilson, P. H., & Edgington, C. (2012). Learning trajectory based instruction: Toward a theory of teaching. *Educational Researcher, 41,* 147–156.

Téllez, K., & Waxman, H. C. (Eds.). (2006). *Preparing quality educators for English language learners.* Mahwah, NJ: Erlbaum.

TESOL International Association. (2013, April). *Implementing the Common Core State Standards for ELs: The changing role of the ESL teacher.* Alexandria, VA: Author.

Thomas, W., Collier, V., & Collier, K. (2011). *English learners in North Carolina, 2010.* Fairfax, VA: George Mason University. Retrieved from http://esl.ncwiseowl.org/resources/dual_language/

Thomas, W. P., & Collier, V. P. (2012). *Dual language education for a transformed world.* Albuquerque, NM: Dual Language Education of New Mexico–Fuente Press.

Tong, F., Lara-Alecio, R., Irby, B., Mathes, P., & Kwok, O. (2008). Accelerating early academic oral English development in transitional bilingual and structured English immersion programs. *American Educational Research Journal, 45,* 1011–1044.

Turner, E., & Celedón-Pattichis, S. (2011). Mathematical problem solving among Latina/o kindergartners: An analysis of opportunities to learn. *Journal of Latinos and Education, 10*(2), 146–169.

Ujifusa, A. (2014). Oklahoma Governor Fallin signs bill to replace common core with new standards. *Education Week, 33*(29).

Uro, G., & Barrio, A. (2013). *English language learners in America's Great City schools: Demographics, achievement, and staffing.* Washington, DC: Council of the Great City Schools.

U.S. Department of Education. (2010). *Race to the top.* Retrieved from http://www2.ed.gov/programs/racetothetop/executive-summary.pdf

U.S. Department of Education. (2013). *Biennial report to Congress on the implementation of the Title III State Formula Grant Program, school years 2008–2010.* Washington, DC: Office of English Language Acquisition, Language Enhancement, and Academic Achievement for Limited English Proficient Students.

Valdés, G. (2001). *Learning and not learning English: Latino students in American schools.* New York: Teachers College Press.

Valdés, G. (2004). Between support and marginalization: The development of academic language in linguistic minority children. *International Journal of Bilingual Education and Bilingualism, 7*(2), 102–132.

Valdés, G., Kibler, A., & Walqui, A. (2014). *Changes in the expertise of ESL professionals: Knowledge and action in an era of new standards.* Alexandria, VA: TESOL International Association. Retrieved from http://www.tesol.org/read-and-publish/newsletters-other-publications/tesol-professional-papers-and-briefs

Valdés, G., MacSwan, J. & Alvarez, L. (2009). *Deficits and differences: Perspectives on language and education.* Washington, DC: National Academies Press.

van Lier, L., & Walqui, A. (2012a, January). *How teachers and educators can most usefully and deliberately consider language.* Paper presented at the Understanding Language Conference, Stanford, CA.

van Lier, L. & Walqui, A. (2012b). *Language and the Common Core State Standards.* Stanford, CA: Understanding Language. Retrieved from http://ell.stanford.edu/papers/language

Vygotsky, L. (1978). *Mind and society: The development of higher psychological processes.* Cambridge, MA: Harvard University Press.

Walqui, A. (2006). Scaffolding instruction for English language learners: A conceptual framework. *International Journal of Bilingual Education and Bilingualism, 9*(2), 159–180.

Walqui, A., Koelsch, N., & Schmida, M. (2012). Persuasion across time and space: Analyzing and producing complex texts. *Understanding Language,* 1–235. Retrieved from ell.stanford.edu/teaching_resources/ela

Walqui, A., & van Lier, L. (2010). *Scaffolding the academic success of adolescent English language learners: A pedagogy of promise.* San Francisco: WestEd.

Wheeler, R., Swords, R., & Carpenter, M. (2004). Codeswitching: Tools of language and culture transform the dialectally diverse classroom. *Language Arts 81*(6), 470–480.

Wiggins, G. P., & McTighe, J. (2005). *Understanding by design.* Alexandria, VA: Association for Supervision and Development.

Wiley, T. G. (1996). Language planning and language policy. In S. McKay & N. Hornberger (Eds.), *Sociolinguistics and language teaching* (pp. 103–147). Cambridge, UK: Cambridge University Press.

Wiley, T. G. (2005). *Literacy and language diversity in the United States.* Washington, DC: Center for Applied Linguistics.

Wiley, T. G. (2008). Language policy and political issues in education. In S. May & N. Hornberger (Eds.), *Encyclopedia of language and education* (2nd ed., vol. 1, pp. 229–242). New York: Springer.

Wiley, T. G., & Rolstad, K. (2014). The Common Core State Standards and the great divide. *International Multilingual Research Journal, 8,* 1–18.

Willey, C. (2010). Teachers developing mathematics discourse communities with Latinas/os. In P. Brosnan, D. Erchick, & L. Flevares (Eds.), *Proceedings of the 32nd annual meeting of the North American Chapter of the International Group of the Psychology of Mathematics Education* (pp. 530–538). Columbus: Ohio State University.

William, D. (2011). *Embedded formative assessment.* Indianapolis, IN: Solution Tree.

Wilson, M. (2009). Measuring progressions: Assessment structures underlying a learning progression. *Journal of Research in Science Teaching, 46,* 716–730.

Wisconsin Center for Educational Research. (2013). *WIDA focus on group work for content learning.* Madison: University of Wisconsin. Retrieved from http://wida.us/get.aspx?id=604

Wong Fillmore, L., & Fillmore, C. (2012, January). *What does text complexity mean for English learners and language minority students?* Paper presented at the Understanding Language Conference, Stanford University, Stanford, CA. Retrieved from http://ell.stanford.edu

Woodburn School District #103 (2011). *Performance supervision and evaluation of licensed teaching professionals program manual.* Woodburn, OR: Author.

World-class Instructional Design and Assessment (WIDA) Consortium. (2009). *The English Learner Can Do* booklet series. Madison: Board of Regents of the University of Wisconsin System, on behalf of the WIDA Consortium. Retrieved from wida.us/standards/CAN_DOs/

World-class Instructional Design and Assessment (WIDA). (2012). English language development standards. Retrieved from http://wida.us/standards/eld.aspx

Yoon, K. S., Duncan, T., Lee, S. W.-Y., Scarloss, B., & Shapley, K. (2007). Reviewing the evidence on how teacher professional development affects student achievement (Issues & Answers Report, REL 2007–No. 033). Washington, DC: U.S. Department of Education, Institute of Education Sciences, National Center for Education Evaluation and Regional Assistance, Regional Educational Laboratory Southwest. Retrieved from http://ies.ed.gov/ncee/edlabs

Zacarian, D. (2004). The road taken: Keeping Tren in school. *Essential Teacher, 1*(2), 11–13.

Zacarian, D. (2006). The road taken: The [im]possibilities of social services. *Essential Teacher, 3*(3), 10–11.

Zacarian, D. (2007a). The road taken: I can't go to college! *Essential Teacher, 4*(4), 10–11.

Zacarian, D. (2007b). The road taken: Mascot or member? *Essential Teacher, 4*(3), 10–11.

Zacarian, D. (2008a). The road taken: Finding the right interpreter is harder than you might think. *Essential Teacher, 5*(2), 10–11.

Zacarian, D. (2008b). The road taken: Joinfostering the missing. *Essential Teacher, 5*(3), 10–11.

Zacarian, D. (2011). *Transforming schools for English learners: A framework for school leaders.* Thousand Oaks, CA: Corwin.

Zacarian, D. (2013). *Mastering academic language: a framework for supporting student achievement.* Thousand Oaks, CA: Corwin.

Zacarian, D., & Haynes, J. (2012). *The essential guide for educating beginning English learners.* Thousand Oaks, CA: Corwin.

Zacarian, D., & Silverstone, M. (2015). *In it together: How student, family and community partnerships advance engagement and achievement in diverse classrooms.* Thousand Oaks, CA: Corwin.

Zehler, A. M., Fleischman, H. L., Hopstock, P. J., Pendzick, M. L., & Stephenson, T. G. (2003). Descriptive study of services to LEP students and LEP students with disabilities. In *Special topic report #4: Findings on special education LEP students* (submitted to U.S. Department of Education, OELA). Arlington VA: Development Associates.

Zehr, M. A. (2007). NCLB seen as a damper on bilingual programs. *Education Week, 5,* 12.

Zwiers, J. (2008). *Building academic language: Essential practices for content classrooms.* San Francisco: Jossey-Bass.

Zwiers, J., O'Hara, S., & Pritchard, R. (2013). *Eight essential shifts for teaching the Common Core to English learners.* Retrieved from http://aldnetwork.org/sites/default/files/pictures/8%20Shifts%20for%20Teaching%20CC%20to%20AELs%20-%20PDF.pdf

Recommended Readings

Abedi, J., & Dietel, R. (2004). Challenges for English language learners in the No Child Left Behind Act. (CRESST Policy Brief No. 7). Los Angeles: National Center for Research in Evaluation, Standards, and Student Testing. Retrieved from http://www.cse.ucla .edu/products/policy/cresst_policy7.pdf

Acosta, B. D., Rivera, C., & Shafer-Willner, L. (2008). *Best practices in state assessment policies for accommodating English language learners: A Delphi study.* Arlington, VA: George Washington University Center for Equity and Excellence in Education.

Adelman, C. (2006). *The toolbox revisited: Paths to degree completion from high school through college.* Washington, DC: U.S. Department of Education.

Anderson, N. C., Chapin, S. C., & O'Connor, C. (2011). *Classroom discussions: Seeing math discourse in action, grades K–6: A multimedia professional learning resource.* Sausalito, CA: Math Solutions.

Anguiano, R. P. V. (2004). Families and schools: The effect of parental involvement on high school completion. *Journal of Family Issues, 25*(1), 61–85.

Arizona Proposition 203. (2008). In J. González (Ed.), *Encyclopedia of bilingual education* (p. 40). Thousand Oaks, CA: Sage. Retrieved from http://knowledge .sagepub.com/view/bilingual/SAGE.xml

Artiles, A. J., Klingner, J., Sullivan, A., & Fierros, E. (2010). Shifting landscapes of professional practices: English learner special education placement in English-only states. In P. Gándara & M. Hopkins (Eds.), *Forbidden language: English Learners and restrictive language policies* (pp. 102–117). New York: Teachers College Press.

Artiles, A. J., Waitoller, F., & Neal, R. (2011). Grappling with the intersection of language and ability differences: Equity issues for Chicano/Latino students in special education. In R. R. Valencia (Ed.), *Chicano school failure and success: Past, present, and future* (3rd ed., pp. 213–234). London: Routledge/Falmer.

Ascenzi-Moreno, L. (2012). *Assessing emergent bilinguals: Teacher knowledge and reading instructional practices.* Unpublished dissertation.

Australian Institute for Teaching and School Leadership and Learning Forward. (2014). *Designing professional learning.* Melbourne, Australia: AITSL.

Bailey, A. (2010). Implications for assessment and instruction. In M. Shatz & L. C. Wilkinson (Eds.), *The education of English language learners: Research to practice* (pp. 222–247). New York: Guilford.

Bilingual Education Act (1968). Pub. L. No. (90-247), 81 Stat. 816.

Bilingual Education Act (1978). Pub. L. No. (95-561), 92 Stat. 2268.

Bird, C. P., Lee, T. S., & Lopez, N. (2013). Leadership and accountability in American Indian education: Voices from New Mexico. *American Journal of Education, 119*(4), 539–564. Retrieved from http://www .jstor.org/stable/10.1086/670959

Brown, K. (2010). Lau v. Nichols. In T. Hunt, J. Carper, T. Lasley, & C. Raisch (Eds.), *Encyclopedia of educational reform and dissent* (pp. 511–513). Thousand Oaks, CA: Sage.

Cadena, A. (1999). *El cuento-historia de los gatos.* Campeche, Mexico: CNCA/Alas y Raíces a los Niños, Gobierno del Estado, Instituto de Cultura Campeche.

Calderón, M. E., & Minaya-Rowe, L. (2011). *Preventing long-term ELs: Transforming schools to meet core standards.* Thousand Oaks, CA: Corwin.

California Proposition 227. (2008). In J. González (Ed.), *Encyclopedia of bilingual education* (p. 110). Thousand Oaks, CA: Sage. Retrieved from http://knowledge .sagepub.com/view/bilingual/SAGE.xml

Castagno, A., & Brayboy, B. (2008). Culturally responsive schooling for indigenous youth: A review of the literature. *Review of Educational Research, 78*(4), 941–993.

Coleman, R., & Goldenberg, C. (2012). The Common Core challenge for ELLs. *Principal Leadership, 12*(5), 46–51. Retrieved from http://www.nuptdc.org/up loads/6/1/8/1/6181665/the_common_core_challenge _for_ells.docx

Cook, H. G., Boals, T., & Lundberg, T. (2011). Developing informed expectations for the academic achievement of English learners. *Phi Delta Kappan, 93*(3), 66–69.

Copple, C., & Bredekamp, S. (Eds.). (2009). *Developmentally appropriate practice in early childhood programs serving children from birth to age 8* (3rd ed.). Washington, DC: NAEYC.

Delgado-Gaitan, C. (2001). *The power of community.* Lanham, MD: Rowman & Littlefield.

Delgado-Gaitan, C. (2004). *Involving Latino families in schools: Raising student achievement through home-school partnerships.* Thousand Oaks, CA: Corwin.

Dixon, L. Q., Zhao, J., Shin, J.-Y., Wu, S., Su, J.-H., Burgess-Brigham, R., Gezer, M. U., & Snow, C. (2012). What we know about second language acquisition: A synthesis from four perspectives. *Review of Educational Research, 82,* 5–60.

Dyrness, A. (2011). *Mothers united: An immigrant struggle for socially just education.* Minneapolis: University of Minnesota Press.

Epstein, J. L., & Sheldon, S. B. (2002). Present and accounted for: Improving student attendance through family and community involvement. *Journal of Educational Research, 95,* 308–318.

Escamilla, K. (2010). *Transitions to biliteracy: Literacy Squared.* Boulder: University of Colorado, BUENO Center for Multicultural Education.

Fuhrman, S. (1993). *Designing coherent education policy.* New York: Wiley.

García, O., Kleifgen, J. A., & Falchi, L. (2008). *From English language learners to emergent bilinguals.* New York: Teachers College, Columbia University, Campaign for Educational Equity.

Gee, J. P. (2008). What is academic language? In A. S. Rosebery & B. Warren (Eds.), *Teaching science to English language learners: Building on students' strengths* (pp. 57–70). Arlington, VA: National Science Teachers Association.

Gonzalez-DeHass, A. R., Willems, P. P., & Doan Holbein, M. F. (2005). Examining the relationship between parental involvement and student motivation. *Educational Psychology Review, 17*(2), 99–123.

Hakuta, K., Zwiers, J., & Rutherford-Quach, S. (2013). *Constructive classroom conversations: Mastering language for the Common Core State Standards*. Retrieved from https://novoed.com/common-core

Haynes, J., & Zacarian, D. (2010). Teaching English language learners across the content areas. Washington, DC: ASCD.

Hernández, J. C., & Gebeloff, R. (2013, August 7). Test scores sink as New York adopts tougher benchmarks. *New York Times.*

Hurtig, J., & Dyrness, A. (2011). Parents as critical educators and ethnographers of schooling. In B. Levinson & M. Pollock (Eds.), *A companion to the anthropology of education*. Oxford, UK: Wiley-Blackwell.

Institute of Medicine and National Research Council. (1997). *Improving schooling for language-minority children: A research agenda*. Washington, DC: National Academies Press.

Johnson, M. (2012). *The 21st century parent: Multicultural parent engagement leadership strategies handbook*. Charlotte, NC: Information Age.

Jojola, T., Lee, T. S., Alacantara, A., Belgarde, M., Bird, C., Lopez, N., & Singer, B. (2010). *Indian education in New Mexico, 2025*. Santa Fe: New Mexico Public Education Department, Indian Education.

Kennedy, E. M. (2008, January 7). How to fix "No Child." *Washington Post*. Retrieved from http://www.washingtonpost.com/wp-dyn/content/article/2008/01/06/AR2008010601828.html

Kieffer, M. J., Rivera, M., & Francis, D. J. (2012). *Practical guidelines for the education of English language learners: Research-based recommendations for the use of accommodations in large-scale assessments*. 2012 update. Portsmouth, NH: RMC Research Corporation, Center on Instruction.

King, K., Artiles, A. J., & Sullivan, A. (2013). Effective reading interventions for English language learners. In R. McWilliam, M. Tankersley, & B. Cook (Eds.), *Effective practices in special education* (pp. 367–383). Upper Saddle River, NJ: Pearson.

Kirst, M. W., & Mazzeo, C. (1996). The rise, fall, and rise of state assessment in California: 1993–96. *Phi Delta Kappan, 78*(4), 319–323.

Klingner, J. (2014). *English language learners: Differentiating between language acquisition and learning disabilities*. Reston, VA: Council for Exceptional Children.

Klingner, J. K., Artiles, A. J., & Barletta, L. M. (2006). English language learners who struggle with reading: Language acquisition or learning disabilities? *Journal of Learning Disabilities, 39*, 108–128.

Lareau, A. (2003). *Unequal childhoods: Class, race, and family life*. Oakland, CA: University of California Press.

Lawrence-Lightfoot, S. (1999). *Respect: An exploration*. Reading, MA: Perseus.

Lawrence-Lightfoot, S. (2003). *The essential conversation: What parents and teachers can learn from each other*. New York: Random House.

Loveless, T. (2012–2013). The Common Core initiative: What are the chances of success? *Educational Leadership, 70*(40), 60–63.

Marschall, M., Rigby, E., & Jenkins, J. (2011). Do state policies constrain local actors? The impact of English only laws on language instruction in public schools. *Publius: Journal of Federalism 41*(4), 586–609.

Martinez, G. (2010). *Native pride: The politics of curriculum and instruction in an urban public school*. New York: Hampton Press.

Moore, C., Shulock, N., Ceja, M., & Lang, D. M. (2007). *Beyond the open door: Increasing student success in the California community colleges*. Sacramento, CA: Institute for Higher Education Leadership and Policy.

National Association for the Education of Young Children (NAEYC). (2012). *The Common Core State Standards: Caution and opportunity for the early childhood education*. Washington, DC: National Association for the Education of Young Children.

National Center for Education Statistics (2013). *The nation's report card: A first look: 2013 mathematics and reading*. (NCES 2014–451). Washington, DC: National Center for Education Statistics, Institute of Education Sciences, U.S. Department of Education.

NGSS Lead States. (2013). *Next Generation Science Standards: For states, by states*. Washington, DC: National Academies Press.

Olsen, L. (2012). *Californians Together presents the Seal of Biliteracy Program*. Long Beach, CA: Californians Together.

Olsen, L. (2014). *The California Campaign for Biliteracy*. Long Beach, CA: Californians Together.

Polikoff, M. S. (2012). The association of state policy attributes with teachers' instructional alignment. *Educational Evaluation and Policy Analysis, 34*(3), 278–294.

Pomerantz, E. M., Moorman, E. A., & Litwack, S. D. (2007). The how, whom, and why of parents' involvement in children's academic lives: More is not always better. *Review of Educational Research, 77*(3), 373–410.

Potowski, K. (2005). *Fundamentos de la enseñanza del español a hispanohablantes en los EE.UU*. Madrid: Arco Libros.

Question 2 (Massachusetts). (2008). In J. González (Ed.), *Encyclopedia of bilingual education* (p. 40). Thousand Oaks, CA: Sage. Retrieved from http://knowledge.sagepub.com/view/bilingual/SAGE.xml

Shavelson, R., & Kurpius, A. (2012). Reflections on learning progressions. In A. Alonzo & A. Gotwals (Eds.), *Learning progressions in science: Current challenges and future direction* (pp. 13–26). Rotterdam, the Netherlands: Sense.

Snow, C. (1998). Bilingualism and second language acquisition. In J. Berko Gleason & N. Bernstein Ratner (Eds.), *Psycholinguistics* (2nd ed., pp. 391–416). New York: Harcourt Brace Jovanovich.

Townsend, D., & Collins, P. (2008). English or Spanish? Assessing Latino/a children in English and in Spanish for risk of reading disabilities. *Topics in Language Disorders, 28*, 61–83.

Tsianina, L. K., & McCarty, T. L. (2006). *To remain an Indian: Lessons in democracy from a century of Native American schooling.* New York: Teachers College Press.

Valdes, G. (1997). Dual-language immersion programs: A cautionary note concerning the education of language-minority students. *Harvard Educational Review, 67*(3), 391–429.

Weis, L., & Fine, M. (2012). Critical bifocality and circuits of privilege: Expanding critical ethnographic theory and design. *Harvard Educational Review, 82*(2), 173–201.

Yanguas, M. (2012). *ELL advocacy: Selecting the right issues and audiences.* Retrieved from http://www.colorin colorado.org/article/50556/

Index

Note: Page numbers followed by b, f, or t refer to boxes, figures, or tables, respectively.